THE
COMPLETE
IDIOT'S
GUIDE® TO

Low-Carb Meals

by Lucy Beale and
Sandy G. Couvillon, M.S., L.D.N., R.D.

ALPHA

A member of Penguin Group (USA) Inc.

Lucy: To my mother, Ann Murphy Rusnock
Sandy: To my three favorite food tasters: Brian, Courtney, and Brad

International Standard Book Number: 1-59257-180-8
Library of Congress Catalog Card Number: 2003113280

06 05 04   8 7 6 5 4

Interpretation of the printing code: The rightmost number of the first series of numbers is the year of the book's printing; the rightmost number of the second series of numbers is the number of the book's printing. For example, a printing code of 04-1 shows that the first printing occurred in 2004.

Printed in the United States of America

Note: This publication contains the opinions and ideas of its authors. It is intended to provide helpful and informative material on the subject matter covered. It is sold with the understanding that the authors and publisher are not engaged in rendering professional services in the book. If the reader requires personal assistance or advice, a competent professional should be consulted.

The authors and publisher specifically disclaim any responsibility for any liability, loss, or risk, personal or otherwise, which is incurred as a consequence, directly or indirectly, of the use and application of any of the contents of this book.

Most Alpha books are available at special quantity discounts for bulk purchases for sales promotions, premiums, fund-raising, or educational use. Special books, or book excerpts, can also be created to fit specific needs.

For details, write: Special Markets, Alpha Books, 375 Hudson Street, New York, NY 10014.

Publisher: *Marie Butler-Knight*
Product Manager: *Phil Kitchel*
Senior Managing Editor: *Jennifer Chisholm*
Senior Acquisitions Editor: *Renee Wilmeth*
Development Editor: *Nancy D. Lewis*
Senior Production Editor: *Christy Wagner*
Copy Editor: *Nancy Wagner*
Illustrator: *Chris Eliopoulos*
Cover/Book Designer: *Trina Wurst*
Indexer: *Brad Herriman*
Layout/Proofreading: *Becky Harmon, Donna Martin*

Contents at a Glance

Contents

What the recipe symbols mean:

▲ Fast

■ Make-ahead

Introduction

There's a certain rhythm to cooking low carb. Once you get into the flow of it, you'll be cooking low carb with joy and delight for the rest of your life.

In this book, you'll find mouth-watering recipes for all your meals, plus daily menu planning. You'll use regular grocery store ingredients and make scrumptious main courses, side dishes, and, yes, even desserts, breads, and chocolate goodies. You'll eat them with confidence, knowing that you are eating healthfully, helping manage your weight, and maintaining your overall well-being.

How This Book Is Organized

This book is divided into six parts:

Part 1, "The Low-Carb Way of Eating," gives you an overview of low-carb eating and cooking. You'll learn which carbs count and which don't, how to use the Glycemic Index, and how to eat a balanced low-carb diet. You'll learn to create a positive mind-set while eating delicious foods in the best portion sizes.

Part 2, "Breakfasts and Lunches," gives you great recipes for both quick and leisurely breakfasts. You'll learn how to make low-carb breakfasts in advance so you can eat on the run. And you'll learn low-carb recipes for packed lunches as well as the kind you eat at home.

Part 3, "Main Dish Entrées," contains recipes for your main meat or fish course. These include yummy beef, pork, poultry, seafood, and fish dishes. You'll use these recipes for dinner and also for lunches and even breakfast.

Part 4, "Main Dish Combinations," gives you recipes for one-pot meals, soups, stews, eggs, cheese, and main-dish salads. "One pot" is the new term for casseroles. With these recipes, you'll have plenty of variety for interesting eating. Many of them contain added vegetables and fruits.

Part 5, "Side Dishes," provides you with recipes for snacks and appetizers for those times when you really need to have a little something to tide you over until the next meal. You'll find recipe chapters for vegetable, fruit, and salad side dishes.

Part 6, "Extras: Treats and Starches," is filled with the comfort foods we all enjoy. You'll find recipes for breads, grains, and potatoes. And if you have a sweet tooth, you'll enjoy our great collection of luscious dessert recipes, plus a whole chapter on chocolate.

Tasty Bites

The sidebars in this book offer low-carb notes and tips, recipe ideas, cooking cautions, and definitions. Here's what to look for:

Table Talk
These entries give good information and notes on the cooking and eating of low-carb foods.

Low-Carb Vocab
The definitions of words and concepts in these boxes increase your knowledge of low-carb eating and cooking.

Hot Potato
Watch out! These warnings help you avoid errors in cooking procedures and things that may hamper your low-carb eating plan.

Recipe for Success
Use these notes on how to serve and enjoy each recipe to increase your dining pleasure.

Acknowledgments

Just as a good recipe tastes best when made with the finest ingredients, a cookbook succeeds best when given helpful and loving support.

Lucy Beale gives loving thanks to her husband, Patrick Partridge, for his caring interest and editing suggestions; to her late mother, Ann Murphy Rusnock, for years ago teaching her how to compose and create recipes; to her co-author, Sandy Couvillon, for her steadfast work and commitment. The following people gave generously of their time and knowledge. Thanks to Rick Mendosa, Lori Beecher, Caryll Cram, Steve Burns, Margarita Guerra, Greg Terrell, Judy Webb, and Greg Davis. Lucy also thanks her newsletter readers and workshop participants who urged her to write a low-carb cookbook for them.

Lucy and Sandy thank Marilyn Allen, Bob DiForio, Coleen O'Shea, and Renee Wilmeth for their guidance in bringing this cookbook into reality.

Sandy Couvillon gives heartfelt thanks to her husband, Brian, for his support and understanding for the many evenings and weekends spent typing and calculating recipes. Much love to Brian and their children, Courtney and Brad, for helping her enjoy years of experimenting with recipes to find healthier and more delicious ways to combine ingredients. Thankfully she had many years of delectable recipes to fall back on from two loving, experienced cooks, her mom, Velma, and her mother-in-law, Stella. Two important family members cannot be left out as they have always been there to lend encouragement, her dad, Jim, and her brother, Jim. Many thanks to her co-author, Lucy, for her enthusiasm and energy that is reflected in this project.

Sincere gratitude and thanks go to her co-workers, who eagerly tasted and honestly rated many recipes for the book. Thanks to her clients who gave input into the types of recipes they needed to make low-carb eating fun. Sandy sends love and hugs to her many friends who supported this endeavor and understood when deadlines had to take first place. Without this love and support of family and friends this project could not have happened nor would it have been such fun.

Special Thanks to the Technical Reviewer

The Complete Idiot's Guide to Low-Carb Meals was reviewed by an expert who double-checked the accuracy of what you'll learn here, to help us ensure that this book gives you everything you need to know about cooking low-carb meals. Special thanks are extended to Susan Derecskey.

Trademarks

All terms mentioned in this book that are known to be or are suspected of being trademarks or service marks have been appropriately capitalized. Alpha Books and Penguin Group (USA) Inc. cannot attest to the accuracy of this information. Use of a term in this book should not be regarded as affecting the validity of any trademark or service mark.

Part 1

The Low-Carb Way of Eating

Low-carb eating is here to stay. It works. It works for you and it makes you feel good. Low-carb cooking is becoming not just a necessity, but an art form.

The challenge with low-carb cooking is to cook up the most delicious foods with the right amount of carbohydrates—enough to satisfy your palate and your tastes, but not so many that you exceed your daily carb allotment. An additional challenge is to make every carbohydrate count nutritionally for your best health, ideal weight, and overall well-being.

Fabulous low-carb cooking eliminates feelings of deprivation and, instead, makes you glad that your foods are satisfying and pleasurable.

Delicious Low-Carb Cooking

In This Chapter

- ◆ Anything but boring low-carb recipes
- ◆ Accommodating your daily carb allotment
- ◆ Counting carbs and the glycemic index

By the time you find this book, you are on a quest. You are committed to eating low carb. This dietary plan is supposed to be good for what seems to be ailing you. People choose low-carb eating as a solution to weight loss, diabetes, high blood pressure, heart conditions, autoimmune diseases, and even depression and anxiety. Low-carb eating works.

However, the dietary limitations of low-carb eating can get very boring really fast. Fortunately, boring eating is not a requirement for eating low carb. Just the opposite can be true. In fact, the opposite has to be true for a person to eat low carb day in and day out over years, in fact, over a lifetime.

As members of the human species, we are programmed biologically to seek out delicious and interesting foods. The good news is, you've found them. With these recipes, you can prepare fabulous dishes for breakfast, lunch, and dinner. They definitely will keep you from ailing with food boredom.

The Carb Count Limit

What constitutes low-carb eating varies with the experts. What we know is that you have to eat some carbs to stay happy and healthy. But the answer to how many isn't clear. The range of acceptable daily amounts swings from 15 to 250, depending on the expert.

Dr. Atkins, who led the movement to eating virtually no carbohydrates, suggested a person start his or her diet by eating only 15 to 20 grams carbohydrates a day for several weeks and slowly adding more, working up to a maintenance level of between 25 and 90. He advised that the maintenance level of carbohydrate intake is determined by the dieter's individual resistance to weight loss. The higher the resistance, the lower the carbohydrate maintenance allotment needs to be.

Low-Carb Vocab

The **low-carb spread-sheet** shows the nutritional count of each recipe so that you can easily plan your eating for a meal, a day, or a week. Use the spreadsheet so you can stay within your carbohydrate allotment.

Other more moderate plans suggest a daily carbohydrate intake of 90 to 100 grams. Another recommends between 125 to 180 grams per day. The most liberal suggests that eating up to 250 grams is fine.

Whatever you choose, we offer you not only recipes but also meal plans to meet your needs. In Appendix C, you will find a *low-carb spreadsheet* listing each recipe in order of the number of carbohydrates per serving. We have also sorted the recipes by main dish, side dish, and dessert, so you can use the spreadsheet to plan a meal or a whole day's worth of meals.

Carb Count Consensus

We calculated the carbohydrate counts of the recipes using the highly reliable sources of the USDA's Nutrient Database and Corinne T. Netzer's *The Complete Book of Food Counts.*

But calculating the carbohydrate count of a recipe isn't precise and exact. The carbohydrate count of an orange depends on where it was grown and how long it was ripened on the vine. A medium orange is an inexact description at best. How thick is the skin? How much actual fruit is in the orange? We don't have any way of knowing these things. So we calculated based on averages.

If you use the amounts of ingredients specified in the recipes and eat the recommended serving amounts or less, you will be eating low carb.

The Bottom Line on Carbohydrates

At the beginning of each recipe, we tally up for you the full carbohydrate count of each serving. However, dietary fiber, which is non-nutritive, is also included in the carbohydrate count available in the reference books. To give you a more accurate carbohydrate count, we have subtracted out the fiber grams to give you the true bottom line.

For example, the carbohydrate count of ¼ cup pecans is 5 grams, and the fiber content is also 5 grams. The *nutritive carbohydrate count* of pecans is 0 grams.

For chocolate chips, though, 16 chips have 9 grams carbohydrates, but only 1 gram fiber, so the nutritive carbohydrate count of the chips is 8 grams.

> **Low-Carb Vocab**
> The **nutritive carbohydrate count** is the actual amount of carbohydrates in a serving. You calculate this by subtracting the amount of dietary fiber in grams from the carbohydrate count of the serving.

Not Going to Extremes

Beware of eating plans that are no carb or virtually no carb. Eating that way for more than a couple weeks can jeopardize your health. You need carbohydrates for your health. They aren't bad for you; in fact, many forms of them are positively wonderful for you. But too much of anything isn't a good thing.

As a nation and now as a world, we are overdoing the carbohydrates. Every fast-food restaurant, virtually every processed food at the store, and every pizza joint loads us up with carbohydrates. Bread sticks, bagels, hamburger buns, french fries, and thick crusts go down so easily and wreak havoc with our weight and our blood sugar levels.

The middle ground is somewhere in between. Eat enough carbohydrates for your health but not so much that you blimp up … or worse. Your body needs the carbohydrates in vegetables and fruits. Our government recommends that we eat a minimum of 5 and preferably 10 servings of fruits or vegetables a day.

> **Hot Potato**
> No-carb and very low-carb diets can be harmful to your health. You could be at risk for reduced kidney function by damaging your kidneys. If you have a history of low kidney function or have high blood pressure, diabetes, or are older than age 65, you are most at risk.

You can meet these recommendations eating low carb, but it is virtually impossible to do this eating no carb. Check out the vegetable, side salads, and fruit chapters. We placed special emphasis on making sure you can prepare fabulous vegetable and fruit side dishes that give your body the vitamins, phytonutrients, and antioxidants it needs.

Not All Carbs Are Created Equal

Years and years ago, when people, mostly dieters, started counting carbohydrates, it was easy. Plenty of carbohydrate counter books listed the counts. Dieters would plan their eating day simply by adding up carbs. If they wanted to eat a donut, they could, without guilt, simply by rearranging their feeding plan for the day.

Things aren't so easy today because we know more, much more. We know that fruits and vegetables are friends. We know we need to eat 5 to 10 servings of fruits and vegetables a day for health and well-being, not to mention dietary fiber.

We also know that not all carbohydrates are created equal. A donut is quite different than broccoli in how a person's blood sugar levels get stimulated. So counting carbohydrates gets a bit messy, if you will. Here's what you need to know:

Low-Carb Vocab

The **glycemic index** is the measurement of how fast a specific carbohydrate causes a rise in a person's blood sugar level. The higher the number on the glycemic index, the faster the rise in blood sugar. You can get a complete list at www.mendosa.com/gilists.htm.

Table Talk

When a person eats a high-glycemic food, blood sugar spikes. As a result, the pancreas gland, in a sense, overreacts and secretes more insulin than the body needs to lower the blood sugar. Leftover insulin causes the body to store yet more fat and makes the person hungry again soon afterward.

- A carb is still a carb, and you count carb grams the same as before.
- The quality of the food containing the carbohydrates may change which foods you choose to eat. This is called the *glycemic index*.

The glycemic index is a compilation of how different carbs affect a person's body. Actual scientific studies were conducted on hundreds of people. They were given different carbs to eat, and afterward, their blood sugar levels were tested.

The studies showed that some carbs made blood sugar levels spike. They are called high glycemic. And some didn't; those are called low glycemic. Some carbs are moderate glycemic because they raised blood sugar levels somewhat but didn't spike them. The carbohydrates that didn't spike blood sugar levels, the low-glycemic ones, are the best carbs to eat.

Low-glycemic carbohydrates are beneficial for those interested in eating low carb for weight loss, diabetes, high blood pressure, heart disease, and so on.

Glycemic Index in Short

The glycemic index only measures foods that are carbohydrates, so you won't find meat or fats in the glycemic index list. The following categories are based on the general ranking of carbohydrates according to the glycemic index. For the sake of simplicity, we have categorized carbohydrates into four broad categories to help explain the glycemic index.

- Highest in the glycemic index ranking are starches that include wheat, rice, corn, white potatoes, and products made from them such as bagels, cereal, and pastas. These products range from about 70 up to 165 and are considered high glycemic. Sweet potatoes and yams aren't included here, as their glycemic index count is low.
- Sugars are rated lower, with sucrose, or table sugar, at 68. Sugars are considered moderate glycemic. This category includes natural sugars such as honey and molasses. These range from about 56 to 69 and are considered medium glycemic.
- Fruits are considered low- to moderate-glycemic foods. This group includes apples, berries, oranges, peaches, pears, and other fruits, and rates range from about 30 to 50. Fifty-five or less is considered low glycemic.
- Vegetables are generally considered low glycemic and range from about 10 to 40. Broccoli, green beans, yams, sweet potatoes, cauliflower, and most other vegetables are in this group.

The carbohydrates with the lowest numbers are best to eat. They help keep your blood sugar on an even keel. So broccoli is better than a donut, table sugar is better than a bagel, an apple is better than sugar, etc., even if the carb counts are exactly the same. Often the lower-glycemic foods have more nutritional value.

For day-to-day eating, choose from fruits and vegetables and perhaps a bit of sugar. Save the starches for eating only occasionally, if at all. You can find a short list of the glycemic index of some ingredients in this book in Appendix B.

Cooking Low Glycemic

The glycemic index is brilliant in that it's comprised of experiments done on actual people. It shows how different carbohydrates actually affect the body. No prior studies have quantified results like the glycemic index has. The studies have required lots of effort over years with willing volunteers.

The glycemic index works for individual foods such as rice, but it doesn't work for combinations of foods. The very fact that the foods are combined changes the way the body reacts to them. For instance, we know that if you combine rice with a fat, such as butter, the glycemic count of the rice is lower than before. We know that if you make a brownie recipe with 5 eggs and ½ pound butter, the affect of the sugar in the brownie isn't the same as if a person ate the same amount of sugar all by itself. The eggs and butter lower the glycemic effect of the sugar. If a meal contains an acidic-tasting food, like a vinaigrette salad dressing, the glycemic index effect of the whole meal is lower.

What we don't know is by how much. The only way to know the glycemic count of a recipe, that is, of a combination of ingredients, is to run the same scientific tests. We didn't do that for this cookbook. No one, as of today, knows how to compute the glycemic index of a recipe without doing elaborate tests on willing volunteers over years.

We believe we would've had plenty of willing volunteers to test the recipes in this book. The food is that good. But we didn't have years and years for the study because we wanted to get this book into your hands right away.

This is our solution for using the glycemic index. We chose to use ingredients that are mostly low to moderate glycemic, with a bias toward low glycemic. For example, we offer you recipes for baked yams but not for white potatoes. In the bread recipes, we use very little wheat but include other low-glycemic flours and proteins.

The ingredients in the recipes, for the most part, are already low glycemic. So you can make these recipes knowing that your eating is comfortably low to moderate glycemic.

The Least You Need to Know

- Eating comfort foods makes for successful low-carb eating.
- Blending carbohydrate counts with glycemic index information best supports your health and weight loss efforts.
- Calculating carbohydrate counts is inexact but close.
- The nutritive carbohydrate count gives you the true bottom line on carbs.
- Eating the serving size amount listed with each recipe helps you calculate an accurate carb count.

Chapter 2

Meal Planning the Low-Carb Way

In This Chapter

- ◆ Eating a well-balanced diet
- ◆ Meeting your daily carbohydrate requirements
- ◆ Adding in comfort foods
- ◆ Planning your daily eating

There was a time when eating low carb meant consuming massive amounts of meat—steaks with lots of butter, chicken with the skin on, pork with lots of fat—and practically nothing else. Those of us who tried the all-protein-and-fat way would awaken in the middle of the night to raid, not the refrigerator, but the breadbox. We craved bread so much it hurt. Not only that, we were bored silly eating such a one-dimensional diet.

Yes, we loved steak, but too much of a good thing became a nightmare ... which could only be soothed and comforted by a sneaky midnight bread raid. Although, come to think of it, mashed potatoes or cookies also worked well to fill the void created by our meat-focused eating regimen.

Neither man nor woman was meant to live on meat alone. We need balance. When we don't get balance in our day-to-day eating, our bodies and spirits pay the price. That's not the way low-carb eating should be. So let sanity prevail! Return to a balanced diet by eating proteins, fats, and enough carbohydrates to control your carbohydrate cravings. You'll more likely reach ideal health, vitality, and size.

Brief History of Low-Carb Eating

Low-carb eating might appear to be a modern phenomenon started a couple decades ago through a few popular diet plans. However, its origins are much earlier than that—in fact, millions of years earlier. We are talking about our prehistoric ancestor, the "caveman." Whether these people lived in caves, jungles, or open savannas, our ancient ancestors just naturally ate low carb.

Hunter-gatherers didn't raise crops or possess domesticated animals. Their diet consisted of meats, fish, eggs, vegetables, fruits, nuts, seeds, and honey. Quite simply, there wasn't anything else to eat. And there certainly weren't any grocery stores offering pre-packaged cookies!

In fact, prehistoric hunter-gatherers didn't have milk or cheese, either. There were no domesticated animals to milk, and, undoubtedly, just the thought of milking an untamed woolly mammoth mama was terrifying enough. Yes, the caveman and woman ate fruits and honey that had some carbohydrates. But prehistoric man never ate enough high-glycemic carbohydrates to contract the diabetes or insulin resistance that is so common today.

Only in the recent history of mankind, within the past 5,000 to 10,000 years, has man eaten cereal grains and, with them, refined sugars. Today foods made from cereal grains and sugar are available on virtually every city and suburban street corner around the world. People often eat these high-carb foods in place of other more nutritious and health-giving foods in both affluent and developing countries.

In eating low carb, you are actually going back to your primitive roots and eating the foods that have sustained mankind for millions of years.

Well-Balanced Eating

The most important thing to know is that you can eat a balanced diet and eat low carb. They are totally consistent. You already know that a well-balanced diet can't include mounds of mashed potatoes, thick-crust pizza, and a big plate of pasta all in the same day. That's called carbohydrate loading. Perhaps you've done carbohydrate loading in the past, and by now you know there's got to be a better way.

Eating in balance is eating the best ratio of fats to proteins to carbs. Ideally, every meal and every snack should contain:

- ◆ **Less than 30 percent fats.** Fats include butter, oils, and the fats in meat, seafood, fish, eggs, and cheese.
- ◆ **About 30 to 40 percent proteins.** Complete proteins come from the animal world and include meat, fish, cheese, eggs, and seafood. Incomplete proteins come from vegetables, such as soy and other legumes plus grains.
- ◆ **About 30 to 40 percent carbohydrates.** If you are on a highly restricted carbohydrate-eating plan, you can choose to eat fruits, vegetables, sugars, milk, and starches that have the fewest carbs and still meet this requirement.

Eating in balance is easy when you understand how to plan meals and know which foods to keep around for snacks and meal preparation.

Nutritional Factors: The "Best"

Some proteins, fats, and carbohydrates are better for you nutritionally than others. So let's review the best choices you can make for each category.

Fats

In this cookbook, we have used the best fats as ingredients in the recipes. They are butter and cold expeller-pressed oils. The oils include mostly olive oil and walnut oil. The only exception is a recipe for a spinach salad that uses bacon fat in the dressing.

We haven't used fats that could contain trans-fatty acids. Also known as partially hydrogenated vegetable oils, trans-fatty acids have been shown to be dangerous to your health. Vegetable oils that are extracted using heat may also contain trans-fatty acids, so we simply didn't use them.

You may also notice that the only fat we use for heating, as in sautéing or baking, is butter. If you heat a vegetable oil, you run the very real risk of it turning into trans-fatty acids.

One important group of fats isn't listed as an ingredient in any of the recipes. We're talking about the *essential fatty acids* (*EFAs*). Your body needs EFAs for health. You get essential fatty acids when you eat cold-water fish, preferably salmon. You can also supplement your intake with EFAs purchased from a health food store.

Low-Carb Vocab

Essential fatty acids are fats that the body needs for health and well-being. They are designated "essential" by the government. This designation means that the body can't manufacture these nutrients from the foods it eats, and, thus, it must get them directly from foods or supplements.

Protein

The best sources of protein are animal products such as meat, fish, seafood, cheese, and eggs. Animal products contain all the nine essential amino acids that the body needs for health and life every day, which makes them *complete proteins*. All the main course dishes in this cookbook are made with complete proteins.

To calculate how much animal protein you need every day, divide your weight in pounds by 2. You need that many grams complete protein. If you weigh 150 pounds, then you need 75 grams complete protein a day. This calculation is a rule of thumb, and you may find that you need somewhat less or more.

Low-Carb Vocab

Complete proteins contain a full complement of the nine essential amino acids the body must get through food. The only sources of complete protein are animal products, such as fish, seafood, meat, eggs, and cheese.

For a low-carb eating plan, vegetable proteins, such as legumes and grains, can't easily meet your needs. Vegetable proteins are "incomplete proteins," lacking one or more of the nine essential amino acids. Each needs to be combined with another incomplete protein to give your body the full daily complement of amino acids.

The foods most often combined are various legumes and grains. Because the grains are high in carbohydrates, food combining doesn't work well for low-carb eating. Eating enough beans and grains to get your daily allotment of protein significantly overloads you with carbohydrates.

So you can make sure you're getting enough complete protein, we've included protein grams per serving in the scorecard after each recipe. You'll find the number of grams protein, the number of grams animal protein, and the number of grams vegetable protein. To insure that you get enough complete protein, add the complete protein listed with each recipe and do a daily total.

Carbohydrates

You really must consider your body's nutritional needs to figure out which carbs to eat. First and foremost, your body needs anywhere from 5 to 10 servings of fruits and vegetables a day. Does that sound like way too much food? It isn't if you put it into perspective. Half of a large-size apple or 1 small apple is 1 serving. So if you eat 1 large apple for breakfast, that counts as 2 servings. As a rule of thumb, 1 serving is ½ cup cooked vegetable or 1 cup raw.

Here's the wisest way to use your carb allotment:

◆ First, eat at least 5 servings vegetables and fruits. If your carb count allows, feel free to eat up to 10 servings.

◆ Next, if you have any carbohydrates left in your daily allotment after you've eaten the fruits and vegetables, choose a comfort food you especially enjoy and eat some of it. You'll find some low-carb comfort foods in the bread, grains, dessert, and chocolate chapters of this book.

The Need for Starches

Nutritionally speaking, your body doesn't need starches or sugars outside the natural sugar in fruit. This means that your body doesn't need such foods as white potatoes, wheat, rice, corn, or table sugar. It doesn't even need chocolate!

Your body can get all the carbohydrate nutrition it requires from eating fruits and vegetables. Vitamins, minerals, and antioxidants are abundant in fruits and vegetables, and many are even exclusive to fruits and vegetables, which means you can't get them from starches and sugars.

Although your body doesn't need starches and sugars, you may want to eat them for other reasons. Starchy and sugary foods provide treats and comfort. In other words, we often eat them for emotional reasons rather than to meet nutritional needs.

If you had to give up starches and refined sugars totally, you could live just fine and be very healthy. Of course, you don't want to. And you don't have to as long as you make them a minor part of your eating plan.

Table Talk
In this cookbook, you'll find many recipes and three whole chapters devoted to comfort foods. Chapter 22 gives you bread recipes, Chapter 23 covers grains, Chapter 24 has desserts, and Chapter 25 presents chocolate. Yes, you can have wonderful treats and comfort foods and still eat low carb.

Putting Together Meals

So how do you actually put together a low-carb meal? Fortunately, you'll find it quite straightforward. Here's what to do:

◆ Choose a main course from Chapters 4 through 16.

◆ If the recipe contains vegetables and fruits, you'll count them as 1 or 2 of your 5 to 10 servings for the day.

♦ If the recipe doesn't include vegetables or fruits, include 2 servings of fruits and vegetables with that meal.

It's really just that simple. With this plan in its most basic form, you'll consume ample complete protein, and you'll eat about 2 servings of vegetables and fruits each meal for a total of 6 for the day. You really don't need to be concerned about getting enough fat. You can assume that adequate fat will come from the main dishes and any additional butter or oil used in the recipes.

Don't Eat This Way

Recently a famous actress was in the news discussing her struggle to *gain* 30 pounds in 6 weeks for her next movie. Her eating program was so loaded with high-carb foods that would make even a carb junkie shudder at what she consumed! Take a look at her eating plan:

♦ **Breakfast:** A Big Mac with large fries, scones with gravy, and a high-fat milkshake

♦ **Lunch:** Pizza, peanut butter with chips, and doughnuts

♦ **Dinner:** Spaghetti with meat sauce with a side of mashed potatoes and butter

Eating like this would make anyone gain 30 pounds quickly. Imagine how many carbs she was eating each meal, let alone each day! Her eating plan had no fruits and vegetables. Why? Because they would have stalled or thwarted her weight gain!

What a great example! Just eat exactly the opposite of how this actress ate to reach your personal size and health goals. You'll be eating in balance and eating low carb.

Meal Recommendations

Let's take a closer look at what does and doesn't work for low-carb meals and also for snacks.

Breakfast

Works:

♦ Bacon, eggs, and fruit.

♦ Egg and cheese omelet with vegetables.

♦ Ham, salmon, chicken, steak, pork chops with vegetables and fruit.

♦ Fast-food egg and sausage "burger" without the bread, plus orange juice.

Doesn't work:

♦ Cereal and milk. Not enough protein, no fruits and veggies, too much starch.

♦ Yogurt with granola and fruit. Not enough protein and too many carbohydrates.

♦ Bagel with cream cheese. Not enough protein, too much starch, no veggies or fruits.

♦ Danish and coffee. Need we say more?

Lunch

Works:

♦ Main dish salad. Plenty of veggies, protein. Even the ones from a fast-food restaurant are good.

♦ Cheese and egg main dish with salad or fruit.

♦ Meat or fish sandwich on one slice of bread from bread recipe in Chapter 22.

♦ Meat, cheese, and vegetable rollups.

♦ Tuna fish salad eaten with a fork and fruit or with crackers from Chapter 22.

Doesn't work:

♦ Submarine sandwich with potato chips.

♦ Corn dog. But add some fruit, and this is passable.

♦ Fettuccine Alfredo with salad. Enough vegetables, but not enough protein and way too many carbs.

♦ Burger, fries, and a soft drink.

Dinner

Works:

♦ Roast beef or steak with asparagus and hollandaise sauce, plus salad.

♦ Meatloaf with "mock" mashed potatoes and salad.

♦ Fried chicken minus the skin with coleslaw and fruit.

♦ Clam mushroom chowder and a tossed romaine salad with capers and salami.

Doesn't work:

- Pizza. To make this work, eat the topping and toss the crust, then add a big salad.
- Pasta primavera with salad. Has virtually no complete protein and possibly few vegetables. Pasta will likely add too many carbs to your daily intake.
- Salsa, chips, and guacamole. Has the veggies, but where's the complete protein? Too many chips equal too many carbs.
- Spaghetti with meat sauce and salad. Chances are good the carb count is way too high unless you serve spaghetti squash in place of the pasta.

Snacks

These don't need to have the same portions of proteins, carbs, and fats as a meal, but they need to be low carb.

Works (all the snack recipes in this book):

- Chicken liver pâté.
- Parmesan crackers.
- Pork on a stick.
- A serving of trail mix.
- Rosemary nuts.
- Fruit with nut butter.
- Low-carb cookies from Chapter 24.

Doesn't work:

- Regular cookies from the store.
- Diet-soda soft drink and popcorn.
- Chips and salsa.
- Cheese and crackers. Instead of regular crackers, use slices of vegetables or simply nothing at all. Or use the cracker recipe in Chapter 22.

As you can tell from reading through these lists, what works is eating a balanced diet that is light on the starches. Getting used to low-carb eating requires you to adopt a different way of thinking about food.

Thinking of Eating

It can be quite a shock when a person first starts eating low carb. It's a shock to your eating habits, a shock to your mind, and certainly a shock to your nervous system. Every part of your body and being wants to know where the doughnuts are. You may be wondering how you can outsmart low-carb eating.

Until you actually experience the good feelings that come from eating low carb and until the doughnut cravings have subsided, you may be rather uncomfortable. But once the good feelings kick in, eating low carb will seem like a natural way to live.

When first starting to eat low carb, make it easy on yourself. Don't spend too much time anticipating food and eating. In that way eating becomes less emotional. Not that you won't enjoy the eating and the preparation, but you won't have to get caught up in feeling deprived or unsatisfied.

Being deprived of your normal starchy comfort foods can make you feel as if someone just stole your favorite teddy bear. Therein lies the problem. If eating were simply a way to sustain life and provide good health, what you eat wouldn't matter much. You'd just eat at meals and then get on with doing more interesting and rewarding activities. But eating is so much more than just chewing and swallowing. Eating is the fulfillment of a sensory and emotional expectation.

The Scorecard

At the beginning of every recipe, we have included a scorecard to let you know the carbohydrate and protein count of a serving. Here's what you might find on the scorecard:

- Total carbohydrates in grams.
- Total fiber in grams.
- Nutritive carbohydrates, the difference between the carbohydrate count and the fiber. This number represents the amount of usable carbohydrates in a serving.
- Total protein in grams.
- Total animal or complete protein. Use this to figure your protein count for the day.
- Total vegetable protein in a serving.

With this information, you can figure your carbohydrate allotment based on the recommendations of your eating plan.

Table Talk _____
The scorecard for a recipe may not contain all the information listed here. For example, some of the meat, fish, and poultry entrées don't contain vegetable protein, so it isn't listed.

All the numbers for the recipes are as accurate as we can make them. But the actual carbohydrate and protein counts of the food you prepare can vary based on the size, ripeness, and type of ingredients you use. Be sure to eat the recommended serving size, and overall, your carb and protein counts will be very close to those listed in the book.

The Least You Need to Know

♦ A balanced diet includes appropriate amounts of carbohydrates, protein, and fats.

♦ Consume vegetables and fruits in your daily carbohydrates before eating starches, treats, and snacks.

♦ Find ways to adapt this new way of eating to your overall life goals.

♦ Use the scorecard at the beginning of each recipe to tally your intake of nutritive carbohydrates and complete protein.

Chapter 3

Cooking the Low-Carb Way

In This Chapter

- ◆ Thinking as a low-carb cook
- ◆ Stocking a low-carb pantry
- ◆ Intelligently selecting ingredients
- ◆ Understanding portions

Cooking low-carb meals isn't much different than cooking as you've always cooked. You'll use the same techniques as before. Most likely, you'll be cooking with more fruits and vegetables, perhaps more meat, and fewer starchy ingredients, but other than that, preparation methods are the same and the cooking and baking methods are similar.

You already know how to cook, so you can easily cook low carb. The main differences won't be in your preparation methods; they'll be in how you think about ingredients and the combination of ingredients. You won't whip up desserts using regular wheat flour, sugar, and eggs, but you'll still whip up desserts. You'll still fix a delicious Italian meat sauce, but instead of serving it over boiled spaghetti or linguine, you'll serve it over spaghetti squash.

You will still delight in preparing and serving good food that you, your family, and your friends still *ooh* and *aah* over.

Preparing a Low-Carb Kitchen

Your pantry may be due for a little low-carb makeover. You don't need to toss out everything in the pantry and start all over again. But you'll use certain ingredients such as sugar and flour less frequently and in smaller quantities than before.

You'll keep more perishable foods in the vegetable crisper and use more eggs, butter, and olive oil. Do some kitchen shelf clearing as a way to make space for your new way of eating. We assume that low-carb eating is not a fad for you, but rather a whole new way of eating, cooking, and living.

You can toss some foods in your pantry. Here's what you can get rid of:

◆ Any vegetable oils that aren't cold expeller-pressed.

◆ Processed and pre-prepared convenience foods that have more than 25 grams carbohydrates per serving.

◆ Any low-fat products, as they have more carbs than the full-fat versions.

◆ High-carb snacks such as breads, crackers, cheese bites, and popcorn.

◆ Sugar-filled sodas.

If in doubt, keep the food item. If you're really attached to your favorite junk food, don't toss it. Keep it around for comfort. If you want to eat it from time to time, eat small amounts and keep a record of how many grams of carbs you eat. Using a daily carb journal will motivate you to avoid mindless snacking and late-night kitchen raids and help in pre-planning your daily menus per your daily carb allotment.

Low-Carb Ingredients

Using regular ingredients makes low-carb cooking much easier and actually less expensive. You don't need to spend hours driving from store to store searching for just the right ingredients—virtually all the ingredients in these recipes can be purchased at a large chain grocery store. You may need to make a trip to the local health food store for some of the ingredients but not many.

Sugars

Although there are plenty of artificial sugars available, we found that plain table sugar, sucrose, works just fine for low-carb cooking. It tastes good and leaves no aftertaste. It works perfectly in baked goods, meaning it browns beautifully and doesn't deteriorate with heat.

The American Diabetes Association (ADA) approves of regular table sugar as a sweetener for diabetics. The ADA suggests counting total carbohydrate intake rather than avoiding sugar. Small amounts of sugar are acceptable, provided that the daily carb intake is within a safe range. A person on a 1,600-calorie-per-day food plan can eat about 200 grams carbohydrates per day.

We chose not to use artificial sweeteners in our recipes because safety and health controversies surround all the artificial sugars available. We decided to avoid the controversy by using what we know works—regular table sugar.

If you're comfortable using a sugar substitute—the best is probably sucralose (brand name Splenda)—you can use it in the recipes. Use the same amount of sucralose as sugar.

The sugars listed here are all moderate glycemic, meaning that they only moderately stimulate a rise in blood sugar. When consumed in serving-size amounts found in the recipes, they're satisfying and great to use for low-carb cooking.

- **Table sugar.** We use as little as needed to give you good taste. Our recipes with sugar have fewer than 20 grams carbohydrates per serving.
- **Molasses.** Choose either light or dark, based on your personal preference. Molasses gives a wonderful "brown sugar" taste with fewer carbs than brown sugar.
- **Brown sugar.** Be sure to measure it unpacked.
- **Honey.** This all-natural sweetener is sweeter than table sugar and excellent for adding sweetness with fewer carbs.

Wheats, Pastas, and Grains

Here's an easy formula to remember: grains = carbs. Yep. It may not be what you want to hear, but you're better off confronting this simple fact directly.

Grains and grain flours are naturally high carb. And unfortunately, there's no magical way—at least none we know of—to make them naturally have fewer carbs. But don't despair. They can be used in recipes in small amounts so you get their taste and texture without all the carbs. Some of our recipes use grain-based ingredients in small amounts, although most avoid their use. Here are some key points:

> **Table Talk** _____
> Make nut flours by pro-
> cessing whole or chopped nuts in
> a food processor. Purchase bulk
> nuts in the grocery store or health
> food store bins. Generally speaking,
> ¾ cup nuts makes 1 cup nut flour.

- Many of our dessert recipes forego wheat flours entirely. Instead we use nut flours. They are out-of-this-world delicious. Our unsuspecting friends love the taste and never have a clue we left out the flour. Nut flours have very few carbs, if any.

- In place of high-carb spaghetti or fettuccine, we use spaghetti squash or shredded vegetables, such as zucchini. The taste is quite wonderful, and using vegetables in place of grain pastas adds more servings of nutrient-packed vegetables to your daily food intake.

- In place of lasagna noodles, we use long slices of zucchini. The zucchini gives you another vegetable serving, it's low carb, and it easily absorbs the flavors of the lasagna sauce and spices—so much so that you won't easily detect the zucchini taste.

- Some recipes just produce better results with flour. For these, we use either whole-wheat flour, rice flour, or white flour in minimum quantities.

- The bread recipes use little to no wheat flour, but instead call for wheat gluten, which gives bread its stick-together-ness. Other bread ingredients include psyllium husks, oat bran, soy powder, whey powder, and, of course, the wonderful nut flours.

- For grains we use quinoa, barley, brown rice, and basmati brown rice because they are lower glycemic than other options. They still have carbs, so be sure to eat the recommended serving amount or less.

- Cornstarch is excellent for thickening sauces, and we use it in some recipes.

Potatoes

Potatoes are also a naturally high-carb food. In general, if you're going to eat low carb, you'll need to limit your potato intake and avoid recipes that are loaded with potatoes. Rather than go completely without potatoes, however, we have devised recipes that let you have some. Consider these few details:

- You'll find recipes for sweet potatoes and yams, which are lower glycemic than white potatoes and have a sweeter taste.

◆ Cauliflower is an excellent vegetable substitute for mashed potatoes and potato salad. When prepared properly, it cooks up to have similar color and texture. If you prepare cauliflower with a little garlic, butter, or gravy, you may find you enjoy it quite a bit.

◆ Potato skins without the insides give you the taste without the carbs.

◆ You can make clam chowder with mushrooms instead of potatoes. You'll never even think of missing the potatoes when you taste this soup.

Fats

Thanks goodness, you can enjoy the mouth-satisfying taste of fat when eating low carb. With all the recent health controversy about trans-fatty acids, we have made sure our recipes use only the fats that are the healthiest for you:

◆ **Olive oil that is cold expeller-pressed.** We use this often but never heat it, as the heating can turn it into trans-fatty acids. In general, the darker the color of the oil, the higher it is in antioxidants.

◆ **Butter.** Butter heats beautifully, and nothing tastes quite like real butter. Use for sautéing, baking, and melting over steamed vegetables.

◆ **Walnut oils and other cold expeller-pressed oils.** You may need to shop at the health food store to find these. They are worth the price. Don't heat them, though.

◆ **Heated bacon fat.** You can heat it safely to use in small amounts, as in a salad dressing.

Dairy

We're no fans of low-fat or skim milk. And the recipes here call for dairy products in their full-fat versions. Why? Because low-fat dairy products usually have more carbs and when used for cooking, don't deliver as satisfying a product. Taste matters! It's amazing how often individuals will eat a much larger quantity of a low-fat food than the regular variety and, in the process, consume more calories and sometimes more fat, too!

◆ **Heavy cream.** Find the thickest, richest cream you can. Go beyond regular whipping cream if heavy cream is available.

◆ **Milk.** Use whole milk.

◆ **Cheeses.** Regular grocery store–quality cheeses work well in these recipes. Save yourself time and use the pre-grated cheeses that come in resealable bags when you can.

◆ **Eggs.** Use large eggs.

Fruits and Vegetables

Make friends with the produce aisle! Vegetables and fruits get heavy emphasis in our cookbook because of their value to your low-carb eating plans. Even though fruits may get a bad rap for containing carbs, they are much lower in carbs than junk food, fast food, and sugared sodas, not to mention french fries! Plus fruits are loaded with valuable vitamins, minerals, phytochemicals, and antioxidants.

There simply aren't any substitutes for fruits and vegetables; fortunately, you don't need substitutes. Purchase produce fresh or frozen and eat about 2 servings each meal. Yes, that's 2 servings for breakfast, lunch, and dinner. You really can't go wrong eating them, but you can definitely go wrong if you don't eat them.

Understanding Portions

Serving sizes in restaurants have grown every year. Super-size fast-food meals are now the norm and no longer a marketing advantage. People are accustomed to eating lots of food—in fact, lots and lots of food—way more than the human body requires.

One wonderful, though sometimes hidden aspect of low-carb eating is that it tends to replace super-size meals with right-size meals. Grain-based foods—just think of bread, cake, and spaghetti—are precisely the kinds of foods we tend to overeat. Most of us who switch to low-carb eating just naturally tend to eat less.

The nutritive carb count of each recipe in the scorecard is directly related to the recommended serving size. Your successful low-carb eating depends on eating the recommended amount or less.

The Least You Need to Know

♦ You can make your pantry low carb by switching out some items for their low-carb counterparts.

♦ Most ingredients for low-carb cooking are available locally.

♦ Regular cooking ingredients can produce great low-carb meals.

♦ Grain-based ingredients and potatoes tend to be high carb, but most other ingredients are not.

♦ Eating smaller portions of low-carb foods will leave you satisfied without overeating.

Part 2

Breakfasts and Lunches

The first meal of the day, breakfast, can supply you with energy to burn for the rest of your day. Yes, eating a good low-carb breakfast sets the stage for a good high-energy day.

Making a quick low-carb breakfast is a high priority in our time-challenged lives. You no longer need to skip breakfast because you don't have anything on hand to eat. These recipes give you countless ways to grab a great breakfast—fast and easy. And one chapter has many recipes for enjoying a leisurely late-morning or weekend brunch.

Pack a delicious low-carb lunch for work or outings and avoid the standard sandwich and chips. Instead, savor meat and cheese rollups, trail mix, and homemade nut butters with fruit.

Chapter 4

Breakfast on the Run

In This Chapter

- Eating our most important meal
- Getting enough complete protein
- Rushing to get out the door

Ah, donuts! We've all loved them, but we also all know they aren't exactly what the nutritionist—or our mother!—would recommend as the ideal way to begin a day. Plus, they are very high carb.

You've heard that a "good breakfast" is your most important meal of the day. Whether or not you eat a good breakfast can determine your overall energy levels and even your moods for hours. A good breakfast is a key way to avoid sudden drops in energy and cravings for a sugar lift come mid-morning. So what constitutes a "good breakfast"? The answer is simple— a low-carb one.

A low-carb breakfast gives you the protein, fat, and enough carbs to stoke your metabolism and get your fat-burning system running on high speed.

But figuring out what to eat for breakfast takes forethought and some planning, especially on those days when you're rushing to get yourself and your family out the door in the mornings. That's why this chapter is devoted to solving the very real problem of how to eat this most important of meals when you're in a rush.

Rise and Shine

Skipping breakfast isn't a great idea. In fact, it's a terrible idea. Your body needs food to "break fast," that is, to restore itself following the long fasting period since supper the night before. Most likely a person hasn't eaten any food for 8 to 12 hours by the time he rises and shines. You want not only to rise but also to shine, and breakfast helps you do just that.

In breaking your fast, you jump-start the body's energy-making machine for the whole day:

◆ Your metabolism goes into high gear when you eat a good, balanced breakfast.

◆ Because your metabolism cues fat-burning, a good, balanced breakfast helps you stay at your ideal size and even lose weight.

◆ Eating a good, balanced breakfast helps keep your energy levels high all day long and into the evening.

◆ As an extra bonus, eating a good, balanced breakfast can keep your moods lifted, your disposition friendly, and your mind and body productive.

"All this from breakfast?" you ask. Absolutely!

A Good, Balanced Breakfast

A good, balanced breakfast provides you with a balanced meal of protein, fat, and carbohydrates. We're not talking about a lot of carbohydrates, but some, because, as you know, you need some carbs for health and energy.

So let's look specifically at what's in a good, low-carb breakfast:

◆ High-quality complete protein that comes from meat, fish, eggs, or cheese. On the average, you need 15 to 20 grams animal protein at each meal, breakfast included. Men may need more.

◆ At least 1 serving either fruits or vegetables, preferably 2.

◆ A modest amount of fat. Yes, fat is absolutely necessary for a healthy diet and a healthy you. You'll get some fat in the eggs, meat, and cheese, plus the butter used for cooking. Fat gives you energy to burn.

As you have probably noticed, cereal just doesn't make the grade, ditto yogurt and granola, and certainly a Danish or bagel washed down with coffee doesn't qualify. So what does?

Think of traditional old-fashioned breakfasts with ham and eggs, omelets, fresh fruit, steak and eggs, or fish. Or what about the sort of thing one might find at a country breakfast in England? Now, that's a good breakfast.

Table Talk

The simple truth is this: What you eat for breakfast can be anything you want. Just because other folks eat a Danish with a cup of coffee doesn't mean you need to. Gosh, you can cook up green beans or asparagus for breakfast if you want. You can fry up a steak or some halibut. How about having a little leftover barbecue? If you enjoy it, that's what counts.

Food That's Ready Fast, Not Fast Food

A leisurely breakfast can be hard to manage in a busy household. Too often there's not enough time, and getting breakfast prepared and eaten when you're rushed is challenging. But it can be lots easier when you know how.

So even though your mornings are rushed, there's still time for a great breakfast. Just get creative. And never forget how important a good breakfast is for your health—and for your family's. Rise and shine with these quick breakfasts.

Microwave Bacon

Prep time: 5 minutes • Cook time: 8 minutes • Serves 4 • Serving size: 2 slices

Each serving has: 5 grams total protein • 5 grams from animal source

8 slices bacon

Line a baking dish with a layer of white paper towels. Arrange bacon slices on the paper towels so that each slice is flat, but they can be touching. Cover with another layer of paper towels.

Place in a microwave on high for 8 minutes or until bacon is done.

To cook more bacon, you can add another layer of bacon on top of the paper towels. Then cover with one more layer of paper towels. Add 1 minute cooking time for each additional slice of bacon.

Variation: Cooked salami, as a substitute for bacon, is great with eggs for breakfast or crumbled into a tossed salad. To cook salami, arrange it in a baking dish as you did the bacon. Depending on the thickness of the salami, cook 30 seconds to 1 minute per slice.

Recipe for Success _____
This method makes great bacon and doesn't smell up the house as much as frying bacon does. You also don't have to dispose of the grease in the pan—simply toss the paper towels in the trash. Keep in mind that some paper towels are made without dyes, inks, and perfumes and are considered hypo-allergenic. Look for towels that are bleached with sodium hydrosulfite whose by-product is oxygen and water, instead of using chlorine, whose by-products are dioxin, furons, and other harmful substances.

Granola

Prep time: 10 minutes   •   Cook time: 1 hour   •   Serves 18   •   Serving size: ½ cup

Each serving has: 20 grams carbohydrate   •   4 grams fiber   •   16 grams nutritive carbohydrate   •   10 grams total protein   •   10 grams from plant source

½ cup (1 stick) butter

2½ cups old-fashioned rolled oats

1 cup sunflower seeds

¾ cup wheat germ

1 cup flaked coconut, unsweetened

½ cup chopped walnuts

1 cup pumpkin seeds

½ cup wheat bran

¼ cup golden raisins

¼ cup dried cranberries

½ cup whole almonds

¼ cup honey

Recipe for Success _____
Use this granola as a side dish for breakfast. Make the main course eggs, meat, fish, or cheese. You can have the granola on the side as a finger food, or eat it topped with some heavy cream, half-and-half, or yogurt. It's also great as a trail mix snack.

Preheat oven to 250°F.

Melt butter in a large, shallow roasting pan on top of the stove. Remove from heat and stir in oats, sunflower seeds, wheat germ, coconut, walnuts, pumpkin seeds, wheat bran, raisins, cranberries, and almonds. Mix well.

Drizzle honey over mixture, and stir until well blended.

Place the pan in the oven, and toast for 1 hour, stirring every 15 minutes. Store in an airtight container.

Microwave Scrambled Eggs

Prep time: 2 minutes • Cook time: 3 minutes • Serves 2 • Serving size: 1 egg

Each serving has: 1 gram nutritive carbohydrate • 10 grams total protein • 10 grams from animal source

1 TB. butter

3 large eggs

1 TB. water

Salt and pepper to taste

Place butter in a glass measuring cup or bowl. Microwave on high for 20 seconds. Mix eggs and water into melted butter until well mixed. Place container in the microwave on high for 1 minute. Stir eggs. Microwave for 1 more minute or until eggs are just a slight bit runny. Let stand 1 minute before serving. Salt and pepper to taste.

Recipe for Success

If you aren't hungry for breakfast, crack some eggs into a glass or plastic container. Add a pat of butter, and cover with the lid. Take the container to work. By the time you get there, the eggs should be well mixed. Cook mixture in a microwave when you get hungry, and you have a perfect breakfast on the run.

Egg Pancake

Prep time: 5 minutes • Cook time: 10 minutes • Serves 1 • Serving size: 1 pancake

Each serving has: 1 gram nutritive carbohydrate • 13 grams total protein • 13 grams from animal source

1 TB. butter

2 eggs, beaten

Salt and pepper to taste

1 TB. chopped onion, bell pepper, tomato, salsa, or chopped cooked meat

Melt butter in a 10-inch skillet over medium-low heat, add beaten eggs, and spread in the skillet. Cook eggs without stirring until set.

Invert the skillet over a plate to allow egg pancake to fall onto the plate.

Sprinkle with salt and pepper or small amount of chopped vegetable or meat. Roll up to eat on the run.

Boiled Eggs

Prep time: 5 minutes • Cook time: 20 minutes • Serves 6 • Serving size: 1 egg

Each serving has: Less than 1 gram carbohydrate • 6 grams total protein • 6 grams from animal source

6 eggs, raw, in shell

Place eggs in a large saucepan without stacking on top of one another. Add enough water to cover tops by 1 inch. Cover the pan and rapidly bring water to a boil.

Table Talk
Eggs have all the amino acids the body needs in the correct proportion; in fact, the egg is the basic standard against which all other protein foods are measured. Who said the egg is not a healthy food?

Remove the pan from heat, and allow it to stand, covered, for 15 minutes. Remove eggs from hot water, and immediately place them into a bowl of cold water. This helps make shells easier to remove and prevents discoloration of yolks.

To remove shells, tap surface of egg to crack; roll egg between hands to loosen shell; and beginning at larger end of egg, peel off shell. It may help to dip egg into the bowl of cold water to ease off shell.

Ham Rollups

Prep time: 10 minutes • Cook time: 0 • Serves 3 • Serving size: 2 rollups

Each serving has: 4 grams carbohydrate • 1 gram fiber • 3 grams nutritive carbohydrate • 28 grams total protein • 28 grams from animal source

6 slices ham

6 slices cheese (your favorite)

6 TB. various fruits or vegetables, matchstick size or chopped

Top ham slice with cheese and various small pieces of fruit or vegetables of choice. Roll up ham; place in sandwich bags if not eaten immediately.

Suggestions for vegetables: bell pepper, radish, celery, broccoli flowerets, raw spinach, tomato, carrot, etc.

Suggestions for fruits: pineapple bits, apple, banana, peach, berries, dried fruits, etc.

Hot Potato

Matchstick size slices of vegetables or small bits of fruit make it easier to roll inside the meat and cheese to prevent falling out the sides. This is a great way to use up leftovers or to get finicky kids to try a new fruit or veggie. The rollups may be heated in the microwave till cheese melts, if desired.

It's important to remember to keep rollups refrigerated because of the high protein content. Be sure to keep on ice if not eaten within 30 minutes. The rollups are great to make ahead of time and portioned into small sandwich or snack bags; grab several to take along for breakfast or a snack.

Egg Rolls

Prep time: 10 minutes • Cook time: 20 minutes • Serves 6 • Serving size: 1 egg roll

Each serving has: 13 grams carbohydrate • 2 grams fiber • 11 grams nutritive carbohydrate • 15 grams total protein • 13 grams from animal source • 2 grams from plant source

6 eggs, beaten

1½ cups milk or cream

½ cup flour

5 green onions, thinly sliced

Salt and pepper to taste

1 cup (4 oz.) shredded cheddar cheese

Preheat oven to 350°F.

Line a 10×15-inch rimmed baking sheet with aluminum foil; coat foil with butter.

Recipe for Success

You can add chopped cooked ham, bacon, sausage, or vegetables to this mixture before baking. If preparing more than one, you can refrigerate the baked rolls. When ready to serve, cut and reheat. The rolls are especially delicious served with salsa!

In a large bowl, whisk together eggs, milk, flour, onions, salt, and pepper. When mixture is smooth, pour evenly onto the baking pan.

Bake for 12 to 15 minutes until set. Sprinkle evenly with cheese and bake 2 minutes or until cheese is melted.

Cool for 5 minutes. Carefully lift the foil (eggs and all) and remove from the baking pan. Starting from smaller end, roll up the eggs, jellyroll style, carefully releasing them from the foil as you roll. Slice into 1-inch pieces and serve.

Open-Face Canadian Bacon Sandwich

Prep time: 10 minutes • Cook time: 5 minutes • Serves 2 • Serving size: 1 slice Canadian bacon and 1 egg

Each serving has: 1 gram nutritive carbohydrate • 14 grams total protein • 12 grams from animal source • 2 grams from plant source

2 Canadian bacon rounds

2 eggs

Salt and pepper to taste

1 slice favorite cheese

2 slices tomato, optional

Slowly warm cooked Canadian bacon in a skillet over medium heat. While meat is warming, break 1 egg into a custard cup or similar small dish. Prick yolk with a fork, season with salt and pepper if desired, cover with a paper towel, and cook in a microwave approximately 45 to 60 seconds.

Place Canadian bacon on small plate, top with egg and tomato (if desired), and cover with ½ cheese slice. Microwave approximately 15 seconds until cheese melts.

Eat as an open-face sandwich.

Recipe for Success

You may add additional vegetables such as mushrooms, bell pepper, chopped onion, etc. If desired, place a second round of Canadian bacon on top of cheese to make a "sandwich."

Make-Ahead Italian Bake

Prep time: 10 minutes • Cook time: 30 minutes • Serves 6 • Serving size:1 square

Each serving has: 13 grams carbohydrate • 2 grams fiber • 11 grams nutritive carbohydrate • 9 grams total protein • 7 grams from animal source • 2 grams from plant source

1 TB. butter	¼ tsp. cayenne
½ cup chopped green onions	2 large eggs, beaten
1 cup sliced mushrooms	½ cup shredded cheddar cheese
1 (14-oz.) can artichoke hearts, drained and chopped	½ cup shredded Swiss cheese
½ tsp. dried oregano	½ cup Italian breadcrumbs

Recipe for Success
This recipe makes a delicious hot or cold snack or even breakfast on the run.

Preheat oven to 350°F.

Melt butter in a skillet, and sauté onions and mushrooms. Combine artichoke hearts with oregano, cayenne, eggs, cheddar and Swiss cheeses, and breadcrumbs; add onion and mushrooms and stir well.

Pour into a buttered 8-inch-square pan. Bake for 30 minutes until set.

Cut into 6 squares. Refrigerate leftovers for the next day.

The Least You Need to Know

- A good breakfast contains complete protein, fruits or veggies, and fat.
- Eating a good, balanced, low-carb breakfast boosts your metabolism.
- Eating a quick, healthy breakfast gives you all the nutrition you need to jump-start your day.
- Eat any meats, fish, eggs, and cheese you like for breakfast, but avoid traditional starch-filled breakfast foods like toast and cereal.

Chapter 5

Leisurely Breakfasts

In This Chapter

- ◆ Taking time for breakfast
- ◆ Planning the meal
- ◆ Selecting brunch ingredients

It's a cozy Saturday morning, and the paper has arrived. Now's the time to relax and enjoy cooking and eating delicious brunch fare. Of course, you can also enjoy these recipes for lunch or dinner or on any day of the week when you have the time. But there's something about a leisurely breakfast that will put a smile on everyone's face and yours, too.

So set the stage for serving these delightful meals with soft classical music playing in the background, flowers on the table, and good china with cloth napkins.

Filled with Goodness

The ingredients in these recipes are selected specifically because they yield a low-carb entrée. Here's a list of what the recipes call for:

- ◆ **Whole-fat dairy products.** Use whole cream, cheese, and milk. Substituting low-fat versions will increase the carbohydrate count.

- ◆ **Vegetables.** As best possible, choose fresh or frozen. Avoid the canned versions, as they have fewer nutrients. We encourage you to try organic vegetables for their purity if you can find them affordably.

- ◆ **Real butter.** Don't use margarine or butter substitutes. If you do, you'll not only compromise flavor and texture, but you'll be eating foods that aren't so great for your overall health. Our simple motto: Butter is better.

- ◆ **Eggs.** Use large eggs. Don't use commercially available egg substitutes, as you may not get the results you want.

- ◆ **Chicken broth.** If you don't have this on hand, you can make an acceptable substitute by using a chicken bouillon cube and water. Just omit the salt in the recipe, as bouillon has plenty of salt.

Whether cooking for family or friends, these recipes are terrific to serve to weekend guests or even before the big game. Your guests will applaud your cooking, want the recipes, and be shocked to learn that dishes that taste so good can be low carb, too.

Eggs Benedict

Prep time: 15 minutes • Cook time: 5 minutes • Serves 6 • Serving size: 2 slices Canadian bacon with 1 egg

Each serving has: 5 grams nutritive carbohydrate • less than 1 gram fiber • 27 grams total protein • 26 grams from animal source • 1 gram from plant source

½ cup (1 stick) butter

4 egg yolks at room temperature

1 TB. fresh lemon juice

1 dozen eggs

12 slices Canadian bacon

½ lb. washed spinach leaves

12 slices tomato

Prepare hollandaise sauce first: Melt butter in a pan or the microwave. Put egg yolks and lemon juice into a blender. Turn on the blender, and slowly pour warm butter into the blender. Whir for a couple seconds. Set aside.

Poach eggs, keeping yolks whole and partially runny. On each plate, place 2 slices Canadian bacon, and top with 4 to 5 spinach leaves and 1 tomato slice. Top with poached egg.

Spoon hollandaise sauce over eggs, and serve right away.

Ham Flan

Prep time: 20 minutes • Cook time: 60 minutes • Serves 6 • Serving size: 1 wedge

Each serving has: 2 grams nutritive carbohydrate • less than 1 gram fiber • 10 grams total protein • 10 grams from animal source

1½ cups cream

1 cup chopped ham

1 TB. chopped green onions

1 tsp. black pepper

4 eggs

Preheat oven to 325°F.

Stirring constantly, heat cream in a saucepan over medium-low heat until small bubbles form. Remove the pan from heat, and stir in ham, green onions, and pepper.

Beat 1 egg in a small bowl, and slowly pour in about 2 tablespoons hot mixture; stir until combined. Beat second egg into this mixture by hand. Pour eggs into slightly cooled mixture in the saucepan. Add last 2 eggs, beating as each is added until completely combined.

Table Talk _____

When adding raw eggs to a hot mixture, always first stir a small portion of the hot mixture into the beaten egg to warm it up. If the raw egg is dumped suddenly into the hot mixture, the protein in the egg will likely coagulate, clump, and partially cook (think scrambled).

Pour mixture into a buttered pie pan, and place in a larger pan of hot water. Bake for 45 minutes until set. Insert a clean knife into custard to be sure it is done. The knife should come out clean when thoroughly cooked. Cut into 6 wedges.

Variation: Try adding 1 cup of your favorite grated cheese to the hot cream and stirring until it melts; then add the rest of the ingredients as instructed. This dish is just as delicious served cold and cut into wedges. It makes a great breakfast on the run or an afternoon snack.

Asparagus Tart

Prep time: 20 minutes   •   Cook time: 60 minutes   •   Serves 6   •   Serving size: 1 wedge

Each serving has: 3 grams nutritive carbohydrate   •   less than 1 gram fiber   •   11 grams total protein   •   10 grams from animal source   •   1 gram from plant source

1½ cups cream	1 tsp. paprika
1 cup grated Swiss cheese	4 eggs
1 TB. diced red onion	½ cup blanched fresh asparagus or drained canned asparagus, cut into bite-size pieces
1 TB. diced bell pepper	
1 tsp. black pepper	

Preheat oven to 325°F.

Stirring constantly, heat cream in a saucepan over medium-low heat until small bubbles form. Add cheese and stir continuously until melted. Remove the pan from heat, and blend in onion, bell pepper, black pepper, and paprika.

Beat 1 egg in a small bowl, and slowly pour in about 2 tablespoons hot mixture; stir until combined. Beat second egg into this mixture with a fork. Pour egg mixture into slightly cooled mixture in the saucepan. Add last 2 eggs, beating as each is added until completely combined.

Line a buttered pie pan with asparagus, and pour mixture into the pan. Place pan into a larger pan of hot water, and bake for 45 minutes, until set.

Insert a clean knife into custard to be sure it is done. The knife should come out clean when thoroughly cooked. Cut into 6 wedges.

Variations: This tart is so refreshing served cold and cut into wedges. It makes a great afternoon pick-me-up snack. Serve with fresh fruit or a light green salad with chopped green apples. If you are not a lover of asparagus, any vegetable may be substituted, such as ½ cup green beans or cooked spinach. This is a great way to use leftover vegetables!

Table Talk
Stirring a small amount of the hot mixture into the egg helps prevent cooking the egg versus dumping the egg into the saucepan and ending up with egg drop soup!

Brunch Egg Casserole

Prep time: day before, 20 minutes • Cook time: 45 minutes • Serves 6 •
Serving size: ⅙ casserole

Each serving has: 12 grams nutritive carbohydrate • less than 1 gram fiber • 30 grams
total protein • 27 grams from animal source • 3 grams from plant source

4 slices whole-wheat bread, crust removed

1 lb. ground sausage or sausage links, thinly
sliced

1 cup chopped vegetable mixture, such as
mushrooms, bell peppers, onions, pimento,
jalapeño peppers, etc.

1 cup (4 oz.) shredded cheddar cheese

6 eggs

1 tsp. dry mustard

Pepper to taste

2 cups cream

Preheat oven to 350°F.

Lightly toast bread and break into small pieces; place bread in a 9×13-inch buttered glass baking
dish.

Brown sausage in a skillet over medium heat. Drain and pat with white paper towels (white
paper towels don't have the added colors that bleed into the food and add mystery ingredients
that are less than healthy). Sprinkle sausage over bread;
next layer with vegetables and cheese.

Recipe for Success

This casserole is best
when it stands 30 minutes
after baking. It's a great dish to have
on hand for company because it
can be frozen in the pan before baking. Remove it from the freezer and
thaw overnight in the refrigerator.

Beat eggs with a fork in a small bowl. Add dry mustard,
pepper, and cream. Beat again.

Pour egg mixture evenly over all ingredients.

Cover with foil and refrigerate overnight.

Remove foil. Bake 45 minutes or until casserole is bubbly and lightly browned on top. Let stand 30 minutes
after baking.

Salmon Soufflé

Prep time: 20 minutes • Cook time: 50 to 60 minutes • Serves 6 • Serving size: ⅙ soufflé

Each serving has: 4 grams nutritive carbohydrate • 19 grams total protein • 19 grams from animal source

1 (15½-oz.) can salmon, drained	4 egg yolks, beaten
3 TB. butter	½ tsp. pepper
3 TB. flour	½ tsp. dill
1 cup cream	4 egg whites, stiffly beaten

Preheat oven to 350°F.

Drain salmon, remove skin and bones, and *flake*.

Melt butter in a saucepan over low heat; gradually add flour and cream, and stir until thickened.

Remove the pan from heat. Stir small amount of hot mixture into beaten egg yolks to keep yolks from coagulating and partially cooking. Now slowly pour egg yolks into hot mixture, stirring constantly. Cook over low heat 1 minute; add pepper, dill, and flaked salmon.

After egg whites are *stiffly beaten*, slowly fold salmon mixture into egg whites; lightly fold egg whites over and over until combined with salmon mixture.

Pour into a buttered 2-quart baking dish. Place the dish in a larger pan of hot water, and bake for 50 to 60 minutes.

Serve immediately.

Variations: This soufflé makes a delightful addition to a company breakfast buffet or light lunch with fresh fruit. There are almost as many variations of this soufflé as you can imagine. In place of the salmon you can add 1 cup grated cheese and stir until it melts or add 1 cup chopped spinach or chopped onions. Let your imagination run wild!

Low-Carb Vocab

To **flake** means to break up with a fork into bite-size pieces. To **stiffly beat** egg whites, use a large bowl and whip with electric mixer until peaks form and stand up straight.

Mexican Omelet

Prep time: 10 minutes • Cook time: 15 minutes • Serves 2 • Serving size: ½ omelet

Each serving has: 18 grams carbohydrate • 3 grams fiber • 15 grams nutritive carbohydrate • 7 grams total protein • 5 grams from animal source • 2 grams from plant source

1 (14-oz.) can chicken broth	1 (4-oz.) can chopped green chilies
¼ cup chopped onion	1 TB. cornstarch (optional)
¼ cup chopped bell pepper	4 eggs, beaten
1 clove garlic, crushed	½ cup grated cheddar cheese
1 (15-oz.) can chopped tomatoes, drained	

To make sauce: Pour chicken broth into a skillet. Add chopped onion, bell pepper, and garlic. Simmer and add tomatoes and chilies. Cook 10 minutes. If not thickened, pour ¼ cup mixture into a glass cup, and stir in cornstarch (if using) until it makes a smooth paste. Pour paste into the skillet, and stir until sauce thickens.

Recipe for Success

If you prefer a spicier omelet, you may add ¼ teaspoon each cumin, chili powder, and oregano along with chopped jalapeño peppers. This makes a great luncheon dish served with fresh fruit. For fluffier, mile-high omelets, beat the egg whites separately and fold them into the yolks before pouring into the omelet pan.

While sauce simmers, heat remaining 4 tablespoons butter in a skillet. Tilt pan so butter coats sides of pan all the way to the top to prevent omelet from sticking. Set pan over medium-low heat. Pour batter into skillet. With a spatula, push egg in from the sides to allow top, uncooked egg to run over to pan. When eggs are set on bottom, immediately add grated cheese and fold omelet in half. Cook another 5 minutes until puffed up.

Remove mixture from the pan, cut into 2 servings, placing ½ omelet on each plate, and pour sauce on top.

For additional omelets, wipe the pan with a paper towel, and repeat for next omelet. You will have enough sauce for about 3 omelets.

German Pancakes

Prep time: 15 minutes • Cook time: 3 minutes • Serves 4 • Serving size: ¼ pancake

Each serving has: 9 grams nutritive carbohydrate • 10 grams total protein • 10 grams from animal source

6 eggs	¼ cup milk
1 TB. sugar	3 TB. butter
2 TB. cornstarch	6 tsp. lemon juice
½ tsp. salt	Powdered sugar
¼ cup water	

Beat eggs with sugar, cornstarch, salt, water, and milk. Heat 2 tablespoons butter in an omelet pan. Pour batter into the pan, and cook as an omelet.

Divide omelet onto 4 plates. Put ½ tablespoon butter and 1 teaspoon lemon juice on each serving. Sprinkle lightly with powdered sugar.

Recipe for Success

German pancakes have a slightly sweet taste, balanced with the lemony butter on top. You can also serve them with the following pancake syrup recipe and omit the lemon juice and powdered sugar. This will be a positive hit every time you serve or eat it. The pancake puffs up when cooking but usually falls before serving. The edges get lightly browned and crusty.

Pancake Syrup

Prep time: 5 minutes • Cook time: 5 minutes • Serves 8 • Serving size: 2 tablespoons

Each serving has: 12 grams nutritive carbohydrate • 0 grams total protein

1 cup water	1 cup no-sugar-added preserves (avoid those sweetened with sugar substitutes)

Heat water in a saucepan until bubbles appear. Slowly add preserves, stirring continuously until completely combined. Cook for 5 minutes until of syrup consistency.

Serve warm or cold.

Easy Cheese Breakfast Soufflé

Prep time: 10 minutes • Cook time: 35 to 40 minutes • Serves 6
• Serving size: ⅙ soufflé

Each serving has: 5 grams nutritive carbohydrate • 17 grams total protein
• 17 grams from animal source

6 eggs

1 cup heavy cream

Salt and pepper to taste

¼ tsp. nutmeg

1 cup grated Swiss or cheddar cheese

½ cup grated Parmesan cheese

Preheat oven to 425°F.

Beat eggs until thick and light. Stir in cream, salt, pepper, and nutmeg. Fold in cheeses. Pour into a well-buttered 1½-quart baking dish or a 10½-inch ovenproof skillet.

Bake 35 to 40 minutes until set.

Crustless Quiche

Prep time: 15 minutes • Cook time: 45 minutes • Serves 8 • Serving size: ⅛ casserole

Each serving has: 4 grams nutritive carbohydrate • 23 grams total protein
• 23 grams from animal source

½ cup (1 stick) butter

2 TB. flour

6 eggs

1 cup milk

1 lb. Monterey Jack cheese, cubed

1 (3-oz.) pkg. cream cheese, softened

2 cups cottage cheese

½ cup diced ham

½ cup chopped spinach

1 tsp. baking powder

½ tsp. salt

1 tsp. sugar

Preheat oven to 325°F.

Melt butter in a small saucepan. Add flour and cook until smooth. Beat eggs and milk. Stir in Monterey Jack cheese, cream cheese, cottage cheese, ham, spinach, baking powder, salt, sugar, and butter-flour mixture. Stir until well blended. Pour into a well-greased 9×13×2-inch pan.

Bake uncovered for 45 minutes.

Recipe for Success

Quiche is wonderful—and easier—made without the crust. You'll enjoy the creamy taste of the eggs and cheeses.

Cranberry Eggs

Prep time: 10 minutes • Cook time: 50 to 60 minutes • Serves 10
• Serving size: ¹⁄₁₀ recipe

Each serving has: 25 grams carbohydrate • 6 grams fiber • 19 grams nutritive carbohydrate
• 5 grams total protein • 2 grams from animal source • 3 grams from plant source

2 eggs	1 cup almond flour
¾ cup sugar	½ cup chopped pecans
½ cup (1 stick) butter, melted	2 cups whole fresh or frozen cranberries

Preheat oven to 325°F.

Combine eggs, sugar, butter, almond flour, pecans, and cranberries. Pour into a greased baking dish. Bake 50 to 60 minutes. Serve warm.

Recipe for Success _____

Use this as a side dish for a leisurely and special breakfast. It's great for the holidays. Add meat such as ham or bacon to balance the sweet-tart taste of this recipe and to get enough complete protein for your meal.

Scrambled Eggs with Tomato and Basil

Prep time: 15 minutes • Cook time: 50 to 60 minutes • Serves 4
• Serving size: ¼ omelet

Each serving has: 3 grams nutritive carbohydrate • less than 1 gram fiber • 13 grams total protein • 13 grams from animal source

8 eggs	2 TB. butter
1 tomato, diced	Salt and pepper to taste
¼ cup chopped fresh basil	

Beat eggs lightly in a bowl. Add tomato and basil. Heat butter in a skillet until melted. Add egg mixture and cook. Stir gently to scramble eggs. Omelet is ready to eat when it is cooked just enough—not runny, but not hard.

Recipe for Success _____
The fresh basil gives a light, refreshing, and aromatic taste to eggs. The tomatoes and basil dress up regular scrambled eggs and leave people asking for your special secret. And guess what? These are so simple to make.

Eggs with Spinach

Prep time: 15 minutes • Cook time: 30 minutes • Serves 6 • Serving size: 1 egg

Each serving has: 8 grams nutritive carbohydrate • less than 1 gram fiber • 14 grams total protein • 13 grams from animal source • 1 gram from plant source

2 TB. butter

2 TB. flour

2 cups cream

1 tsp. white pepper

1 (10-oz.) pkg. frozen spinach, thawed and squeezed dry

6 eggs

1 cup shredded cheddar or Mozzarella cheese

Preheat oven to 350°F.

Heat butter in a pan and add flour, stirring constantly until thick. Add cream and pepper and stir until well blended.

Line bottom of a buttered oblong baking dish with spinach. Make 6 indentations in spinach, and break 1 egg into each.

Pour cream sauce over eggs, and sprinkle with cheese.

Bake for 30 minutes.

Recipe for Success _____
You can easily change this basic recipe with additions of various seasonings. In spinach cups, place red onion rings, bell pepper, mushrooms, or olives before adding the raw egg. Then, garnish with green onions, chilies, or chopped tomato before serving.

The Least You Need to Know

◆ Brunch entrées are easily and naturally low carb.

◆ Using the specified ingredients ensures a delicious low-carb brunch.

◆ Add 2 servings of fruit and/or vegetables to each entrée for a balanced and healthy meal.

◆ If your brunch occasion calls for something sweet, choose from desserts and chocolate in Chapters 24 and 25.

Chapter 6

Lunches

In This Chapter

- ◆ Choosing foods for lunch
- ◆ Thinking outside the lunch box
- ◆ Making lunches without sandwiches

A woman walked up to the counter at the local deli, and seeing that they didn't offer salads, ordered a ham and cheese sandwich, hold the bread. Without batting an eyelash, the deli owner declared, "I can do that." The paper plate she received held ham, cheese, lettuce, and a deli pickle plus mustard and mayonnaise packets.

This scene is being played out more and more—at delis, fast-food drive-thru lanes, and even at submarine sandwich shops. If a restaurant can't or won't hold the bread, some of us simply ask for a fork and knife and eat the insides of the sandwich. We put the bread on hold for ourselves. The *insides* of the sandwich make for a perfect lunch.

Today the more progressive, popular fast-food restaurants offer interesting and inexpensive salads filled with greens, vegetables, and chicken or beef. The trend toward low carb is now well established, and eating a low-carb lunch is easier than it's ever been.

Lunch Is Important

Lunch isn't something to be taken lightly—perhaps eaten lightly, but not taken lightly. That's why we've included a chapter on lunches in this cookbook. You may need to adjust your thinking about lunch and modify a few of your well-established midday eating habits. This chapter will help.

Some of you who eat lunch at a restaurant every day have figured out how to eat low carb. But many folks are still stuck in the "fries and burger" rut. Or they take a lunch to work occasionally (or want to) and haven't figured out what to pack. Even eating a low-carb lunch at home can be tricky.

Packing low-carb lunches for the kids can be rough, too. If they want to eat at school, the prime choice is usually one basic starch or another. The entrées offered are now such things as pizza or some other fast food … hold the vegetables and fruit, which definitely is not good.

Don't despair, because a healthy lunch is important. And you don't want to skip lunch. Eating lunch keeps your energy high and can avert late-day fatigue. It will also help maintain your metabolism at a higher level, which is helpful if you're trying to lose weight or maintain a healthy weight. But as you know, too heavy a lunch can lead to right-after-lunch lethargy and fatigue. Eating a low-carb lunch lets you avoid the "down" feeling.

The Sandwich Struggle

The basic sandwich presents a problem for anyone trying to eat low carb. The problem, of course, is the bread. As of this writing, there really aren't any yummy commercial low-carb breads available. And they certainly aren't offered in restaurants, and that includes fast-food restaurants.

Until the time comes that you can purchase healthy low-carb bread, you have two choices: You can skip the bread, or you can bake low-carb bread at home and use it for your lunches. Our bread recipes in Chapter 22 are great if you want a sandwich.

A little self-discipline goes a long way, too. Just think to say "Hold the bread," and you'll hardly notice its absence.

Salad to Go

Prep time: 20 minutes • Cook time: 0 • Serves 1 • Serving size: 2 cups

Each serving has: 30 grams carbohydrate • 5 grams fiber • 25 grams nutritive carbohydrate • 24 grams total protein • 18 grams from animal source • 6 grams from plant source

Mixed greens	Nuts
Various vegetables	Seeds
Fresh fruits	Salad dressings
Leftover meats	4 oz. portion cups
Cheese, grated or small cubes	Paper lunch bags

See suggestions that follow for a variety of ingredients to make these delicious salads.

Wash and dry all greens, vegetables, and fruits. In separate quart baggies, place 1½ cups greens, squeeze out as much air as possible, and seal. In separate sandwich-size baggies, mix ½ cup sliced or chopped vegetables, ¼ cup cut-up fruits, ¼ cup leftover meats, and a toppings combination including 1 tablespoon each cheese, nuts, or seeds.

Prepare favorite salad dressing recipes, and pour 2 to 4 tablespoons dressing into small plastic containers.

In each paper lunch bag, place one of each various baggies and a salad dressing cup. Each lunch bag will contain greens, veggies and/or fruit, meat and/or cheese, nuts and seeds, as well as a portion of salad dressing or lemon juice.

If need be, don't forget a napkin, eating utensils, and salad bowl!

Ingredient suggestions:

Greens: Choose red leaf, green leaf, raw baby spinach, romaine, Bibb, shredded cabbage, or mixed greens in a bag that include arugula, radicchio, and dandelion.

Raw vegetables: Celery, peppers, cucumbers, carrots, mild onions, broccoli, cauliflower, yellow squash, mushrooms, snow peas, shelled soybeans, radishes, jicama, avocado, and cherry or grape tomatoes are simply delicious raw.

Canned vegetables: Other veggie choices are mushrooms, artichoke hearts, hearts of palm, asparagus, pearl onions, cut green beans, olives, chilies, and water chestnuts.

Fruits: It is best to bag whole fruit and cut up as needed to prevent browning or becoming mushy or watery. Crisp green apples are delicious on salads, as are fresh berries such as blueberries or strawberries, pineapple tidbits, raisins or any dried fruit, mandarin oranges, grapes, kiwi, cantaloupe, fresh mangos, pears, or peaches. If you decide to cut fruits, sprinkle them with lemon juice to slow down browning.

Recipe for Success _____
Do you see that the world of salads is limited only by your own imagination and creative genius? If we omitted your favorite ingredient from this list, then by all means bag it for your next salad to go! You can substitute lemon juice for salad dressing.

Meats: Leftover meats can be anything from last night's dinner or canned tuna, salmon, or chicken. Boiled eggs or leftover ham or sausage from breakfast can also be added to your salad.

Cheese: Any cheese cut into small bite-size cubes or grated, such as cheddar, Swiss, Parmesan, blue, or feta works well.

Nuts and seeds: These can include, peanuts, macadamias, walnuts, almonds, pecans, pistachios, pine nuts, cashews, coconut, flaxseeds, or sesame seeds.

Cold Cut Rollups

Prep time: 5 minutes • Cook time: 0 • Serves 6 • Serving size: 1 rollup

Each serving has: 1 gram nutritive carbohydrate • less than 1 gram fiber • 14 grams total protein • 14 grams from animal source

Lettuce leaves

½ lb. sliced luncheon meat (ham, turkey, roast beef, or pastrami)

½ lb. thinly sliced cheese (American, cheddar, Swiss, or provolone)

Mayonnaise

Mustard

Toothpicks

Place lettuce leaves on work space. Top with a slice each of meat and cheese. Spread cheese with mayonnaise and mustard to taste. Roll up and secure with a toothpick.

Recipe for Success _____
You can prepare rollups the night before and have them ready for a quick breakfast. Eat with an apple or other fruit, and you have a good breakfast. You can also pack these in a school lunch box. They are great with dill pickles as a condiment.

Chicken Couscous

Prep time: 10 minutes • Cook time: 0 • Serves 6 • Serving size: ¼ cup

Each serving has: 9 grams carbohydrate • 2 grams fiber • 7 grams nutritive carbohydrate • 17 grams total protein • 15 grams from animal source • 2 grams from plant source

1 cup couscous

1½ cups boiling chicken broth

2 cups diced cooked chicken

2 large tomatoes, diced

¼ cup chopped green onion

¼ cup sliced radishes

½ cup chopped cucumber

¼ cup olive oil

¼ cup lemon juice

¼ cup snipped fresh parsley

¼ cup minced fresh mint leaves or 1 TB. dried mint

Salt and pepper to taste

Pine nuts or slivered almonds for garnish (optional)

Place couscous in a 2-quart casserole dish or bowl, and cover with boiling chicken broth; cover and let sit for 10 minutes until stock is absorbed.

In a medium bowl, combine chicken, tomatoes, green onion, radishes, and cucumber.

In a pint-size screw-top jar, combine olive oil, lemon juice, parsley, mint, salt, and pepper; shake well.

If couscous does not absorb all liquid, drain before adding dressing and chicken.

Pour olive oil dressing over couscous, fluff with fork, and mix in chicken and vegetable mixture. Sprinkle with nuts (if using) and serve.

Recipe for Success

The flavors in this recipe mellow and blend together better if allowed to sit 30 minutes or longer. This dish is just as wonderful served cold and is a snap to make ahead of time for that special luncheon. Serve with Congealed Asparagus Salad and Parmesan Crackers, and you will still have plenty of room for scrumptious Chocolate Soufflé for dessert.

Scotch Eggs

Prep time: 20 minutes • Cook time: 30 minutes • Serves 6 • Serving size: 1 egg

Each serving has: 4 grams carbohydrate • 1 gram fiber • 3 grams nutritive carbohydrate • 24 grams total protein • 23 grams from animal source • 1 gram from plant source

2 TB. chopped fresh parsley

¼ tsp. sage, optional

1 tsp. onion powder

1 lb. bulk sausage

6 hard-boiled eggs, peeled

2 beaten eggs

⅓ cup oat bran or ground oatmeal

Preheat oven to 350°F.

Stir parsley, sage, and onion powder into sausage. Divide sausage into 6 even portions, and shape each into a 4-inch circle. Flatten and wrap around 1 peeled hard-boiled egg, covering egg completely.

Roll each sausage egg in beaten egg and then in oat bran. Bake on a buttered sheet pan for 30 minutes or until sausage is completely cooked.

Remove eggs from pan and serve. If making in advance, place cooled eggs in individual snack bags, and refrigerate up to 1 week.

Table Talk

Using scissors to snip fresh parsley and other twiggy herbs and spices is usually much easier than trying to chop. It's easy to snip a handful of green onions and keeps you from bruising the delicate foods.

Egg Salad and Variations

Prep time: 15 minutes   •   Cook time: 0   •   Serves 6   •   Serving size: ½ cup

Each serving has: 2 grams nutritive carbohydrate   •   13 grams total protein   •   13 grams from animal source

12 hard-boiled and peeled eggs, chopped

½ tsp. salt

½ tsp. pepper

3 to 4 TB. mayonnaise

Combine eggs, salt, and pepper and mix to a paste with a fork. Add just enough mayonnaise to moisten. This makes basic egg salad. You can add any of the following variations to this mixture.

Variation 1:

½ cup chopped crisp-fried bacon

Variation 2:

½ cup baby shrimp

½ tsp. curry powder

Variation 3:

¼ cup chopped pecans

2 TB. flax seeds

Variation 4:

½ cup chopped ham

½ tsp. Dijon mustard

1 TB. chopped fresh parsley

¼ tsp. chopped fresh dill

Variation 5:

½ cup minced smoked salmon

1 tsp. minced onion

1 TB. capers

1 TB. lemon juice

Variation 6:

Sour cream to moisten rather than mayonnaise

1 mashed anchovy

1 tsp. chopped chives

1 TB. chopped fresh cilantro

Variation 7:

1 mini can tuna

¼ tsp. minced garlic

½ cup chopped celery

Recipe for Success _____

The possibilities for egg salad are endless and all appetizing. Here's one for every day of the week, but feel free to add in your own favorite meats, cheeses, and condiments.

Nut Butter Spreads

Prep time: 15 minutes • Cook time: 0 • Makes 1½ cups nut butter • Serving size: 2 tablespoons

Each serving has: 0 grams carbohydrate • 4 grams total protein • 4 grams from animal source

2 cups peanuts, almonds, pecans, macadamias, cashews, or filberts

Recipe for Success
Purchase nuts in bulk to get the best prices. Nut butters are great for late-afternoon snacks. You can even eat the butters plain by the spoonful.

Place nuts in a food processor or blender. Process until nut butter forms. You may need to scrape the side of the bowl several times to blend thoroughly.

Serve on vegetables, such as celery, jicama slices, carrot sticks, or cucumber slices.

You can also serve as a spread on fruit, such as bananas, peaches, melon, pears, apples, and oranges.

Beef and Pork Skewers

Prep time: 20 minutes • Cook time: 1½ hours • Serves 12 • Serving size: 1 skewer

Each serving has: less than 1 gram carbohydrate • 16 grams total protein • 16 grams from animal source

¾ lb. beef, cut into ½-inch cubes

¾ lb. pork, cut into ½-inch cubes

2 TB. butter

Salt and pepper

Recipe for Success
Eat these warm when they come out of the oven and cold for lunches and breakfasts. They also make a great after-school or after-work snack. You can even take these along for a picnic lunch while hiking or bicycling.

Preheat oven to 325°F.

Alternate beef and pork onto wooden 6-inch skewers. Brown well in butter. Sprinkle meat with salt and pepper. Place meat in an ovenproof dish. Cover meat with water. Cover the pan.

Cook for 1 hour.

Eat like a chicken leg or remove meat from sticks. These can be eaten cold as well.

Mexican Layers with Veggies

Prep time: 45 minutes plus time to chill • Cook time: 0 • Serves 6 • Serving size: ½ cup

Each serving has: 15 grams carbohydrate • 5 grams fiber • 10 grams nutritive carbohydrate • 15 grams total protein • 2 grams from animal source • 13 grams from plant source

½ cup mayonnaise

½ cup chopped fresh cilantro

¼ cup lime juice

1 tsp. cumin

½ tsp. black pepper

1 head lettuce, shredded

1 (15 oz.) can black beans, rinsed and drained

8 oz. cheddar cheese, shredded

1 large bell pepper, chopped

3 green onions, chopped

3 tomatoes, chopped

In a food processor, combine mayonnaise with cilantro, lime juice, cumin, and black pepper.

Either on a large platter or in a large glass bowl, layer ingredients in the following order: ½ lettuce, ⅓ mayonnaise mixture, ½ beans, cheese, bell pepper, onions, and tomatoes. Repeat layers and top with remaining mayonnaise mixture.

Cover and chill 1 to 2 hours.

Recipe for Success

This is a meal in itself but has very little animal protein. You may slice boiled eggs on top or serve with one of the beefsteak recipes or the Pork and Beef Skewers. Baked apples make a great dessert, adding that additional serving of fruit to your day.

Layered Salad

Prep time: 15 minutes plus overnight marinating　•　Cook time: 0　•　Serves 6　• Serving size: 1 cup salad with 2 tablespoons dressing

Each serving has: 10 grams carbohydrate　•　3 grams fiber　•　7 grams nutritive carbohydrate　• 30 grams total protein　•　26 grams from animal source　•　4 grams from plant source

1 cup sour cream

2 oz. (½ cup) crumbled feta or blue cheese

½ tsp. dried dill weed or 1 TB. fresh

½ tsp. dried basil or 1 TB. fresh

½ tsp. crushed red pepper

4 cups fresh spinach, bite-size pieces

2 large tomatoes, chopped, or 1 cup cherry tomatoes cut in half

1 cup (½ lb.) sliced mushrooms

1 cup small green peas, frozen

1 cup chopped cauliflower

1½ cups crumbled cooked bacon

4 green onions, chopped

For the dressing: In a blender or food processor, combine sour cream, feta cheese, dill weed, basil, and red pepper until smooth.

In a serving dish, layer vegetables one at a time beginning with torn spinach leaves on bottom. Add tomatoes, mushrooms, peas, and cauliflower, and pour on dressing. Sprinkle top with bacon and green onions.

Cover and refrigerate overnight.

Recipe for Success

Serve in individual bowls along with White Chili, or for a light luncheon. Sausage Cheese Muffins with Frosty Fruit for dessert can accompany the salad.

The Least You Need to Know

◆ The new lunch box includes complete protein, fruit, vegetable, and an optional sweet treat.

◆ An inexpensive commercial low-carb bread isn't available, so either bake your own or hold the bread.

◆ Keep your refrigerator stocked with foods for lunch—such as cold cuts, eggs, leftovers, and cheese.

◆ Eating a low-carb lunch lets you avoid the after-lunch letdown and fatigue.

Part 3

Main Dish Entrées

The centerpiece of your meals is a low-carb main dish made with delectable meats, poultry, fish, or seafood. The meat can be roasted, marinated, grilled, boiled, or even cooked in the oven in bags.

Appealing spices and aromas greet you as you sit down to enjoy these main dishes. The tastes are satisfying, whether savory or sweet, as they deliver high-quality complete protein to stoke your metabolism and give you tip-top nutrition.

Chapter 7

Beef Dishes

In This Chapter

- ◆ Eating the energizing meat
- ◆ Purchasing beef
- ◆ Dressing it up or down
- ◆ Planning meals with beef

Whatever form it comes in—steaks, roast beef, or hamburgers—beef is a favorite. It's hearty fare, real stick-to-your-ribs—but not fattening—kind of food and for good reason. The very intensity and rich taste of beef makes it ideal for eating low carb because, as you know, getting plenty of high-quality protein is a big factor in eating low carb.

Beef gives that to you and more. By itself, it has no carbohydrates, yet it offers plenty of protein, vitamins, and minerals. Beef is filled with the highest concentration of B vitamins and trace minerals of any single food. It supplies ample amounts of the vitamin B_{12} that you can't get from vegetables alone. Oh, and it simply tastes good, too!

Get an Energy Lift

Beef is one of the perfect foods for staying energized all day long. It contains purines, which are a major component of nucleic acids. Nucleic acids are metabolized into energy more slowly than carbohydrates. Practically speaking, what does that mean? By eating beef you may be able to boost your metabolic burn rate and keep your energy level high through stressful and taxing situations. In short, beef is a great food for our busy lives.

You don't need to eat very much beef to stay energized. Typically, you only need 3 ounces cooked beef, which is about the size of a deck of cards. Yes, we have all been to restaurants that offer 16-ounce T-bone steaks or prime rib. Just think, you could eat five meals from that amount of beef! So avoid the mega-portions or share your entrée with a friend … or two or three!

Table Talk
Four ounces raw meat yields about 3 ounces cooked—the weight listed in menus is always the pre-cooked raw weight.

Those 3 ounces cooked beef contain about 26 grams high-quality complete protein. A good formula for healthy adults is that you need about ½ gram protein per day for each pound you weigh. So a woman who weighs 150 pounds needs about 75 grams of protein a day. A man who weighs 200 needs about 100 grams protein a day. So even 3 ounces beef goes a long way to getting you the protein you need.

Beef for Your Body

If you have a heavy-duty day ahead of you, whether it's a day of business travel, hot and heavy negotiations, or hitting the ski slopes, go ahead and have some beef for breakfast. Your body will thank you.

While most of us won't cook up a feast for breakfast using the recipes here, they will make great breakfast from last night's dinner leftovers. You might also be surprised at how little time it takes to cook a small steak or meat patty for breakfast. Add some vegetables or fruit, and you are ready to roll into action.

Table Talk
Recent research indicates that eating lean beef combined with a lower-carbohydrate diet is excellent for weight loss. Of course, portion control is important, too. No matter how much you love beef, don't overeat. Three to five ounces is plenty.

Eating beef can also be good for your heart, but you'll definitely need to eat modest quantities. Be sure to cut off all the visible fat. That is saturated fat, and you don't need any extra. Choose lean cuts or cook slowly so the fat melts out of the meat and into the pot. Cooking in the slow cooker does this well, as does roasting or boiling the beef.

Leaner cuts of beef include flank steak and beef tenderloin. If the label says loin or round, the meat is lean. Fattier cuts include chuck roasts and rib eye steaks.

Spicing Up the Beef

The ingredients we use in our recipes enhance the flavor of beef because we use strong flavors:

♦ Spices and pepper

♦ Chili and south-of-the-border ingredients such as cayenne

♦ Mushrooms

♦ Onions and garlic

♦ Cheeses

♦ Tangy condiments such as vinegar and soy sauce

Table Talk

Rubs and pastes (also known as wet rubs) are ground spices and herbs rubbed into meat for additional flavoring, but are not tenderizers. Rubs work best when using dry heat to cook the meat by baking, broiling, or grilling. Cover the meat with the spice mixture using enough force to be sure the spices adhere to the meat. The thicker the rub or the longer it will stay on the meat before cooking, the greater the flavor.

The recipes in this chapter give you a wide variety of tastes and preparation methods. Included are plain and fancy steaks, roasts, and ethnic selections. Here are a few pleasant things you'll discover as you cook more beef recipes:

♦ Many beef recipes are fast and easy to prepare.

♦ Beef can be very economical, especially if you eat modest quantities.

♦ You'll get better at knowing what spices work well with beef the more you cook it.

Beef contains no dietary fiber. To get plenty of fiber in a beef meal, it's important to add side dishes of vegetables and fruits, either cooked or raw. At least 2 servings, or even 3, will give you plenty of fiber and a meal's worth of phytonutrients and antioxidants … plus great eating.

Slow Cooker Pot Roast

Prep time: 5 minutes • Cook time: 4 hours • Serves 8 • Serving size: 4 ounces

Each serving has: 0 grams carbohydrate • 32 grams total protein • 32 grams from animal source

3 lb. beef chuck roast   ½ tsp. coarsely ground black pepper

Recipe for Success
The slow cooker is an easy way to prepare beef roasts without slaving in the kitchen all day. The meat is moist and can be cut with a fork. Serve with plenty of vegetables. Use the pan drippings to make gravy, or serve with horse-radish, chutney, or barbecue sauce.

Put beef into a slow cooker, season with pepper, and cover with the lid. Turn on high and cook for 4 to 6 hours or until the meat is so tender it can be cut with a fork.

Variations: This recipe is the easiest way to get cooked beef for tacos, barbecued beef, salads, and other recipes. Reheat or serve cold for lunches and snacks. You can vary the flavor each time you cook a roast by adding additional seasonings to the slow cooker. Suggestions include ½ cup beef broth or tomato sauce, onions, garlic, bell pepper, oregano, salsa, etc.

Beef-Jicama Chalupas

Prep time: 15 minutes • Cook time: 2 minutes • Serves 6 • Serving size: ¾ cup

Each serving has: 14 grams carbohydrate • 9 grams fiber • 5 grams nutritive carbohydrate • 19 grams total protein • 16 grams from animal source • 3 grams from plant source

2 cups shredded cooked beef from Slow Cooker Pot Roast (recipe earlier in this chapter)

1 cup commercial salsa

1 small can corn

1 small can diced green chilies

½ cup shredded cheddar or Monterey Jack cheese

2 cups shredded jicama

2 tomatoes, diced

In a shallow, microwave-safe dish, mix beef, salsa, corn, and chilies. Heat on medium for about 1 minute, until warm. Top with cheese, and microwave until just melted.

Divide jicama onto 6 dinner plates. Spoon beef mixture on jicama, and top with diced tomatoes.

Marinated London Broil

Prep time: 15 minutes plus marinating time • Cook time: 15 minutes • Serves 6
• Serving size: 4 ounces

Each serving has: 2 grams nutritive carbohydrate • less than 1 gram fiber • 33 grams
total protein • 32 grams from animal source • 1 gram from plant source

1 to 2 lb. flank steak	¼ cup olive oil
3 TB. red wine vinegar	¼ tsp. coarsely ground black pepper
1 clove garlic, minced	2 cups sliced mushrooms
¼ tsp. crushed red pepper	2 TB. butter
2 TB. soy sauce	

Place steak and vinegar, garlic, crushed red pepper, soy sauce, olive oil, and black pepper into a
resealable bag. Marinate for 2 to 4 hours or overnight in the refrigerator.

Cook on the grill or broil in the oven until done to taste, about 3 minutes on a side.

At the same time, sauté mushrooms in butter in a heavy skillet until tender. Slice meat very
thin, and top with mushrooms.

Variations: Marvelous and economical, this recipe makes great leftovers for breakfast. You can
also roll up pieces of fruit in the thin slices and send them to school with the kids. This steak is
perfect for fajitas, chalupas, or topping your favorite green salad for lunch.

Low-Carb Vocab

Marinades are a blend of seasonings, oil, and acidic liquid. The acid in the
marinade tenderizes meat and adds flavoring. Wine may be substituted for
juice or vinegar in marinades; use white wine for a milder flavor for more delicate proteins such as fish or poultry. A red wine gives a stronger, more robust flavor and is usually
used with red meat, game, and pork.

Sirloin with Lemon Sauce

Prep time: 15 minutes   •   Cook time: 15 minutes   •   Serves 6   •   Serving size: 4 ounces

Each serving has: 2 grams nutritive carbohydrate   •   less than 1 gram fiber   •   33 grams total protein   •   32 grams from animal source   •   1 gram from plant source

4 TB. butter

1 cup finely chopped green onions

½ bay leaf

½ tsp. dried thyme

1½ cups dry red wine

3½ lb. boneless beef sirloin steak, about 1½ inches thick

3 TB. minced fresh parsley

1 TB. fresh lemon juice

In a large, heavy skillet, melt 2 tablespoons butter over high heat. Sauté onions, bay leaf, and thyme until onions are transparent, about 2 to 3 minutes. Add wine and cook until reduced by ⅓.

Recipe for Success

Lemon adds lots of piz-zazz to a dinner steak. Garnish with lemon twists. You can serve with rich or simple side dishes, such as creamed vegetables or a tossed vegetable salad.

Remove bay leaf, and pour sauce from the skillet and reserve. In the same skillet over high heat, sear steak for 1½ minutes per side. Turn heat to medium, and let skillet cool slightly; add sauce, remaining 2 tablespoons butter, parsley, and lemon juice. Cook for an additional 2 to 4 minutes per side, depending on taste.

Cut steak into 2-inch diagonal strips, and serve with red wine sauce from skillet.

Mustard Brisket

Prep time: 10 minutes   •   Cook time: 4 hours   •   Serves 6   •   Serving size: 4 ounces

Each serving has: 2 grams nutritive carbohydrate   •   32 grams total protein   •   32 grams from animal source

1 (3-lb.) beef brisket, trimmed of excess fat

2 cups water

6 cloves garlic, peeled and sliced

⅓ cup spicy mustard

1 tsp. cracked peppercorns

1 tsp. dried tarragon

¼ cup diced green onions

Preheat oven to 325°F

Place brisket in a large baking pan. Add water to bottom of the baking pan. Cut slits all around brisket, and insert slices of garlic deep into meat.

In a small bowl, combine mustard, peppercorns, tarragon, and green onions. Rub mixture into brisket, covering well all over.

Cover pan and bake for 4 hours or until meat is tender.

Rubbed Beef Steak

Prep time: 15 minutes plus marinating time • Cook time: 15 minutes • Serves 6 • Serving size: 4 ounces

Each serving has: 4 grams nutritive carbohydrate • 32 grams total protein • 32 grams from animal source

1 (3-lb.) flank steak pierced on all sides with fork	1 TB. black pepper
	2 TB. paprika
Butter	1 tsp. crushed red pepper
1 TB. garlic powder	1 tsp. salt
3 TB. oregano	¼ cup dry mustard

Place steak in a glass dish.

In a small bowl, blend garlic powder, oregano, black pepper, paprika, red pepper, salt, and dry mustard.

Spread rub onto all sides of flank steak, especially pushing into areas pierced with fork. Cover meat thoroughly, pressing rub onto meat. Cover dish, and refrigerate for several hours or overnight.

Preheat broiler. Butter broiler pan, and place steak on pan. Throw away any remaining seasoning from marinating raw meat. Set pan 4 inches from broiler unit, and broil on each side 5 minutes or until meat thermometer registers 145°F.

Recipe for Success

This steak can just as easily be grilled, if desired. Serving with Vibrant Peppers and Tomatoes, Mock Mashed "Potatoes," and Frosty Fruit ensures the entire rainbow of colors and plenty of vitamins.

Beef Steak over Greens

Prep time: 15 minutes plus marinating overnight • Cook time: 20 minutes • Serves 6 • Serving size: 4 ounces meat over 1 cup greens

Each serving has: 9 grams carbohydrate • 2 grams fiber • 7 grams nutritive carbohydrate • 35 grams total protein • 33 grams from animal source • 2 grams from plant source

¼ cup olive oil

¼ cup Worcestershire sauce

1 tsp. garlic powder

1 tsp. cayenne

1 (3-lb.) flank steak

8 oz. sour cream

4 TB. prepared horseradish

2 TB. lemon juice

1 TB. chopped fresh parsley

Salt and pepper to taste

6 cups mixed salad greens (red leaf, butternut, romaine, baby spinach, etc.)

3 cucumbers, peeled and sliced

Combine olive oil, Worcestershire sauce, garlic powder, and cayenne in a gallon-size freezer bag. Add steak, seal bag, and refrigerate overnight. Turn bag occasionally to spread marinade over all surfaces of steak.

In a pint jar with a screw-type lid, combine sour cream, prepared horseradish, lemon juice, parsley, salt, and pepper. Refrigerate till needed.

Heat grill to medium-high heat. Remove steak from marinade, and throw away marinade. Place steak off direct heat, and close lid on grill; cook 8 to 10 minutes per side or until desired doneness.

While meat is cooking, wash and dry greens, and tear into bite-size pieces. Toss with cucumber slices, and place 1 cup salad mix in individual bowls or on plates.

Cut steak into thin slices and place over greens. Drizzle with horseradish sauce and serve.

Variations: Grilled steak makes wonderful fajitas as well as served over greens. Serve with Baked Onions and Garbanzo Bean Salad. Pear Compote makes the perfect ending to this satisfying meal. The leftover grilled steak makes delicious cold beef for breakfast or snacks, or bag up leftovers to add to tomorrow's mixed salad.

Hot Potato

Be sure to throw away the marinade and do not be tempted to reuse it. It is a breeding ground for bacteria. Never use left-over marinade that raw meat soaked in as a basting sauce.

Marinated Beef Kabobs

Prep time: 20 minutes plus marinating time   •   Cook time: 15 minutes   •   Serves 6
•   Serving size: 1 skewer

Each serving has: 8 grams carbohydrate   •   2 grams fiber   •   6 grams nutritive carbohydrate
•   33 grams total protein   •   32 grams from animal source   •   1 gram from plant source

2 TB. lemon or lime juice	2 lb. boneless beef, cut into 1-inch cubes
2 TB. olive oil	2 large bell peppers, cut into 1¼-inch pieces
2 tsp. sesame oil	18 whole mushrooms
2 TB. water	12 grape or cherry tomatoes, leave whole
1 TB. spicy mustard	2 zucchini, cut into 1-inch slices
1 tsp. honey	2 large onions, cut into 1¼-inch pieces
1 tsp. basil	Butter
1 tsp. crushed red pepper	

In a large bowl, combine lemon juice, olive oil, sesame oil, water, spicy mustard, honey, basil, and red pepper; add beef, red bell peppers, mushrooms, tomatoes, zucchini, and onions. Toss well and allow to marinate in refrigerator at least 2 hours or even overnight; turn occasionally.

Alternately thread beef and vegetables onto 6 large skewers.

Butter a broiler pan, and place kabobs on the pan 3 to 4 inches from heat. Broil 9 to 12 minutes for medium-rare to medium-done, turning occasionally to prevent overbrowning surface.

Hot Potato

If using wooden skewers, be sure to soak them in water for 1 hour before using to prevent them from burning.

Recipe for Success

If you prefer to grill, place kabobs over medium-hot coals and grill uncovered 8 to 11 minutes, turning occasionally. You may place beef and vegetables in a wire basket instead of threading onto skewers, if desired. For a fabulous next-day luncheon salad, double this recipe to have plenty of leftovers. Top a mixed green salad and sprinkle with sesame seeds and balsamic vinegar. Running late for work the next day? Grab a leftover skewer for a high-protein, high-vitamin breakfast!

Beef with Vinaigrette Sauce

Prep time: 10 minutes • Cook time: 30 minutes • Serves 6 • Serving size: 4 ounces with 2 tablespoons sauce

Each serving has: 1 gram nutritive carbohydrate • 32 grams total protein • 32 grams from animal source

1 (3-lb.) flank steak, grilled	1 tsp. black pepper
½ cup olive oil	½ tsp. crushed red pepper
2 TB. red wine vinegar or seasoned vinegar	1 tsp. dried rosemary or other herb of choice
2 cloves garlic, minced	

Slice cooked steak on the diagonal, against the grain, and arrange on a platter.

Combine olive oil, vinegar, garlic, black pepper, red pepper, and rosemary. Pour vinaigrette sauce over steak and serve.

Sautéed Steak with Green Peppercorns

Prep time: 10 minutes plus 1 hour marinating time • Cook time: 20 minutes • Serves 4 • Serving size: ½ steak, approximately 6 ounces

Each serving has: Less than 1 gram nutritive carbohydrate • 42 grams total protein • 42 grams from animal source

Green peppercorns	Salt and pepper to taste
2 (1-lb.) steaks, ¾ to 1 inch thick	½ cup beef stock, red wine, dry white wine, or vermouth
2 TB. butter	
2 TB. oil	2 to 3 TB. softened butter

Press peppercorns onto both sides of meat. Place in a dish, cover, and refrigerate 1 hour.

Heat butter and oil in a heavy skillet over medium-high heat until butter foam begins to subside. With grease very hot but not burning, sauté steak on each side for 3 to 4 minutes. Steak will be medium-rare when a bit of red juice begins to ooze at surface.

Remove steak to a hot platter, and season to taste with salt and pepper. Keep warm while completing sauce.

Pour grease out of the skillet. Add stock and set the skillet over high heat. Scrape juices with a wooden spoon while rapidly boiling down liquid until it is reduced almost to syrup.

Remove from heat, and swirl softened butter into liquid until it is absorbed. Butter will thicken liquid into a light sauce.

Pour sauce over steak and serve.

Recipe for Success

Steak with peppercorns seems to be a combination made in cook's heaven. The peppercorns add flavor and seem to make the steak more tender. Serve with at least one mildly seasoned side dish to prevent spice overload. Bland steamed peas, carrots, or broccoli would be great.

Beef Tandoor

Prep time: 15 minutes plus overnight marinating time • Cook time: 1½ hours • Serves 6 • Serving size: ¾ cup

Each serving has: 5 grams nutritive carbohydrate • 32 grams total protein • 32 grams from animal source

1 onion, coarsely chopped	¼ cup chopped red pepper
3 cloves garlic, chopped	¼ cup red wine vinegar
1 tsp. minced fresh ginger	¼ cup olive oil
½ tsp. cumin	2 lb. beef stew meat
2 TB. coriander	4 TB. butter
1 TB. turmeric	

Blend onion, garlic, ginger, cumin, coriander, turmeric, red pepper, red wine vinegar, and olive oil into thick marinade.

Thoroughly coat meat, and marinate in the refrigerator overnight.

In a heavy pot, brown meat in melted butter over high heat. Lower heat and simmer about 1 to 1½ hours until tender. Stir occasionally.

Beef Stroganoff

Prep time: 15 minutes   •   Cook time: 10 minutes   •   Serves 6   •   Serving size: ½ cup

Each serving has: 2 grams nutritive carbohydrate   •   less than 1 gram fiber   •   32 grams total protein   •   32 grams from animal source

1½ lb. sirloin steak	½ tsp. salt
6 TB. butter	½ tsp. coarsely ground black pepper
¼ onion, chopped	1 TB. paprika
½ cup sliced mushrooms	½ cup heavy cream

Cut meat into slices ½ by 2 inches. Heat butter in a heavy pan. Sauté onion and mushrooms for about 3 minutes until tender. Add steak and cook for about 5 minutes or until tender. Season with salt, pepper, and paprika.

Slowly stir in cream. Heat without boiling. Serve at once.

Pot Roast with Caraway, Orange, and Ginger

Prep time: 30 minutes   •   Cook time: 5 to 7 hours   •   Serves 8   •   Serving size: 4 ounces

Each serving has: 5 grams carbohydrate   •   1 gram fiber   •   4 grams nutritive carbohydrate   •   32 grams total protein   •   32 grams from animal source

4 to 5 lb. boneless chuck roast or eye of round	1 bay leaf
4 TB. butter	2 TB. grated orange peel
2 medium onions, chopped	1 TB. paprika
½ cup chopped carrots	1 tsp. caraway seeds
2 cups water	1½ cups sour cream
1 cup Burgundy wine	2 TB. dill
6 cloves garlic	2 TB. ginger

Recipe for Success
This recipe, which has a Scandinavian flavor, is great for a winter fireside dinner.

Preheat oven to 275°F.

In a roasting pan, brown roast in butter. Remove roast from the pan, and sauté onions and carrots until tender. Add water, wine, garlic, bay leaf, orange peel, paprika, and caraway seeds to the pan. Heat to boiling and add roast.

Cover and bake for 5 to 7 hours or until tender.

Remove roast from the pan. Skim off fat. In the roasting pan, blend sour cream, dill, and ginger. Cook over low heat for 10 to 15 minutes. Don't boil.

Slice meat into thin slices and serve with sauce.

≈~

Beef Fajitas

Prep time: 15 minutes plus 2 to 3 hours marinating time • Cook time: 15 minutes
• Serves 6 • Serving size: 4 ounces beef with 3 tablespoons vegetables

Each serving has: 3 grams carbohydrate • 1 gram fiber • 2 grams nutritive carbohydrate
• 32 grams total protein • 32 grams from animal source

¼ cup vinegar	1 medium onion, sliced
½ cup olive oil	1 green pepper, cut into strips
¼ cup lime juice	1 red pepper, cut into strips
1 clove garlic, mashed	2 TB. butter
¼ tsp. cumin	Sour cream
¼ tsp. crushed red pepper	Guacamole
½ tsp. coriander	Salsa (optional)
1½ lb. flank steak	

Prepare marinade by combining vinegar, olive oil, lime juice, garlic, cumin, red pepper, and coriander in a resealable bag. Place beef in the bag, seal, and marinate 2 to 3 hours or overnight in the refrigerator.

When ready to cook, remove steak from the bag, saving marinade.

Boil marinade for 20 minutes to kill bacteria before serving over meat. Let simmer until ready to serve.

Slice steak into thin slices.

Saute onion and red and green peppers in butter in a heavy skillet. Cook until crisp-tender. Remove to a side platter. Sauté steak until cooked through. Stir in marinade. Add onion and peppers.

Serve topped with sour cream, guacamole, and salsa (if using). Guacamole and salsa may add more carbs to the scorecard.

Recipe for Success

Fajitas combine the best of south-of-the-border tastes with our American desire for meats and vegetables. Eat these fajitas with a fork instead of as tortillas, as they contain lots of carbohydrates.

≈~

Blue Cheese Rib Eyes

Prep time: 10 minutes • Cook time: 10 to 15 minutes • Serves: 4 • Serving size: 6 ounces

Each serving has: less than 1 gram nutritive carbohydrate • 43 grams total protein • 42 grams from animal source • 1 gram from plant source

2 lb. rib eye steaks   4 TB. crumbled blue cheese

2 TB. butter

Fry steak in butter to desired doneness. Turn off the stove. Divide blue cheese, and sprinkle over top of steaks. Let melt. Serve.

Garlic Roast

Prep time: 24 to 48 hours marinating time • Cook time: 6 hours • Serves 6 • Serving size: 4 ounces

Each serving has: 6 grams nutritive carbohydrate • 32 grams total protein • 32 grams from animal source

1 (3- to 5-lb.) chuck roast   3 TB. olive oil

4 to 6 cloves garlic, cut into slivers   2 cups strong coffee

1 cup vinegar   2 cups water

1 TB. garlic powder   Salt and pepper to taste

1 TB. onion powder

Preheat oven to 225°F.

Recipe for Success
Serve this tender roast with Southern Greens, Tasty Turnips, and Marinated Tomato slices. But remember to save room for a slice of Chocolate Amaretto Cheesecake.

Pierce meat and insert slivered garlic cloves all over roast. Place meat in a heavy plastic bag, pour vinegar over meat, and sprinkle with garlic and onion powders. Cover and refrigerate for 24 to 48 hours. Turn every 12 hours.

Place oil in a heavy pan, and heat over medium heat. Add roast and brown on all sides. Pour coffee and water over meat, cover, and place in oven; bake for 4 to 6 hours. Season with salt and pepper 20 minutes before serving.

Stuffed Steak

Prep time: 30 minutes • Cook time: 60 minutes • Serves 6 • Serving size: 1 (6-ounce) steak

Each serving steak has (stuffing varies): 0 grams nutritive carbohydrate • 42 grams total protein • 42 grams from animal source

Pecan Stuffing adds: 9 carbohydrates and 2 grams fiber for 7 grams nutritive carbohydrate • 4 grams from plant source

Pesto Stuffing adds: 2 grams carbohydrate and less than 1 gram fiber for 2 grams nutritive carbohydrate • 9 grams from plant source

Roasted Pepper Stuffing adds: 1 gram nutritive carbohydrates • 2 grams from plant source

6 oz. boneless top sirloin steak per person, cut 1½ to 2 inches thick

Worcestershire sauce or red wine for basting

Stuffing of choice (see suggestions that follow)

Preheat oven to 350°F or grill, depending on cooking method desired.

Cut slit through center of each steak to within ½ inch of edge. This will form a pocket to hold stuffing.

If steaks will be grilled, heat coals to medium-hot and place steaks to the side to smoke for about 20 minutes, turning frequently until steaks are of desired doneness. If needed, brush with Worcestershire sauce or red wine to keep moist.

If steaks will be baked, place steaks in a buttered roasting pan; add ½ cup water to pan, and sprinkle steaks with a few tablespoons Worcestershire sauce or red wine. Bake 1 hour or until steaks reach desired doneness.

Choose from the following stuffings:

Pecan Stuffing

Pecan Stuffing has: 9 grams carbohydrate • 4 grams total protein • 4 grams from plant source

½ cup pecans (may substitute any nut)

2 TB. apple or orange juice

½ cup parsley leaves

1¼ cups fresh fruit (apples, pears, etc.)

¼ cup dried fruit (cranberries, apricots, raisins, etc.)

Combine pecans, juice, parsley, fresh fruit, and dried fruit in a food processor. Chop the ingredients by pulsing the processor.

Pesto Stuffing

Pesto Stuffing has: 4 grams carbohydrate • 9 grams total protein • 9 grams from plant source

1½ cups fresh basil leaves (for milder flavor substitute parsley)

2 cloves garlic

¼ cup pine nuts (may substitute any nut)

¾ cup grated fresh Parmesan cheese

½ cup olive oil

Process basil, garlic, and nuts into thick paste; add cheese and process until very thick. Slowly add oil and continue to process until combined well.

Roasted Pepper Pesto Stuffing

Roasted Pepper Stuffing has: 4 grams carbohydrate • 2 grams total protein • 2 grams from plant source

¼ cup pesto from Pesto Stuffing (recipe earlier in this chapter)

1 small jar roasted red pepper (or substitute pimiento or dried tomatoes)

2 TB. minced garlic

Combine pesto, red pepper, and garlic well.

Your Choice Stuffing

Combine your favorite herbs and 1 vegetable or fruit with 2 tablespoons liquid if ingredients appear dry.

The Least You Need to Know

- ◆ Beef gives you energy with high concentrations of B vitamins and trace elements.
- ◆ Eating beef works for fat-restricted diets as well as low-carb.
- ◆ Beef works well with other strong flavors.
- ◆ Add vegetable and/or fruit side dishes to your beef main course meals.

Chapter 8

Ground Meat Dishes

In This Chapter

- ◆ Versatility of ground meat
- ◆ Making everyday food
- ◆ Choosing your fat content

Start with a pound of ground meat, and you can seemingly do almost anything, at least as far as a good meal is concerned. Ground meat is versatile and blends comfortably with many flavors, such as Italian, German, Greek, Mexican, Asian, and good old American.

Ground meat main-course dishes are usually easy to make and easy to serve. While most of us think of ground meat as something reserved for family dinners, you can proudly take several of the recipes in this chapter, such as lasagna and meatloaf, to potluck dinners or serve them to company.

Ground meat by itself has no carbohydrates. In these recipes, the carbohydrates come from other ingredients that add flavor, texture, and taste. Beef, pork, veal, and turkey are the most common types of ground meat.

We suggest you always keep a couple pounds ground meat in the freezer, so you'll always have some high-quality complete protein on hand for dinner. You can defrost it quickly in the microwave and have it ready to cook within 6 minutes.

Table Talk
To quickly defrost 1 pound ground meat in the microwave, set power level to defrost. Place meat, uncovered, on a microwave dish or tray. Defrost for 3 minutes. Scrape off softened meat and set aside. Break up remaining block and microwave on defrost for 2 to 3 more minutes.

Cooking Ground Meat

Not all ground beef is the same. It comes prepackaged with varying amounts of fat. The amounts range from 20 percent all the way down to 4 percent. The fat percentage you choose depends on your personal taste preference. Factors to consider when making your choice include (1) how you are going to cook the beef, (2) if you like the taste of fat in your food, and (3) what your personal dietary restrictions are. If you need to eat lower fat, then go for the lower percentages of fat in your ground beef.

Ground turkey ranges between 7 to 15 percent fat, so don't be fooled by thinking that if it's turkey, it has to be low fat. Ground pork is about 15 percent. Sausage is higher at about 25 percent.

When ground meat is cooked, whether browned for a dish like spaghetti, or baked as for a meatloaf, much of the fat is cooked out. This is called shrinkage. The fattier ground meats shrink down to less volume as the fat cooks out. Draining the fat from the meat leaves far less fat in the food. So let taste be the deciding factor in purchasing ground meat.

Picadille Dip

Prep time: 20 minutes • Cook time: 30 minutes • Serves 8 • Serving size: ½ cup

Each serving has: 11 grams carbohydrate • 3 grams fiber • 8 grams nutritive carbohydrate • 32 grams total protein • 28 grams from animal source • 4 grams from plant source

1 lb. sausage	1 tsp. garlic salt
1 lb. ground beef	½ tsp. black pepper
4 chopped green onions	½ TB. sugar
1 tsp. cumin	1 cup diced pimiento
1 cup toasted slivered almonds	1 can tomatoes with jalapeños
1 tsp. dried oregano	2 small cans tomato sauce

Cook and drain sausage and beef. Add onions, cumin, almonds, oregano, garlic salt, pepper, sugar, pimiento, tomatoes with jalapeños, and tomato sauce; simmer 30 minutes.

Recipe for Success

You can serve Picadille Dip in small soup bowls and eat with a spoon or serve it with vegetable scoops, such as celery, jicama, and zucchini. Put over a bed of shredded jicama for eating as an open-face taco. You can even serve it over spaghetti squash as a main dish.

Fruit-Stuffed Meat Loaf

Prep time: 30 minutes • Cook time: 1½ hours • Serves 6 • Serving size: 1 slice

Each serving has: 16 grams carbohydrate • 2 grams fiber • 14 grams nutritive carbohydrate • 32 grams total protein • 30 grams from animal source • 2 grams from plant source

1½ lb. ground beef chuck	¼ cup chopped dried apricots
½ lb. ground lean pork	¼ cup fresh chopped parsley
2 eggs, lightly beaten	½ cup chopped onion
½ cup soft breadcrumbs	½ tsp. sage
1½ tsp. salt	¼ tsp. dried thyme
¼ tsp. black pepper	½ cup beef broth
¼ cup raisins	

Preheat oven to 350°F.

Combine beef, pork, eggs, breadcrumbs, salt, and pepper in a bowl and mix well. Spread mixture in a rectangle about ½-inch thick on a large piece of heavy-duty aluminum foil.

Combine raisins, apricots, parsley, onion, sage, thyme, and beef broth; mix thoroughly. Spread over meat loaf mixture, then roll up meat and filling like a jellyroll. Bring foil up around the roll, and fold over to seal.

Place the package on a foil-lined baking sheet, and bake 1 hour. Open the foil to allow surface to brown, and bake 30 minutes longer. Let cool 5 minutes, and slice into 6 servings.

Recipe for Success

Meat loaf is so versatile! Use it for a hot meal, serve it cold for lunches and breakfasts. Have a late-afternoon snack with a half-slice. It definitely will tide you over until a late dinner. This meat loaf has extra flair with the fruit stuffing.

Wild Rice and Beef Casserole

Prep time: 40 minutes • Cook time: 1 hour • Serves 6 • Serving size: ¾ cup

Each serving has: 10 grams nutritive carbohydrate • less than 1 gram fiber • 30 grams total protein • 26 grams from animal source • 4 grams from plant source

4 cups boiling water

¾ cup wild rice

1 lb. ground beef

3 cups chicken broth

1½ tsp. salt

1 bay leaf

1 TB. soy sauce

½ tsp. curry powder

½ cup (1 stick) butter

⅓ cup finely chopped onion

1 lb. mushrooms, sliced

½ lb. sharp cheddar cheese, grated

Recipe for Success

Wild rice has a strong enough flavor to enhance the beef in this recipe. This dish has a higher carb count than other beef recipes, so serve it with very low-carb vegetable dishes such as steamed vegetables and a tossed salad.

Preheat oven to 350°F.

Pour boiling water over rice, and let stand 15 minutes. Meanwhile, brown beef in a skillet and drain.

Drain rice; add broth, salt, bay leaf, soy sauce, and curry powder to rice.

Melt butter in a heavy skillet, add onion, and sauté until tender. Add mushrooms and sauté 3 minutes. Add browned beef, and stir over medium heat for about 5 minutes.

Combine rice mixture with meat mixture in a 9×14-inch casserole. Top with cheese, and bake 1 hour. Remove bay leaf before serving.

Eggplant with Ground Beef

Prep time: 15 minutes • Cook time: 1 hour • Serves 6 • Serving size: ½ cup

Each serving has: 9 grams carbohydrate • 2 grams fiber • 7 grams nutritive carbohydrate • 20 grams total protein • 18 grams from animal source • 2 grams from plant source

1 large eggplant, peeled and diced

1 lb. lean ground beef

1 large onion, chopped

1 large bell pepper, chopped

1 stalk celery, diced

1 clove garlic, minced

1 (15-oz.) can diced tomatoes, drained and juice reserved

½ cup liquid from tomatoes

1 TB. tomato paste

Salt and black pepper to taste

1 cup grated cheddar cheese

Preheat oven to 350°F.

Boil diced eggplant for 5 minutes and set aside. Brown beef and drain. To meat in the skillet add onion, bell pepper, celery, and garlic; sauté 10 minutes or until onions are clear. Add drained tomatoes, ½ cup liquid, tomato paste, salt, pepper, and eggplant mixture; simmer 30 minutes covered.

Pour mixture into a buttered casserole dish, and top with grated cheese.

Bake 20 minutes.

Recipe for Success

This is an easy dish to serve after a long, busy day. Any leftovers will freeze well for a quick lunch another day. Pair this casserole with Fresh Cranberry Salad and steamed broccoli.

Table Talk

Plan ahead when using the food processor to chop fresh seasoning vegetables. It takes no more work to put in an extra onion or bell pepper, etc. Package your chopped veggies in amounts you usually need for sautéing, and freeze in small freezer bags. This makes cooking a breeze when needing a few veggies to sauté for a dish. Rule of thumb is one chopped medium onion or bell pepper is equal to about ½ cup each. Of course, you do not have to be exact with seasoning vegetables as you cook to your family's taste preferences.

Portobello Pizzas

Prep time: 20 minutes • Cook time: 10 minutes • Serves 6 • Serving size: 2 mushroom pizzas

Each serving has: 9 grams carbohydrate • 2 grams fiber • 7 grams nutritive carbohydrate • 17 grams total protein • 11 grams from animal source • 6 grams from plant source

½ lb. ground beef	6 (¼-inch) slices tomato
1 small onion, diced	1 tsp. oregano
12 (5- to 6-inch) portobello mushrooms	1 tsp. black pepper
½ cup olive oil	1 cup shredded mozzarella cheese
¼ cup freshly grated Parmesan cheese	Butter

Preheat oven to 375°F.

Crumble and brown beef in a skillet with diced onions; drain and keep warm.

Recipe for Success

These mini pizzas use the portobello mushrooms for a base. They are wonderful appetizers as well as being highlighted as the main dish. Serve with basmati rice pilaf, Green Beans Almandine, and mixed fresh fruit.

Clean mushrooms by wiping with a damp paper towel. Brush mushrooms with olive oil on both sides. In a large skillet, warm 1 tablespoon olive oil; add mushrooms and brown on both sides.

Place mushrooms on a buttered baking sheet. Cover with Parmesan cheese, and add ground beef. Place 1 tomato slice on each mushroom, top with oregano and pepper, and sprinkle with mozzarella cheese.

Bake for 10 minutes.

Hot Potato

Never store mushrooms in plastic bags. Refrigerate in containers that allow air to circulate around each mushroom, as moisture will cause mushrooms to deteriorate quickly.

Chili Meat Loaf

Prep time: 30 minutes • Cook time: 50 minutes • Serves 10 • Serving size: 1 (½-inch) slice

Each serving has: 9 grams carbohydrate • 2 grams fiber • 7 grams nutritive carbohydrate • 33 grams total protein • 31 grams from animal source • 2 grams from plant source

2 TB. butter	2 tsp. cumin
1 medium onion, diced	4 tomatoes, diced
1 red bell pepper, diced	1 lb. ground beef
2 tsp. minced garlic	½ lb. ground sausage
2 fresh jalapeño peppers, diced	2 eggs, lightly beaten
2 TB. chili powder	1 cup frozen corn kernels
2 tsp. salt	1 cup (4 oz.) grated sharp cheddar cheese
2 tsp. oregano	

Preheat oven to 350°F.

In a large skillet, heat butter and sauté onion, bell pepper, garlic, jalapeños, chili powder, salt, oregano, and cumin. Cover and cook, stirring occasionally, until vegetables are soft, about 10 minutes. Add tomatoes and cook another 10 minutes. Remove from heat to cool.

Combine ground beef and sausage. Add cooked mixture plus eggs and corn. Press into two 9×5-inch loaf pans.

Bake 50 minutes. Pour off any pan juices. Sprinkle cheese over loaves, and return to oven until cheese melts. Cool 5 minutes, and cut each loaf into 5 slices to serve.

Recipe for Success
This recipe is a tangy alternative to meat loaf. Serve with salsa and guacamole salad. Leftovers are great for lunches and breakfasts.

Stuffed Green Peppers

Prep time: 20 minutes • Cook time: 30 minutes • Serves 4 • Serving size: 1 stuffed pepper

Each serving has: 10 grams carbohydrate • 3 grams fiber • 7 grams nutritive carbohydrate • 34 grams total protein • 30 grams from animal source • 4 grams from plant source

4 green peppers	1 lb. ground beef
Boiling water	2 eggs, lightly beaten
2 slices bacon, diced	Salt and pepper to taste
2 TB. butter	¼ tsp. dried parsley
1 small onion, diced	¼ tsp. dried basil
¾ cup chopped celery	

Preheat oven to 350°F.

Cut a slice from the top of each pepper, and remove seeds and membrane. Cook pepper shells in boiling water for 5 minutes. Drain well.

Recipe for Success

The green peppers in this recipe make a tidy package for the seasoned ground beef mixture. Plus the peppers add yet more flavor. Serve with one more vegetable and a light mousse or fruit soufflé for dessert.

In a heavy skillet, cook bacon until crisp. Remove bacon and add butter, onion, and celery, and sauté until tender. Remove mixture and set aside. Brown and drain ground beef. Add vegetable mixture back into the skillet, and set off heat. Stir in eggs, salt, pepper, parsley, and basil.

Fill pepper shells with meat mixture, and place in a greased baking dish. Pour hot water to a depth of ¼ inch around peppers. Bake 30 minutes.

Cabbage Rolls

Prep time: 20 minutes   •   Cook time: 1 hour   •   Serves 6   •   Serving size: 2 rolls

Each serving has: 10 grams carbohydrate   •   2 grams fiber   •   8 grams nutritive carbohydrate   •   10 grams total protein   •   8 grams from animal source   •   2 grams from plant source

1 large head cabbage	2 TB. Worcestershire sauce
1 lb. ground meat	1 tsp. lemon juice
1 medium onion, diced	Salt and pepper to taste
1 egg	1 cup water
½ tsp. cinnamon	1 (8-oz.) can tomato sauce
1 (6-oz.) can tomato paste	1 sliced bell pepper

Preheat oven to 350°F.

Remove 12 large leaves from cabbage, and parboil until softened. Trim off thick portion of each leaf.

In a bowl, mix together meat, diced onion, egg, cinnamon, tomato paste, Worcestershire sauce, lemon juice, salt, and pepper.

Line the bottom of a baking dish with extra cabbage leaves, and cover with water.

Place mound of meat mixture on each cabbage leaf, roll up, and place seam size down in cabbage-lined dish. Pour on tomato sauce, and top with green pepper slices.

Cover the pan, and bake 1 hour.

Recipe for Success
This meat stuffing is wonderful in hollowed out zucchini or eggplant boats. Serve with Garbanzo Bean Salad and Curried Fruit Skewers.

Spaghetti Sauce

Prep time: 25 minutes • Cook time: 1 hour • Serves 6 • Serving size: ¾ cup

Each serving has: 9 grams carbohydrate • 2 grams fiber • 7 grams nutritive carbohydrate • 14 grams total protein • 7 grams from animal source • 7 grams from plant source

1 onion, chopped	¼ cup green olives, sliced
½ cup sliced mushrooms	½ tsp. fennel seeds
1 tsp. minced garlic	1 tsp. salt
2 TB. butter	½ tsp. black pepper
1 lb. ground beef	2 TB. tomato paste
1 tsp. dried oregano	1 (28-oz.) can whole tomatoes
¼ cup black olives, sliced	

In a large heavy pot, sauté onion, mushrooms, and garlic in butter until tender. Remove from pan and set aside. Place ground beef in the pan and brown; drain. Return onion mixture to the pan, and add oregano, black and green olives, fennel seeds, salt, pepper, and tomato paste. Cut whole tomatoes into quarters, and add to the pot. Blend thoroughly.

Simmer for 1 hour, stirring occasionally. Add water as needed.

Variation: If you're in a rush to get the spaghetti sauce made, try this: Brown 1 pound ground beef in a heavy skillet. Add 1 large container commercially prepared spaghetti sauce. Then add more of the seasonings you like—onion salt, minced garlic, crushed red pepper, fennel seed, oregano, and whatever else sounds good to you. Continue to cook a couple minutes and serve.

Recipe for Success

Everyone loves spaghetti. You can double this or even triple it to feed a crowd. Serve it over cooked spaghetti squash. You can spoon sauce into half a squash for each serving, or remove the spaghetti-type fibers first from the squash shells.

Tamale Pie

Prep time: 30 minutes • Cook time: 50 minutes • Serves 6 • Serving size: ¾ cup

Each serving has: 23 grams carbohydrate • 4 grams fiber • 19 grams nutritive carbohydrate • 11 grams total protein • 7 grams from animal source • 4 grams from plant source

1 lb. lean ground beef	2 TB. chili powder
1 onion, chopped	Salt and black pepper to taste
1 green bell pepper, chopped	1 (15-oz.) can drained kidney beans
1 jalapeño pepper, diced (optional)	1 cup whole-kernel corn, drained
2 TB. taco seasoning	2 (8-oz.) cans tomato sauce
1 tsp. minced garlic	

Preheat oven to 400°F.

In a large skillet, brown ground beef. Drain off excess fat. Combine meat, onion, green pepper, jalapeño (if using), taco seasoning, garlic, chili powder, salt, and black pepper. Cook over medium heat until tender.

Using a 9×9-inch glass baking dish, place a layer of meat sauce on the bottom. Then layer with kidney beans. Add more meat sauce; top layer with corn; and add remaining meat mixture. Pour tomato sauce over all.

Bake for 20 minutes.

Recipe for Success
This pie uses no crust, but the layering makes for a festive presentation. Serve it with shredded cheddar cheese, salsa, and guacamole or avocado salad.

Hamburger with Mushrooms and Cream

Prep time: 15 minutes • Cook time: 15 minutes • Serves 6 • Serving size: ½ cup

Each serving has: 4 grams carbohydrate • 1 gram fiber • 3 grams nutritive carbohydrate • 9 grams total protein • 9 grams from animal source

1 lb. ground beef	1 tsp. tarragon
½ cup minced onions	1 cup sliced mushrooms
1 tsp. salt	1 cup heavy cream
¼ ground pepper	1 cup sour cream

Brown ground beef and onions together; drain off excess fat. Add salt, pepper, tarragon, and mushrooms. Cook 5 minutes. Add heavy cream, simmer uncovered for 10 minutes, and stir in sour cream.

Recipe for Success

Serve this creamy, rich beef dish over basmati rice or, for a lower carb count, serve over Vegetable Pasta. Steamed vegetables make a light accompaniment to this heavier dish. Serve it as a wonderful hot dip with vegetable scoops instead of higher-carb crackers and chips. Celery sticks, squash rounds, large bell pepper squares, and jicama circles make great scoopers!

Lasagna

Prep time: 20 minutes   •   Cook time: 45 minutes plus standing time   •   Serves 8   •   Serving size: 1 section

Each serving has: 6 grams nutritive carbohydrate   •   less than 1 gram fiber   •   17 grams total protein   •   16 grams from animal source   •   1 gram from plant source

1 lb. ground beef

1 (15-oz.) can tomato sauce

1 garlic clove, minced

1 tsp. basil

2 tsp. rosemary

1½ cups ricotta cheese

½ cup grated Parmesan cheese

1 egg

1½ lb. zucchini, cut lengthwise into ¼-inch slices

4 oz. shredded mozzarella cheese

Recipe for Success

Don't let the zucchini fool you. It takes on the wonderful Italian aromatic flavors of the lasagna and provides a great low-carb way to layer the cheeses and meat. Plus, the zucchini adds another vegetable to the meal.

Preheat oven to 350°F.

Brown ground beef in a large skillet and drain. Stir in tomato sauce, garlic, basil, and rosemary. Heat to boiling. Reduce heat and simmer about 10 minutes.

Mix ricotta, ¼ cup Parmesan, and egg in small bowl.

In 9×13-inch greased baking pan, layer zucchini, cheese mixture, meat sauce, and mozzarella. Repeat. Sprinkle ¼ cup grated Parmesan on top.

Bake for 45 minutes. Let stand 20 minutes before serving. Slice into 8 servings.

Chinese Meatballs

Prep time: 20 minutes • Cook time: 40 minutes • Serves 6 • Serving size: 12 meatballs

Each serving has: 13 grams carbohydrate • 6 grams fiber • 7 grams nutritive carbohydrate • 29 grams total protein • 28 grams from animal source • 1 gram from plant source

Each ¼ cup sauce serving has: 13 grams nutritive carbohydrate • less than 1 gram total protein

1 TB. soy sauce	1 TB. molasses
1½ lb. ground beef	½ cup vinegar
¼ cup minced celery	2 TB. cornstarch
¼ cup minced water chestnuts	2 TB. soy sauce
2 cloves garlic, minced	½ cup pineapple juice
½ cup oat bran or ground oatmeal	½ cup pineapple tidbits
2 eggs, beaten	½ green pepper, cut into strips
1 cup tomato juice	

Preheat oven to 350°F.

Mix 1 tablespoon soy sauce with ground beef, celery, water chestnuts, garlic, oat bran, and eggs. Form into 72 (1-inch) balls. Bake for 30 minutes.

For sauce, combine tomato juice, molasses, vinegar, cornstarch, soy sauce, pineapple juice, pineapple tidbits, and green pepper. Cook for 3 minutes or until slightly thickened. Add meatballs and simmer for 10 minutes. Remove meatballs from sauce, and serve alone for fewer carbohydrates.

Recipe for Success

As a main dish with an Asian flair, serve with Ginger Carrots and Mandarin Orange Spinach Salad. Make the meatballs miniature-size, and serve with the warm sauce over fresh baby spinach for a delicious sweet-and-sour wilted salad; garnish with slivered almonds.

Italian Meatballs

Prep time: 20 minutes   •   Cook time: 30 minutes   •   Serves 6   •   Serving size: 12 meatballs

Each serving has: 7 grams carbohydrate   •   6 grams fiber   •   1 gram nutritive carbohydrate
•   35 grams total protein   •   34 grams from animal source   •   1 gram from plant source

1½ lb. ground beef	½ tsp. dried oregano
2 eggs, beaten	¼ tsp. dried basil
½ cup oat bran or ground oatmeal	¼ tsp. dried marjoram
¼ cup minced onion	¼ tsp. crushed red pepper
3 cloves garlic, minced	

Table Talk
For convenience, you may substitute Italian seasoning mix for the herb mixture in this recipe.

Preheat oven to 350°F.

Combine beef, eggs, oat bran, onion, garlic, oregano, basil, marjoram, and red pepper. Form into 72 (1-inch) meatballs. Bake for 30 minutes.

Serve meatballs in your favorite Italian sauce over Vegetable Pasta or Egg Pancakes. Also, meatballs rolled up in large romaine leaves make great finger food!

The Least You Need to Know

◆ The versatility and convenience of ground meat lets you create interesting low-carb main courses.

◆ Use the ground meat—beef, sausage, turkey, or pork—that appeals to you in these recipes.

◆ Keep ground meat as a staple in your freezer for quick meals.

◆ Purchase ground meat with the fat percentage that meets your taste and dietary requirements.

Chapter 9

Pork, Ham, and Veal Dishes

In This Chapter

- Cooking with pork
- Choosing pork and veal for meals
- Recognizing many cuts and choices

For many of us, just the smell of bacon cooking on a Saturday morning mesmerizes us enough to make us roll out of bed and stumble into the kitchen for breakfast. The aroma is irresistible. The enticing smell of pork ribs on the grill or Grandma's baked ham for holidays and special occasions elicits the same ardor.

The truth is, we love ham, bacon, and ribs. We love pork. It tastes good, and now we know it is also good for us. Pork contains plenty of essential amino acids to stoke metabolism. Plus, it's a cook's delight. Pork blends well with many other foods and is enhanced with many different spices and herbs. And best of all, pork has no carbs and is ideal for a low-carb eating plan.

Myths and Half-Truths

Pork has been subject to bad media spin for hundreds of years. So let's clear the air on the truth about pork.

Pork definitely has fat, as does any other meat. Through roasting and grilling the fattier cuts, such as ribs and ham, some of the fat is rendered out of the meat. The cooked pork you eat contains far less fat than it did before cooking.

Pork loin and pork chops often have very little to no marbling of fat and, so, contain less fat, even before cooking. Trimming the visible fat from such cuts either before or after cooking helps reduce your fat intake even further.

Part of pork's bad rep comes from earlier methods used to raise pigs that resulted in uncooked pork containing a dangerous parasite called trichinosis. But a recent report from the USDA states that only 1 in 1,000 pigs are now found to contain the trichinosis parasite. But just in case, never eat raw or partially cooked pork. Cooking the meat to an internal temperature of 137°F kills the parasite. To be safe, pork needs to be cooked to an internal temperature of 160°F. The cooked meat must be white or grayish throughout, without a trace of pink. When pricked with a fork, the juices must run clear and not be even slightly pink.

Hot Potato

When handling all raw meats and fish, but especially chicken and pork, be sure to wash all utensils and cutting boards thoroughly in hot soapy water to avoid contamination and prevent disease.

Tenderizing the White Meats

The light cuts of pork, such as tenderloin and chops, can turn out tough and chewy because these cuts have virtually no fat marbling and tight muscle fibers. However, marinades can solve the problem. Marinades contain an acidic liquid, usually vinegar, alcohol, or soy sauce, that helps break down the tight muscle fibers and makes the meat more tender and easier to chew. Some of the ingredients in our recipes also serve to tenderize the meat, such as sauerkraut, apples, and wine.

Veal is also a light meat that has relatively little fat and very tight muscle fibers. We can use two preparation methods to make the veal tender. First, we can pound thin slices of veal with a meat hammer to break up the muscle tissue. Pounding makes the meat quite thin. The second way to tenderize veal is by marinating.

Country Pâté

Prep time: 1½ hours • Cook time: 1½ hours • Serves 25 • Serving size: 1 (½-inch) slice

Each serving has: 1 gram nutritive carbohydrate • less than 1 gram fiber • 13 grams total protein • 12 grams from animal source • 1 gram from plant source

¾ lb. bacon	½ tsp. ground allspice
1 TB. butter	1 pinch ground cloves
1 onion, chopped	1 pinch ground nutmeg
1 lb. pork (½ fat, ½ lean), ground	2 small eggs, lightly beaten
½ lb. veal, finely chopped	½ cup heavy cream
½ lb. chicken livers, finely chopped	Salt and pepper to taste
½ cup shelled pistachios	½ lb. ham, cut in thin strips
2 cloves garlic, crushed	1 bay leaf

Preheat oven to 350°F.

Line a 2-quart baking dish with a tight lid with bacon, reserving a few slices for the top.

Melt butter in a small pan, and sauté onion until soft but not brown. Combine with pork, veal, chicken livers, pistachios, garlic, allspice, cloves, nutmeg, eggs, heavy cream, salt, and pepper. Check seasoning. It should have a generous amount of salt and pepper.

Spread ⅓ mixture in the baking dish. Layer with half ham strips and repeat.

Recipe for Success

Pâté is wonderful for eating low carb. This pâté is great for meals, appetizers, and snacks. The combination of meats is very European.

Cover with last third of meat mixture. Lay remaining slices of bacon on top, then top with bay leaf.

Set the baking dish in a shallow roasting pan filled with 2 to 3 inches hot water. Bake 1⅓ hours. Remove bay leaf.

Cool pâté until it is tepid before removing lid. Refrigerate 3 days or up to a week before serving.

As a first course, slice and serve on lettuce (perhaps butter lettuce) with small dill pickles.

Pork Chops and Cabbage

Prep time: 10 minutes • Cook time: 1 hour • Serves 8 • Serving size: 1 pork chop and 1 cup vegetables

Each serving has: 9 grams carbohydrate • 2 grams fiber • 7 grams nutritive carbohydrate • 32 grams total protein • 31 grams from animal source • 1 gram from plant source

¼ cup olive oil

8 pork chops, about ½ inch thick

2 medium onions, sliced

1 clove garlic, chopped

1 (28-oz.) can tomatoes (2½ to 3 cups)

1 head cabbage (about 2 lb.), coarsely shredded

1 tsp. salt

⅛ tsp. pepper

⅛ tsp. dried sage

1 cup dry red wine

Recipe for Success

The chops turn out tender and delicious with the taste of cabbage in the red wine. This recipe has 2 servings of vegetables, so consider this dish a complete meal.

Preheat oven to 350°F.

Heat oil over medium heat in a large skillet. Brown chops 3 minutes on each side. Remove to a casserole.

In the same skillet, sauté onions and garlic 3 minutes. Stir in tomatoes, and add cabbage, salt, pepper, sage, and wine. Spread mixture over chops.

Bake for 60 minutes or until cabbage and chops are tender. Check occasionally. You can prepare this in advance and refrigerate. (If refrigerated, allow 15 minutes additional baking time.)

Veal Marsala with Cream

Prep time: 15 minutes • Cook time: 10 minutes • Serves 4 • Serving size: 5 ounces

Each serving has: 13 grams nutritive carbohydrate • less than 1 gram fiber • 39 grams total protein • 35 grams from animal source • 4 grams from plant source

2 TB. vegetable oil	Salt and pepper to taste
3 TB. butter	½ cup dry Marsala
1¼ lb. thin veal scallops	⅓ cup heavy cream
3 TB. flour	

Heat oil and butter in a large skillet over high heat. Dredge veal scallops in flour one at a time, coating both sides.

As butter foam begins to subside, put veal in the skillet, but don't put any more in the skillet than will fit without overlapping.

Brown veal quickly on both sides; about 30 seconds per side is enough if the cooking grease is hot. When browned on both sides, transfer to a large platter. Season meat on the platter with salt and pepper to taste.

Add Marsala to the skillet and stir, scraping cooking residues loose from the bottom of the pan. When Marsala has begun to boil away, add cream and stir constantly over high heat until cream blends with juices in the pan into a thick, dark sauce.

Turn heat to medium and add veal. Simmer for 5 minutes, and serve with sauce.

Recipe for Success
This is a classic cooking method for veal. The wonderful blending of tastes is sweet, plus the meat cuts with a fork.

Marinated Pork Tenderloin

Prep time: 15 minutes plus 24 hours marinating time • Cook time: 2½ hours • Serves 10 • Serving size: 4 ounces

Each serving has: 1 gram nutritive carbohydrate • less than 1 gram fiber • 30 grams total protein • 30 grams from animal source • 0 grams from plant source

½ cup dry white wine

¼ cup vegetable oil

6 TB. Dijon mustard

¼ cup chopped mushrooms

2 TB. soy sauce

2 TB. fresh lemon juice

2 TB. minced onion

2 TB. butter

½ tsp. celery seed

½ tsp. salt

½ tsp. freshly ground black pepper

1 (5-lb.) pork loin roast, boned, rolled, and tied

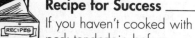

Recipe for Success

If you haven't cooked with pork tenderloin before, now is the time. The meat is tender, lean, and loves to take up the flavors of spices and mushrooms. You'll soon become friends with this tasty cut of pork.

In a large bowl, mix together wine, oil, mustard, mushrooms, soy sauce, lemon juice, onion, butter, celery seed, salt, and pepper. Place pork roast in a rectangular baking pan, and pour marinade over meat. Cover and refrigerate 24 hours, turning occasionally.

Place tenderloin with marinade into a roasting pan. Roast at 350°F for 2½ hours or to an internal temperature of 155°F to 160°F.

Pork Chops with Spaghetti

Prep time: 20 minutes   •   Cook time: 1 hour   •   Serves 4   •   Serving size: 1 (6-ounce) pork chop with ½ cup squash

Each serving has: 14 grams carbohydrate   •   3 grams fiber   •   11 grams nutritive carbohydrate   •   46 grams total protein   •   44 grams from animal source   •   2 grams from plant source

1 large spaghetti squash	⅛ tsp. crushed red pepper
4 thick-cut pork chops	1 tsp. dried rosemary
8 TB. butter	2 cups chopped tomatoes
4 TB. grated Parmesan cheese	¼ cup chopped fresh parsley
½ tsp. minced garlic	½ tsp. salt
¼ tsp. freshly ground black pepper	

Preheat oven to 350°F.

Place spaghetti squash in a baking dish, and bake for 1 to 1½ hours or until done. To test for doneness, prick skin with a fork. If the fork enters easily, squash is done. While squash is baking, prepare the pork chops.

Melt 4 tablespoons butter in a large, heavy skillet. Add garlic, black pepper, red pepper, and rosemary. Add pork chops and brown slowly. Add tomatoes, parsley, and salt. Cover and simmer for 20 minutes. Uncover and cook 20 more minutes until pork chops are tender.

When squash is done, split open with a knife and scoop out and discard seeds. Take a fork and scrape inside of squash. The flesh comes out in strands—like spaghetti. Toss strands with 4 tablespoons butter and Parmesan cheese.

Place spaghetti squash strands on a platter, arrange chops on spaghetti, and pour sauce over all.

 **Table Talk**

You can also cook the spaghetti squash in the microwave as you would a baked potato. Prick the skin with a fork in several places. Microwave on high for 12 to 15 minutes. Cut open and scoop out seeds. Then use a fork to separate and remove the strands from the shells.

Pork Chops with Raisins and Walnuts

Prep time: 10 minutes plus 2 to 3 hours marinating time • Cook time: 20 minutes
• Serves 4 • Serving size: 1 pork chop

Each serving has: 12 grams carbohydrate • 1 gram fiber • 11 grams nutritive carbohydrate
• 47 grams total protein • 42 grams from animal source • 5 grams from plant source

4 pork chops	¼ tsp. freshly ground black pepper
¼ cup bourbon	1 clove garlic, minced
½ cup water	2 TB. raisins
2 TB. apple juice	¼ cup walnuts
¼ tsp. cayenne	

Put pork chops, bourbon, water, apple juice, cayenne, pepper, garlic, raisins, and walnuts into a large, resealable plastic bag. Marinate 2 to 3 hours at room temperature or overnight in the refrigerator.

Recipe for Success

This recipe has a surprising flavor. The bourbon imparts a great and unusual taste, but don't worry about the alcohol—it evaporates during cooking. And the walnuts taste *so* good!

When you are ready to cook, remove pork chops to a heavy skillet, and fry until cooked through. At the same time, put marinade—including raisins and walnuts (they're the best part)—into a small saucepan. Bring to a boil and reduce sauce to ½ volume.

Remove pork chops to a serving platter and pour sauce over pork chops.

Veal Chops with Tarragon

Prep time: 20 minutes   •   Cook time: 10 minutes   •   Serves 4   •   Serving size: 1 veal chop

Each serving has: 2 grams nutritive carbohydrate   •   30 grams total protein   •   30 grams from animal source

4 veal chops, about ¾- to 1-inch thick	¼ cup (½ stick) butter
4 TB. olive oil	1 TB. chopped fresh tarragon
2 TB. lemon juice	¼ tsp. minced garlic
4 fresh tarragon leaves, leaves rolled or bent to release flavor	¼ tsp. salt
	¼ tsp. pepper

Place veal chops in a resealable plastic bag. Put in olive oil, lemon juice, and tarragon. Close bag and marinate 2 to 3 hours or overnight in refrigerator. Turn over bag occasionally to marinate chops on all sides.

To make tarragon butter, melt butter in the microwave with tarragon, garlic, salt, and pepper. Set aside.

Heat a heavy skillet and brown chops. Cook for about 4 minutes per side, basting with marinade. Serve topped with tarragon butter.

Variation: Substitute basil for tarragon in this recipe. It will be just as delicious.

Recipe for Success _____
These veal chops are easy to prepare. They are quite tender when marinated and cooked or grilled quickly. Serve for special occasions and to special guests.

Curried Pork Chops with Apricots

Prep time: 30 minutes • Cook time: 40 minutes • Serves 4 • Serving size: 1 pork chop with ¼ cup sauce

Each serving has: 9 grams nutritive carbohydrate • less than 1 gram fiber • 43 grams total protein • 42 grams from animal source • 1 gram from plant source

1 medium onion, chopped	4 pork chops
3 TB. butter	4 dried apricot halves, chopped
1 TB. flour	¼ cup water
1 TB. curry powder	1 cup sliced mushrooms
¾ cup white wine	6 TB. butter
Salt and pepper to taste	Salt and pepper to taste

Make sauce first. Sauté onions in butter until just tender. Sprinkle with flour, and add curry powder. Cook 1 to 2 minutes, stirring, and add white wine. Season with salt and pepper. Simmer while cooking pork chops.

Recipe for Success

The apricots and mushrooms enhance the mild curry taste. But don't let it fool you; the combination makes your mouth sing. And it sure doesn't taste like low carb.

Put chopped apricots with water into a small bowl, and microwave for 1 minute, until water boils. Remove and let stand to let apricots get tender and soft.

Sauté mushrooms over high heat in 3 tablespoons butter. In a separate skillet, sauté pork chops in 3 tablespoons butter until browned on both sides.

Top pork chops with apricots, then curry sauce. Season with salt and pepper. Spread mushrooms over sauce, cover the skillet, and cook gently for 30 minutes or until done.

Pork Chops with Apples

Prep time: 20 minutes   •   Cook time: 10 to 15 minutes   •   Serves 4   •   Serving size: 1 pork chop and 1 apple

Each serving has: 21 grams carbohydrate   •   5 grams fiber   •   16 grams nutritive carbohydrate   •   42 grams total protein   •   42 grams from animal source   •   less than 1 gram from plant source

4 pork chops

3 TB. butter

4 medium cooking apples, such as Fuji, Golden Delicious, or Granny Smith

Salt and pepper to taste

Preheat oven to 300°F.

Sauté pork chops on both sides in butter to brown, and then continue cooking at a high temperature for 10 minutes, turning once after 5 minutes.

Core apples and cut into thin slices. Leave skins on.

Arrange pork chops in a shallow oven dish, and pour pan juices over chops. Arrange apple slices around chops. Season with salt and pepper. Bake for about 10 to 15 minutes, until apples are tender.

Recipe for Success

With just 3 ingredients plus salt and pepper, you can make these interesting pork chops. They have a sweetness with a light tang from the apples.

Pork Chops with Sauerkraut

Prep time: 15 minutes • Cook time: 1 hour • Serves 6 • Serving size: 1 pork chop and ½ cup sauerkraut

Each serving has: 9 grams carbohydrate • 4 grams fiber • 5 grams nutritive carbohydrate • 43 grams total protein • 42 grams from animal source • 1 gram from plant source

6 pork chops, ¾ to 1 inch thick	¼ cup water
3 TB. butter	¼ tsp. caraway seeds
2 lb. drained sauerkraut	¼ tsp. freshly ground black pepper
1 TB. molasses	

Sauté pork chops in butter to brown on both sides.

Mix sauerkraut, molasses, water, caraway seeds, and pepper in an oven casserole. Place pork chops on top of the mixture. Cover and bake about 1 hour.

Recipe for Success
Sauerkraut, notably low in carbs, gives the pork chops a highly tangy and interesting flavor. The caraway seeds add authenticity to this recipe, adapted from Middle European cuisine. Baked apples are a great accompaniment.

Oven BBQ Ribs

Prep time: 15 minutes • Cook time: 1 hour 15 minutes • Serves 6 • Serving size: approximately 5 to 6 ribs

Each serving has: 18 grams nutritive carbohydrate • 44 grams total protein • 42 grams from animal source • 2 grams from plant source

6 lb. spareribs, cut into serving-size pieces	4 to 5 dashes hot pepper sauce
Boiling water	2 onions, minced
1 cup ketchup	2 cloves garlic, minced
⅓ cup Worcestershire sauce	1 tsp. paprika
2 TB. soy sauce	1 tsp. dry mustard
½ cup water	1 tsp. black pepper
¼ cup lemon juice	¼ tsp. ginger

Preheat oven to 450°F.

Parboil ribs in a large pot for 5 minutes. Drain and set aside.

Combine ketchup, Worcestershire sauce, soy sauce, water, lemon juice, hot pepper sauce, onions, garlic, paprika, mustard, black pepper, and ginger in a saucepan. Bring to a boil, reduce heat, and simmer until thickened.

Low-Carb Vocab

Parboil means to boil partially or for a short time. In this recipe, parboiling the ribs removes some of the fat and precooks them.

While sauce simmers, line a roasting pan with heavy foil, and place ribs on foil and cover. Bake for 15 minutes, and remove from the oven. Reduce heat to 350°F. Pour sauce over ribs, covering well. Cover the pan with foil, and bake 1 hour. Check every 15 minutes, basting as needed.

Green Tomatoes and Ham

Prep time: 15 minutes • Cook time: 40 minutes • Serves 6 • Serving size: 4 ounces ham with ½ cup vegetables

Each serving has: 13 grams carbohydrate • 2 grams fiber • 11 grams nutritive carbohydrate • 30 grams total protein • 26 grams from animal source • 4 grams from plant source

1 (2-lb.) (or 2 smaller) ham slice, ¾ inch thick, fully cooked	2 TB. brown sugar
5 medium green tomatoes, sliced ¼ inch thick	1 tsp. tarragon
3 onions, sliced ¼ inch thick	1 tsp. dry mustard
2 TB. Worcestershire sauce	½ tsp. black pepper

Preheat oven to 350°F.

On top of the stove, brown ham on both sides; place in the bottom of a baking dish. Place tomato and onion slices on top of ham; sprinkle with Worcestershire sauce, brown sugar, tarragon, mustard, and black pepper. Cover dish and bake 40 minutes.

Recipe for Success

This is a deliciously simple dish ready to eat in under an hour. Use your favorite seasonings to make this dish uniquely yours. Bell pepper rings give additional flavor, or try sprinkling with a bit of cinnamon or basil.

Herbed Pork Chops

Prep time: 10 minutes • Cook time: 30 minutes • Serves 6 • Serving size: 1 pork chop

Each serving has: 3 grams nutritive carbohydrate • less than 1 gram fiber • 42 grams total protein • 42 grams from animal source

6 pork chops, ¾ inch thick	1 tsp. dried rosemary
2 TB. butter	1 tsp. dried thyme
2 whole cloves	1 tsp. garlic powder
1 onion	1 tsp. black pepper
1 tsp. dried oregano	½ cup water
1 tsp. dried marjoram	

Preheat oven to 350°F.

Brown both sides pork chops in butter; set aside.

Insert cloves into onion, and add to the pot with pork chops.

Sprinkle oregano, marjoram, rosemary, thyme, garlic powder, and black pepper over pork chops. Add water and bake covered 30 minutes.

Recipe for Success _____

For a complete dinner in one pot, use a Dutch oven and layer cabbage sections over top of pork chops, then top with sliced carrots, thick slices of onion, bell pepper, tomatoes, or thinly sliced sweet potatoes. Any mixture of these vegetables will add flavor and be ready to eat with the pork chops.

Mushroom-Gingered Ham Slice

Prep time: 20 minutes plus 1 hour marinating time • Cook time: 40 minutes • Serves 6 • Serving size: 5 ounces ham with ¼ cup sauce

Each serving has: 12 grams nutritive carbohydrate • less than 1 gram fiber • 29 grams total protein • 28 grams from animal source • 1 gram from plant source

1 tsp. dry mustard

1 tsp. ground ginger

½ cup white wine

2 lb. ham slice, 1 to 2 inches thick, fully cooked

2 TB. butter

1 onion, minced

2 cloves garlic, minced

1 stalk celery, sliced

1 cup cream

1 (8-oz.) can mushrooms or 1 pint fresh mushrooms, sliced

3 TB. butter

1 TB. cornstarch

¼ cup water

Preheat oven to 425°F.

Blend together mustard, ginger, and wine, and pour over ham slice. Refrigerate for 1 hour, turning occasionally.

Drain ham, reserving liquid. Melt butter in a skillet and brown ham. Remove ham, place in a baking dish, and set aside. In the same skillet, melt additional butter, if needed, to sauté onions, garlic, and celery.

Recipe for Success

Make ham into a delectable and unusual taste treat. Serve with salad and a vegetable, such as asparagus, green beans, or peas.

When vegetables are tender, add marinade and cream to the skillet; heat to simmering, stir in mushrooms, and simmer 10 minutes.

Mix cornstarch into water to form smooth paste, and slowly stir into sauce mixture, cooking and stirring constantly until thickened. Pour over ham slice in the baking dish, and bake 20 minutes.

Veal Parmesan

Prep time: 20 minutes • Cook time: 30 minutes • Serves 6 • Serving size: 4 ounces

Each serving has: 20 grams carbohydrate • 2 grams fiber • 18 grams nutritive carbohydrate • 42 grams total protein • 38 grams from animal source • 4 grams from plant source

3 TB. butter	¼ tsp. Italian herb mixture
1 onion, minced	1½ lb. veal cutlets, thinly sliced
3 cloves garlic, minced	¾ cup Parmesan cheese
1 (28-oz.) can Italian-seasoned tomato pieces	¼ cup finely ground breadcrumbs
8 oz. tomato sauce	1 egg, slightly beaten
Salt and pepper to taste	3 TB. olive oil
¼ tsp. dried basil	½ lb. mozzarella cheese slices

Preheat oven to 350°F.

Melt butter in a skillet and sauté onion and garlic until tender. Add tomatoes, tomato sauce, salt, pepper, basil, and herb mixture; simmer 10 minutes.

Pound cutlets until very thin. Combine ½ cup Parmesan cheese and breadcrumbs. Dip cutlets into egg and then into breading mixture, covering well. In a separate skillet, heat olive oil and brown cutlets on both sides.

Recipe for Success

This recipe is a classic Italian favorite that's also low carb. Serve with spaghetti squash and sliced tomatoes on lettuce. It's wonderful because you get the terrific tastes of the Mediterranean without the pasta.

In one layer, place cutlets in a large baking dish, and pour ⅔ sauce over top. Layer mozzarella slices over sauce, and pour remaining tomato sauce on top of cheese. Sprinkle remaining Parmesan cheese over all and bake, uncovered, for 30 minutes.

Smothered Pork Chops

Prep time: 15 minutes • Cook time: 1 hour • Serves 6 • Serving size: 1 pork chop

Each serving has: 8 grams nutritive carbohydrate • less than 1 gram fiber • 44 grams total protein • 42 grams from animal source • 2 grams from plant source

1 TB. butter	2 cups chicken broth
6 thick pork chops	1 cup sliced carrots
2 onions, chopped	1 TB. cornstarch
½ bell pepper, chopped	¼ cup water
1 tsp. minced garlic	1 tsp. Worcestershire sauce

Recipe for Success

This hearty pork dish includes plenty of vegetables. Add a tossed salad with a mild dressing such as Green Goddess to balance the savory taste of the sauce.

Melt butter in a skillet, and brown pork chops on both sides. Remove from the pan and set aside. In the same skillet, sauté onions, bell pepper, and garlic until tender. Add chicken broth and carrots to the skillet, and bring to a simmer.

Mix cornstarch into water, and stir to a smooth paste; add to the skillet, and stir to thicken. Add Worcestershire sauce and pork chops to the skillet. Cover and cook over low heat for 1 hour or until meat is cooked.

The Least You Need to Know

- Pork is a delicious meat that can be prepared in a wide variety of intriguing ways.
- Pork cuts can be low fat or high fat. Let your taste preferences guide you.
- Veal and pork are light meats that take well to marinating or tenderizing with other recipe ingredients.
- Cook pork to a minimum internal temperature of 137°F, and clean work areas thoroughly.
- Pork and veal contain no carbohydrates and offer complete protein so they are great for low-carb eating.

Chapter 10

Poultry Dishes

In This Chapter

- ◆ The ease of cooking with chicken
- ◆ Interchanging chicken and turkey
- ◆ Tasty and varied low-carb meals with chicken

Perhaps you most enjoy the breast meat of a chicken or turkey. Or maybe you love the dark meat and delight in savoring the turkey legs at Thanksgiving. Whichever part you prefer, recipes in this chapter can satisfy your appetite.

Chicken is the most adaptable of meats. It can be roasted, stewed, sautéed, or cooked on the grill. And it can even be baked on top of an opened can of beer!

Chicken has a comparatively mild, almost bland taste, so it readily takes on the flavors of other ingredients in a recipe. Here you'll find recipes for chicken combined with a wide variety of both sweet and hot spices, plus many different fruits, meats, and condiments. Chicken contains less fat than other meats so you can cook it with butter and cream to create a richer taste or with water or bouillon for a lighter-tasting meal.

Another No-Carb Food

Chicken has no carbohydrates. Hooray! Rather, it contains high-quality complete protein and both saturated and unsaturated fats. So chicken cooked without other ingredients is totally carb free. Unfortunately, eating plain chicken without other ingredients would get boring really fast. It would also eliminate lots of wonderful, delicious chicken meals.

It's the other ingredients in these recipes that add to the carb count. These ingredients include fruits, spices, condiments, nuts, and vegetables plus some flour or corn-starch used as thickeners. We have minimized the use of thickeners, and you can omit them if you want to reduce the carb count further. But as you can tell by glancing through these recipes, the carb count is already low and should meet your requirements for low-carb meals.

Table Talk _____

We figure that if you're going to spend your time cooking a delicious chicken meal, you may as well make plenty so you can have leftovers for breakfast or lunch the next day. Best of all, you can relax about what low-carb meal to have the next day for breakfast and/or lunch. Because many of the recipes taste great cold as well as heated, they are perfect for sack lunches.

What Goes with Chicken (or Turkey)

As you plan your chicken meals, always make sure you have two servings of either fruits and/or vegetables at your meal. For instance, serve a tossed salad and steamed vegetable for a wholesome, delicious, and balanced meal. Or substitute fresh fruit for the salad.

You want to "eat a rainbow" as best you can at every meal, so think of side dishes with tomatoes, green vegetables, colorful salad greens, in-season fruit, or a tangy salsa.

And if you have room left in your stomach, add in a treat from the dessert or chocolate recipes.

With the exception of Roast Turkey, we have written all the recipes in this chapter using chicken, but you can substitute turkey for all these recipes except Beer Bottom Smoked Chicken. We don't want you to impale a turkey on that can of beer. Use a chicken only for that recipe, please.

Otherwise, choose turkey or chicken based on what sounds good to you that day. Turkey is a tasty alternative that adds variety and can be quite economical.

Paprika Chicken

Prep time: 30 minutes • Cook time: 40 minutes • Serves 6 • Serving size: 1 breast or 1 leg and thigh

Each serving has: 6 grams carbohydrate • 1 gram fiber • 5 grams nutritive carbohydrate • 33 grams total protein • 32 grams from animal source • 1 gram from plant source

2 large onions	5 strips bacon, cooked and coarsely crumbled
1 clove garlic	1 cup dry white wine
2 cups mushrooms, cut in quarters	½ tsp. salt
3 TB. butter	¼ tsp. pepper
4 lb. chicken, cut in pieces	Cayenne to taste
2 TB. paprika	¾ cup heavy cream

Chop onions, garlic, and mushrooms coarsely. Heat butter in a heavy pan and sauté chicken, onions, garlic, and mushrooms until chicken is well browned on all sides. Sprinkle with paprika. Add bacon, white wine, and enough water to cover. Season with salt, pepper, and a small pinch of cayenne. Cover the pan and cook about 35 minutes.

Remove chicken pieces with a slotted spoon and boil sauce down until slightly thick. Put chicken back into sauce. Add cream, stir, and taste for seasoning.

Recipe for Success _____

Family and friends will exclaim, "This is chicken?!" This decadently rich dish with its creamy sauce has a deep reddish-brown color. When we serve this at a party, friends seem to end up licking the serving bowl. You can substitute water for the wine, if you like. This is a rich and hearty main dish, so serve with lighter fare, such as a fresh salad with a tangy dressing and a side of steamed veggies with butter.

Pine Nut Chicken

Prep time: 20 minutes • Cook time: 35 minutes • Serves 8 • Serving size: 1 breast

Each serving has: 7 grams carbohydrate • 1 gram fiber • 6 grams nutritive carbohydrate • 38 grams total protein • 32 grams from animal source • 6 grams from plant source

1½ cups pine nuts, finely chopped	¼ tsp. salt
3 TB. cornmeal	1 egg white
2 TB. chopped fresh cilantro	3 TB. Dijon mustard
2 cloves garlic, minced	1½ tsp. water
½ tsp. dried sage	8 boneless, skinless chicken breasts, halves, or thighs
½ tsp. cayenne	

Table Talk
Pine nuts come from the piñon pine tree, which grows wild in the southwestern United States and in Mediterranean countries. They contain more protein per weight than any other nut.

Preheat oven to 375°F, and grease a large baking dish.

Combine pine nuts, cornmeal, cilantro, garlic, sage, cayenne, and salt in a bowl. Add egg white and stir. Transfer to a shallow dish.

In a small bowl, combine mustard and water. Spread mixture evenly over chicken. Roll chicken in pine nut mixture, and press to coat evenly. Arrange in the baking dish.

Bake until coating is crisp and browned, about 35 minutes.

Recipe for Success
If you are not familiar with pine nuts, then you need to get familiar! They have a delightful taste. That said, you can use other nuts in place of the pine nuts. Select from pecans, almonds, walnuts, or peanuts, and the carb count stays basically the same. Make ahead and serve cold for picnics and outing. Try this recipe with Confetti Salsa and a side dish of spicy green beans.

Chicken Stir-Fry with Fruit

Prep time: 20 minutes plus marinate for 2 hours • Cook time: 10 minutes • Serves 6 • Serving size: ¼ cup

Each serving has: 9 grams carbohydrate • 1 gram fiber • 8 grams nutritive carbohydrate • 33 grams total protein • 30 grams from animal source • 3 grams from plant source

2 tsp. white wine	½ cup snow peas
1 tsp. soy sauce	4 green onions
¼ tsp. grated fresh ginger	3 TB. peanut oil
1 tsp. cornstarch	1 cup green grapes
½ tsp. sugar	1 cup cubed cantaloupe
½ tsp. salt	1 TB. garlic, minced
¼ tsp. pepper	⅓ cup peanuts, chopped
3 boneless, skinless chicken breasts, cut into strips	

Combine white wine, soy sauce, ginger, cornstarch, sugar, salt, and pepper in a bowl and mix well. Add chicken to this mixture, and refrigerate for 2 hours or longer.

Slice snow peas and onions diagonally into ½-inch pieces.

Heat a wok or a large skillet over high heat for 45 seconds. Add 1 tablespoon peanut oil, and swirl evenly to coat. Add snow peas and onions. Stir-fry for 1 minute or until snow peas are bright green. Add grapes and cantaloupe. Stir-fry for 1 minute. Remove with a slotted spoon, and wipe the wok with a paper towel.

Reheat the wok, add 2 tablespoons peanut oil, and heat. Add garlic and stir-fry for 30 seconds. Add chicken and cook 2 minutes or more, stirring until cooked through.

Return fruit and vegetables to the wok. Cook for 1 minute until heated through. Serve immediately. Garnish with peanuts.

Recipe for Success

Cantaloupe isn't just for breakfast! Melon can be cooked quickly, as in stir-frying. You can substitute other fruits, such as pineapple, raisins, apples, and papaya for the fruit in this recipe. Other nuts such as walnuts, cashews, pecans, pine nuts, almonds, or even macadamias will work as substitutes for the peanuts. This is a meal all by itself, but if you want more, go with a low-carb side dish like a salad or a simple vegetable like sliced tomatoes.

Rosemary Roasted Chicken

Prep time: 10 minutes • Cook time: 60 minutes • Serves 6 • Serving size: 1 breast or 1 leg and thigh

Each serving has: 8 grams nutritive carbohydrate • 32 grams total protein • 32 grams from animal source

4 lb. baking chicken

Salt and freshly ground pepper to taste

3 cloves garlic, cut into halves

4 sprigs fresh rosemary

1 TB. chopped fresh rosemary or 1 to 2 tsp. dried

Recipe for Success

Don't be timid with rosemary! Rosemary is a wonderfully aromatic herb, and the kitchen will be filled with wonderful smells as the chicken bakes. The recipe is also terrific if you substitute tarragon for the rosemary. This dish is perfect for dinner or a picnic. For a great side dish, serve asparagus with hollandaise sauce.

Preheat oven to 400°F.

Remove giblets and neck from chicken cavity. Rinse chicken and pat dry. Season inside and out with a generous mixture of salt and pepper. Put garlic and rosemary sprigs in the cavity, and pat chopped rosemary on the outside of chicken.

Place chicken, breast side down, on a rack in a roasting pan. Bake for 30 minutes, basting with pan juices every 10 minutes. Turn chicken breast side up, and roast for 30 minutes longer or until chicken is cooked through and the outside is crisp and brown.

Chicken with Olives and Capers

Prep time: 20 minutes plus marinate overnight • Cook time: 1 hour • Serves 8
• Serving size: 1 breast or 1 leg and thigh

Each serving has: 5 grams nutritive carbohydrate • less than 1 gram fiber • 32 grams total protein • 32 grams from animal source

2 (2½-lb.) chickens, cut into pieces	½ cup dried apricot halves
1 TB. minced garlic	¼ cup pitted green olives
2 TB. dried oregano	¼ cup capers
1 tsp. salt	3 bay leaves
½ tsp. freshly ground pepper to taste	½ cup white wine
¼ cup red wine vinegar	¼ cup chopped fresh cilantro
¼ cup olive oil	

In a large bowl, combine chicken, garlic, oregano, salt, pepper, vinegar, olive oil, apricots, olives, capers, and bay leaves. Cover and let marinate, refrigerated, overnight.

The next day, preheat the oven to 350°F.

Arrange chicken in a single layer in 1 or 2 shallow baking pans, and spoon marinade evenly over chicken. Pour white wine into pan(s).

Bake for 1 hour, basting frequently with pan juices. Chicken is done when thigh pieces, pricked with a fork, have a clear yellow rather than a pink juice.

To serve, remove bay leaf and sprinkle chicken with cilantro. Serve pan juices separately.

Recipe for Success

Expect to hear a few "Wows!" with this recipe. It's great for a buffet dinner because the chicken is so tender your guests can easily cut it with a spoon (just in case you run out of knives and forks!). The recipe can be doubled or tripled for a crowd. You can substitute a little water for the white wine. As this is a rich and hearty main course, select light and rather plain side dishes, such as a tossed salad and steamed vegetables.

Italian Baked Chicken

Prep time: 15 minutes   •   Cook time: 25 minutes   •   Serves 6   •   Serving size: ½ breast

Each serving has: less than 1 gram carbohydrate   •   21 grams total protein   •   21 grams from animal source

½ cup freshly grated Parmesan cheese

2 TB. minced fresh parsley

½ tsp. minced garlic

1 tsp. dried oregano

1 tsp. dried basil

¼ tsp. crushed red pepper

½ tsp. freshly ground black pepper

3 whole chicken breasts, boned, skinned, and halved

3 TB. butter, melted

Recipe for Success

Delicious served hot or cold, this dish can be on the table in less than an hour. The Parmesan cheese and spices add some low-carb zing to the chicken. Serve with a Caesar salad and steamed vegetables such as broccoli, Brussels sprouts, or green beans.

Preheat oven to 375°F.

Combine Parmesan, parsley, garlic, oregano, basil, red pepper, and black pepper in a shallow dish. Dip chicken into melted butter and then into cheese mixture. Place into a shallow baking pan. Drizzle remaining butter over chicken, and sprinkle with any remaining cheese mixture.

Bake for 25 minutes or until tender.

Chicken Piccata

Prep time: 10 minutes   •   Cook time: 15 minutes   •   Serves 6   •   Serving size: ½ breast

Each serving has: 4 grams nutritive carbohydrate   •   less than 1 gram fiber   •   22 grams total protein   •   21 grams from animal source   •   1 gram from plant source

3 whole chicken breasts, boned, skinned, and halved

3 TB. flour

¼ tsp. salt

¼ tsp. pepper

¼ cup butter

½ cup white wine

¼ cup fresh-squeezed lemon juice

2 TB. capers

Pound chicken between 2 sheets of waxed paper until ¼ inch thick. Dredge chicken in flour that has been seasoned with salt and pepper. Melt butter in a heavy skillet until sizzling. Sauté chicken breasts in butter until light brown, about 3 minutes per side. Add wine, lemon juice, and capers to chicken, and let boil 3 minutes or until cooked thoroughly, turning chicken in sauce.

Variation: Veal Piccata is another wonderful way to get the piccata flavor into your mouth. Substitute veal in this recipe, and the amount of carbohydrates stays the same.

 Table Talk

Eating foods that are acidic lowers the glycemic index of the food. The lower the glycemic index, the less it increases blood sugar levels in the body, which is what you want to avoid by eating low carb. This recipe contains capers, which are acidic.

 Recipe for Success

The tanginess of the lemon juice and capers creates the magical taste of this dish. Serve garnished with lemon wedges and fresh parsley. Recommended side dishes are spaghetti squash with tomato sauce and tossed salad with Italian vinaigrette. Or complete your meal with steamed carrots with zucchini and red peppers sprinkled with oregano or basil.

Curried Chicken

Prep time: 10 minutes • Cook time: 20 minutes • Serves 6 • Serving size: 1 breast or 1 leg and thigh

Each serving has: 9 grams carbohydrate • 1 gram fiber • 8 grams nutritive carbohydrate • 33 grams total protein • 32 grams from animal source • 1 gram from plant source

1 large onion, chopped coarsely	½ tsp. freshly ground pepper
2 TB. butter	1 TB. curry powder
1 (3- to 4-lb.) chicken, cut into pieces	1 green pepper, cut into ½-inch squares
1 TB. flour	½ cup sliced fresh peaches
2 cups chicken bouillon	2 TB. raisins
½ tsp. minced garlic	1 TB. butter
1 tsp. salt	3 TB. slivered almonds

In a large skillet, sauté onion in butter. Add chicken and brown. Slowly stir in flour. Add chicken bouillon, and stir until slightly thickened. Add garlic, salt, pepper, and curry powder; cook over medium-low heat for 15 to 20 minutes.

In a separate skillet, sauté green pepper, peaches, and raisins in butter until warmed and soft. Serve chicken with fruit sauce, and sprinkle with slivered almonds.

Recipe for Success

To lower the carb count, you can omit the fruit sauce but keep the slivered almonds. You can also serve the following condiments with the curried chicken without increasing the carb count much: chopped hard-cooked eggs, shredded coconut, chopped black or green olives, chopped salted peanuts, chopped crisp bacon. If you add the following condiments, the carb count does increase: orange marmalade, store-bought chutney, sweet pickle relish, crushed pineapple.

Artichoke Chicken with Mushrooms

Prep time: 15 minutes • Cook time: 1 hour • Serves 6 • Serving size: 1 breast or
1 leg and thigh

Each serving has: 9 grams carbohydrate using sherry; 5 with broth • 2 grams fiber • 7 grams
nutritive carbohydrate with sherry or 3 grams nutritive carbohydrate with broth • 34 grams
total protein • 32 grams from animal source • 2 grams from plant source

1 (2- to 3-lb.) chicken, cut into pieces	2 TB. lemon or lime juice
Salt and pepper to taste	1 (14-oz.) can artichokes, drained
2 TB. butter	1 cup heavy cream
½ lb. mushrooms, sliced	½ cup sliced green onions
½ cup sherry or chicken broth	½ cup plain yogurt

Season chicken pieces with salt and pepper. Melt
butter in a large skillet. Brown chicken on both sides,
about 5 minutes per side. Add mushrooms, sherry,
and lemon juice.

Bring to a boil, and reduce heat to a simmer. Cover
and cook 45 minutes or until chicken is done. Add
artichokes and cream and stir, cooking for 5 more
minutes. Mix in green onions and yogurt. Let simmer until hot.

Recipe for Success

We love the combination
of artichokes, mushrooms,
and chicken—they seem made for
each other. To make this recipe lower
in fat but higher in carbs, you can
substitute evaporated skim milk for
the heavy cream and use low-fat
yogurt instead of plain yogurt.

Basil Stuffed Chicken

Prep time: 25 minutes • Cook time: 60 minutes • Serves 6 • Serving size: ¼ chicken

Each serving has: 3 grams nutritive carbohydrate • 45 grams total protein • 45 grams from animal source

2 TB. butter

½ onion, chopped

4 cloves chopped garlic

3 TB. fresh basil leaves or 1 TB. dried

1 egg

½ cup shredded Swiss cheese

Black pepper to taste

6 chicken quarters, leave skin intact

Recipe for Success

You can use spinach, curly parsley, cilantro, or shredded zucchini in place of the basil. Put a baked yellow squash casserole in the oven to cook with the chicken and your meal is complete.

Preheat oven to 400°F.

Melt butter in a 2-quart pan over medium heat. Sauté onion and garlic, and cook until tender, about 2 minutes, stirring often. Remove from heat; add basil, egg, cheese, and pepper.

Carefully loosen chicken skin on each quarter by pushing your finger between skin and meat to form a pocket. Spoon stuffing into each pocket.

Place chicken in a 9×13-inch buttered baking dish, and bake 50 minutes or until tender.

Beer Bottom Smoked Chicken

Prep time: 20 minutes, plus 6 hours marinating time   •   Cook time: 2 hours   •   Serves 6
•   Serving size: 1 breast or 1 leg and thigh

Each serving has: 2 grams nutritive carbohydrate   •   32 grams total protein   •   32 grams from animal source

½ cup lime juice

½ cup orange juice

⅓ cup olive oil

1 TB. minced garlic

¼ cup minced fresh cilantro

½ tsp. cayenne

1 minced, seeded jalapeño pepper (or amount desired)

Salt and pepper to taste

1 (2- to 3-lb.) whole chicken

1 can light beer

Mix together lime juice, orange juice, olive oil, garlic, cilantro, cayenne, jalapeño, salt, and pepper. Use amount of spicy peppers as desired for your taste. Remove and refrigerate ½ cup marinade to use for basting during grilling.

Wash chicken and remove and throw away gizzards, etc. Place chicken in a large resealable plastic bag, and pour in marinade. Squeeze excess air from the bag, and refrigerate at least 6 hours or overnight. Turn occasionally. Throw away marinade when removing chicken for cooking.

Preheat grill to medium-hot. Place a roasting pan on the grill. Open the beer can, and carefully insert the can into chicken cavity. Push chicken onto the can so it will not tip over on the grill. Set the can and chicken in the roasting pan on the grill off the direct fire, and close the grill cover.

Beer will boil during cooking, basting chicken on the inside.

Using ½ cup reserved marinade, brush chicken every 20 minutes. Smoke chicken about 2 hours or until a meat thermometer inserted into the thickest portion of chicken registers 180°F.

Recipe for Success

This is a terrific recipe for party cooking—it makes for quite a lively and, perhaps, silly discussion. The double basting causes the chicken to be very moist.

Chinese Chicken

Prep time: 35 minutes, plus cooking time for chicken • Cook time: 20 minutes
• Serves 6 • Serving size: 1 cup

Each serving has: 10 grams carbohydrate • 1 gram fiber • 9 grams nutritive carbohydrate
• 32 grams total protein • 30 grams from animal source • 2 grams from plant source

1 (3- to 4-lb.) chicken	1 (14-oz.) can Chinese vegetables, drained
2 TB. butter	1 (8-oz.) can bean sprouts, drained
1 cup chopped celery	Pepper to taste
1 cup chopped onion	1 (8-oz.) can sliced water chestnuts, drained
2 cups chicken broth	1 TB. cornstarch
1 TB. molasses	1 cup water
3 TB. soy sauce	

Cook and shred chicken; set aside until ready to add to vegetable mixture.

Melt butter in a Dutch oven, and sauté celery and onion until tender. Add chicken broth, molasses, soy sauce, vegetables, bean sprouts, pepper, and water chestnuts to pot. Simmer slowly until bubbly.

Add cornstarch to water, and stir until a paste forms. Slowly add paste to pot, and stir to thicken to gravy consistency.

Add chicken and simmer 10 minutes.

Recipe for Success _____

You may add additional vegetables to this recipe, such as fresh mushrooms, snow peas, or various colored bell peppers. You can substitute cooked beef for the chicken. Serve over a small serving of rice, if desired, which does increase carbohydrate count. Seasonal mixed fresh fruit is a delicious addition to a Chinese meal as well as a broth-based soup appetizer.

Chicken Macadamia

Prep time: 15 minutes • Cook time: 45 minutes • Serves 6 • Serving size: 1 breast or 1 leg and thigh

Each serving has: 18 grams carbohydrate • 2 grams fiber • 16 grams nutritive carbohydrate • 34 grams total protein • 32 grams from animal source • 2 grams from plant source

2 TB. butter

1 (3½-oz.) jar macadamia nuts

2 eggs, beaten

2 TB. olive oil

2 TB. soy sauce

1 tsp. powdered ginger

¼ tsp. pepper

2 TB. brandy, optional

1 medium onion, minced

¼ cup cold water

¼ cup plus 1 TB. cornstarch

2 to 3 lb. chicken, cut into pieces

Butter

½ medium green pepper, diced

½ medium red pepper, diced

1 cup water

1 chicken bouillon cube

2 TB. brown sugar

2 TB. cider vinegar

3 oz. pineapple juice

Preheat oven to 350°F.

Melt butter in a shallow oven pan. Add nuts and roast until light brown, about 15 minutes. Be sure to stir often to prevent burning. Place nuts into a small food processor or nut chopper, and slightly chop for later use at serving time.

Using a blender or mixer, combine eggs, oil, soy sauce, ginger, pepper, brandy, onion, water, and ¼ cup cornstarch to make batter. Soak chicken in batter for at least 20 minutes. Pan-fry chicken in small amount of butter until done.

While chicken is soaking, place green and red peppers and water in a saucepan, and bring to boil. Add bouillon cube and brown sugar. Simmer. Mix vinegar with 1 tablespoon cornstarch to make a smooth paste. Slowly add cornstarch paste to simmering liquid. Cook 1 to 2 minutes until sauce is thick and clear. Add pineapple juice and heat.

Arrange warm chicken on a platter, pour sauce over, and sprinkle with toasted nuts.

Recipe for Success

This recipe, with its Asian flavor, is so delicious that it's worth the effort. If preferred, use ½ teaspoon brandy flavoring instead of the brandy.

Chicken Breasts Stuffed with Mushrooms and Spinach

Prep time: 30 minutes • Cook time: 45 minutes • Serves 6 • Serving size: 1 breast

Each serving has: 6 grams nutritive carbohydrate • less than 1 gram fiber • 38 grams total protein • 35 grams from animal source • 3 grams from plant source

½ cup chopped onion	6 boneless, skinless chicken breasts
½ tsp. crushed dried oregano	1 to 2 TB. flour
1 clove garlic, minced	⅓ cup cream
6 TB. butter	¼ cup chicken broth
4 cups fresh spinach	1 clove garlic, minced
1 cup chopped mushrooms	2 TB. lemon juice
4 TB. Parmesan cheese	1 tsp. spicy mustard
4 oz. goat's milk cheese	Salt and pepper to taste
6 TB. red wine	

Preheat oven to 350°F.

Sauté onion, oregano, and ½ garlic clove in 3 tablespoons butter. Add spinach and mushrooms; cook until spinach is wilted. Remove from heat.

Stir in Parmesan and goat's milk cheeses and 3 tablespoons wine.

Pound chicken breasts to flatten; divide stuffing and place in center of each breast. Wrap chicken around stuffing to form a roll. Secure with wooden toothpicks.

Lightly dust breasts with flour. Sauté in remaining 3 tablespoons butter until lightly browned; remove chicken to a baking dish, and bake for 30 minutes.

Meanwhile, add cream, broth, remaining 3 tablespoons wine, garlic, lemon juice, mustard, salt, and pepper to pan juices; cook until sauce is slightly thickened.

Serve sauce over chicken.

Recipe for Success

Tuck a bit of parsley and colorful yellow and orange strips of bell peppers around the chicken for a pretty presentation. Steamed cauliflower makes a wonderful substitute for higher-carb potatoes. Steam cauliflower and mash, if desired, with a bit of butter and cream; serve with additional sauce as you would gravy and potatoes! Fresh strawberries make a colorful plate as well as give a touch of natural sweetness.

Company Chicken Spaghetti

Prep time: 30 minutes   •   Cook time: 40 minutes   •   Serves 6   •   Serving size: 1 cup

Each serving has: 6 grams nutritive carbohydrate plus 5 grams for ½ cup squash   •   38 grams total protein plus 2 grams for ½ cup squash   •   36 grams from animal source   •   2 grams from plant source plus 2 grams for ½ cup squash

2 lb. chicken, cooked and shredded	¼ cup white wine, optional
2 spaghetti squash, cooked and shredded	1 tsp. garlic powder
2 TB. cornstarch	½ tsp. crushed red pepper
1 cup chicken broth	1 tsp. dry mustard
1 cup cream	1 TB. butter
1 cup sour cream	8 oz. sliced mushrooms
1 cup freshly grated Parmesan cheese, ¼ cup reserved	Salt and pepper to taste
	Paprika
2 TB. lemon juice	

Preheat oven to 350°F.

Save broth from cooking chicken. Debone chicken and tear or shred into bite-size pieces.

Cut spaghetti squash in half lengthwise, and place on a buttered baking sheet. Cook for 20 minutes or until soft. Take a fork and scrape inside meat from squash, making spaghettilike strings. Set aside.

While squash is baking, make basic white sauce by stirring cornstarch into chicken broth until smooth. Add cream, sour cream, Parmesan cheese, lemon juice, wine (if using), garlic powder, red pepper, and mustard.

Melt butter in a skillet and sauté mushrooms; slowly stir in cream sauce mixture, and simmer until bubbly.

Mix sauce and chicken together, and pour into a buttered 3-quart baking pan. Sprinkle top with paprika and additional Parmesan cheese.

Bake for 30 to 40 minutes. Serve over ½ cup spaghetti squash.

Recipe for Success

Make this recipe ahead and freeze it, but don't sprinkle with paprika and cheese before freezing. Instead, do this after thawing and before putting in the oven. White grape juice may be substituted for wine, if preferred, although the juice will add additional carbohydrates. Side dishes should be vibrant in color and simple because this dish is so rich. Steamed green beans with almonds or a beautiful mixed green salad with lots of fresh veggies makes a wonderful companion dish.

Roasted Turkey Breast

Prep time: 5 minutes • Cook time: 1 to 1½ hours • Serves 6 • Serving size: 4 ounces

Each serving has: 1 gram nutritive carbohydrate • 25 grams total protein • 25 grams from animal source

1 (2-lb.) fresh turkey breast

½ cup chicken broth or bouillon cube in water

1 TB. dried rosemary

1 tsp. garlic powder

1 tsp. dried thyme leaves

1 tsp. dried oregano leaves

½ tsp. black pepper

Hot Potato

Cooking turkey until it registers 170°F on the thermometer is the safest way to be sure it is well done. Poultry is not a meat we eat medium-rare! A good rule of thumb is to cook about 20 minutes per pound.

Preheat oven to 325°F.

Combine seasonings in a small dish.

Rinse turkey breast, dry, and place into a shallow baking dish. Add broth and water to just below upper rim of baking dish.

Rub rosemary, garlic powder, thyme, oregano, and pepper onto turkey breast.

Bake 1 hour or until temperature registers 170°F on a meat thermometer.

The Least You Need to Know

◆ Chicken and turkey contain no carbohydrates and plenty of complete protein.

◆ Chicken and turkey are complemented by a wide variety of flavors, from tangy and spicy to sweet and fruity.

◆ For side dishes, add two or more vegetables and/or fruits.

◆ Leftover chicken dishes make for yummy breakfasts and lunches.

◆ You can substitute turkey for chicken in all the recipes in this chapter except Beer Bottom Smoked Chicken.

Seafood Main Dishes

In This Chapter

◆ Making seafood a part of your low-carb eating

◆ Cooking seafood with many different flavors

◆ Enjoying the rich taste of seafood

Seafood is our no-carb treat from the oceans. The many varieties of seafood—shrimp, crab, crawfish, and lobster just to name a few—can make eating low carb an absolute delight and certainly anything but boring.

Cooked plain and served with drawn butter and some fresh lemon wedges, seafood is wonderful. It adds flavor when included in a recipe with, among others, sun-dried tomatoes, artichokes, or fennel.

Low-carb seafood recipes are great to make if you thrive on a busy lifestyle. They are easy to prepare and quick to make because seafood cooks in just minutes. Plus, seafood offers a high amount of complete protein.

Ingredients for Seafood

Seafood tastes best with the best ingredients. These recipes call for the following kinds of ingredients:

- **Heavy cream.** Many of the recipes call for cream. Be sure to use real cream and do not substitute fake cream, milk, skim milk, or even half-and-half. The results will be puny, and quite frankly, you will have wasted your money on purchasing the seafood.

- **Sun-dried tomatoes.** You can purchase sun-dried tomatoes in oil by the jar and also dried in plastic or cellophane bags. For these recipes, it's easiest to use sun-dried tomatoes straight from the jar, but you can reconstitute the ones in bags by soaking them in warm water until they plump.

- **Butter.** Always use real butter. Only butter will do, so don't try using fakes or margarines. They don't work well for sautéing, and they can't deliver the wonderful taste of real butter.

However you cook it, seafood is an excellent choice for a lifetime of low-carb eating. With its abundant amounts of complete protein, you can enjoy it frequently.

Shrimp with Sun-Dried Tomatoes

Prep time: 15 minutes • Cook time: 12 to 15 minutes • Serves 4 • Serving size: ¼ pound shrimp

Each serving has: 9 grams carbohydrate • 2 grams fiber • 7 grams nutritive carbohydrate • 14 grams total protein • 13 grams from animal source • 1 gram from plant source

1 garlic clove, minced

¼ cup butter

1 lb. large shrimp, peeled

¼ cup sun-dried tomatoes

1 green bell pepper, cut into ½-inch pieces

1 (6½-oz.) jar marinated artichoke hearts

½ cup pineapple, cut into chunks

Sauté garlic in butter in a Dutch oven. Add shrimp, tomatoes, pepper, artichoke hearts, and pineapple. Cover and heat for 12 to 15 minutes until warm throughout.

Shrimp, Crab, and Artichokes au Gratin

Prep time: 30 minutes   •   Cook time: 30 minutes   •   Serves 6   •   Serving size: ¾ cup

Each serving has: 10 grams carbohydrate   •   2 grams fiber   •   8 grams nutritive carbohydrate
•   32 grams total protein   •   30 grams from animal source   •   2 grams from plant source

¼ cup butter	¾ cup heavy cream
½ lb. fresh mushrooms, sliced	2 cups (8 oz.) grated, sharp cheddar cheese
1 clove garlic, minced	½ cup dry white wine
2 TB. finely minced green onions	2 (7½-oz.) cans king crab, flaked and drained
1 TB. flour	1 lb. shrimp, cooked and peeled
½ tsp. pepper	1 (10-oz.) pkg. frozen artichoke hearts, cooked and drained

Preheat oven to 375°F.

Melt butter in a skillet; add mushrooms, garlic, and green onions; sauté for 5 minutes.

Remove from heat and stir in flour, pepper, and cream. Slowly bring to a boil, stirring, and remove from heat. Add ½ cup cheese, and stir until melted. Stir in wine.

Combine sauce, crab, shrimp, artichokes, and 1 cup cheese. Pour into a buttered 2-quart casserole, and top with remaining 1 cup cheese.

Bake uncovered for 30 minutes or until bubbly and lightly browned.

Recipe for Success

The combination of artichokes with crab and shrimp is a savory success. Baked like this, the dish can travel to potlucks or simply to the kitchen table. Serve with a side dish of salad or fruit.

Crab Cakes with Mustard Creole Sauce

Prep time: 25 minutes • Cook time: 10 minutes • Serves 4 • Serving size: 1 cake

Each serving has: 8 grams nutritive carbohydrate • 21 grams total protein • 20 grams from animal source • 1 gram from plant source

1 lb. fresh lump crabmeat	¼ cup dry white vermouth
2 TB. finely chopped green onions	1 tsp. white wine vinegar
1 TB. white wine	1 tsp. chopped green onions
1 TB. plus 2 tsp. Dijon mustard	½ cup heavy cream
1 TB. lemon juice	1 TB. chopped, peeled, red bell pepper
3 TB. mayonnaise	½ tsp. tarragon
White pepper to taste	1 TB. unsalted butter
1 egg white, slightly beaten	Salt to taste
2 TB. finely crushed saltine crackers	Cayenne to taste
Butter for sautéing	Lemon wedges

To make crab cakes, combine crabmeat, greens onions, white wine, 1 tablespoon Dijon mustard, lemon juice, mayonnaise, and white pepper in a bowl and mix gently. Add egg white and cracker crumbs to hold the mixture together and mix gently. Shape into 4 patties.

Sauté in butter in a skillet for 3 to 4 minutes on each side or until golden brown.

To make Mustard Creole Sauce, boil vermouth, vinegar, and green onions in a small, heavy saucepan until the mixture is reduced to 2 tablespoons. Add cream, red bell pepper, and tarragon. Boil until thickened and reduced to about ⅓ cup, stirring constantly.

Reduce the heat to medium-low. Whisk in vermouth-vinegar mixture and remaining Dijon mustard. Cook for 30 seconds. Whisk in butter. Season with salt and cayenne. Keep warm until ready to serve. Serve crab cakes topped with Mustard Creole Sauce and lemon wedges.

Recipe for Success

Tarragon makes every entrée special. Adding it to crab cakes, you have a down-home delight. Crab cakes are good hot or cold. Use leftovers—if there are any—for lunch and breakfast.

Crabmeat Florentine

Prep time: 20 minutes   •   Cook time: 45 minutes   •   Serves 8   •   Serving size: ¾ cup

Each serving has: 6 grams carbohydrate   •   2 grams fiber   •   4 grams nutritive carbohydrate   •   13 grams total protein   •   10 grams from animal source   •   3 grams from plant source

4 (10-oz.) pkg. frozen spinach

2 TB. chopped green onions

2 cloves garlic, minced

¼ cup butter

1 TB. flour

1 cup heavy cream

1 cup water

¼ cup white wine

Chopped fresh parsley to taste

2 TB. grated Parmesan cheese

Salt and white pepper to taste

1 lb. lump crabmeat

Low-Carb Vocab

Florentine in a recipe usually means a savory main dish or side dish made with spinach. This recipe combines carbs and spinach for a delectable main dish meal. Serve with a light side dish such as steamed vegetables or a raw fruit combination salad.

Preheat oven to 350°F.

Cook spinach in a saucepan according to package directions and drain well. Place in a greased 3-quart casserole.

Sauté green onions and garlic in a small skillet with 2 tablespoons butter until onions are tender.

Melt remaining butter in a saucepan, stir in flour, and add cream and water gradually, stirring constantly. Cook until thickened, stirring constantly. Add wine, parsley, sautéed green onions, Parmesan cheese, salt, and pepper. Stir in crabmeat, and pour mixture over spinach.

Bake for 45 minutes or until bubbly.

Crawfish Creole

Prep time: 10 minutes • Cook time: 30 minutes • Serves 4 • Serving size: 1 cup

Each serving has: 9 grams carbohydrate • 1 gram fiber • 8 grams nutritive carbohydrate • 28 grams total protein • 26 grams from animal source • 2 grams from plant source

1 medium onion, chopped	½ TB. cayenne
1 bunch green onions, chopped	½ TB. white pepper
1 green bell pepper, chopped	1 lb. crawfish tails
1 cup butter	1 cup white wine
1 TB. Creole seasoning	1 cup heavy cream

Sauté onion, green onions, and bell pepper in butter in a skillet until onion is translucent. Add Creole seasoning, cayenne, and white pepper. Cook for 1 minute. Add crawfish tails and white wine. Simmer, covered, for 25 minutes.

Add cream and simmer for 5 minutes, stirring constantly.

Crabmeat au Gratin

Prep time: 20 minutes • Cook time: 15 minutes • Serves 6 • Serving size: 1 individual dish or approximately ½ cup

Each serving has: 7 grams nutritive carbohydrate • 30 grams total protein • 30 grams from animal source • 0 grams from plant source

2 TB. butter	1½ cup cream
2 TB. chopped fresh parsley	1 TB. sherry
¾ cup chopped green onions	2 lb. lump crabmeat
1 TB. cornstarch	¾ cup (3 oz.) grated cheddar cheese
½ tsp. dry mustard	

Preheat oven to 375°F.

Melt butter in a pan over medium heat, and sauté parsley and green onions until tender.

Combine cornstarch and dry mustard, add cream, and stir until this makes a smooth paste. Slowly add this to onion mixture, and stir until smooth and thick. Remove from heat, and stir in sherry. Add crabmeat and mix gently.

Pour into individual serving dishes or one large baking dish. Sprinkle with cheese, and bake 15 minutes or until cheese is melted and bubbly.

Sautéed Shrimp in Artichoke Sauce

Prep time: 25 minutes   •   Cook time: 5 minutes   •   Serves 4   •   Serving size: ¼ pound shrimp with ¼ cup sauce

Each serving has: 15 grams carbohydrate   •   3 grams fiber   •   12 grams nutritive carbohydrate   •   23 grams total protein   •   20 grams from animal source   •   3 grams from plant source

28 large shrimp (22 to 30 per lb.), peeled, deveined

Creole seasoning

¼ cup (½ stick) butter

3 green onions, thinly sliced

2 (14-oz.) cans artichoke hearts, chopped and drained

½ cup dry white wine

1 cup heavy cream

Dash cayenne

Salt and freshly ground black pepper to taste

2 TB. chopped fresh parsley

Sprinkle shrimp with Creole seasoning. Heat 2 tablespoons butter in a skillet over medium-high heat. Add shrimp and sauté until cooked.

Heat remaining butter in a skillet. Add green onions. Sauté until onions are soft but not brown. Add artichoke hearts and wine. Simmer for 5 minutes or until heated through. Stir in cream and season with cayenne, salt, and black pepper.

Arrange shrimp on individual serving plates. Spoon sauce over shrimp, and sprinkle with parsley.

Recipe for Success

This recipe has a Southern taste with a beloved combination of artichokes and shrimp. To devein shrimp, remove the dark thread that runs up the back of the shrimp. The easiest way to do this is to make a cut with a small knife along the dark matter and then remove it.

Shrimp with Fennel and Green Beans

Prep time: 30 minutes • Cook time: included in prep time • Serves 4 • Serving size: ¼ pound shrimp

Each serving has: 5 grams carbohydrate • 1 gram fiber • 4 grams nutritive carbohydrate • 20 grams total protein • 19 grams from animal source • 1 gram from plant source

1 lb. large (22 to 30 per lb.) shrimp, peeled	½ cup sliced fennel stalks
4 TB. butter	1 cup green beans
1 garlic clove, minced	2 TB. sesame seeds
½ tsp. dried parsley	

Sauté shrimp in butter with garlic and parsley until cooked to taste. At the same time, steam fennel and green beans until tender.

Place shrimp in a serving dish, add fennel and green beans, and pour garlic butter sauce over all. Sprinkle with sesame seeds and serve warm.

Recipe for Success _____

Fennel is similar to celery and grows with stalks and leaves. The seeds add great flavor to Italian dishes, and the stalks can be used like celery, as in this recipe. The taste is refreshing and slightly exotic. This unusual combination of tastes is quick and easy to prepare.

BBQ Shrimp

Prep time: 5 minutes • Cook time: 25 minutes • Serves 6 • Serving size: ¼ pound, approximately 1 dozen

Each serving has: 2 grams nutritive carbohydrate • less than 1 gram fiber • 26 grams total protein • 26 grams from animal source • 0 grams from plant source

3 TB. butter	2 TB. cracked black pepper
1 large onion, chopped finely	1 tsp. cayenne
½ cup chopped celery	¼ cup Worcestershire sauce
½ cup Italian salad dressing	2 TB. steak sauce
1 TB. minced garlic	1 TB. lemon juice
1 TB. paprika	3 lb. large (22 to 30 per lb.) shrimp, unpeeled

Melt butter in a cast-iron skillet or other heavy skillet, and sauté onion and celery until tender. Add Italian dressing, garlic, paprika, black pepper, cayenne, Worcestershire sauce, steak sauce, and lemon juice; stir well until it begins to boil. Add shrimp and simmer 15 minutes or until shrimp turn pink.

Recipe for Success

"Real" BBQ shrimp is served in the shell and with rolls of paper towels—even newspaper has been seen as the tablecloth of choice! Die-hard seafood eaters even eat the shells. You can cheat a little and serve this delicious dish in a more civilized manner by peeling the shrimp before cooking—just be sure not to overcook. You will also need to reduce the amount of black and red peppers because you will not be seasoning through the shells. Without the peelings, you can eat the dish with a fork on good china and with cloth napkins!

Crab-Stuffed Eggplant

Prep time: 10 minutes   •   Cook time: 1 hour   •   Serves 6   •   Serving size: ½ eggplant

Each serving has: 8 grams carbohydrate   •   4 grams fiber   •   4 grams nutritive carbohydrate
•   17 grams total protein   •   17 grams from animal source   •   0 grams from plant source

3 medium-size eggplants

3 TB. olive oil

4 cloves garlic, minced

1 onion, chopped

¼ cup shredded carrot

3 TB. sliced celery

2 TB. chopped fresh parsley

Salt and pepper to taste

1 TB. lemon juice

1 TB. cornstarch

½ cup cream

1 tsp. white pepper

¼ tsp. salt

2 cups crabmeat

Paprika

Recipe for Success

Sprinkle shredded Parmesan cheese on top 5 minutes before finished cooking, if desired. You may substitute imitation crabmeat, but if you do, then delete the additional salt in the recipe. A festive way to serve seafood is to add marinated veggies or spinach with hot bacon dressing.

Preheat oven to 375°F. Butter a baking pan.

Cut eggplants in half lengthwise, and place cut side down onto the pan. Bake until eggplant is soft, about 35 minutes, and cool. Scoop out meat from eggplants and chop. Set shells aside.

Heat oven to 425°F. In a skillet, heat oil and sauté garlic, onion, carrot, celery, and parsley until vegetables are tender. Add chopped eggplant, salt, pepper, and lemon juice; cook 5 minutes.

Combine cornstarch, cream, white pepper, and salt; add to vegetable mixture, stirring constantly over low heat for 5 minutes until thickened and smooth.

Gently combine crabmeat with mixture, and spoon into eggplant shells. Place eggplant on a baking sheet, and sprinkle with paprika. Bake 15 to 20 minutes or until hot.

Creamed Cajun Seafood

Prep time: 30 minutes   •   Cook time: 30 minutes   •   Serves 6   •   Serving size: ¾ cup

Each serving has: 7 grams carbohydrate   •   1 gram fiber   •   6 grams nutritive carbohydrate
•   26 grams total protein   •   25 grams from animal source   •   1 gram from plant source

8 oz. cream cheese, cubed	1 TB. garlic powder
3 TB. butter	½ tsp. cayenne
1 lb. crawfish tails, cooked and peeled	1 cup cream
½ cup chopped onion	1 cup grated Swiss cheese
½ cup chopped bell pepper	2 TB. sherry
1 (8-oz.) pkg. fresh mushrooms, coarsely chopped	½ cup chopped pecans

Preheat oven to 350°F.

In a double boiler over simmering water, melt cream cheese.

Melt butter in a skillet, and sauté crawfish tails, onion, bell pepper, mushrooms, garlic powder, and cayenne until vegetables are tender. Add cream, Swiss cheese, and sherry, stirring until cheese is melted and mixture is well combined.

Pour into a baking pan, and sprinkle pecans on top. Bake 30 minutes.

Variation: For a divine meal, use a grilled or baked fish fillet as a base, and top with a mixture of the shrimp or crawfish and lump crabmeat in the cream sauce.

Recipe for Success

If desired, you can bake the seafood in individual ramekins, or small baking dishes. You may substitute any seafood for the crawfish tails. Use shrimp, crab, fish, or any mixture of several. Vary the seasonings to suit your taste; if you desire additional hot flavor, add several drops of your favorite hot sauce or ¼ cup salsa. This sauce is delicious served over scrambled or poached eggs or your favorite vegetable.

Crawfish Étouffée

Prep time: 30 minutes • Cook time: 30 minutes • Serves 6 • Serving size: 1 cup

Each serving has: 10 grams carbohydrate • 1 gram fiber • 9 grams nutritive carbohydrate • 37 grams total protein • 34 grams from animal source • 3 grams from plant source

¼ cup butter	1 tsp. cayenne
1 onion, chopped	1 tsp. paprika
1 bell pepper, chopped	2 cups chicken broth or seafood stock
½ cup chopped celery	¼ cup chopped fresh parsley
1 tsp. minced garlic	1 lb. crawfish tails, cooked and peeled or
¼ cup flour	1 lb. cooked peeled shrimp

Melt butter in a Dutch oven, and sauté onion, bell pepper, celery, and garlic. Add flour, cayenne, and paprika, stirring constantly until brown, about 10 minutes. Be careful it does not stick or burn. Add chicken broth and parsley, and stir until thick and simmering. Stir in crawfish or shrimp, and cook until heated through, about 5 minutes.

Low-Carb Vocab

Étouffée means "smoth-ered." But in today's lingo, expect étouffée to have a slightly browned butter and flour taste, which is very elegant and unusual.

Variations: Traditionally, this wonderful dish is piled over white rice. Use lower-glycemic basmati rice or brown rice if you decide to use rice, and count the added carbohydrates. You can enjoy this étouffée without the rice. Étouffée seasonings and vegetable mixtures are sold in grocery stores and specialty food stores—just cook up a batch and freeze to have on hand to season any vegetable or meat dish. This saves you time because you don't have to chop and sauté each time you get ready to cook.

Shrimp Scampi

Prep time: 10 minutes • Cook time: 15 minutes • Serves 6 • Serving size: 1 dozen shrimp

Each serving has: 3 grams nutritive carbohydrate • 26 grams total protein • 26 grams from animal source • 0 grams from plant source

¼ cup butter	1 tsp. paprika
¼ cup lemon juice	1 tsp. black pepper
¼ cup chopped green onions	2 drops hot sauce or ½ tsp. cayenne
2 TB. minced garlic	6 dozen (22 to 30 per lb.) raw shrimp, peeled
1 TB. Worcestershire sauce	

In a large skillet or a Dutch oven, melt butter. Mix lemon juice, green onions, garlic, Worcestershire sauce, paprika, black pepper, and hot sauce into melted butter. Add shrimp and stir to coat well. Stir and cook over medium heat until shrimp are pink. Watch closely so as not to overcook.

Summer Quick Shrimp

Prep time: 5 minutes • Cook time: 10 minutes • Serves 6 • Serving size: 1 dozen shrimp

Each serving has: 4 grams nutritive carbohydrate • 18 grams from animal source • less than 1 gram from plant source

3 TB. butter	½ tsp. cayenne
1 bunch green onions, sliced	Crab boil, dry or liquid
4 cloves garlic, minced	6 dozen (22 to 30 per pound) large raw shrimp, peeled
1 TB. Worcestershire sauce	

In a skillet, melt butter and sauté green onions and garlic until tender. Stir in Worcestershire sauce, cayenne, and crab boil mix, if you have that available in your area grocery. Add shrimp and cook until shrimp turn pink, about 5 minutes.

Variations: Shrimp cooked in this manner is quicker than steamed or boiled and is delicious served over a green salad. Poured hot with the sauce over baby spinach results in a wonderful wilted salad. Or add cream to the skillet and make a delectable cream of shrimp soup. If it needs to be thicker, add a bit of cornstarch paste made with water. Chop shrimp before cooking, and serve soup in demitasse cups for a quick and easy appetizer.

The Least You Need to Know

- ◆ Seafood meals are an excellent choice for low-carb eating.
- ◆ Today's grocery stores and fish markets offer a wide variety of fresh and frozen seafood year-round.
- ◆ Eat seafood steamed with drawn butter and lemon juice or in more elaborate dishes—either way seafood is a no-carb food.
- ◆ Seafood meals add variety to low-carb eating.

Fish Main Dishes

In This Chapter

- ◆ Enjoying a vast selection of fish
- ◆ Benefiting from essential fats in cold-water fish
- ◆ Using new low-carb "breading" options

The vast variety of fish in the oceans and streams is astounding. Most of us have only eaten a few different kinds—salmon, tuna, halibut, and perhaps trout. Yet the oceans and streams have hundreds of edible species of fish, all with no carbohydrates. Even if you don't think of yourself as a fish eater, it's time you give fish a try.

Preparing fish is usually simple. But beware: Plain fish can be rather boring and ordinary, which is exactly what you *don't* want when you are eating low carb. The recipes in this chapter can make fish not only interesting but also positively scrumptious! Grill fish, poach it, fry it, bake it, then add seasonings and sauces that make it tasty and terrific.

Those Cold-Water Fish

Many of the recipes in this chapter call for cold-water fish, such as salmon, halibut, tuna, and trout. These varieties of fish deserve special mention because they contain nutrients that you need to be healthy.

These nutrients are called essential fatty acids, also known as EFAs. Eating just one serving a week can improve the health of your heart, reduce blood pressure, enhance moods, and improve brain function. In addition, they aid in the prevention of arthritis. Essential fatty acids aid in weight loss and weight management.

Low-Carb Vocab

Essential is a term used by the government to designate a nutrient necessary to the body that has to be ingested or eaten. Your body can't manufacture an essential nutrient.

These fats, known as omega-3, 6, and 9 fatty acids, are deemed *essential* because you need to get them through your diet. Your body can't manufacture them by itself from other food you consume, as it can other fats.

Fish Ingredients

Here are notes and ideas for ingredients used in these recipes.

- Some of the fish recipes call for using finely chopped nuts in place of the traditional breading. This dramatically reduces the number of carbohydrates in the dish and adds interesting flavors. To chop finely, process in a food processor or blender.

- Use butter to grease a baking dish. Avoid using vegetable oils to grease baking dishes. They don't hold up to heat well and can become carcinogenic.

- Adding tangy, sweet, or savory ingredients is the key to making otherwise plain fish interesting to eat. In these recipes, you'll find macadamia nuts, lime juice, dill, tomatoes, black pepper, even olives, capers, and a mango salsa.

Table Talk

The best oil to use for heating and baking is butter. It holds up well to heat. Don't use vegetable oils, such as olive, walnut, canola, or safflower for cooking. The oils break down when heated and can be harmful to your overall health.

It's these other ingredients that bring fish to your palate in a pleasing and appetizing way. Eat a fish entrée at least once a week, and you'll get out of any low-carb eating rut you may be in.

Crispy Black Pepper Salmon

Prep time: 15 minutes plus 30 minutes marinating time   •   Cook time: 20 minutes
•   Serves 4   •   Serving size: 1 fillet

Each serving has: 6 grams nutritive carbohydrate   •   37 grams total protein   •   35 grams from animal source   •   2 grams from plant source

½ cup dry white wine	1 medium onion, peeled and very thinly sliced
¼ cup Worcestershire sauce	4 (6-oz.) salmon fillets
1 cup chicken broth	2 TB. freshly cracked black pepper
¼ tsp. salt	2 TB. butter
Dash white pepper	1 bunch fresh spinach, washed, stemmed, and dried

In a resealable plastic bag, combine wine, Worcestershire sauce, chicken broth, salt, and white pepper. Add onion and salmon. Seal and chill at least 30 minutes.

Spread black pepper on a large plate. Remove salmon, reserving marinade and onion. Press both sides of salmon into pepper to coat and set aside. In a large skillet, heat butter over medium heat. Add onion to skillet. Cook until onion is soft, about 5 minutes. Remove with a slotted spoon and set aside.

Increase heat to medium-high. Place salmon, flesh side down, in the skillet and cook until crisp and browned, about 4 minutes per side. When salmon is just cooked through, about 6 to 10 minutes, remove from the skillet.

Add spinach to the skillet, and cook until limp. Divide spinach equally among the plates. Cook marinade until reduced by ½, and divide equally over salmon.

Recipe for Success
Salmon has a sturdy flavor and texture that can embrace the intense flavors of black pepper and spinach. With one vegetable in the spinach, this meal needs only a side salad or fruit to make a balanced meal.

Mediterranean Halibut

Prep time: 20 minutes   •   Cook time: 15 minutes   •   Serves 4   •   Serving size: 1 fillet

Each serving has: 6 grams carbohydrate   •   1 gram fiber   •   5 grams nutritive carbohydrate   •   42 grams total protein   •   41 grams from animal source   •   less than 1 gram from plant source

4 Italian plum tomatoes, seeded and diced	½ cup crumbled feta cheese, divided
2 TB. chopped Kalamata olives	2 TB. minced shallots
¼ cup drained capers	2 TB. chopped fresh basil
1 tsp. minced garlic	Salt and freshly ground black pepper
3 TB. olive oil, divided	1 TB. butter
3 TB. fresh lemon juice, divided	4 (6-oz.) halibut fillets
¼ cup dry white wine	

In a glass bowl, combine tomatoes, olives, capers, garlic, 2 tablespoons olive oil, 1½ tablespoons lemon juice, wine, ¼ cup feta, shallots, basil, salt, and pepper to taste. Let stand at room temperature.

Preheat oven to 425°F. Grease the bottom of a shallow baking dish with butter. Season both sides of halibut with salt and pepper to taste. Place in the prepared baking dish. Squeeze remaining 1½ tablespoons lemon juice over halibut and top with tomato mixture. Sprinkle with remaining ¼ cup cheese.

Recipe for Success

The Greek–Mediterranean flavors make this halibut dish interesting and delicious.

Bake until just cooked through, about 15 minutes. Arrange halibut on individual serving plates and spoon pan juices on top.

Variation: You can substitute salmon, trout, or any other sturdy fish, such as red snapper for the halibut in this recipe.

Red Snapper with Mango Salsa

Prep time: 25 minutes plus 30 minutes marinating time   •   Cook time: 20 minutes   •   Serves 4   •   Serving size: 1 fillet

Each serving has: 18 grams carbohydrate   •   1 gram fiber   •   17 grams nutritive carbohydrate   •   30 grams total protein   •   29 grams from animal source   •   1 gram from plant source

¼ cup fresh lime juice	1 TB. chopped fresh cilantro
2 TB. chopped fresh cilantro	½ tsp. sugar
2 tsp. olive oil	½ tsp. cumin
4 (4- to 5-oz.) red snapper fillets	⅛ tsp. salt
¼ tsp. salt	⅛ tsp. pepper
¼ tsp. black pepper	Dash hot sauce
1 cup chopped Roma tomatoes	2 TB. fresh lime juice
1 cup chopped mango	2 TB. chopped fresh cilantro
1 TB. chopped red onion	

To marinate red snapper, combine lime juice, 2 tablespoons cilantro, and olive oil in a large shallow dish and mix well. Place fish in marinade, turning to coat. Marinate, covered, in the refrigerator for 30 minutes, turning once.

Drain fish and discard marinade. Sprinkle with salt and pepper. Place in a grilling basket. Grill over medium-hot (350°F to 400°F) coals for 10 minutes on each side or until fish flakes easily. Place fish on a serving platter.

To make mango salsa, mix tomatoes, mango, red onion, cilantro, sugar, cumin, salt, pepper, hot sauce, and lime juice in a medium bowl.

Spoon room temperature Mango Salsa evenly over top of fish, and sprinkle with remaining 2 tablespoons cilantro.

Recipe for Success

Fruit salsa is a healthful accompaniment to fish and can also count as 1 serving of fruits and vegetables for the day. This red snapper dish has a modern Southwest taste. The salsa contributes virtually all the carbohydrates in this dish, so you can cut your serving of the salsa in half and only get 9 grams carbohydrates.

Grilled Catfish with Mustard Sauce

Prep time: 15 minutes • Cook time: 10 minutes • Serves 10 • Serving size: 1 fillet

Each serving has: 4 grams nutritive carbohydrate • 32 grams total protein • 32 grams from animal source • 0 grams from plant source

¼ cup chopped onion

3 TB. butter

1 TB. flour

¼ tsp. dry mustard

1½ cups milk

1¼ cups shredded mild cheddar cheese

¾ cup white wine

1 TB. green onion tops

½ tsp. salt

¼ tsp. white pepper

10 (5-oz.) catfish fillets

Recipe for Success

Catfish prepared any way at all is wonderful. And with this mustard sauce, it is deeply satisfying and interesting. A good tip for cooking fish is to measure its thickness; for best flavor it should be no more than 1 inch thick.

In a large skillet, sauté onion in butter until translucent. Stir in flour and dry mustard. Cook for 1 minute, stirring constantly. Continue constant stirring as you add milk, and cook until thickened; add cheese and cook until cheese melts.

Add wine, green onion tops, salt, and white pepper; mix well. Place fish on the grill rack or in a greased fish basket. Heat coals until gray or set dial on gas grill to medium-high temperature. Grill for 5 to 8 minutes or until fish flakes easily. Serve with sauce.

Five-Pepper Tuna

Prep time: 15 minutes   •   Cook time: 10 minutes   •   Serves 4   •   Serving size: 1 steak

Each serving has: 7 grams nutritive carbohydrate   •   27 grams total protein   •   27 grams from animal source   •   0 grams from plant source

5 TB. five-pepper blend	¼ cup cognac
4 (8-oz.) tuna steaks	½ cup chicken broth
Salt to taste	2 TB. Dijon mustard
2 TB. butter	1 cup heavy cream

Crush pepper blend, and spread on a plate or cutting board. Press tuna steaks into crushed pepper, turning to coat both sides. Sprinkle steaks with salt.

Melt butter in a sauté pan over high heat. Add steaks. Cook for 3 minutes on each side for rare or until steaks flake easily. Remove steaks to a warm platter.

Drain excess butter from the pan. Add cognac and cook over high heat, stirring to deglaze the pan. Add broth, mustard, and cream. Cook until sauce is reduced by ½. Spoon sauce over tuna steaks and serve.

Recipe for Success

The five-pepper blend, which can be purchased at a specialty food store, adds spicy heat, while the cream cools the palate. This is a different way to prepare fresh or frozen tuna.

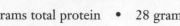

Baked Salmon with Spinach Sauce

Prep time: 25 minutes • Cook time: 1 hour • Serves 8 • Serving size: 1 fillet

Each serving has: 1 gram nutritive carbohydrate • 29 grams total protein • 28 grams from animal source • 1 gram from plant source

8 (4- to 5-oz.) salmon fillets

3 to 5 scallions, thinly sliced

1 lemon, thinly sliced

Salt and ground black pepper to taste

½ cup spinach leaves

1 cup regular mayonnaise

1 to 2 TB. lemon juice

1 cup (2 sticks) butter

Preheat oven to 350°F.

Lay each piece of salmon on a square piece of aluminum foil. Place some scallions and 1 lemon slice on each piece of salmon. Sprinkle with salt and pepper to taste. Fold the foil around fish, and fold the edges over to seal. Bake for about 1 hour.

Recipe for Success

Baking the salmon in the foil "bag" keeps it very moist, tender, and tidy for cleanup. The sauce adds a nice tang to the salmon.

While fish is cooking, make sauce. Chop spinach in a food processor. Add mayonnaise and lemon juice, and process until blended. Melt butter and add slowly to spinach mixture until butter is thoroughly blended and sauce is thick.

Remove fish from the oven. Unwrap the foil, remove fish, and put on individual serving plates. Serve spinach sauce on the side.

Pecan Trout

Prep time: 25 minutes   •   Cook time: 15 to 20 minutes   •   Serves 6   •   Serving size: 1 fillet

Each serving has: 8 grams carbohydrate   •   6 grams fiber   •   2 grams nutritive carbohydrate   •   37 grams total protein   •   33 grams from animal source   •   4 grams from plant source

2 cups pecan halves	¼ tsp. salt
1 TB. flour	¼ tsp. pepper
2 eggs	6 (3- to 4-oz.) trout fillets

Preheat oven to 375°F.

In a food processor or blender, process 1½ cups pecans until very finely chopped. Mix with flour, and put in a shallow pan.

Place remaining ½ cup pecans in the microwave in a dish, and cook on high for 2 to 3 minutes until toasted.

Beat eggs with salt and pepper until blended. Dip each trout fillet into egg mixture and then into pecan mixture. Coat thoroughly and place in a buttered shallow baking dish. Bake for 15 to 20 minutes until trout is white and flakes.

Serve garnished with ½ cup toasted pecan halves.

Recipe for Success

Finely chopped pecans are a terrific substitute for breading on trout. Use freshly caught trout or purchase it from the fish section of the grocery store. The pecans keep the dish low carb compared to using flour or breading and add crunch plus flavor.

Tuna Fish Cakes

Prep time: 10 minutes • Cook time: 8 minutes • Serves 4 • Serving size: 1 cake

Each serving has: 1 gram nutritive carbohydrate • 13 grams total protein • 13 grams from animal source • 0 grams from plant source

1 egg	¼ tsp. cayenne
1 (6½-oz.) can albacore tuna, drained	Salt and pepper to taste
1 TB. chopped green onions	3 TB. butter
2 TB. chopped green pepper	¼ cup grated Parmesan cheese
3 TB. chopped celery	

Recipe for Success

This recipe makes a satisfying quick dinner. If dinner is on the run, add fresh apples and carrot sticks for a balanced meal. You can also make tuna fish cakes and keep them in the refrigerator to pack for lunch or eat for breakfast.

Beat egg slightly in a bowl. Add tuna, green onions, green pepper, celery, cayenne, salt, and pepper. Mix thoroughly.

Heat butter in a heavy skillet until melted and hot. Form tuna mixture into 4 cakes and place in skillet, cooking for 3 minutes per side. In the last minute, top each tuna cake with 1 tablespoon Parmesan cheese.

Salmon with Olives and Lemon

Prep time: 20 minutes • Cook time: 5 to 8 minutes • Serves 4 • Serving size: 1 fillet

Each serving has: less than 1 gram nutritive carbohydrate • 35 grams total protein • 35 grams from animal source • 0 grams from plant source

4 (5- to 6-oz.) salmon fillets	Salt and pepper to taste
1 lemon	½ cup water
6 green olives stuffed with pimientos	

Preheat oven to 500°F.

Place salmon on a foil-lined baking sheet. Cut lemon into ⅓-inch slices. Cut olives into ¼-inch slices. Place lemon and olive slices over salmon. Salt and pepper to taste. Pull up the sides of the foil and add water. Cover with foil, and seal the edges securely.

Oven "poach" salmon for 5 to 8 minutes or until cooked throughout so that the middle is not raw and is the same color as the outside of the fish.

Recipe for Success

This recipe gives a tangy Mediterranean taste to salmon. Cooking in the foil makes the salmon very tender and flaky. You can also grill the foil bag over high heat for 15 to 20 minutes.

Salmon with Macadamia Lime Butter

Prep time: 15 minutes • Cook time: 10 to 16 minutes • Serves 4 • Serving size: 1 salmon steak

Each serving has: 3 grams nutritive carbohydrate • less than 1 gram fiber • 36 grams total protein • 35 grams from animal source • 1 gram from plant source

5 TB. butter

3 TB. lime juice

2 TB. ground macadamia nuts

4 (5- to 6-oz.) salmon steaks

Salt and pepper to taste

To make butter sauce, melt butter in a small bowl in the microwave. Stir in lime juice and chopped macadamia nuts.

Season salmon steaks with salt and pepper. Cook salmon steaks on a gas or charcoal grill. Grill, covered, for 5 to 8 minutes per side until fish is cooked. Remove to a serving platter, and top with butter sauce.

Table Talk

This dish scores a home run. Quick and easy to prepare, the mixture of lime, butter, and macadamia nuts makes this salmon dish appealing to eaters of all ages. Use nut flour or ground nuts for breading on fish and meats. It actually adds more flavor than regular breading made with wheat, while it lowers the carb count and the glycemic index of the food. Plus, the nuts contain more nutrients.

Blackened Fish

Prep time: 5 minutes plus time to prepare spice mixture   •   Cook time: 5 minutes
•   Serves 6   •   Serving size: 1 fillet

Each serving has: 1 gram nutritive carbohydrate   •   30 grams total protein   •   30 grams
from animal source   •   0 grams from plant source

2 tsp. onion powder	1 tsp. white pepper
2 tsp. cayenne	1 tsp. oregano
1 tsp. black pepper	1 pinch sage
1 tsp. thyme	2 TB. butter
1 TB. garlic powder	2 TB. melted butter
1 TB. paprika	6 (5-oz.) fish fillets
1 tsp. salt	Lemon wedges for serving

Combine onion powder, cayenne, black pepper, thyme, garlic powder, paprika, salt, white pepper, oregano, and sage to create the Cajun Spice Mix. Store extra in a sealed jar in the refrigerator. Use the mixture in other Cajun recipes or anytime a spicy taste is desired.

In a cast-iron skillet, heat butter to just short of smoking.

Wash fish and pat dry. Coat each side with melted butter, and sprinkle Cajun spice liberally on both sides. Cook fish 1 minute until the side down begins to char, quickly flip fish over, and cook the other side in the same manner.

Serve with lemon wedges.

Recipe for Success
The Cajun Spice Mix is just as delicious when used to season grilled, baked, or pan-fried fish. Serve with Southern Greens or Creamed Cabbage, Cajun Dirty Rice, Minty Fruit, and your favorite dessert. Each tablespoon equals 1 gram carbohydrate.

Hot Potato
The cast-iron skillet has to be almost white hot for the fish to blacken and not burn. The blackening process happens quickly and may produce a lot of smoke. Some folks prefer to use this method of cooking outdoors on a fish cooker.

Salmon in Dill Sauce

Prep time: 15 minutes • Cook time: 8 minutes • Serves 6 • Serving size: 1 steak with ¼ cup sauce

Each serving has: 4 grams nutritive carbohydrate • 35 grams total protein • 35 grams from animal source • 0 grams from plant source

2 tsp. dried dill weed or 2 TB. chopped fresh	1 cup plain yogurt
½ tsp. white pepper	2 TB. finely chopped red onion
2 TB. spicy prepared mustard	6 (4- to 6-oz.) salmon steaks
1 TB. white wine vinegar	Olive oil
1 tsp. honey	

Combine dill, white pepper, mustard, vinegar, honey, yogurt, and onion. Refrigerate until ready to serve.

Brush salmon steaks with olive oil, and grill 5 to 8 minutes per side, depending on thickness of steaks.

Place salmon on serving platter, and drizzle each with Dill Sauce. Save any leftover sauce for use later.

Recipe for Success

The Dill Sauce is delicious as a vegetable dip or salad dressing. You can also refrigerate the salmon and serve it cold over fresh baby spinach leaves. If desired, poach or bake the salmon instead of grilling it. It is delicious cooked by any method, and leftover salmon makes the perfect breakfast protein.

Trout Dinner in a Bag

Prep time: 15 minutes • Cook time: 30 minutes • Serves 6 • Serving size: 1 fillet with 1 cup vegetables

Each serving has: 15 grams carbohydrate • 4 grams fiber • 11 grams nutritive carbohydrate • 32 grams total protein • 29 grams from animal source • 3 grams from plant source

½ cup chopped green onion

1 tsp. white pepper

6 (4- to 5-oz.) trout fillets (or use any fish desired)

1 lb. fresh or frozen whole green beans

3 medium turnips, peeled and sliced

6 carrots, shredded or chopped

6 TB. butter

6 sprigs fresh parsley

Preheat oven to 350°F.

In a small bowl, combine green onion and pepper and set aside.

Put a large baking bag in a baking pan. Place fillets, green beans, turnips, and carrots in the bottom of the bag. Sprinkle with onion-pepper mixture; top each fillet with 1 tablespoon butter and 1 sprig parsley.

Recipe for Success

Within the cooking bag is a complete meal for 6 people! As each person gets 1 cup vegetables, this equals 2 servings vegetables—the least you need for a meal.

Close the bag, and cut vent holes according to manufacturer's directions. Bake for 30 minutes until fish flakes and vegetables are tender.

Variation: If preferred, you can place each fillet and ⅙ of all ingredients into individual foil packets and serve them on plates. This basic recipe is delicious when using poultry in place of the fish; increase cooking time accordingly for the poultry.

The Least You Need to Know

♦ Fish is a wise nutritional choice for low-carb eating.

♦ The varieties of fish are endless, and the tastes, diverse and interesting.

♦ Use marinating and nut coatings to make tasty fish main dishes.

♦ Cold-water fish contain essential fatty acids you need for a strong body, a healthy heart, and weight loss.

Part **4**

Main Dish Combinations

The combination of ingredients—proteins, fats, and vegetables—prepared and cooked together delivers great food and eating value. Here are recipes for timesaving one-pot meals, plus soups and stews. They feature all your favorite meats and ingredients.

Eggs and cheese blend well together to deliver creamy entrees complemented with vegctables, herbs, and spices. Main dish salads meet your highest expectations for interesting tastes and textures.

One-Pot Meals

In This Chapter

- ◆ Slow cooking with the oven, stove, or slow cooker
- ◆ Converting recipes for the slow cooker
- ◆ A convenient balanced meal in a pot

Casseroles are back in popularity but under a different name—one-pot meals. Just toss delicious low-carb ingredients into a baking dish, Dutch oven, or slow cooker; return sometime between 2 to 8 hours later; and voilà—dinner is ready.

We know your lifestyle is busy. You rush to keep up with multiple demands at work, at home, and even at play. You want to eat low carb, yet fast food beckons at every corner. One-pot meals let you add some stability and order into your day and your eating. Best of all, you can easily make your one-pot meals low carb and totally scrumptious.

Your Choice of Cookware

One-pot cooking requires different kinds of cookware. Our recipes use the following types:

- ◆ **Oven casserole.** Use a glass or enameled baking dish. Some recipes require a lid. You can put the pot in the oven before you leave for work or play.

- **Dutch oven.** Usually made from cast iron, the Dutch oven is used for top-of-the-stove cooking. The cast iron evenly distributes heat and is ideal for low-temperature simmering.

- **Slow cooker.** This electrical appliance cooks at a very low temperature. It may take 4 to 8 hours to cook a pot roast, but it is ideal for when you will be away from home for hours. It uses very little electricity, and the newer models clean up easily, as the crockery cooking chamber comes out and can go into the dishwasher. Don't lift the lid on your slow cooker during cooking. Every time you do, it can take the pot 20 minutes to return to its previous cooking temperature.

With one-pot meals, you cook vegetables and meat together so you get both complete protein and at least one vegetable and often two—a balanced and nutritious meal. You can serve each of these recipes by itself or add one more vegetable or salad as a side dish if you prefer. These vegetable and meat combinations are low-carb and are hearty enough to serve you and your entire family.

Adapting for the Slow Cooker

You can adapt any of these recipes to cook in the slow cooker. Just follow these guidelines:

- **Vegetables.** Dense vegetables like carrots and other root vegetables should be cut no larger than 1-inch thick and placed in the bottom of the pot because they take longer to cook. Other vegetables, such as tomatoes and parsley, can be put on top of the meat or mixed in with it.

- **Liquids.** Decrease the quantity of liquids in slow cooking to about half the recipe's recommended amount. One cup liquid is usually plenty.

- **Herbs and spices.** Whole herbs release flavors over time, so they are a good choice for slow cooking. Ground herbs and spices lose pungency when slow cooked, so add them near the end of cooking, about an hour before serving. As in all cooking, taste and adjust seasonings, if necessary, before serving.

- **Milk/cheese.** Add these during the last hour, as they don't hold up well during slow cooking.

- **Preparation.** Browning meats first in a heavy skillet can enhance flavor. This also decreases the amount of fat in the food. For a special taste treat, after browning, deglaze the skillet with wine, a little vinegar, lemon, or broth, and add the liquid to the pot.

Follow this time guide for converting regular one-pot recipes for the slow cooker.

Conventional Recipe	Low (200°F)	High (300°F)
15 to 30 minutes	4 to 6 hours	1½ to 2 hours
35 to 45 minutes	6 to 10 hours	3 to 4 hours
50 minutes to 3 hours	8 to 18 hours	4 to 6 hours

One-Pot Ingredients

One-pot recipes lend themselves to the use of almost any ingredient imaginable. Fresh ingredients are best, of course, as they contain more nutrients, but because everything is cooked all together, you can often use canned ingredients and not notice much difference in taste.

Peasant Beef Casserole

Prep time: 15 minutes • Cook time: 5 hours • Serves 8 • Serving size: ¾ cup

Each serving has: 13 grams carbohydrate • 3 grams fiber • 10 grams nutritive carbohydrate • 31 grams total protein • 28 grams from animal source • 3 grams from plant source

2 lb. beef stew meat, cubed

2 cups frozen peas

1½ cups sliced carrots

2 large onions, chopped

¾ cup water

3 tomatoes, chopped

¼ cup chopped fresh parsley

1 tsp. salt

¼ tsp. pepper

Preheat oven to 275°F.

Mix meat, peas, carrots, onions, water, tomatoes, parsley, salt, and pepper in a 3-quart casserole with a tight lid. Bake, covered, for 5 hours.

Variation: To spice up this recipe, add ¼ teaspoon each rosemary, basil, and oregano for an Italian taste. Add ¼ teaspoon each dried cilantro and crushed red pepper plus a small can of green chilies for a Mexican flavor. Or add 1 lemon, sliced, and 8 to 10 green olives for a piquant taste. Serve with a salad or fruit and you have a complete balanced meal.

Meat and Cheese Loaf

Prep time: 20 minutes • Cook time: 1½ hours • Serves 12 • Serving size: 1 slice

Each serving has: 7 grams carbohydrate • 1 gram fiber • 6 grams nutritive carbohydrate • 29 grams total protein • 29 grams from animal source • less than 1 gram from plant source

2 lb. ground beef chuck	½ tsp. freshly ground black pepper
1½ cups grated Swiss cheese	1 tsp. celery salt
2 eggs, lightly beaten	2 cups milk
½ cup chopped onion	¼ cup dry breadcrumbs
½ cup chopped green pepper	4 slices lean bacon
1½ tsp. salt	

Preheat oven to 350°F.

Mix together beef, Swiss cheese, eggs, onion, green pepper, salt, black pepper, celery salt, milk, and breadcrumbs. Pack into a large loaf pan or 2 smaller loaf pans. Top with bacon, and bake 1 to 1½ hours. Cool for 5 minutes, and slice loaf into 12 portions.

Recipe for Success

This recipe is a variation on meat loaf—both cheese and meat in a loaf. Prepare enough for one meal, and use the leftovers for lunch and dinner. Good side dishes include green vegetables such as broccoli, spinach, green peas, and green beans.

Braised Beef with Italian Herbs

Prep time: 20 minutes • Cook time: 1½ to 2 hours • Serves 6 • Serving size: 4 ounces

Each serving has: 6 grams nutritive carbohydrate • less than 1 gram fiber • 43 grams total protein • 43 grams from animal source • 0 grams from plant source

2 TB. flour	1 small carrot, minced
Salt and pepper to taste	1 stalk celery, minced
3 to 4 lb. rump or chuck roast	1 cup chopped tomatoes
¼ cup butter or bacon fat	½ tsp. dried oregano
1 cup beef broth or water	½ tsp. dried rosemary
1 small onion, minced	2 whole cloves
1 clove garlic, minced	1 cup red wine

Combine flour, salt, and pepper, sprinkle on waxed paper or platter, and roll meat in seasoned flour mixture.

Heat butter in a Dutch oven or heavy saucepan with a tight-fitting lid.

Brown meat well on all sides over medium heat for about 15 to 20 minutes. Add beef broth, onion, garlic, carrot, celery, tomatoes, oregano, rosemary, cloves, and wine. Simmer over low heat 1½ to 2½ hours or until meat is tender.

Remove meat to a serving platter. Prepare this recipe 1 day ahead of time or freeze.

Variation: You can make this in a slow cooker by putting all ingredients except flour and butter directly into the slow cooker and cooking on high for 6 to 7 hours.

Beef Ratatouille Pie

Prep time: 30 minutes • Cook time: 45 minutes • Serves 8 • Serving size: 1 wedge

Each serving has: 15 grams carbohydrate • 2 grams fiber • 13 grams nutritive carbohydrate • 24 grams total protein • 21 grams from animal source • 3 grams from plant source

1½ lb. extra-lean ground beef

½ cup chopped red bell pepper

1 cup tomato purée

½ tsp. dried oregano

3 tsp. salt, plus additional to taste

¼ tsp. freshly ground black pepper, plus additional to taste

1 medium eggplant, quartered and thinly sliced

2 small zucchini, thinly sliced

2 small yellow squash, thinly sliced

4 TB. butter

1 tsp. dried thyme, crumbled

1 large yellow onion, peeled, quartered, and sliced

1 large red onion, peeled, quartered, and sliced

2 small green bell peppers, cored, seeded, and thinly sliced

1 tsp. minced garlic

½ lb. ripe tomatoes, chopped

1½ tsp. dried basil

½ cup minced fresh parsley leaves

Garnish:

3 TB. minced fresh parsley leaves

Freshly grated Romano cheese

Preheat oven to 350°F.

In a large bowl, combine beef, red bell pepper, ½ cup purée, oregano, 1 teaspoon salt, and ¼ teaspoon pepper. Press into bottom and sides of a 10-inch deep-dish pie pan. Bake 20 minutes. Remove from oven, leaving oven on. Drain and set aside.

Sprinkle eggplant, zucchini, and yellow squash with remaining 2 teaspoons salt. Let stand 30 minutes to release moisture, then pat dry. In a skillet with a lid, heat 2 tablespoons butter over high heat. Add eggplant, zucchini, and yellow squash, and cook 3 minutes. Stir in thyme. Transfer to a plate.

In the same skillet, heat remaining 2 tablespoons butter over high heat. Add yellow and red onions and green bell peppers, and cook just until soft. Stir in garlic, tomatoes, and remaining ½ cup tomato purée. Cover, reduce heat to medium, and cook 5 minutes. Remove cover and cook until juices have evaporated. Add basil and ½ cup parsley, and season with salt and pepper to taste.

Recipe for Success

This is a complete balanced meal as it is. You get complete protein from the meat and plenty of vegetables. The higher carbs come from the vegetables in the pie. Plus, it tastes great.

Spread about ⅓ tomato mixture evenly over prepared meat shell. Cover with ½ eggplant mixture. Add another ⅓ tomato mixture, and cover with remaining eggplant mixture. Top with remaining tomato mixture. Cover with foil and bake 25 minutes. Remove foil and continue baking 20 minutes. Garnish with 3 tablespoons parsley, and sprinkle with Romano. Cut into 8 wedges before serving.

Veal Italian Style

Prep time: 25 minutes • Cook time: 1 hour • Serves 6 • Serving size: ¼ cup

Each serving has: 3 grams nutritive carbohydrate • 28 grams total protein • 28 grams from animal source • Less than 1 gram from plant source

¼ cup butter	¼ tsp. dried rosemary
2 lb. boneless veal, cut into 1-inch cubes	¼ tsp. dried oregano
1 medium onion, chopped	½ tsp. salt
2 stalks celery, cut into 1-inch pieces	¼ tsp. pepper
2 cups sliced fresh mushrooms	1 cup dry white wine

Preheat oven to 350°F.

Melt butter in a casserole on the stove. Add veal and brown on all sides for 10 minutes. Add onion, celery, and mushrooms; sauté 5 minutes. Add rosemary, oregano, salt, pepper, and wine. Cover and bake for 1 hour, stirring occasionally.

Recipe for Success

This recipe adds the taste and aroma of Italian cooking without any high-carb pasta. If you prefer, substitute 1 cup water plus 1 teaspoon vinegar for the wine. The wine or vinegar helps tenderize the meat as it cooks, and this small amount doesn't change the taste of the recipe. You can also cook this in a slow cooker on low for 4 to 6 hours. Serve with puréed cauliflower and Baked Tomatoes Italiano.

Peppered Tenderloin Casserole

Prep time: 30 minutes • Cook time: 30 minutes • Serves 6 • Serving size: ¾ cup

Each serving has: 11 grams carbohydrate • 1 gram fiber • 10 grams nutritive carbohydrate • 29 grams total protein • 28 grams from animal source • 1 gram from plant source

6 TB. butter	1 medium onion, chopped
2 lb. beef tenderloin or boneless sirloin, cut into ¼-inch strips	1 green pepper, sliced
	1 red pepper, sliced
1 tsp. salt	2 celery stalks, chopped
½ tsp. black pepper	2 tomatoes, cut into wedges
⅛ tsp. dried sage	¼ cup soy sauce
⅛ tsp. dried cumin	2 TB. apple cider vinegar
2 cups quartered mushrooms	2 TB. tomato paste
2 cloves garlic, minced	

Preheat oven to 325°F.

Heat 3 tablespoons butter in a heavy skillet, and quickly brown beef on all sides. Put beef into a 4-quart casserole. Sprinkle with salt, pepper, sage, and cumin, and stir to mix.

Recipe for Success
Great for serving a crowd or for a potluck dinner, this casserole has the flavor of fajitas in one pot. Serve it all by itself or with guacamole or avocado salad.

Sauté mushrooms in 3 tablespoons butter. Add garlic, onion, red and green peppers, and celery. Sauté for an additional 3 minutes. Put mixture into the casserole and add tomatoes.

Put soy sauce, vinegar, and tomato paste into the skillet and cook, stirring to loosen browned particles. Pour over meat and vegetables in the casserole. Toss lightly to mix.

Bake 30 minutes or until meat is tender and mixture is bubbling.

Basil Pot Roast

Prep time: 15 minutes • Cook time: 2½ to 3 hours • Serves 6
• Serving size: 4 ounces beef with 1 carrot and ½ cup cauliflower

Each serving has: 15 grams carbohydrate • 3 grams fiber • 12 grams nutritive carbohydrate
• 31 grams total protein • 29 grams from animal source • 2 grams from plant source

1 (4- to 5-lb.) pot roast	1 TB. ground black pepper
2 TB. olive oil or butter	2 TB. fresh basil or 1 TB. dried
1 (16-oz.) can tomato sauce	1 tsp. dried oregano
½ cup red wine	1 cup beef broth
2 onions, chopped	6 large carrots, cut in half
5 cloves garlic, minced	3 cups mashed cooked cauliflower

Preheat oven to 350°F.

In a Dutch oven, brown roast on all sides in hot oil.

To make sauce, combine tomato sauce, red wine, onions, garlic, black pepper, basil, oregano, and beef broth. Pour over meat in the pot and cover. Bake 2½ to 3 hours until roast is tender.

Add carrots the last 40 minutes of baking time.

Recipe for Success

The gravy is delicious served over mashed cauliflower instead of potatoes. By itself, this is a complete balanced meal, as you have the carrots and cauliflower for vegetables. If you like, add a fruit salad for something light with the meal.

Slow Cooker Italian Brisket

Prep time: 15 minutes • Cook time: 11 hours • Serves 6 • Serving size: 4 oz. brisket

Each serving has: 5 grams nutritive carbohydrate • 30 grams total protein • 30 grams from animal source • less than 1 gram from plant source

1 (2- to 3-lb.) boneless brisket, partially frozen	1 TB. molasses
2 cups spaghetti sauce (purchased or home-made)	½ tsp. Italian seasoning
	¼ tsp. cayenne
2 onions, chopped	2 TB. Worcestershire sauce
1 bell pepper, chopped	6 oz. shredded white cheese (mozzarella, Swiss, provolone, Parmesan, etc.)
2 TB. cornstarch	

Hot Potato

It is easier to slice beef when it is partially frozen. Use this technique when you need slices for stir-fry or fajitas.

Thinly slice beef diagonally across the grain. In a bowl, combine spaghetti sauce with onions, bell pepper, cornstarch, molasses, Italian seasoning, cayenne, and Worcestershire sauce. Place beef in a slow cooker, and cover with seasoned sauce. Cover and cook on high for first hour; turn to low for 10 hours. Serve with shredded cheese on top.

Recipe for Success

Put together this recipe the day before and add to the slow cooker early in the morning to be ready for supper. Or if you prefer to cook ahead and just reheat, add it to the slow cooker to reheat 2 to 3 hours before serving time. Use 1 slice Low-Carb Bread for a wonderful open-face Italian sandwich; remember to add additional carbohydrates. Serve with Nine-Day Coleslaw and Chocolate Mousse for dessert.

Stewed Chicken

Prep time: 10 minutes • Cook time: 3 to 10 hours in slow cooker • Serves 6
• Serving size: 4 ounces

Each serving has: 4 grams carbohydrate • 1 gram fiber • 3 grams nutritive carbohydrate
• 28 grams total protein • 28 grams from animal source

1 whole chicken	½ tsp. salt
1 TB. garlic powder	2 TB. Worcestershire sauce
2 TB. dried parsley	¼ cup water
½ tsp. cayenne	3 onions, halved
½ tsp. ground black pepper	

Wash and dry chicken, removing and discarding neck and giblets from cavity. Mix together garlic powder, parsley, cayenne, black pepper, and salt. Season inside cavity with spices and Worcestershire sauce. Pour water into a slow cooker, and place chicken inside the pot. Lay onion pieces around chicken and cover. Cook on low 10 hours or high for 3; read manufacturer's instructions.

Serve immediately or refrigerate separately from broth to use later.

Recipe for Success _____

This is such an easy way to get de-boned chicken for recipes. The meat just falls off the bone. Refrigerate the chicken and de-bone the next day, and chill the broth and remove congealed fat the next day. Thicken broth for gravy or use as stock for recipes. Freeze broth in ice cube trays and use for seasoning as needed.

Jambalaya

Prep time: 20 minutes plus time to prepare shrimp • Cook time: 15 minutes • Serves 6 • Serving size: 1 cup

Each serving has: 30 grams carbohydrate • 3 grams fiber • 27 grams nutritive carbohydrate • 34 grams total protein • 30 grams from animal source • 4 grams from plant source

2 chicken bouillon cubes

1½ cups boiling water

2 TB. butter

2 onions, chopped

1 bell pepper, chopped

¼ cup chopped celery

½ cup raw basmati rice

1 (28-oz.) can whole tomatoes, cut in quarters

1½ tsp. Cajun spice mix

2 lb. shrimp, cooked, peeled, and chopped

¼ cup finely chopped green onions, for garnish

Dissolve chicken bouillon cubes in boiling water and set aside.

In a Dutch oven, melt butter and sauté onions, bell pepper, and celery until tender. Add chicken bouillon and raw rice; simmer 15 minutes. Add tomatoes and Cajun spice mix, and simmer 5 minutes until rice is done. Add shrimp and simmer just until heated.

Serve garnished with green onion.

Recipe for Success _____

Any seafood or mixture may be substituted for shrimp. Chicken with sausage makes a great jambalaya as well. Rice is included in this dish and adds 11 carbs per serving. Omit the rice and only use 1 cup water if you want to have fewer carbs. The carb count without the rice is 19 grams per serving. Serve with a large mixed green salad.

Your Choice Stir-Fry

Prep time: 30 minutes • Cook time: 15 minutes • Serves 6 • Serving size: 3 ounces meat, 2½ cups vegetables

Each serving has: 7 grams carbohydrate • 7 grams fiber • 0 grams nutritive carbohydrate • 25 grams total protein • 21 grams from animal source • 4 grams from plant source

Protein	Veggie A	Veggie B	Crunch	Necessities
1 lb. beef top round, partially frozen and thinly sliced	1 cup broccoli florets	1 cup fresh mushrooms, thinly sliced	1 cup walnut pieces	⅓ cup water; 2 tsp. cornstarch
1 lb. boneless pork, partially frozen and thinly sliced	1 cup fresh asparagus, cut into 1-inch lengths	2 cups chopped Chinese cabbage	1 cup dry-roasted peanuts	2 TB. soy sauce; 1 TB. dry sherry (or bouillon granules and water)
2 whole large boneless chicken breasts, skinned and cut into 1-inch pieces	2 large carrots, thinly bias sliced	1 cup pea pods, halved length-wise	2 stalks celery, thinly sliced	2 TB. oil; 1 clove garlic, minced; 4 green onions, thinly sliced
1 lb. medium shrimp, peeled and deveined	½ cup cauliflower florets, thinly sliced	2 medium tomatoes, cut into wedges and seeded	1 (8-oz.) can sliced water chestnuts, drained	½ cup bean sprouts or bamboo shoots, no liquid

Choose ingredients from each of the first four columns. Use all ingredients in the last column, Necessities, in every recipe. Prepare all ingredients as needed before the cooking begins.

Combine water, cornstarch, soy sauce, and sherry, and set aside.

In a covered saucepan, cook Veggie A in boiling salted water for 3 minutes. Drain well and set aside.

In a large wok or a skillet, heat oil and stir-fry garlic and green onions. Add Crunch ingredient and bean sprouts. Stir fry 1 to 2 minutes. Remove from the pan and set aside.

Add more oil, if needed. Add ½ Protein choice, and stir-fry 2 to 3 minutes or until browned. Remove from the pan and set aside while cooking remaining Protein choice. Return all Protein food to pan, and add Crunch ingredient mixture.

Stir in soy sauce mixture, and cook until thickened and bubbly. Stir in Veggies A and B; cover and heat 1 minute.

Recipe for Success _____

With this recipe, you can have stir-fry for days and never end up with the same combo! Mix and match additional great veggies such as bell pepper, red onion, or Brussels sprouts; vary the nuts and add sesame seeds. A great party idea is to have guests choose their own ingredients and cook in separate electric woks or skillets. Add additional carbohydrate if served over rice.

Eggplant and Meat Casserole

Prep time: 15 minutes • Cook time: 30 minutes • Serves 6 • Serving size: ⅙ recipe

Each serving has: 14 grams nutritive carbohydrate less than 1 gram fiber • 29 grams total protein • 21 grams from animal source • 8 grams from plant source

1 lb. ground beef	1 tsp. dried oregano
2 (8-oz.) cans tomato sauce	2 eggplants
¼ cup Italian seasoned breadcrumbs	3 egg whites, slightly beaten
2 TB. Parmesan cheese	1 cup shredded mozzarella cheese

Preheat oven to 350°F.

Brown beef and drain. Mix in tomato sauce and set aside.

Combine breadcrumbs, Parmesan cheese, and oregano and set aside.

Peel eggplants and slice lengthwise into thin lasagnalike strips. Dip eggplant in egg whites and then into breadcrumb mixture. Bake slices on a baking sheet for 20 minutes.

In a buttered oblong baking dish, layer eggplant "noodles," ⅓ beef mixture, and ⅓ cheese; repeat layers until all ingredients are used. Bake 10 minutes or until cheese melts and lasagna is bubbling. Slice into 6 servings.

The Least You Need to Know

◆ One-pot meals give you ultimate convenience and low-carb eating.

◆ Cook one-pot meals when you are away from home for a while, simply relaxing, or too busy to be in the kitchen.

◆ Give one-pot meals flavor and aroma variety with international or regional flavors.

◆ One-pot meals give you a nutritionally balanced meal.

◆ You can convert any one-pot meal for cooking in the slow cooker.

14

Low-Carb Soups and Stews

In This Chapter

◆ Cooking comfort food like Mother's chicken soup
◆ Varying your standard noodle soup
◆ Boosting your immune system

For many of us, when the weather turns cold and damp, soups and stews offer both comfort and nutrition. They ward off the damp. They overcome the chill in our bodies. They warm our hands and mouth and seem to heat our whole insides.

Maybe it's the pleasure that comes from slurping up a liquid-based dish, but eating soups and stews seems to evoke feelings of an earlier time and causes us to remember Mama's nurturing cooking. They seem to nurture the whole body. And yes, chicken soup really is good for what ails you!

A good soup is special. A cup of something delicious at the start of a meal delights the palate. A whole bowl of a hearty soup can serve as a meal in itself. A stew seems ideal for a winter evening when you want to keep the cold outside while you, your family, and your friends warm your insides inside!

Ladle the Soup, Hold the Noodles

Traditional soups and stews often have noodles, rice, or potatoes, but these ingredients aren't at all necessary to taste or goodness. The recipes in this chapter give soups and stews a distinctly modern twist. So don't expect to find starchy foods such as potatoes or rice. Just forget about those starches! You don't need them.

These recipes add more of what your body needs and actually yearns for. What's that? More vegetables that support you in health and also help you with weight management. But the rich taste remains with the use of such ingredients as heavy cream, cheese, and legumes.

As you and your body get accustomed to the flavor and crisp taste of these soups and stews, you'll prefer leaving out the high-carbohydrate starches.

Good for What Ails You

Nothing soothes the yucky feeling of a cold like a bowl of chicken soup. Scientists have actually figured out why. Chicken soup has anti-inflammatory properties and boosts the immune system. The soup also helps stop the movement of neutrophils, which are cells that are released by viral infections such as colds and flu and result in increased mucus production. Thus, soup helps dry up your runny nose.

In this chapter, you'll find an old-country recipe for chicken soup and a quite modern one for tortilla soup, also made with chicken. But you don't need to have a cold or the flu to enjoy these soups and stews. They're wonderful any time.

 Table Talk

Serve soups and stews for any meal. Yes, they taste great for lunch, but what about breakfast? A hearty soup or stew may be just the right breakfast before a day of skiing, snowshoeing, or hiking. They can even be just the right thing before school and even before work. You don't need to limit your breakfast eating to the standard expected fare. Perk up your day and the days of your loved ones with soups and stews, low-carb, of course, for breakfast, too.

Beef Soup with Vegetables

Prep time: 30 minutes • Cook time: 3 hours • Serves 10 • Serving size: 1 cup

Each serving has: 6 grams carbohydrate • 2 grams fiber • 4 grams nutritive carbohydrate • 30 grams total protein • 29 grams from animal source • 1 gram from plant source

2 lb. beef brisket, cut into chunks	½ cup spinach
1 carrot	½ cup peas
½ head cabbage	1 (14½-oz.) can tomatoes
3 spears asparagus	1 bay leaf
1 stalk celery	1 pinch dried thyme
1 small bunch parsley	1 pinch dried oregano
1 small onion	Salt and pepper to taste
½ cup string beans	

Put beef in a large pot or a Dutch oven. Cover with cold water, and boil for ½ hour. During this time, cut carrot, cabbage, asparagus, celery, parsley, onion, string beans, and spinach into 1-inch chunks.

Skim the pot carefully, then add all cut vegetables plus peas, tomatoes, bay leaf, thyme, and oregano. Add salt and pepper to taste.

Simmer very slowly for 3 hours. Remove bay leaf. Serve with horseradish for meat.

 **Hot Potato** _____

Be sure to check the pot about every half-hour to make sure it is simmering enough but not boiling. You may need to add water from time to time to keep the water level high enough to cook the vegetables.

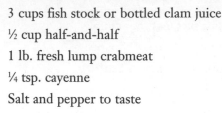

Sweet Red Pepper and Crab Bisque

Prep time: 25 minutes • Cook time: 20 minutes • Serves 6 • Serving size: ¾ cup

Each serving has: 8 grams carbohydrate • 1 gram fiber • 7 grams nutritive carbohydrate • 16 grams total protein • 13 grams from animal source • 3 grams from plant source

2 TB. butter

1 cup chopped onion

1 cup chopped celery

1 cup chopped red bell pepper

1¼ tsp. seafood spice blend

3 cups fish stock or bottled clam juice

½ cup half-and-half

1 lb. fresh lump crabmeat

¼ tsp. cayenne

Salt and pepper to taste

Recipe for Success
Add one more vegetable or fruit to this cream-based soup to have a balanced meal.

Melt butter in a heavy, medium saucepan over low heat. Add onion, celery, red pepper, seafood spice blend, and fish stock or clam juice. Cook, covered, for 10 minutes, stirring occasionally.

Add half-and-half. Bring to a simmer. Stir in crabmeat. Season with cayenne, salt and pepper. Cover and turn off the heat. Let stand for 2 minutes. Ladle into soup bowls.

Mexican Meat Soup

Prep time: 20 minutes • Cook time: 1 hour • Serves 8 • Serving size: ¾ cup

Each serving has: 4 grams nutritive carbohydrate • less than 1 gram fiber • 31 grams total protein • 30 grams from animal source • 1 gram from plant source

2 lb. round steak, cut into cubes

1 lb. pork shoulder, cut into cubes

3 TB. butter

1 (4-oz.) can diced green chilies

3 green onions, chopped

3 sprigs mint

½ tsp. minced garlic

¼ cup chopped fresh parsley

1 pinch cumin

½ tsp. ground cloves

6 cups water

1 cup tomato juice

Salt and pepper to taste

Brown steak and pork in butter, and add chilies, onions, mint, garlic, parsley, cumin, and cloves into a large pot with a lid. Add water, tomato juice, salt, and pepper to taste. Cover tightly and simmer for 1 hour.

Mexican Chicken Avocado Soup

Prep time: 25 minutes • Cook time: 15 minutes • Serves 6 • Serving size:1 cup

Each serving has: 9 grams carbohydrate • 2 grams fiber • 7 grams nutritive carbohydrate • 15 grams total protein • 13 grams from animal source • 2 grams from plant source

1 TB. olive oil	1 tomato, diced
1 small onion, coarsely chopped	1½ tsp. salt
2 large garlic cloves, minced	1 tsp. sugar
1 TB. chili powder	¼ tsp. pepper
2 tsp. cumin	2 large chicken breasts
½ tsp. dried oregano	½ cup corn
6 cups chicken stock	1 avocado, sliced

Heat olive oil in a skillet. Add onion and sauté until onion is translucent. Add garlic, chili powder, cumin, and oregano. Sauté for 1 minute.

Add chicken stock, diced tomato, salt, sugar, and pepper. Bring to a boil. Add chicken. Simmer, covered, about 15 minutes or until chicken is cooked through. Remove chicken to a plate and cool slightly.

Shred chicken, discarding skin and bones. Add corn to soup. Simmer until corn is tender. Add shredded chicken. Simmer for 1 minute. Ladle into soup bowls. Top with avocado slices.

Note: You can prepare soup 1 to 3 days in advance. Chill, covered, in the refrigerator and reheat before serving.

Recipe for Success

This recipe is a favorite variation of regular chicken soup. The hot spices enhance the healing and comforting aspects of chicken soup. And the exotic taste is just right for a special meal. The two vegetables—the corn and avocado—make this a balanced meal.

White Chili

Prep time: 10 minutes plus 24 hours soaking time • Cook time: 6 hours • Serves 10 • Serving size: 1 cup

Each serving has: 22 grams carbohydrate • 5 grams fiber • 17 grams nutritive carbohydrate • 32 grams total protein • 28 grams from animal source • 4 grams from plant source

1 lb. dry white northern beans	1 TB. dried oregano
7 cups chicken broth	1 TB. ground cumin
2 cloves garlic, minced	½ tsp. ground cloves
1 large white onion, chopped	1 (7-oz.) can diced green chilies
1 TB. ground white pepper	5 cups diced cooked chicken breast
1 tsp. salt	1 TB. diced jalapeño pepper (optional)

Recipe for Success

Beans are great for fiber and, combined with the chicken, make this a hearty dish. The south-of-the-border spices make this hot. To cool the temperature, omit the jalapeño pepper. Add avocado salad or guacamole on lettuce to make this a balanced meal.

Soak beans in water to cover for up to 24 hours; drain.

In a slow cooker or a large kettle, combine beans, 5¼ cups chicken broth, garlic, onion, white pepper, salt, oregano, cumin, and cloves. Simmer, covered, for at least 5 hours until beans are tender, stirring occasionally.

Stir in green chilies, diced chicken, and remaining 1¾ cups chicken broth. For a hotter taste, add jalapeño (if using). Cover and simmer for 1 hour.

Spoon chili into bowls.

Clam Chowder with Mushrooms

Prep time: 20 minutes • Cook time: 10 minutes • Serves 6 • Serving size: ¾ cup

Each serving has: 8 grams nutritive carbohydrate • less than 1 gram fiber • 5 grams total protein • 5 grams from animal source • less than 1 gram from plant source

2 TB. chopped green onions	2 (6½-oz.) cans chopped clams with juice
1 clove garlic, minced	2 cups water
4 TB. butter	Salt and pepper to taste
1 lb. mushrooms, sliced	⅛ tsp. nutmeg
2 TB. chopped fresh parsley	1½ cups whipping cream
2 TB. flour	

Sauté green onions and garlic in butter. Add mushrooms and parsley, and cook 3 minutes longer. Sprinkle with flour and stir. Add clams with juice, water, salt, pepper, and nutmeg. Bring to a boil, and simmer for 5 minutes. Add cream and reheat but don't boil.

Recipe for Success

Try this clam chowder—it's filling, it's rich, it's creamy, and the mushrooms blended with the clams are fabulous.

Chicken Soup with Paprika

Prep time: 20 minutes plus 30 minutes after cooking • Cook time: 1½ hours • Serves 6 • Serving size: 1 cup

Each serving has: 2 grams nutritive carbohydrate • less than 1 gram fiber • 32 grams total protein • 32 grams from animal source • less than 1 gram from plant source

1 (4-lb.) chicken	½ tsp. thyme
2 carrots, cut into 1-inch slices	1 bay leaf
2 leeks, trimmed and washed	2 tsp. butter
1 tsp. salt	3 eggs
Freshly ground pepper to taste	2 TB. chopped fresh parsley
2 tsp. paprika	

To a soup kettle with 3 quarts water, add chicken, carrots, leeks, salt, pepper, paprika, thyme, and bay leaf. Bring water to a boil, and skim off any matter that rises to the top. Lower heat and simmer for 1½ hours. Remove bay leaf.

Remove chicken and let cool. Remove skin and debone chicken. Remove all nerves and tendons, and cut chicken into bite-size pieces.

Melt butter in a large skillet, and pour in eggs to make a very thin omelet. Cool and cut into shreds.

Add chicken, omelet shreds, and parsley to bouillon. Heat before serving.

Recipe for Success

This is just the type of soup to use for a cold day, a head cold, and a heartwarming meal. And it tastes even better reheated. Serve with green beans, a salad, and a brownie or cookie for dessert.

Basic Cream Soup

Prep time: 5 minutes • Cook time: 15 minutes • Serves 4 • Serving size: ½ cup

Each serving has: 7 grams nutritive carbohydrate • less than 1 gram fiber • 2 grams total protein • 1 gram from animal source • 1 gram from plant source

1 cup cream

1 TB. cornstarch

½ tsp. ground white pepper

½ tsp. cayenne

¼ tsp. salt

½ cup minced onion or 3 TB. onion flakes

1 lb. mushrooms, chopped, or 1 (8-oz.) can

1 TB. butter

Recipe for Success

This is a wonderful fresh substitute for canned cream soups in any recipe. Substitute celery, cooked chicken, or other seasonings of choice for the mushrooms.

In a cup, mix ¼ cup cream with cornstarch until smooth paste is formed. Over low heat, combine remaining cream, cornstarch mixture, white pepper, cayenne, salt, and onion. Stir constantly until mixture thickens, about 8 to 10 minutes. Remove from heat, and strain out onions through a mesh strainer.

Sauté mushrooms in butter until softened; add strained soup, and stir over medium-low heat about 5 minutes or until thoroughly cooked.

Beef-Vegetable Burgundy Stew

Prep time: 10 minutes • Cook time: 2 hours • Serves 6 • Serving size: 1 cup

Each serving has: 9 grams carbohydrate • 4 grams fiber • 5 grams nutritive carbohydrate • 29 grams total protein • 29 grams from animal source • less than 1 gram from plant source

1 TB. butter

1½ lb. lean stew meat, cut into 1-inch pieces

1 tsp. thyme

1 tsp. black pepper

1½ cups beef broth

¼ cup Burgundy wine

1 TB. minced garlic

1½ cups sliced carrots

1 cup pearl onions or 2 onions, quartered

1 (10-oz.) pkg. frozen English peas or soybeans

2 TB. cornstarch

2 TB. water

Melt butter in a Dutch oven, and brown beef cubes. Season with thyme and pepper. Stir in broth, wine, and garlic. Bring to a boil, reduce heat, cover, and simmer 1½ hours.

Add carrots, onions, and peas; cover and simmer 30 minutes or until vegetables are tender.

Mix cornstarch and water until smooth paste forms; add to stew and cook, stirring, until mixture is boiling and gravy thickens.

Recipe for Success

Let this hearty soup meant for cold wintry nights simmer while you begin your meal with Caesar Salad.

Cajun Black Bean Soup

Prep time: 30 minutes • Cook time: 1 hour • Serves 6 • Serving size: 1 cup

Each serving has: 19 grams carbohydrate • 8 grams fiber • 11 grams nutritive carbohydrate • 7 grams total protein • 2 grams from animal source • 5 grams from plant source

2 cups cooked black beans, cooking liquid reserved

2 TB. butter

2 onions, chopped

¼ cup Basic Cajun Flour (see Basic Cajun Flour Roux recipe later in this chapter)

1½ quarts beef or chicken broth

1 lemon, thinly sliced and seeds removed

1 TB. garlic powder

2 tsp. Cajun seasoning mix

½ cup dry sherry

Salt to taste

Hot sauce to taste

2 hard-boiled eggs, peeled and chopped

Mash 1 cup beans through a sieve; save remaining cup and set aside.

In a Dutch oven, melt butter and sauté onions. Add Basic Cajun Flour to the Dutch oven with 1 cup broth. Over medium heat, stir until well blended. Add rest of broth, mashed beans, and 2 cups reserved liquid from beans or enough water to make 2 quarts liquid for soup; stir well.

Add sliced lemon, garlic powder, Cajun seasoning, sherry, salt, and hot sauce. Simmer, covered, 1 hour.

Serve in bowls topped with chopped egg.

Recipe for Success

One cup may not be enough of this Cajun delight! This soup makes a wonderful appetizer served in demitasse cups, as it is warm and inviting; just a taste won't fill up your guests before dinner but will make them beg for your recipe. It freezes well, so make a large amount to have on hand for those winter afternoons.

Sweet-and-Sour Stew

Prep time: 25 minutes plus marinating overnight • Cook time: 1 hour 15 minutes
• Serves 6 • Serving size: ¾ cup

Each serving has: 16 grams carbohydrate • 2 grams fiber • 14 grams nutritive carbohydrate
• 37 grams total protein • 35 grams from animal source • 2 grams from plant source

2 lb. beef or pork, cut into cubes	½ cup pineapple juice
½ cup soy sauce	2 cups water
1 clove garlic, minced	2 TB. vinegar
4 TB. butter	1 tsp. molasses
1 green bell pepper, cut in strips	1 cup drained pineapple chunks, water-packed
2 medium onions, sliced	4 tomatoes, cut into wedges

Put meat into a resealable bag. Add soy sauce and garlic. Marinate overnight in the refrigerator.
Preheat oven to 350°F.

Recipe for Success

Here we have a taste of Asia—the sweet-and-sour taste—in a one-pot meal. Be sure to use water-packed pineapple. If you use juice-packed, the carb count increases by 7.

Remove meat from marinade and discard marinade.

Sauté meat in 3 tablespoons butter until browned. Put into a large casserole. Sauté green pepper and onions in remaining 1 tablespoon butter. Add to the casserole. Combine pineapple juice, water, vinegar, and molasses, stirring to blend. Pour over meat. Top with pineapple chunks and tomatoes.

Cover and bake for 1 hour and 15 minutes or until meat is tender.

Catfish Stew

Prep time: 10 minutes • Cook time: 40 minutes • Serves 6 • Serving size: 1 cup

Each serving has: 12 grams carbohydrate • 2 grams fiber • 10 grams nutritive carbohydrate • 35 grams total protein • 33 grams from animal source • 2 grams from plant source

2½ lb. catfish nuggets (or cut fish fillets into bite-size nuggets)	6 cloves garlic, minced (1 TB.)
	2 drops Tabasco or other hot sauce (optional)
Salt and pepper to taste	1 (8-oz.) can tomato sauce
2 TB. butter	1 cup water
5 large onions, sliced	2 TB. Worcestershire sauce

Season fish with salt and pepper to taste and set aside.

Melt butter in a Dutch oven or stew pot, and sauté onions and garlic until soft. Stir in Tabasco sauce (if using). Place fish nuggets on top of vegetables. In a small bowl, combine tomato sauce, water, and Worcestershire sauce. Pour this mixture on top of fish, and simmer until fish flakes easily, about 30 minutes. Do not stir, as this will break up fish.

Recipe for Success _____

This recipe is better if it's made early enough to allow the seasonings to be absorbed. You may add a bit more water, if desired, more juice, or serve over Vegetable Pasta as a sauce. Add your favorite seasoning vegetables such as bell pepper, celery, mushrooms, etc. A salad and a luscious dessert completes this fish lover's meal.

Lentil Soup

Prep time: 10 minutes plus 1 hour cooking time for lentils • Cook time: 6 to 8 hours
• Serves 8 • Serving size: ¾ cup

Each serving has: 23 grams carbohydrate • 10 grams fiber • 13 grams nutritive carbohydrate
• 4 grams total protein • 0 grams from animal source • 4 grams from plant source

1½ cups dried lentils, soaked overnight and drained

4½ cups water

1 beef bouillon cube

1 onion, chopped

2 carrots, chopped

1 stalk celery, thinly sliced

1 TB. olive oil

2 cloves garlic, minced

1 bay leaf

½ tsp. dried oregano

½ cup tomato sauce

2 TB. Worcestershire sauce

Recipe for Success

This hearty soup warms you on a chilly day and gives you energy to burn. Because it is low in complete protein, serve it as a side dish with meat, cheese, or pâté. Include a vegetable or salad, and you have a balanced meal.

Simmer lentils in 4½ cups water 1 hour or until almost tender. Dissolve bouillon cube in hot liquid, and transfer liquid and lentils to a slow cooker.

In a skillet, sauté onion, carrots, and celery in oil until tender; add to the slow cooker. Add garlic, bay leaf, and oregano. Cook, covered, on low for 6 to 8 hours.

Add tomato sauce and Worcestershire sauce. Stir well, cover, and cook on high 30 minutes or until flavors are well blended. Remove bay leaf and serve.

Red Bean and Ham Soup

Prep time: 10 minutes   •   Cook time: 10 hours   •   Serves 8   •   Serving size: ¾ cup

Each serving has: 23 grams carbohydrate   •   7 grams fiber   •   16 grams nutritive carbohydrate
•   19 grams total protein   •   12 grams from animal source   •   7 grams from plant source

1 lb. ham, cooked and diced	1 TB. soy sauce
3 cups cooked red beans	1 tsp. brown sugar
1 large red onion, chopped	1 tsp. cayenne
1 (16-oz.) can tomatoes, diced tomatoes	½ tsp. dried basil
1 cup tomato sauce	

Place ham, red beans, red onion, tomatoes, tomato sauce, soy sauce, brown sugar, cayenne, and basil into a slow cooker; cook on low 8 to 10 hours. Add water as needed.

Recipe for Success
If you have a ham bone, add it to the pot for more delicious flavor. Add additional vegetables as you desire, and just calculate additional carbohydrates. This recipe makes a great base for a mixed vegetable soup for a cold winter day. Substitute leftover Thanksgiving turkey and the carcass for a wonderful heart- and tummy-warming November meal.

Rich Cheesy Soup

Prep time: 10 minutes • Cook time: 30 minutes • Serves 6. • Serving size: 1 cup

Each serving has: 12 grams carbohydrate • 1 gram fiber • 11 grams nutritive carbohydrate • 11 grams total protein • 10 grams from animal source • 1 gram from plant source

3 cups chicken broth

1½ TB. cornstarch

¼ cup butter

½ cup minced onion

½ cup diced celery

½ cup diced carrots

¼ cup flour

3 cups cream

1 cup shredded cheddar cheese

½ tsp. ground white pepper

½ tsp. cayenne

2 TB. chives or finely chopped green onions

Recipe for Success

This soup makes a wonderful accompaniment to a salad or served as a delightful sauce over steamed vegetables. Add or substitute additional cheeses as desired; Swiss cheese gives it a totally new flavor.

In a cup, mix ½ cup cool chicken broth and cornstarch until a smooth paste forms; set aside.

In a stock pot, melt butter and sauté onion, celery, and carrots over low heat. Add flour and cook until thickened.

Add remaining chicken broth and cornstarch mixture, and simmer, stirring constantly. Pour in cream, and stir until smooth and bubbly. Add cheese, white pepper, and cayenne; stir until all cheese is melted and soup is smooth.

Sprinkle with chives when serving.

Basic Gumbo and Variations

Prep time: 1 hour plus cooking time for meat • Cook time: 2 hours • Serves 10
• Serving size: 1½ cups

Each serving has: 14 grams carbohydrate • 1 gram fiber • 13 grams nutritive carbohydrate
• 32 grams total protein • 30 grams from animal source • 2 grams from plant source

2 TB. butter	½ tsp. cayenne
3 stalks celery, chopped	Salt and pepper to taste
1 cup finely chopped onion	1 tsp. Cajun Spice Mix (optional; see Blackened Fish recipe in Chapter 12)
3 garlic cloves, minced	
3 qt. broth, stock, etc.	6 cups cooked poultry or other meat choice (if using seafood it will cook in gumbo)
1¼ cups Basic Cajun Flour (see Basic Cajun Flour Roux recipe later in this chapter)	
	1 bunch green onions, chopped
1 TB. Worcestershire sauce	*Filé powder* (optional)
½ cup chopped fresh parsley or ¼ cup dried	

Melt butter in a skillet, and sauté celery, onion, and garlic. Bring broth to boiling, and stir in Basic Cajun Flour until smooth; add sautéed vegetables, Worcestershire sauce, parsley, cayenne, salt, pepper, and Cajun Spice Mix (if using).

Add meat and simmer 2 hours for flavors to blend well. Add additional broth or water, if needed. If using seafood, add seafood for the last 30 minutes of cooking time. Add green onions the last 10 minutes of cooking. Serve with filé powder (if using).

The flavor is best if made at least 1 day in advance. Freezes well.

Low-Carb Vocab

Filé powder is ground sassafras root and is used in Southern-style cooking. It can be found in both grocery stores and specialty food stores.

Recipe for Success

Cajuns take their gumbo seriously! There are as many varieties of gumbo as there are people who eat it. Okra is said by some to be the main ingredient; others won't touch a gumbo if it has okra. Many use okra as the thickening agent. The basic recipe here omitted okra, but feel free to add 1 cup fresh or frozen okra if desired. The meat or seafood can be anything you want. You can use varieties of seafood such as shrimp, crawfish, crab (both flaked and in the shell), and oysters. Use wild game such as duck or squirrel as well as link sausage, rabbit, or chicken. Mix and match whatever you want. Just have fun and enjoy!

Basic Cajun Flour Roux

Prep time: 5 minutes • Cook time: 30 minutes • Serving size: 1 tablespoon

Each serving has: 5 grams nutritive carbohydrate • less than 1 gram fiber • 1 gram total protein • 0 grams from animal source • 1 gram from plant source

4 cups flour

Use 4 cups flour or whatever amount you want to make; stir into a cast-iron skillet over high heat. You must stir constantly with a wire whisk for the entire 25 minutes or until flour is the color of brown sugar.

If the skillet gets too hot, flour may start to brown too rapidly. Immediately remove from heat, and stir to cool flour; return to heat, and lower temperature a little if need be. After flour is the right color, continue to stir until it cools. Pour into covered container.

Recipe for Success

This roux is simply browned flour. You can also make roux the traditional way with equal portions of butter and flour. Sometimes you can find jars of roux in grocery stores. Make this recipe for Basic Cajun Flour Roux ahead of time and store indefinitely in the freezer. Roux is the secret to making gumbo taste like gumbo and not soup.

Make a 4-cup batch and refrigerate or freeze any extra for another recipe. Use it to thicken any soup or dish to which you want to give a rich nutty flavor. To make Basic Cajun Flour Roux, you must be able to give it undivided attention for 25 to 30 minutes to brown the flour. If it burns just a little it must be thrown away or the entire gumbo will taste burned!

Shrimp Dinner Boil

Prep time: 20 minutes • Cook time: 30 minutes • Serves 6 • Serving size: 12 large shrimp plus ½ ear corn and ½ onion

Each serving has: 15 grams carbohydrate • 3 grams fiber • 12 grams nutritive carbohydrate • 18 grams total protein • 17 grams from animal source • 1 gram from plant source

1 lemon, cut into wedges

2 to 3 TB. crab boil or other seafood seasoning

¼ cup salt

1 TB. black pepper

6 dozen large shrimp (22 to 30 per lb.) still in shell

3 large ears corn, cut in half or use 6 small frozen ears of corns

3 onions, cut in half

In a large stock pot, bring 1½ gallons water to a boil. Add lemon, crab boil, salt, and pepper.

Boil for 10 minutes. Add shrimp, corn, and onions, and bring back to boil. Boil 5 minutes; remove from heat and allow to stand covered 10 to 15 minutes. Pour into a large colander, or carefully spoon out vegetables and then drain shrimp.

Recipe for Success
This can be considered a modified Louisiana Crawfish boil ... only much easier and cooked indoors. Serve with ketchup seasoned with Tabasco or other hot sauce.

Southern Chili

Prep time: 20 minutes • Cook time: 2 hours • Serves 6 • Serving size: 1 cup

Each serving has: 23 grams carbohydrate • 5 grams fiber • 18 grams nutritive carbohydrate • 31 grams total protein • 27 grams from animal source • 4 grams from plant source

1 lb. ground beef

1 large onion, chopped

1 green pepper, chopped

1 (14.5-oz.) can tomatoes with jalapeños or chilies

1 (8-oz.) can tomato sauce

1 (14½-oz.) can kidney beans, do not drain

2 tsp. chili powder

1 tsp. Cajun spice mixture

1 bay leaf

1 cup shredded cheddar cheese, for garnish

1 cup sour cream, for garnish

3 green onions, chopped, for garnish

Recipe for Success
Omit beans if you wish and adjust seasonings to your preference for hot or mild flavors. If you like a more tomato flavor, add 1 small can tomato paste and 1 can diced tomatoes.

Brown beef and drain well; return to the skillet. In the same skillet, sauté onion and bell pepper until tender. Add tomatoes, tomato sauce, kidney beans, chili powder, Cajun spice mixture, and bay leaf; simmer 2 hours or pour into a slow cooker and heat on low 5 or more hours. Remove bay leaf before serving. Garnish with shredded cheddar cheese, sour cream, and chopped green onions.

Spicy Seafood Stew

Prep time: 45 minutes • Cook time: 45 minutes (includes standing time) • Serves 10 • Serving size: 1 cup

Each serving has: 11 grams carbohydrate • 1 gram fiber • 10 grams nutritive carbohydrate • 21 grams total protein • 19 grams from animal source • 2 grams from plant source

¼ cup butter

2 cups chopped onion

½ cup chopped celery

1 cup chopped green bell pepper

2 TB. minced garlic

4 cups chicken broth

1 (28-oz.) can stewed tomatoes, any seasoning

1 tsp. dill weed

1 tsp. black pepper

½ tsp. cayenne

1½ lb. shrimp, peeled and deveined

2 dozen fresh or frozen crab fingers

1 (10-oz.) container oysters

½ cup chopped green onions

Hot sauce (optional)

Recipe for Success

Use your favorite seafood in this easy stew; omit any suggested seafood if undesirable or hard to obtain in your area. Chicken and pork link sausage work just as well in this stew and make for a great "mock gumbo." Add okra to thicken, if desired.

Melt butter in a Dutch oven, and sauté onion, celery, bell pepper, and garlic until tender. Add chicken broth, tomatoes, dill weed, black pepper, and cayenne. Simmer, uncovered, 20 minutes.

Add shrimp, crab fingers, and oysters. Add water or broth if additional juice is desired; cover and simmer 10 minutes. Stir in green onions and hot sauce (if using). Remove from heat and allow to stand covered 10 minutes before serving.

The Least You Need to Know

- Soups and stews warm the heart and the body for cold- and damp-weather meals.
- Scientists have actually found out why chicken soup is so good for colds and the flu.
- Low-carb soups and stews provide a complete balanced meal and go well with warm fruit side dishes.
- Soups and stews are great for all meals—dinner, lunch, or breakfast.

Chapter 15

Egg and Cheese Main Dishes

In This Chapter

- ◆ Keeping eggs and cheese on hand
- ◆ Recognizing good-for-you nutrition
- ◆ Making delicious meals with eggs and cheese

When you read the term "egg and cheese" dishes, please don't think "macaroni and cheese." Instead, expect even better. Yes, if you love the taste of eggy-cheesy food, you'll love the recipes in this chapter.

Egg and cheese dishes are great for any meal. Most of these recipes were created as dinner fare, but serve them whenever you want a rich, creamy taste and texture. For instance, an omelet, normally thought of as breakfast food, makes a hearty supper when filled with meat, cheese, or vegetables. (We have recipes for omelets in Chapter 5.)

Combinations of eggs and cheese yield different kinds of low-carb meals. Take a break from eating meat and vary your cuisine.

The Care of Eggs

Unless otherwise specified, these recipes call for whole eggs. Only whole eggs will work. Don't use eggs that come in any container other than an eggshell. Use no plastic milk-type cartons, no bottles, and no preprocessing. Also, don't substitute egg whites for whole eggs. You lose nutritional value.

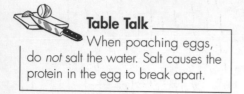

Table Talk When poaching eggs, do *not* salt the water. Salt causes the protein in the egg to break apart.

Eggs will keep in the refrigerator for several weeks without going stale. But they are best when eaten within a week of purchase.

Grating Cheese

Want to save a few minutes of your busy life? Purchase pre-grated cheese. If for some reason it's not available already grated or you got a great deal on a block of cheese, you'll need to grate it using one of these methods:

- **With a hand grater.** This takes some elbow grease. Use a hand grater that can be draped over a bowl so the cheese falls inside neatly. One advantage of a hand grater is that you actually burn calories as you cook.
- **With a food processor.** Use the grating attachment and put the cheese down the feeder tube while applying pressure with the pusher. It's quick and easy.

The Good Stuff in Eggs and Cheese

Eggs and cheese are both usually included under dairy products (although we suspect the chickens who laid the eggs would disagree). Both eggs and cheese offer good nutritional value in terms of protein and carbs. A cooked large egg has more than 6 grams complete protein and less than 1 gram carbohydrates.

The nutritional value of cheese varies based on the kind of cheese. One-quarter cup grated Parmesan contains 9 grams complete protein and 1 gram carbohydrate. The same amount of cheddar cheese has 6 grams complete protein and 1 gram carbohydrate.

Eggs and cheese are great for cooking because they blend with virtually every vegetable and fruit, spice and herb. Plus, eggs offer a soothing taste of their own, which can be spiced up with just the distinctive flavor of the added cheese.

Once upon a time, health experts thought that consuming eggs directly contributed to heart disease. Now they know better. Scientific studies show that consuming egg yolks doesn't appreciably elevate blood cholesterol levels. The lecithin found naturally in eggs may actually help the body clear out cholesterol. The real health concern isn't the cholesterol contained in the food you consume; it's the cholesterol level in your blood. Get that checked by your physician.

So there you have it. Not only are eggs not bad, they actually are good for you. So enjoy.

Whether you are eating low-carb for health reasons, heart reasons, or weight reasons, eggs and cheese combinations make excellent main dishes. Make a complete, balanced meal by adding vegetable and/or fruit side dishes to these recipes. Keep it light, as the dishes tend to be quite rich all by themselves. So think fresh salads, crudités, and fresh fruit platters.

 Hot Potato
Purchase fresh, large eggs for these recipes. Open the carton and make sure none of them are cracked before you put the eggs in your grocery cart. Be careful when loading them into the car. Even eggs in cartons can crack and ultimately leak. Yuck.

Asparagus Cheese Pie

Prep time: 20 minutes • Cook time: 35 minutes • Serves 8 • Serving size: ⅛ pie

Each serving has: 6 grams nutritive carbohydrate • less than 1 gram fiber • 20 grams total protein • 19 grams from animal source • 1 gram from plant source

1 lb. asparagus, trimmed, 6 spears reserved for top, the rest cut into ½-inch pieces	1 tsp. freshly ground black pepper
5 eggs	½ tsp. ground nutmeg
15 oz. ricotta cheese	3 green onions, chopped, including tops
1 tsp. salt	½ lb. bacon, crisply cooked and crumbled

Preheat oven to 375°F.

To a large pan of boiling water, add asparagus pieces, and cook 3 minutes. Drain, dry, and set aside.

In a large bowl, combine eggs, ricotta, salt, pepper, and nutmeg. Whisk to blend, and carefully stir in green onions, crumbled bacon, and cooked asparagus.

Spoon into a greased pie pan, and arrange reserved asparagus spears on top. Bake until firm, about 35 minutes.

Luncheon Egg Ring

Prep time: 30 minutes   •   Cook time: 45 minutes   •   Serves 8   •   Serving size: ⅛ ring

Each serving has: 10 grams nutritive carbohydrate   •   35 grams total protein   •   34 grams from animal source   •   1 gram from plant source

8 eggs	1½ cups milk
2 cups milk, scalded	½ lb. mushrooms, sliced
1½ tsp. salt	1 lb. cooked chicken or 1 lb. crab
1 tsp. *onion juice*	2 tsp. lemon juice
1 pinch cayenne	¼ tsp. paprika
5 TB. butter	Salt and pepper to taste
2 TB. flour	

Preheat oven to 300°F.

Beat eggs slightly. With a whisk, mix in scalded milk, salt, onion juice, and cayenne. Strain egg mixture through cheese cloth or a fine strainer. Pour into a well-oiled, 8½-inch ring mold. Set in a shallow roasting pan filled with ½ inch hot water, and bake 45 minutes or until firm.

In a large saucepan, melt 3 tablespoons butter, and stir in flour with a whisk. When blended, add milk, stirring constantly, until smooth and thickened. Remove from heat.

Low-Carb Vocab

Onion juice is a liquid seasoning similar to garlic juice and is packaged in a bottle. It can be found in the condiment aisle of your grocery store.

In a heavy skillet, sauté mushrooms in remaining 2 tablespoons butter over medium-high heat for 3 to 5 minutes or until juices are fairly well absorbed. Add to cream sauce with chicken. Add lemon juice, paprika, salt, and pepper to taste. Heat to simmer, but do not boil.

When egg ring is baked, carefully loosen from mold with a knife, and invert on a warm platter. Fill center and surround with cream mixture.

Chile Relleno and Crab Casserole

Prep time: 20 minutes • Cook time: 45 minutes • Serves 8 • Serving size: ½ chile

Each serving has: 8 grams nutritive carbohydrate • 38 grams total protein • 37 grams from animal source • 1 gram from plant source

4 (7-oz.) cans whole, mild green chilies	¼ cup flour
1 lb. Montercy Jack cheese	½ tsp. salt
5 eggs	Dash black pepper
1 (6½-oz.) can flaked crabmeat	4 cups (1 lb.) grated mild cheddar cheese
1¼ cups milk	

Preheat oven to 350°F.

Slit chilies lengthwise on one side. Remove seeds and drain. Slice Monterey Jack cheese into ¼-inch-thick slices, and place cheese inside chilies. Place stuffed chilies in an ungreased 3-quart baking dish or a soufflé dish.

Mix eggs, crabmeat, milk, flour, salt, and pepper well; pour over chilies. Sprinkle top with grated cheddar cheese. Bake uncovered for 45 minutes.

Recipe for Success
This recipe puffs up beautifully. It's a bit crusty on the outside, but it's creamy inside. It's fancy enough for guests and simple enough for dinner with your family.

Lemon Cheese Pie

Prep time: 20 minutes • Cook time: 30 minutes • Serves 12 • Serving size: ¹⁄₁₂ pie

Each serving has: 18 grams nutritive carbohydrate • 3 grams total protein • 3 grams from animal source • less than 1 gram from plant source

1 cup sugar, divided	1½ TB. finely grated lemon zest
1½ TB. cardamom	⅓ cup sour cream
¼ cup plus 2 tsp. butter, softened	3 egg yolks
1 (8-oz.) pkg. cream cheese, softened	

Preheat oven to 350°F.

In a small bowl, combine ½ cup sugar and cardamom. In a large bowl, beat ¼ cup butter and ½ cup sugar until smooth. Add cream cheese and lemon zest, and beat until fluffy. Blend in sour cream and egg yolks.

Pour into a buttered pie pan or quiche baking dish. Bake until golden brown and crisp, about 30 minutes. Cool and slice.

Table Talk

To make a low-carb pie crust, try this: Process 1 cup either almonds or pecans in a food processor until they turn into a flour, which is actually very finely chopped nuts. Add 1 egg and ⅓ cup butter. Process as for pie dough. Spread dough into bottom of pie dish, and bake at 400°F for 10 to 13 minutes or until lightly browned. Let cool and fill. You can rebake this with filling.

Cheese Apple Bake

Prep time: 25 minutes   •   Cook time: 50 minutes   •   Serves 6   •   Serving size: 5 slices apple

Each serving has: 16 grams nutritive carbohydrate   •   2 grams total protein   •   2 grams from animal source   •   less than 1 gram from plant source

4 medium baking apples, such as Fugi, Golden Delicious, or Granny Smith, peeled, cored, and cut into eighths

½ cup water

2 tsp. fresh lemon juice

1 TB. sugar

¼ tsp. ground cinnamon

⅛ tsp. salt

½ cup shredded cheddar cheese

Recipe for Success

Here's an apple treat that's low carb. The cheddar cheese adds complete protein. If you like more of a natural taste, don't peel the apples. Your children will find these hard to pass up—adults will, too!

Preheat oven to 350°F.

In a shallow dish, arrange apple slices. Sprinkle with water and lemon juice. In a small bowl, combine sugar, cinnamon, and salt. Sprinkle over apples.

Bake for 45 minutes or until apples are tender. Uncover. Top with shredded cheese. Bake for 5 more minutes or until cheese melts.

Smoked Salmon Cheesecake

Prep time: 30   •   Cook time: 2 hours, 20 minutes   •   Serves 12   •   Serving size: 1 slice

Each serving has: 5 grams nutritive carbohydrate   •   14 grams total protein   •   14 grams from animal source   •   less than 1 gram from plant source

4½ TB. butter

¼ cup dry breadcrumbs

¾ cup grated Gruyère cheese

½ tsp. dill weed

1 medium onion, chopped

1 (8-oz.) pkg. cream cheese

4 eggs

⅓ cup half-and-half

½ tsp. salt

½ lb. smoked salmon, coarsely chopped

Preheat oven to 325°F.

Butter an 8- or 9-inch springform pan, using about 1½ tablespoons butter.

In a small bowl, combine breadcrumbs, ¼ cup Gruyère cheese, and dill. Sprinkle mixture in the prepared pan, turning and tapping to coat evenly.

In a heavy skillet over low heat, melt remaining 3 tablespoons butter. Add onion, cover, and cook until soft, about 10 minutes.

Recipe for Success

This cheesecake even has a cheese crust! The combination of Gruyère cheese and smoked salmon is unique. The recipe makes plenty, so invite a crowd. Eat any leftovers for breakfast and lunch.

In a food processor, blend cream cheese. Add eggs, remaining ½ cup Gruyère cheese, half-and-half, and salt. Process until smooth. By hand, stir in cooked onion and most of salmon, reserving 2 tablespoons. Pour into the prepared pan. Top with remaining salmon.

Set the pan in a large roasting pan filled with enough water to come halfway up the sides of the springform pan. Bake 80 minutes. Turn the oven off, and cool cheesecake in the oven with the door slightly ajar.

Cool to room temperature before removing the sides of pan. Cut into 12 slices, and serve at room temperature.

Chorizo Omelet

Prep time: 25 minutes • Cook time: 5 minutes • Serves 6 • Serving size: 1 wedge

Each serving has: 6 grams carbohydrate • 1 gram fiber • 5 grams nutritive carbohydrate • 18 grams total protein • 18 grams from animal source • 0 grams from plant source

10 oz. *chorizo* sausage

1 cup finely chopped onion

1 clove garlic, minced

1 TB. butter

1 cup chopped green bell peppers

1 (4-oz.) jar pimiento, chopped

9 eggs

½ tsp. salt

¼ tsp. freshly ground black pepper

In a large skillet, crumble chorizo and sauté until lightly browned. Drain and discard drippings. Remove chorizo, and in the same skillet, sauté onion and garlic in butter. Add green peppers and pimiento, and cook 1 minute more. Stir in sausage.

In a large bowl, beat eggs with salt and pepper. Pour eggs over vegetables and sausage in the large skillet. Cook on one side, and then flip over. You may need to cut omelet in half, and turn each side separately. Cut each half into 3 wedges before serving.

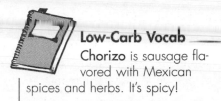

Low-Carb Vocab

Chorizo is sausage flavored with Mexican spices and herbs. It's spicy!

Eggs with Spinach

Prep time: 25 minutes • Cook time: 10 minutes • Serves 4 • Serving size: ¼ recipe which includes 2 eggs

Each serving has: 13 grams nutritive carbohydrate • less than 1 gram fiber • 19 grams total protein • 18 grams from animal source • 1 gram from plant source

3 TB. butter

3 TB. flour

2 cups milk

½ tsp. dried ginger

½ tsp. dried rosemary

½ tsp. dried thyme

½ tsp. celery seed

Salt and pepper to taste

½ cup chopped, cooked spinach

8 hard-boiled eggs, sliced

In a heavy saucepan, melt butter. Add flour all at once and mix well. Cook a few minutes over low heat until butter-flour mixture is pale gold. Stir in milk with a wire whisk, stirring until mixture thickens.

Season with ginger, rosemary, thyme, celery seed, salt, and pepper. Gently stir in spinach and eggs. Chill before serving.

Table Talk

If you're going to make 1 hard-boiled egg, you may as well make a half-dozen or more. Eat them for snacks or make the Pickled Eggs in Chapter 18. It's convenient to have hard-boiled eggs around, but just remember to eat them within a couple days.

Spinach and Ricotta Pie

Prep time: 25 minutes • Cook time: 50 minutes • Serves 8 • Serving size: 1 slice

Each serving has: 8 grams nutritive carbohydrate • less than 1 gram fiber • 19 grams total protein • 18 grams from animal source • 1 gram from plant source

1 (10-oz.) pkg. frozen spinach, finely chopped

2 TB. butter

4 oz. prosciutto

1 garlic clove, minced

3 eggs

¾ cup grated Parmesan cheese

1 (15-oz.) pkg. ricotta cheese

Salt to taste

Recipe for Success

This is good-for-you food—low carb, complete protein, and a Mediterranean flavor. Serve with a tossed salad with romaine or Bibb lettuce. Choose a fruit soufflé or lemon mousse for dessert.

Preheat oven to 375°F.

Cook spinach until tender. Drain and squeeze dry. Heat butter in a small skillet. Add prosciutto and cook for 3 minutes. Stir in garlic, and remove from heat.

Beat eggs until lightly lemon colored. Add Parmesan cheese, ricotta cheese, spinach, prosciutto, and salt, and mix lightly.

Pour into a greased soufflé dish. Bake for 50 minutes or until done. Cut into 8 portions to serve.

Cheesy Baked Eggs

Prep time: 10 minutes • Cook time: 15 minutes • Serves 6 • Serving size: 1 egg

Each serving has: 3 grams nutritive carbohydrate • 11 grams total protein • 11 grams from animal source • 0 grams from plant source

4 TB. butter

1 onion, finely chopped

Salt and cayenne to taste

1 cup grated cheddar cheese

6 eggs

½ cup heavy cream or chicken broth

Preheat oven to 350°F.

Melt butter in a skillet, and sauté onion until tender. Butter 6 individual baking dishes, and layer onions on the bottom, topped with salt, cayenne, and ½ cheese. Gently break each egg (without breaking yolks) onto cheese. Cover with cream, and top with remaining cheese.

Cover dishes with foil, and bake 15 minutes until yolks are set and whites are cooked.

Recipe for Success

Add additional seasonings to taste such as basil, dill, and oregano, or add shredded vegetables layered on top of onions such as squash or carrots. Refrigerate leftovers and eat the next day.

Cold Egg Cream Salad

Prep time: 20 minutes plus time to chill • Cook time: 0 minutes • Serves 6 • Serving size: 2 halves with sauce

Each serving has: 5 grams nutritive carbohydrate • 8 grams total protein • 8 grams from animal source • 0 grams from plant source

6 hard-boiled eggs	3 TB. minced onion
2 egg yolks, beaten	¼ cup minced celery
2 TB. warm vinegar	½ cup cream, whipped
2 TB. butter	¼ cup mayonnaise
½ tsp. sugar	6 sprigs fresh parsley
¼ tsp. salt	1 tsp. paprika
½ tsp. ground black pepper	

Peel boiled eggs, and cut in half. Place in a serving bowl and set aside. Beat together egg yolks and warm vinegar, and cook over low heat, stirring until thickened. Set aside.

In a separate bowl, cream butter, sugar, salt, pepper, onion, and celery. Stir in egg mixture and cool.

Fold in whipped cream and mayonnaise.

Pour dressing over eggs in the serving bowl; garnish with parsley and paprika. Refrigerate and serve cold.

Recipe for Success

This dish is perfect for those lazy dog days of summer. It makes a nice cool dish for a weekend brunch.

Sausage Muffins

Prep time: 15 minutes • Cook time: 25 minutes • Serves 12 • Serving size: 1 muffin

Each serving has: 3 grams nutritive carbohydrate • 22 grams total protein • 22 grams from animal source • 0 grams from plant source

½ lb. pork sausage, bulk

12 eggs

½ cup chopped onion

¼ cup chopped green bell pepper

½ tsp. ground black pepper

½ tsp. salt

¼ tsp. garlic powder

½ cup shredded sharp cheddar cheese

Recipe for Success

With no flour, these muffins are very low carb. They make the perfect breakfast, or use them as an accompaniment to soup and salad for lunch. When made in the tiny muffin tins, they make the perfect appetizer or party food.

Preheat oven to 350°F.

Brown sausage and drain. In a separate bowl, beat eggs; add onion, bell pepper, black pepper, salt, and garlic powder. Stir in sausage and cheese.

Spoon into 12 muffin cups. Bake 20 to 25 minutes. Test doneness by inserting a knife into center of a muffin. Muffins are done when the knife comes out clean.

The Least You Need to Know

♦ You get complete protein and low-carb eating with egg and cheese main dishes.

♦ Egg and cheese combinations are so versatile they blend well with a wide variety of fruits and vegetables.

♦ Egg and cheese meals are often quick and easy to make.

♦ Keep eggs and cheese in your refrigerator just in case you need them for a delicious dinner.

Chapter

16

Salads Make a Meal

In This Chapter

- ◆ Not your everyday boring salads
- ◆ Salads mean low carb and high fiber
- ◆ Only the freshest ingredients

"More salads?" you're thinking. "Please, no." If you've been trying to eat healthy and eat low carb, the thought of more salads seems downright depressing. We understand. After years of salads for lunch, we're tired of salads, too. There's only so much lettuce anyone needs to eat in his or her lifetime.

So we promise this chapter will be filled with pleasant surprises, including some delicious main dish salads. We want you to toss out what's boring and instead toss salad ingredients with the most fragrant and wonderful dressings imaginable. You'll use walnut oil, chilies, and cilantro. You'll add curry and steak, even fennel and salami. You'll load your salads with dried cranberries, pine nuts, and capers.

These are salads fit for a king and for you. They're totally scrumptious, very low carb, and almost—shall we say—exciting! So read on, get out the salad bowl, and have fun. Great eating awaits you.

Low-Carb Salads

Vegetable salads are naturally low carb. With the main dish salads in this chapter, you also get plenty of complete protein because we include protein-rich ingredients. The total carb count, though, is somewhat higher than meat-only meals. That's because all vegetables contain carbohydrates. However, of all the categories of carbohydrates—starches, sugars, fruits, and vegetables—vegetables have the lowest counts.

A main course salad can supply you with 3, 4, or even 5 servings of fruits and vegetables. In other words, in 1 meal you can consume the 5 servings that equal your minimum daily quota. The salad dressings add the fat you need to have a balanced meal.

Here's more good news. The lettuces and vegetables in these salads add fiber to your diet. Some people think that one drawback of a low-carb diet is a lack of dietary fiber. This is not true. Vegetables and fruits, such as you find in these recipes, give you plenty of fiber. You can definitely eat low carb *and* high fiber, especially if you conscientiously eat 5 to 10 servings of vegetables and fruits each day.

Salad Ingredients

For most of these recipes you'll use raw vegetables, so you want the highest quality you can get. Organically grown versions are often available if you prefer them. In any case, go for the freshest and ripest you can find.

- **Fresh greens.** Select the freshest and ripest lettuces and vegetables. If the selection at the grocery store doesn't look that great, ask one of the produce specialists to bring out the back stock. Chances are good it's fresh and crisp.

- **Home grown.** If you have a vegetable garden, you already know the delights of fresh-picked lettuce and tomatoes. Vegetables don't get any better than home-grown, although we suspect the sweat and love that went into growing them makes them taste even more delicious.

- **Oils.** Use only expeller-pressed oils. If an oil has been processed in any other way, it has been heated. Heat destroys the taste and the nutritional value. Plus, heat-processed oils can add unhealthy trans-fatty acids to your otherwise healthy salad. Store all expeller-pressed oils except olive oil in your refrigerator. Otherwise they may get rancid and end up tasting terrible.

 Hot Potato
Some farmers' markets offer home and locally grown produce. But some vendors cheat. Be careful if you buy at the farmer's market that you aren't purchasing produce grown in another country!

- **Lemon and lime juice.** Your best choice is fresh squeezed. The second best choice is bottled organic fresh-squeezed juice with no preservatives. Your worst choice is bottled juice with preservatives.

♦ **Vinegars.** Vinegars are a delectable world unto themselves. Your choices include red or white wine vinegars. There are many balsamic vinegars and a wide range of flavored varieties—red raspberry, tarragon, orange—you name it. When you find a favorite, use it in these recipes wherever vinegar is called for.

Pleasurable Salads

Eat salads because they taste good. Forget that they are also good for you, as that kind of thinking can ruin a delicious meal. Deep down, your body actually hungers for lots of this kind of food, so regularly make it part of your eating.

If you have room left after eating your salad, enjoy a wonderful dessert from the low-carb dessert or chocolate chapters (24 and 25).

Pacific Seafood Salad

Prep time: 20 minutes plus 1 hour marinating time • Cook time: 0 • Serves 6
• Serving size: ⅙ recipe

Each serving has: 18 grams carbohydrate • 4 grams fiber • 14 grams nutritive carbohydrate
• 24 grams total protein • 22 grams from animal source • 2 grams from plant source

¼ cup olive oil

3 TB. red wine vinegar

1 TB. fresh lemon juice

2 tsp. Dijon mustard

1 tsp. anchovy paste

¼ tsp. freshly ground black pepper

1 lb. cooked tiny shrimp, bay scallops, or a combination of both

4 tsp. freshly grated Parmesan cheese

3 medium avocados, peeled and halved

12 oz. Monterey Jack cheese, shredded

Combine oil, vinegar, lemon juice, mustard, anchovy paste, and pepper in a lidded jar and shake well. Pour dressing over seafood, and add Parmesan cheese; mix well. Marinate for 1 hour.

Place 1 avocado half in each of 6 individual ramekins. Divide seafood evenly among avocados. Sprinkle with Monterey Jack cheese. Place ramekins under heated broiler until cheese melts. Serve immediately.

Recipe for Success

Many favorite flavors combine here for a refreshing main course salad. You can omit the anchovy paste and add 1 teaspoon capers, if desired.

Hot Chicken Salad

Prep time: 10 minutes plus time to cook and debone chicken • Cook time: 20 minutes • Serves 6 • Serving size: ¾ cup

Each serving has: 8 grams carbohydrate • 2 grams fiber • 6 grams nutritive carbohydrate • 20 grams total protein • 17 grams from animal source • 3 grams from plant source

2 cups cooked, deboned chicken, cut into small pieces, ¼ cup broth reserved

2 TB. butter

2 cups diced celery

½ cup slivered almonds

1 cup chopped green onions

¼ cup mayonnaise

8 oz. cream cheese, softened

Salt and pepper to taste

2 TB. lemon juice

Paprika, for garnish

Chill reserved chicken broth, and remove congealed fat. Set aside cut-up chicken.

Preheat oven to 400°F.

Melt butter in a skillet, and sauté celery, almonds, and green onions till soft.

Recipe for Success

This recipe is delicious served hot or cold. Substitute walnuts for almonds, and you'll get additional healthy omega-3 fats.

In a bowl, combine mayonnaise and cream cheese, and stir into a paste. Add reserved chicken broth, salt, pepper, and lemon juice, stirring well until smooth. Add chicken and sautéed celery, almonds, and onions. Pour into a buttered baking dish.

Sprinkle with paprika, and bake for 20 minutes.

Steak Salad

Prep time: 20 minutes plus 2 to 3 hours marinating time • Cook time: 0 • Serves 6 • Serving size: 1 cup

Each serving plain salad has: 6 grams carbohydrate • 2 grams fiber • 4 grams nutritive carbohydrate • 23 grams total protein • 22 grams from animal source • 1 gram from plant source

3 cups rare roast beef, cut in thin strips

2 tomatoes, cut in wedges

1 green bell pepper, cut in strips

1 cup sliced celery

⅓ cup sliced green onions

⅓ cup sliced fresh mushrooms

4 cups mixed greens, such as Bibb, leaf, or romaine lettuce, or Savoy cabbage

Marinade #1:

Each serving has: 5 grams carbohydrates for 3 tablespoons marinade

½ cup teriyaki sauce

⅓ cup dry sherry

⅓ cup salad oil

3 TB. white vinegar

½ tsp. ground ginger

Marinade #2:

Each serving has: 1 gram carbohydrate for 3 tablespoons marinade

½ tsp. salt

¼ tsp. pepper

3 dashes Tabasco sauce

¼ tsp. Worcestershire sauce

2 tsp. lemon juice

¼ cup red wine vinegar

1½ cups salad oil

2 TB. green peppercorns

Combine beef, tomatoes, green pepper, celery, onions, and mushrooms.

In a screw-top jar, combine ingredients for marinade of your choice. Shake well. Pour over beef mixture. Toss to coat well. Cover and refrigerate 2 or 3 hours.

Drain, reserving marinade.

Place greens in a large salad bowl; top with marinated meat and vegetables. Pass reserved marinade for dressing.

Recipe for Success

Rare roast beef isn't used often in salads, but the meat takes well to highly flavored marinades such as the ones in this recipe.

Scallop Salad

Prep time: 20 minutes • Cook time: 10 minutes • Serves 4 • Serving size: ¼ recipe

Each serving has: 8 grams carbohydrate • 2 grams fiber • 6 grams nutritive carbohydrate • 6 grams total protein • 4 grams from animal source • 2 grams from plant source

½ cup dry white wine	½ tsp. salt
¼ lb. bay scallops	½ tsp. freshly ground black pepper
6 TB. virgin olive oil	1 clove garlic, minced
1 TB. red wine vinegar	1 medium tomato, chopped
1 TB. balsamic vinegar	1 small cucumber, chopped
1 TB. fresh lemon juice	2 stalks celery, chopped
1 TB. minced fresh parsley	1 small head red leaf lettuce
1 tsp. sugar	1 head Bibb lettuce, torn into pieces

To make salad, in a small saucepan, bring wine to a slow boil. Add scallops and cook until no longer transparent; drain.

To make dressing, combine olive oil, red wine vinegar, balsamic vinegar, lemon juice, parsley, sugar, salt, pepper, and garlic in lidded jar and shake well.

Recipe for Success

The fresh ocean taste of scallops gives this salad a vacation feeling. You can enjoy it even in the winter months.

Pour ⅓ dressing over scallops; chill.

In a separate bowl, marinate tomato, cucumber, and celery in another ⅓ dressing; chill.

To serve, line 4 plates with red leaf lettuce. Top with Bibb lettuce. Divide marinated vegetables among the 4 plates. Arrange scallops on vegetables, and drizzle with remaining ⅓ dressing.

Seafood with Curried Chutney Dressing

Prep time: 30 minutes • Cook time: 0 • Serves 8 • Serving size: ⅛ recipe

Each serving has (without dressing): 17 grams carbohydrate • 3 grams fiber • 14 grams nutritive carbohydrate • 29 grams total protein • 25 grams from animal source • 4 grams from plant source • 3 tablespoons dressing equals 10 grams carbohydrates

2 TB. peach or mango chutney	4 stalks celery, chopped
1 cup mayonnaise	4 green onions, chopped
2 TB. tarragon vinegar	1 lb. lump crabmeat
2 TB. vegetable oil	1 lb. shrimp, cooked, peeled, and deveined
2 tsp. curry powder	1 cup cashews, toasted
¼ cup half-and-half	1 cup coconut, toasted
1 head lettuce, torn into pieces	1 cup raisins

To make dressing, combine peach chutney, mayonnaise, vinegar, vegetable oil, curry powder, and half-and-half. Mix well.

To make salad, combine lettuce with celery and green onions; toss well. Arrange crabmeat and shrimp on top of lettuce, and drizzle with dressing. Sprinkle cashews, coconut, and raisins to taste over salad.

Recipe for Success

This mixture has all the best tastes of curry in one dish—the cashews, coconut, raisins, and chutney. It transports you—at least in your taste buds—to a more exotic locale.

Table Talk

To toast coconut in the oven, set temperature to 350°F. Spread coconut in a thin layer in a large shallow baking pan. Put pan in oven and toast for about 10 minutes, stirring every couple minutes until just lightly browned. It's best to toast the cashews separately, as they take longer to turn golden brown.

Halibut Salad with Carrots and Fennel

Prep time: 30 minutes plus 30 minutes marinating time • Cook time: 10 minutes
• Serves 6 • Serving size: 1 halibut fillet plus ⅙ carrot and fennel mixture

Each serving has: 11 grams carbohydrate • 2 grams fiber • 9 grams nutritive carbohydrate
• 23 grams total protein • 23 grams from animal source • 0 grams from plant source

6 (4-oz.) halibut fillets	½ cup red vinegar
2 TB. olive oil	¼ cup olive oil
3 TB. orange juice	**For dressing:**
1 TB. minced fresh ginger root	2 TB. orange juice
1 TB. freshly ground black pepper	1 tsp. orange rind
1 tsp. minced, seeded jalapeño pepper	½ cup olive oil
For carrot-fennel salad:	2 tsp. Dijon mustard
2 cups shredded carrots	2 tsp. red wine vinegar
2 cups shredded fennel bulb	Salt and pepper to taste

Marinate halibut fillets in olive oil, orange juice, ginger root, black pepper, and jalapeño pepper for at least 30 minutes. Before cooking halibut, combine carrots, fennel, vinegar, and oil. Make dressing by combining orange juice, orange rind, olive oil, mustard, vinegar, salt, and pepper.

Recipe for Success
This recipe is a whole meal in a salad. The combination of fennel and carrots is unusual and enhances the halibut.

Grill halibut over medium-high heat for about 4 minutes per side. Baste with marinade.

Spoon carrot-fennel salad onto individual serving plates. Place halibut fillets on top of salad. Spoon about 1 tablespoon dressing over each serving of halibut.

Chicken Cole Slaw

Prep time: 30 minutes plus 24 hours chill time • Cook time: 5 minutes • Serves 10 • Serving size: $^1/_{10}$ recipe

Each serving has: 9 grams carbohydrate • 1 gram fiber • 8 grams nutritive carbohydrate • 15 grams total protein • 13 grams from animal source • 2 grams from plant source

3 cups shredded chicken	½ cup slivered almonds
1 head cabbage, sliced into ⅜-inch strips	⅓ cup olive oil
2 green onions, sliced	¼ cup cider vinegar
2 carrots, grated	1 tsp. celery seed
1 green bell pepper, sliced into ¼-inch strips	2 TB. sugar
1 red bell pepper, sliced into ¼-inch strips	1 tsp. salt
1 (8-oz.) can water chestnuts	½ tsp. freshly ground black pepper

In a large bowl, combine chicken, cabbage, green onions, carrots, green and red bell peppers, water chestnuts, and almonds.

In a saucepan, heat oil, vinegar, celery seed, sugar, salt, and pepper to boiling. Pour over salad, toss, and refrigerate for 24 hours.

Recipe for Success

Who would have thought to put chicken into a vinaigrette coleslaw? The results are simply good eating.

Salmon Salad with Pickles and Raisins

Prep time: 15 minutes • Cook time: 0 • Serves 3 • Serving size: ⅓ recipe

Each serving has: 8 grams carbohydrate • 1 gram fiber • 7 grams nutritive carbohydrate • 14 grams total protein • 13 grams from animal source • 1 gram from plant source

1 (6½-oz.) can salmon	3 TB. pecans, coarsely chopped
1 hard-boiled egg, chopped	2 TB. mayonnaise
1 small sweet gherkin pickle, chopped	Salt and freshly ground pepper to taste
1 TB. raisins	

In a small bowl, break apart salmon with a fork. Add egg, pickle, raisins, and pecans. Mix together with mayonnaise. Add salt and pepper to taste.

Variation: Substitute albacore tuna for salmon. Albacore contains more essential fatty acids than regular tuna.

Recipe for Success

Serve this with raw vegetables such as jicama, carrots, and celery on a bed of lettuce, or with sliced apples, pears, and peaches. Eat the salad with a fork. Any way you eat it, the pecans, raisins, and pickles make this an interesting salad.

Oriental Spinach Salad

Prep time: 25 minutes • Cook time: 0 • Serves 8 • Serving size: ⅛ recipe

Each serving has: 8 grams carbohydrate • 1 gram fiber • 7 grams nutritive carbohydrate • 10 grams total protein • 9 grams from animal source • 1 gram from plant source

1 cup walnut oil	8 oz. fresh bean sprouts
½ cup red wine vinegar	1 (8-oz.) can water chestnuts
1 TB. molasses	4 hard-boiled eggs, sliced
2 TB. ketchup	¼ cup cashews
1 TB. Worcestershire sauce	8 strips crisply fried bacon, crumbled
1 small onion, quartered	8 slices crisply fried salami, crumbled
1 (10-oz.) pkg. fresh spinach	

To make dressing, combine walnut oil, red wine vinegar, molasses, ketchup, Worcestershire sauce, and onion in a blender or food processor. Process on high for a couple minutes.

Wash, dry, and remove stems from spinach, then tear into pieces. Add bean sprouts, water chestnuts, eggs, cashews, bacon, and salami. Toss with dressing.

Recipe for Success

This recipe makes a light main-course salad. For convenience and easier cleanup, use the microwave to cook the bacon and salami.

Artichokes Stuffed with Shrimp

Prep time: 25 minutes • Cook time: 1 hour for artichokes • Serves 4 • Serving size: 1 artichoke plus ¼ shrimp-mayonnaise mixture

Each serving has: 8 grams carbohydrate • 3 grams fiber • 5 grams nutritive carbohydrate • 6 grams total protein • 5 grams from animal source • 1 gram from plant source

4 large artichokes

1 TB. Dijon mustard

2 TB. lemon juice

¼ cup mayonnaise

½ tsp. tarragon

Salt and freshly ground pepper to taste

1 (6-oz.) can baby shrimp (get the really small ones)

Steam artichokes over boiling water for 1 hour or until done. Cool. When cool, carefully open out artichoke leaves, and with a spoon, scrape out inner inedible part just above artichoke heart.

In a small bowl, combine mustard, lemon juice, mayonnaise, tarragon, salt, and pepper. Drain shrimp and stir into mayonnaise mixture.

Spoon shrimp mixture into hollowed-out part of each artichoke.

Recipe for Success

Use the artichoke leaves to scoop out the shrimp for eating. When you finish eating the leaves, enough dressing should remain to eat the heart. It takes time to eat this salad—a major advantage to slowing down stress and enjoying the meal.

Beef Salad with Capers

Prep time: 30 minutes plus 3 hours marinating time • Cook time: 0 • Serves 8 • Serving size: ⅙ recipe

Each serving has (without dressing): 6 grams carbohydrate • 2 grams fiber • 4 grams nutritive carbohydrate • 30 grams total protein • 28 grams from animal source • 2 grams from plant source • 2 tablespoons dressing contain 3 carbohydrates

4 tsp. capers

4 TB. fresh lemon juice

½ cup red wine vinegar

4 tsp. Dijon mustard

1 cup olive oil

½ tsp. freshly ground black pepper

1 tsp. sugar

1½ lb. rare roast beef, cut into 1-inch strips

¾ lb. fresh string beans, trimmed, blanched, and sliced

½ lb. mushrooms, sliced

3 tomatoes, cut into wedges

1 (14-oz.) can hearts of palm, cut into rings

1 bunch watercress, washed and stems removed

1 head romaine lettuce, torn into bite-size pieces

Prepare dressing by combining capers, lemon juice, vinegar, mustard, oil, pepper, and sugar. Pour about ½ over beef, and marinate in the refrigerator for at least 3 hours.

Recipe for Success

This is a completely balanced meal all by itself. It feels as if you are eating a rainbow. And you are—a rainbow of vegetables.

Remove from refrigerator and add beans, mushrooms, tomatoes, hearts of palm, and watercress. Add additional dressing as needed.

Place lettuce on individual serving plates. Top with meat mixture.

Save extra salad dressing for later use.

Aslan Smoked Turkey Slaw

Prep time: 20 minutes plus chill time • Cook time: 5 minutes • Serves 6 • Serving size: 1 cup

Each serving has: 18 grams carbohydrate • 3 grams fiber • 15 grams nutritive carbohydrate • 19 grams total protein • 16 grams from animal source • 3 grams from plant source

1 cup fresh or frozen pea pods	½ small red onion, sliced
2 TB. brown sugar	½ small red onion, chopped
¼ cup rice vinegar	1 cup frozen green peas
3 TB. olive oil	Salt and pepper to taste
1 TB. sesame oil	1 lb. smoked turkey, cut into small cubes or thin strips
4 cups shredded Chinese cabbage	6 red lettuce leaves
1 cup shredded carrot	

Blanch pea pods in boiling water for 2 minutes. Drain and set aside. Combine brown sugar, rice vinegar, olive oil, and sesame oil in a saucepan over medium heat and simmer.

In a large bowl, combine cabbage, carrot, sliced onion, chopped onion, pea pods, peas, salt, and pepper. Pour hot dressing over all and toss well. Add turkey and toss; chill. Serve 1 scoop in each lettuce leaf.

Recipe for Success

What a light refreshing meal this is with just the right touch of sweet and sour with crunch! Serve with Parmesan Crackers and tossed fresh fruit salad for a light lunch.

Basil Turkey with Peppers

Prep time: 20 minutes • Cook time: 5 minutes • Serves 6 • Serving size: ½ cup turkey with 1 cup spinach salad

Each serving has: 12 grams carbohydrate • 3 grams fiber • 9 grams nutritive carbohydrate • 27 grams total protein • 22 grams from animal source • 5 grams from plant source

2 TB. olive oil

1 green bell pepper, cut into 1-inch pieces

1 red bell pepper, cut into 1-inch pieces

1 TB. minced garlic

3 cups cubed cooked turkey

¼ cup chopped fresh basil or 1 tsp. dried

6 TB. coarsely chopped macadamia nuts

¼ cup balsamic vinegar

6 cups raw baby spinach leaves

3 cups grape or cherry tomatoes, sliced in half

6 TB. chopped red onion

Recipe for Success

This is a different take on the traditional hot spinach salad. Substitute any seafood or meat for the turkey for a change of flavor.

Heat olive oil in a skillet, and sauté peppers and garlic until tender. Mix in turkey cubes, basil, nuts, and vinegar; stir and cook for 5 minutes over medium heat.

Serve ½ cup turkey mixture over baby spinach with ½ cup sliced grape tomatoes and 1 tablespoon chopped red onion. Pour any remaining hot dressing over salad; if needed, sprinkle salad with additional balsamic vinegar and olive oil.

Chicken and Fresh Fruit Salad

Prep time: 20 minutes plus 30 minutes chill time • Cook time: 0 • Serves 6
• Serving size: 1 cup

Each serving has: 20 grams carbohydrate • 1 gram fiber • 19 grams nutritive carbohydrate
• 33 grams total protein • 32 grams from animal source • 1 gram from plant source

3 cups cooked, boneless, cubed chicken

2 cups cubed watermelon or cantaloupe

3 cups cubed pears or peaches

1 cup chopped fresh mushrooms

½ lb. blue cheese, crumbled

2 cups sour cream

1 tsp. sugar

6 large lettuce leaves, such as romaine or Bibb lettuce

6 sprigs fresh mint, for garnish

¼ cup slivered almonds, for garnish

Combine chicken, watermelon, pears, mushrooms, blue cheese, sour cream, and sugar. Toss gently, then chill.

Serve on lettuce leaf, and garnish with mint sprig and a sprinkle of slivered almonds.

Recipe for Success _____

This recipe is a complete meal as is. Add a vegetable, if you prefer, or save room for a rich chocolate dessert such as Chocolate Soufflé or a Double Chocolate Brownie—now that's planning ahead!

Grilled Fish Salad

Prep time: 15 minutes • Cook time: 15 minutes to grill fish • Serves 6 • Serving size: 1 cup

Each serving has: 13 grams carbohydrate • 1 gram fiber • 12 grams nutritive carbohydrate • 32 grams total protein • 29 grams from animal source • 3 grams from plant source

6 (5-oz.) fish fillets, baked or grilled

1 cup fresh baby spinach leaves, torn into bite-size pieces

4 cups fresh red leaf or green leaf lettuce, torn into bite-size pieces

1 cup shredded cabbage

½ cup sliced mushrooms

½ cup chopped green onions

6 marinated artichoke hearts, cut in half

For Garlic Mayonnaise:

2 tsp. garlic powder, or 1 tsp. garlic juice (can be found in the condiment section of your grocery store)

¾ cup mayonnaise

Recipe for Success

This salad is actually best made with leftover grilled or baked fish. So next time you decide to have fish, cook extra to have on hand for this dish! It is such a light meal that you have room for a cup of soup and any scrumptious dessert.

Grill or bake fish as desired. Place fish on individual plates.

In a large bowl, toss together spinach leaves, lettuce, cabbage, mushrooms, green onions, and artichoke hearts. Serve salad on top of hot or cold fish. Combine garlic powder and mayonnaise, and drizzle each salad with 2 tablespoons Garlic Mayonnaise, vinaigrette, or other dressing of choice.

Layered Roast Salad

Prep time: 30 minutes plus chill time   •   Cook time: 0   •   Serves 6   •   Serving size: 1 cup

Each serving has (dressing included): 20 grams carbohydrate   •   4 grams fiber   •   16 grams nutritive carbohydrate   •   25 grams total protein   •   22 grams from animal source   •   3 grams from plant source

4 cups shredded lettuce	½ cup chopped green onions
2 cups cauliflower florets	2 cucumbers, chopped
1 cup shredded carrots	1¼ cups Green Goddess Dressing (recipe in Chapter 20)
½ cup sliced celery	
1 lb. cooked roast beef, cut into bite-size pieces	Paprika
1 cup chunky salsa	Fresh parsley sprigs

In a large salad bowl, layer lettuce, cauliflower, carrots, celery, roast beef, salsa, green onions, and cucumbers. Spread Green Goddess dressing over top, and refrigerate at least 30 minutes or overnight.

Just before serving, sprinkle with paprika for color, and add a few parsley sprigs for garnish.

Recipe for Success _____

Vary this basic recipe to suit your taste. Use chicken instead of beef or Ranch dressing instead of Green Goddess; use any vegetables you prefer. This makes a beautiful presentation layered and served in a deep glass bowl.

Roast Beef Scoop

Prep time: 15 minutes • Cook time: 0 (using leftover or pre-cooked roast beef)
• Serves 6 • Serving size: ½ cup

Each serving has: 8 grams carbohydrate • 1 gram fiber • 7 grams nutritive carbohydrate
• 18 grams total protein • 16 grams from animal source • 2 grams from plant source

½ cup mayonnaise

¼ cup cream

¼ cup sour cream

¼ cup grated Parmesan cheese

½ tsp. cayenne

½ tsp. dill weed

12 oz. shredded cooked roast beef (2 cups)

1 cup shredded carrots

½ cup chopped bell pepper

Lettuce leaves

Recipe for Success

Serve Roast Beef Scoop with marinated vegetables and tomato slices. Green Goddess dressing makes a great dip for raw vegetable snacks.

Combine mayonnaise, cream, sour cream, Parmesan cheese, cayenne, and dill weed in a food processor. Add roast beef, carrots, and bell pepper, and pulse just until combined.

Serve a scoop on lettuce leaves. You can also roll up lettuce leaves, and eat them as a rollup or with a fork.

Roasted Vegetable-Fruit-Beef Salad

Prep time: 15 minutes • Cook time: 30 minutes • Serves 6 • Serving size: 1 cup mixed greens with 1 cup topping

Each serving has: 19 grams carbohydrate • 1 gram fiber • 18 grams nutritive carbohydrate • 35 grams total protein • 32 grams from animal source • 3 grams from plant source

2 zucchini, cut into 1-inch medallions	¼ cup balsamic vinegar
2 large red bell peppers, cut into 1-inch strips	1 TB. minced garlic
2 onions, cut into 1-inch pieces	1 tsp. dried rosemary
18 mushrooms	1 tsp. ground black pepper
12 cherry tomatoes	4 TB. olive oil
12 cubes cantaloupe	1½ lb. beef steak, cut into strips
12 grapes	6 cups mixed greens

Preheat oven to 425°F.

Place zucchini, bell peppers, onions, mushrooms, tomatoes, cantaloupe, and grapes on a greased baking sheet. Mix together vinegar, garlic, rosemary, white pepper, and 2 tablespoons olive oil. Drizzle dressing on vegetables and fruit, and roast in oven for 30 minutes, stirring once.

Stir-fry beef strips in a skillet in remaining 2 table-spoons olive oil until done, about 10 minutes.

Arrange beef strips over mixed greens, and top with hot vegetables and fruit. If additional dressing is needed, sprinkle with olive oil and balsamic vinegar.

Recipe for Success

Roasted fruit is an unusual treat for many; experiment with other fruits or even double up on veggies and omit fruit for a lower carb count.

Turkey-Apple Salad

Prep time: 15 minutes plus chill time • Cook time: 0 • Serves 6 • Serving size: ¾ cup

Each serving has: 19 grams carbohydrate • 2 grams fiber • 17 grams nutritive carbohydrate • 35 grams total protein • 32 grams from animal source • 3 grams from plant source

2 cups diced, cooked, boneless turkey or chicken

2 cups diced red or green apples

½ cup chopped walnuts or other nuts of choice

½ cup chopped celery

½ cup mayonnaise

2 TB. brown sugar

3 TB. spicy brown mustard

Dash dried rosemary

Salt and pepper to taste

6 red lettuce leaves

Recipe for Success

What a refreshing summer lunch this is or the perfect take-along meal any time of the year! Serve with a cold fruit or vegetable soup for a completely satisfying meal.

Combine turkey, apples, walnuts, and celery; set aside.

In a small bowl, combine mayonnaise, brown sugar, mustard, rosemary, salt, and pepper.

Combine mayonnaise mixture with turkey mixture and chill. Serve a scoop of turkey salad on a red lettuce leaf.

The Least You Need to Know

- Main dish salads are a superb, delicious way to eat a balanced meal.
- Main dish salads are wonderfully varied, interesting, and delicious.
- Make salad dressings with olive oil and other expeller-pressed raw oils such as walnut oil.
- Salads are deeply satisfying when you can get beyond eating them because they are good for you.

Part 5

Side Dishes

Snacks and appetizers give you plenty of variety for in-between-meals munching and entertaining. From Parmesan crackers to a chocolate chip cheese appetizer, these low-carb treats satisfy your hunger and your taste buds.

Vegetables, fruits, and side salads rate a chapter each. You'll have an easy time eating enough fruits and vegetables with these low-carb recipes. Prepare them to accompany main dish entrees in Parts 1 and 2, and get set to love eating your veggies!

Chapter 17

Appetizers

In This Chapter

◆ Eating before meals
◆ Recognizing low-carb appetizers
◆ Eating low carb at cocktail parties
◆ Making a meal of appetizers

Cocktail parties are one of the easiest places to eat low carb naturally—provided the host or hostess prepared traditional appetizers such as meatballs, water chestnuts wrapped in bacon, crudités, cheese cubes, chicken livers wrapped in bacon, shrimp cocktail, or deviled eggs.

The list of delicious low-carb tidbits goes on and on. You could make a whole meal of low-carb appetizers … and plenty of us have done just that! At a party you may want to forego the chips, but, happily, you usually can enjoy the dip. When you are hungry for appealing bites of low-carb foods, traditional appetizers such as vegetables, meats, fish, and cheese make for delightful eating.

Unfortunately, party givers are serving breads and starchy foods in place of low-carb fare at many of today's cocktail buffets. If you go to one of these parties, you may still need to choose carefully what you eat.

And remember, when it's your turn to throw a party, make sure your spread includes lots of low-carb yummies.

Bite-Size Low Carb

Virtually all traditional appetizers are low carb. You can usually expect to find meats, fish, cheese, or seafood, with or without vegetables and fruit. The recipes in this chapter are mostly high protein plus a couple vegetable offerings. Definitely, they are no starch and totally delicious.

On the menus of many restaurants, the appetizers look more appealing than the entrées. So go ahead and order one or two appetizers and a side salad for your meal. You'll be totally satisfied. It's also a good approach to consider for your own meals and parties.

Beauty, the saying goes, lies in the eye of the beholder. This may explain why appetizers are so appealing. Presented well, appetizers look marvelously delicious. Fortunately, even the simplest appetizers can appear quite elegant. We know you have better things to do than spend unnecessary time in the kitchen, so these recipes use simple preparation techniques whenever possible.

Table Talk

Have you ever showed up hungry to a party only to discover that there isn't any low-carb food to eat? Picking the chunks of chicken out of the chicken salad definitely seems out of place and unappreciative. To prevent this scenario from happening again, take the hostess a gift of a low-carb appetizer. Make sure the one you prepare has plenty of complete protein. Cook enough for everyone to enjoy and for you to have your fair share … and maybe seconds.

History of Before-Meal Hunger

Very few people can actually wait to eat until dinnertime—at least not people we know. Only those mythological people we have never met can actually go from lunch until 7 or 8 P.M. in the evening without eating. If we have to wait 7 or 8 hours before eating again, when dinner is finally served, we don't eat, we inhale. This is not good. Rapidly consuming food often leads to overeating, creating indigestion and weight gain.

Appetizers solve this problem. Traditionally, appetizers are served anywhere from ½ to 1 hour or even 2 hours before dinner. The length of time often depends on how much alcohol people are willing to drink before they eat, but that's another matter entirely.

The appetizer is the traditional solution to the problem of acute "I'm-ready-to-eat-the-napkins" ravenous hunger. It contains enough food and nourishment to tide you over until dinner is served. The key is to eat a few appetizers but not too many, or dinner won't seem appealing.

As to the alcohol consumption at this pre-dinner time, you'll need to judge how much is fine, how much is enough, and how much is sloppy. Too much will obviously impair your ability to enjoy your food.

Parmesan Snacks

Prep time: 5 minutes   •   Cook time: 10 minutes   •   Serves 8   •   Serving size: ⅛ recipe or 0.4 ounce cheese

Each serving has: 1 gram nutritive carbohydrate   •   8 grams total protein   •   8 grams from animal source   •   0 grams from plant source

1 (6-oz.) pkg. shredded Parmesan cheese

Preheat oven to 400°F.

Spread cheese in a thin layer on a cookie sheet. Bake for 10 to 12 minutes until cheese is lightly toasted and browned. Cool, break into pieces, and serve.

Recipe for Success _____

Everyone likes these Parmesan snacks—they disappear really fast. If you should have any left over, crumble and sprinkle on salads and steamed vegetables.

Chocolate-Chip Cheese Ball

Prep time: 20 minutes plus 3 hours chill time   •   Cook time: 0   •   Serves 20   •   Serving size: ½₀ ball or 2½ tablespoons

Each serving has: 4 grams carbohydrate   •   1 gram fiber   •   3 grams nutritive carbohydrate   •   1 gram total protein   •   1 gram from animal source

1 (8-oz.) pkg. cream cheese, softened

½ cup (1 stick) butter (no substitutes), softened

¼ tsp. vanilla extract

¼ cup confectioners' sugar

2 TB. brown sugar

¾ cup miniature semi-sweet chocolate chips

¾ cup finely chopped pecans

In a mixing bowl, beat cream cheese, butter, and vanilla until fluffy. Gradually add confectioners' and brown sugars; beat just until combined. Stir in chocolate chips.

Cover and refrigerate for 2 hours. Place cream cheese mixture on a large piece of plastic wrap; shape into a ball.

Refrigerate for at least 1 hour. Just before serving, roll cheese ball in pecans.

Brie Stuffed with Sun-Dried Tomatoes and Basil

Prep time: 20 minutes • Cook time: 0 • Serves 6 • Serving size: ⅙ recipe

Each serving has: 5 grams carbohydrate • 1 gram fiber • 4 grams nutritive carbohydrate • 9 grams total protein • 8 grams from animal source • 1 gram from plant source

½ cup chopped fresh basil

10 oil-packed sun-dried tomatoes, drained and oil reserved

2 garlic cloves, peeled

¼ tsp. freshly ground black pepper

1 tsp. fresh lemon juice

1 wedge Brie cheese (about ½ lb.), thoroughly chilled

Recipe for Success

You can eat this delicious appetizer with a fork or spread on slices of jicama, celery root, and other vegetables. You may prepare this recipe 1 day in advance. Serve chilled or at room temperature.

In a food processor, combine basil, sun-dried tomatoes, garlic, pepper, and lemon juice. Process until paste forms. Add oil from sun-dried tomatoes or olive oil if texture is very dry. Mixture needs to be spreadable, but not runny.

Cut Brie in half horizontally. Spread bottom half with reserved sun-dried tomato mixture, and top with remaining half, pressing halves together firmly. Chill in the refrigerator, then bring to room temperature before serving.

Lobster with Mango

Prep time: 20 minutes • Cook time: 0 • Serves 6 • Serving size: ⅙ recipe, about ½ cup lobster plus ⅙ mango and sauce

Each serving has: 14 grams carbohydrate • 1 gram fiber • 13 grams nutritive carbohydrate • 27 grams total protein • 27 grams from animal source • less than 1 gram from plant source

1 tsp. minced ginger root	2 mangos, halved and pitted
4 TB. olive oil	1½ cups cooked lobster meat
2 TB. lemon juice	4 sprigs fresh mint

Recipe for Success

Serve this simple, tasty, and exotic recipe as an appetizer or increase the serving size and serve as a main dish salad on a bed of Bibb lettuce. You can also substitute shrimp for the lobster.

Mix ginger root with olive oil and lemon juice and set aside.

Remove pulp from mangoes, and cut into bite-size pieces. Divide among 4 small plates. Place lobster meat beside mango, and top with a sprig of mint.

Spoon ginger sauce on top of lobster and mango, and serve.

Lobster Pâté

Prep time: 15 minutes plus several hours chill time • Cook time: 0 • Serves: 10 • Serving size: ¼ cup

Each serving has: 2 grams nutritive carbohydrate • 17 grams total protein • 17 grams from animal source

1 (8-oz.) pkg. regular cream cheese, softened	⅛ tsp. fresh chopped cilantro
¼ cup dry white wine	1½ cups lobster meat, finely chopped
½ tsp. salt	

Beat cream cheese and wine with salt and cilantro until smooth. Stir in lobster. Cover and refrigerate several hours or more.

Smoked Salmon Spread

Prep time: 15 minutes plus 1 hour chill time • Cook time: 0 • Serves: 6 • Serving size: ¼ cup

Each serving has: less than 1 gram nutritive carbohydrate • 4 grams total protein • 4 grams from animal source

4 oz. smoked salmon	Freshly ground black pepper to taste
2 dashes Tabasco sauce	½ cup whipping cream
2 dashes Worcestershire sauce	

Hot Potato

The pâtés and spreads in this chapter are low carb. Be sure to follow our serving suggestions to keep them low carb. Don't eat them with regular crackers or breads, or the carb count will go up fast.

In a food processor, process salmon, Tabasco sauce, Worcestershire sauce, and pepper until smooth. Whip cream in a bowl until stiff peaks form. Fold in salmon mixture. Refrigerate for 1 hour or more.

Serve on individual plates on top of lettuce leaves, or serve as a dip with vegetable crudités, such as carrots, jicama, and celery.

Eggplant Spread

Prep time: 10 minutes • Cook time: 35 minutes • Serves 6 • Serving size: ½ cup

Each serving has: 5 grams nutritive carbohydrate • less than 1 gram fiber • less than 1 gram total protein

2 large eggplants	20 green olives, pitted
1¼ cups fresh basil or 1 TB. dried	Salt and pepper to taste
2 TB. minced garlic	

Recipe for Success

This makes a great filling for lettuce leaf rollups or spread on cucumber or raw turnip rounds. If using for raw veggie dip and it needs to be thinned, stir in cream until desired consistency.

Preheat oven to 375°F.

Butter a baking pan, and cover with foil if desired. Cut eggplants in half lengthwise, and lay cut side down on the pan. Bake until eggplant is soft, about 35 minutes. Cool.

Scrape meat out of eggplant shells. Blend in food processor with basil, garlic, olives, salt, and pepper. Let stand at room temperature before serving.

Avocado Margarita

Prep time: 20 minutes • Cook time: 0 • Serves 8 • Serving size: ⅛ recipe

Each serving has: 4 grams carbohydrate • 2 grams fiber • 2 grams nutritive carbohydrate • less than 1 gram total protein • less than 1 gram from plant source

1 TB. minced onion	Juice of 1 lime
2 TB. chopped fresh cilantro	2 medium avocados
Salt and pepper to taste	1 medium-size tomato, chopped

In a small bowl, mix onion, cilantro, salt, pepper, and lime juice.

Cut open avocados, remove pits, and spoon out fruit into a bowl. With a spoon, cut any big chunks of avocado into smaller ones, but keep chunks quite large—1 inch square is fine. Add chopped tomato. Add onion mixture, and stir gently to blend.

Recipe for Success

The secret is in the lime juice and the big chunks of avocado. When Margarita brought this to a potluck, it was gone before we could turn around for seconds. We loved it.

Spinach Cheese Squares

Prep time: 15 minutes • Cook time: 35 minutes • Serves 20 • Yield: 40 squares • Serving size: 2 squares

Each serving has: 4 grams nutritive carbohydrate • 8 grams total protein • 7 grams from animal source • 1 gram from plant source

½ cup (1 stick) butter	1 tsp. salt
3 eggs	1 tsp. baking powder
½ cup flour	1 lb. Monterey Jack cheese, grated
1 cup milk	4 cups chopped fresh spinach

Preheat oven to 350°F.

Melt butter in a 9×13-inch pan.

Beat eggs, adding flour, milk, salt, and baking powder. Add cheese and spinach to the bowl, mixing well.

Pour mixture into the pan, and bake 35 minutes. Cool before serving. Cut into squares.

Deviled Eggs

Prep time: 25 minutes plus chill time • Cook time: 0 • Serves 6 • Serving size: 4 halves

Each serving has: 1 gram nutritive carbohydrate • 13 grams total protein • 13 grams from animal source

12 hard-boiled eggs

Mayonnaise

Salt and freshly ground pepper to taste

¼ tsp. paprika

Peel and cut each egg in half lengthwise, and gently remove yolks, saving whites to refill.

Put all yolks in a bowl, and gently moisten with just enough mayonnaise so they hold together. Add salt and pepper to taste and paprika. Refrigerate until serving.

You can repack eggs with yolk mixture as is, or you can add more zest. Here are some choices:

These additions will have little effect on the carb count:

Recipe for Success

Deviled eggs contain terrific protein and work well as hostess gifts for parties or to take to potluck dinners. It seems everyone loves deviled eggs—they're usually gone within 10 minutes of setting out the serving tray.

- Dry mustard
- Cayenne
- Curry powder
- Caviar
- Minced ham, bacon, or beef
- Grated Parmesan or Roquefort cheese
- Chopped fresh cilantro, basil, rosemary, or tarragon
- Chopped ginger
- Chutney

These could slightly increase carb count:

Table Talk

Adding grated Parmesan cheese to any of the combinations—whether sweet or savory—enhances the flavor and will have guests asking for your "secret" ingredient.

- Chopped black or green olives
- Capers
- Chopped dill pickles
- Minced onion

Baked Avocado

Prep time: 20 minutes • Cook time: 10 minutes • Serves 6 • Serving size: ½ avocado

Each serving has: 12 grams carbohydrate • 4 grams fiber • 8 grams nutritive carbohydrate • 8 grams total protein • 3 grams from animal source • 5 grams from plant source

3 large avocados	¼ cup finely chopped red bell pepper
1 lemon	2 TB. finely chopped onion
Salt to taste	½ tsp. cayenne
3 hard-boiled eggs, peeled and chopped	¼ cup mayonnaise
¼ cup finely chopped celery	3 TB. chopped pine nuts, almonds, or walnuts, for garnish

Preheat oven to 400°F.

Cut avocados in half, leaving peel intact; remove pit. Cut lemon in half, and sprinkle each cut side of avocado with lemon juice to prevent browning; sprinkle with salt.

Combine eggs, celery, red bell pepper, onion, cayenne, and mayonnaise.

Fill each avocado half with scoop of egg mixture, and place on baking pan. Bake 10 minutes. Sprinkle with nuts and serve.

Recipe for Success

Cooked chicken or seafood may be added to mixture to fill avocados, if desired. For the main dish, make a larger batch with added protein and bake in a casserole dish without the avocado. To serve, place lettuce or cabbage leaf onto a plate, scoop cooked mixture onto the leaf, and top with sliced avocado.

Baked Swiss Onion Dip

Prep time: 15 minutes • Cook time: 30 minutes • Serves 24 • Serving size: ¼ cup

Each serving has: 6 grams nutritive carbohydrate • less than 1 gram fiber • 4 grams total protein • 4 grams from animal source • less than 1 gram from plant source

3 sweet onions, chopped in large pieces

2 TB. butter

8 oz. shredded Swiss cheese (2 cups)

1 cup sour cream

1 cup mayonnaise

¼ cup white wine

½ tsp. cayenne

1 tsp. white pepper

1 tsp. garlic powder

Recipe for Success

This is great as a dip for raw vegetables or small cubes of meat. It makes a delicious rich sauce to serve over vegetables such as cauliflower or broccoli—all your guests will want this recipe!

Preheat oven to 375°F.

In a large skillet over medium heat, sauté onions in butter until tender. Add cheese, sour cream, mayonnaise, wine, cayenne, pepper, and garlic powder to the pan; stir well until blended.

Pour mixture into a baking dish, and bake 30 minutes. Let stand 10 minutes before serving.

Broccoli Seafood Dip

Prep time: 15 minutes • Cook time: 15 minutes • Serves: 16 • Serving size: ¼ cup

Each serving has: 3 grams nutritive carbohydrate • less than 1 gram fiber • 10 grams total protein • 10 grams from animal source • less than 1 gram from plant source

2 TB. butter

½ cup finely chopped onion

½ lb. mushrooms, sliced

1 (10-oz.) pkg. frozen chopped broccoli

1 tsp. Worcestershire sauce

8 oz. processed cheese block, chopped into small pieces

1 tsp. black pepper

½ tsp. cayenne

1 lb. cooked crawfish tails, peeled shrimp, or crabmeat

1 cup sour cream

1 TB. cornstarch (optional)

¼ cup water (optional)

Melt butter in a skillet, and sauté chopped onion and mushrooms until tender; add broccoli, Worcestershire sauce, cheese, black pepper, and cayenne, and stir until heated through. Stir in seafood and sour cream, and bring to simmer for 5 minutes. If not thick enough, mix cornstarch and water until smooth paste forms, and add to dip. Serve with vegetable dippers.

Variations: Substitute cooked ground beef or shredded chicken for the seafood. As a main dish, serve over Vegetable Pasta.

Table Talk
To make a cornstarch paste, stir cornstarch into water until it dissolves without lumps and then add it to the hot mixture. A wire whisk works well for this.

Chicken Quesadillas

Prep time: 20 minutes   •   Cook time: 20 minutes   •   Serves 6   •   Serving size: 1 tortilla

Each serving has (without the tortilla): 6 grams carbohydrate   •   3 grams fiber   •   3 grams nutritive carbohydrate   •   27 grams total protein   •   22 grams from animal source   •   5 grams from plant source (The tortilla by itself has 18 grams of carbohydrate.)

2 TB. butter	6 whole-wheat flour tortillas
1 red bell pepper, chopped	⅔ cup shredded cheddar cheese
3 green onions, chopped	⅔ cup shredded Monterey Jack cheese
1 TB. minced garlic	¾ cup sour cream
2 chicken breasts, cooked and shredded or cubed	¾ cup guacamole
½ cup finely chopped fresh cilantro or parsley	1½ cups salsa

Preheat oven to 250°F.

Melt butter in a large skillet, and sauté bell pepper, onions, and garlic. Stir in chicken and cilantro and heat.

If you prefer not to use tortillas, as each adds 18 carbohydrates to the recipe, see the following Recipe for Success sidebar. If the extra 18 carbohydrates fits into your daily budget, then proceed with the rest of this recipe.

Moisten tortillas with water and heat in a large skillet, about 30 seconds on each side, or wrap wet tortillas in a paper towel and heat in the microwave 15 to 20 seconds.

Open tortilla and place 2 tablespoons chicken mixture in center, top with 1½ tablespoons each cheddar and Monterey Jack cheeses, and fold in half. Set aside until all tortillas are filled.

Recipe for Success

To lower your carb count by 18 per tortilla, pile up the ingredients on a plate, warm in microwave a few seconds to melt the cheese, and top with sour cream and guacamole … just as tasty! Another option is to fill a cabbage leaf instead of a tortilla and heat in the same manner to melt the cheese.

Heat a large skillet, or fire up the grill. Add 1 or 2 quesadillas, and cook over medium heat for 2 to 3 minutes. Flip and cook until cheese is completely melted, another minute or so.

Repeat with all tortillas, stacking them on baking sheet and keeping them warm in the oven while cooking others.

To serve, place 1 quesadilla on a plate, cut into 4 wedges, and top each wedge with ½ tablespoon each sour cream and guacamole. Pour ¼ cup salsa into individual ramekins for each plate to dip wedges.

Hot Crab Dip

Prep time: 10 minutes • Cook time: 25 minutes • Serves 6 • Serving size: ¼ cup

Each serving has: 2 grams nutritive carbohydrate • less than 1 gram fiber • 10 grams total protein • 10 grams from animal source

1 (7-oz.) can crab or fresh lump crabmeat

1 (8-oz.) pkg. cream cheese, at room temperature

½ tsp. horseradish

1 TB. sherry or cream

2 TB. chopped onion

2 tsp. minced garlic

1 tsp. ground white pepper

¼ cup shredded cheese of choice

Preheat oven to 375°F.

Blend crab, cream cheese, horseradish, sherry, onion, garlic, and white pepper, and pour into a greased baking dish. Bake for 15 minutes, sprinkle with shredded cheese, and return to oven for 10 minutes or until cheese is melted and bubbly.

Serve with vegetable scoopers.

Recipe for Success _____

Use this basic creamy dip to create your own unique dip. Add in whatever seasonings you prefer, such as dill weed or basil. Change the protein base to shredded chicken or chipped beef, etc. You can also add chopped artichoke hearts, asparagus, spinach, or broccoli. Top with nuts, or for a unique blend of flavors you might add golden raisins. Let your creative juices flow!

Marinated Crab Fingers

Prep time: 10 minutes plus overnight marinating time • Cook time: 0 • Serves 6 • Serving size: 3 tablespoons

Each serving has: 4 grams nutritive carbohydrate • less than 1 gram fiber • 5 grams total protein • 5 grams from animal source

1 cup finely chopped green or white onion	½ tsp. sugar
1 tsp. dried basil	3 TB. balsamic vinegar
1 tsp. dry mustard	1 TB. lemon juice
1 TB. minced garlic or 1 tsp. garlic powder	1 TB. Worcestershire sauce
½ tsp. salt	2 TB. white wine or white cran-apple juice made without added sugars or sweeteners
½ tsp. ground black pepper	2 TB. olive oil
½ tsp. cayenne	1 lb. crab fingers or crab claws

In a medium bowl with a tight-fitting lid, combine onion, basil, dry mustard, garlic, salt, pepper, cayenne, sugar, vinegar, lemon juice, Worcestershire sauce, wine, and olive oil; shake well. Add crab fingers, and gently shake to cover well. Marinate in refrigerator overnight, turning over several times to coat fingers well.

Drain marinade before serving.

Recipe for Success

The marinade makes a delicious salad dressing. Serve crab fingers over red leaf lettuce as a salad. Sprinkle with parsley. This dressing also makes a wonderful dipping sauce for artichoke leaves.

Eat crab fingers just like you would artichoke leaves. Grab the claw by the pincher hook and bite, pulling off the meat with your teeth.

Mushroom "Caviar"

Prep time: 30 minutes plus chill time   •   Cook time: 0   •   Serves 6   •   Serving size: 2 tablespoons

Each serving has: 2 grams nutritive carbohydrate   •   less than 1 gram plant protein

½ lb. mushrooms, finely chopped

1 onion, finely chopped

2 TB. olive oil

Juice of 1 lemon

Pepper to taste

In a skillet over low heat, sauté mushrooms and onion in oil until tender. Add lemon juice and pepper, and simmer 15 to 20 minutes. Refrigerate and serve chilled.

Recipe for Success

Surprise your guests and serve this caviar at your next party. It is great served in Belgium endive leaves or small celery boats. Make plenty, as it goes fast. This mushroom caviar also makes a great topping on salads and vegetables or use as a garnish for cheese balls.

Olive Cheese Bites

Prep time: 20 minutes plus freezing overnight • Cook time: 15 minutes • Serves: approximately 50 • Serving size: 2 pieces

Each serving has: 3 grams nutritive carbohydrate • less than 1 gram fiber • 2 grams total protein • 1½ grams from animal source • ½ gram from plant source

2½ cups grated cheddar cheese

¾ cup butter, softened

1¼ cups all-purpose flour

1 tsp. cayenne

1 tsp. paprika

100 small stuffed olives

Recipe for Success

These bites make a great "bread" to eat with salad. Just be sure to know your carb budget for the day, as they are almost too good to stop eating! Package a portion size in a small baggie and take it along for an afternoon pick-me-up snack. The kids will love being treated to these and sliced fruit after school.

These bites should be made at least 1 day in advance to allow for freezing.

On day of baking, preheat oven to 400°F.

Blend cheese and butter; stir in flour, cayenne, and paprika, and mix well. Wrap 1 teaspoon cheese mixture around each olive; cover completely.

Best if frozen at this stage and baked from frozen state. To freeze, place on sheet pans and freeze until firm; if desired, remove to freezer storage bags until ready to bake.

Place cheese bites on baking sheet, and bake 15 minutes. They can also be frozen after baking.

Party Cheese Log

Prep time: 20 minutes plus chill time • Cook time: 0 • Serves 6 • Serving size: 4 slices

Each serving has: 4 grams carbohydrate • 1 gram fiber • 3 grams nutritive carbohydrate • 14 grams total protein • 13 grams from animal source • 1 gram from plant source

1 (8-oz.) pkg. cream cheese	1 TB. Worcestershire sauce
8 oz. grated cheddar cheese or crumbled blue cheese	3 TB. cran-apple juice
¼ cup grated onion	¼ cup dried beef, shredded
	¼ cup finely chopped pecans

Mix together cream cheese, cheddar cheese, onion, Worcestershire sauce, cran-apple juice, and beef. Shape into a log, cover with foil, and refrigerate until firm. Just before serving, roll in pecans. Or if preferred, pecans can be mixed into log before shaping.

Slice into 24 pieces.

Recipe for Success

Serve on small plates—top a lettuce leaf with a slice and eat with a fork. Or eat casually with your fingers or on sliced vegetables such as jicama, carrots, or celery.

Seafood Mold

Prep time: 10 minutes plus chill time • Cook time: 10 minutes • Serves 10 • Serving size: 1 slice

Each serving has: 10 grams carbohydrate • 10 grams total protein • 8 grams from animal source • 2 grams from plant source

1½ cups Basic Cream Soup recipe (recipe in Chapter 14)

1 (6-oz.) can shrimp

6 to 8 oz. cream cheese

¼ cup finely chopped green onions

2 envelopes plain gelatin

1 cup cold water

1 cup mayonnaise

½ tsp. cayenne

1 cup finely chopped celery

¼ cup finely chopped bell pepper

1 (10-oz.) pkg. frozen crab

Recipe for Success

If desired, this recipe may be molded in individual molds and served as a salad or appetizer on a leaf of romaine or red leaf lettuce. Garnish with black olive slices and pimiento strips. One can cream of shrimp soup may be substituted for the Basic Cream Soup and canned shrimp.

Combine soup, shrimp, cream cheese, and green onions; heat to simmer.

Dissolve gelatin in cold water; add to warm mixture with mayonnaise and stir well.

Add cayenne, celery, bell pepper, and crab to mixture, stir to combine, and remove from heat.

Pour into mold, and refrigerate until set. Cut into 10 slices, and serve with raw vegetables.

Spinach Artichoke Dip

Prep time: 10 minutes • Cook time: 6 minutes • Serves 12 • Serving size: ¼ cup

Each serving has: 5 grams carbohydrate • 2 grams fiber • 3 grams nutritive carbohydrate • 9 grams total protein • 8 grams from animal source • 1 gram from plant source

2 (10-oz.) pkg. frozen spinach

½ cup chopped green onions

1 (8-oz.) pkg. cream cheese

8 oz. sour cream

¼ cup Parmesan cheese

1 (14-oz.) can artichoke hearts, drained and cut

Pepper to taste

2 to 3 drops hot sauce or ½ tsp. cayenne

8 oz. Monterey Jack cheese, shredded

Cook spinach and drain well; squeeze out excess moisture with white paper towels.

In a microwave-safe serving dish, combine spinach, green onions, cream cheese, sour cream, Parmesan cheese, artichoke hearts, pepper, and hot sauce; mix well.

Microwave 4 minutes, sprinkle with cheese, and cook 2 minutes longer or until cheese melts.

Serve with vegetable scoopers.

Recipe for Success

This is a favorite appetizer at many restaurants served with high-carb chips. You can serve a delectable platter of a variety of raw vegetables in various shapes and sizes knowing you are enhancing your vitamin intake plus enjoying a variety of flavors.

The Least You Need to Know

- ◆ Traditional appetizers are low carb, but at today's parties, appetizers are often high carb.
- ◆ Eat appetizers before meals, or enjoy a whole meal by consuming several.
- ◆ Take along low-carb, high-protein appetizers to parties so you aren't tempted by high-carb choices.
- ◆ Appetizers take the edge off your hunger, making it easier to eat a normal-size meal.

Chapter 18

Snacks

In This Chapter

- The appeal of snacks
- Timing your snacks
- Snacking with conscious attentiveness

Yes, it's time for a snack. We all love snacks. Whether we eat them in the late afternoon as a pick-me-up or for an energy boost during challenging outdoor activities, snacks are a very real part of most everyone's eating.

You may have been told to avoid snacking if you're watching your weight. You know how hard that is … and how unnatural. The good news is that you can have your snacks provided you budget them into your overall daily carbohydrate budget. Just follow the general guidelines found in Chapter 1. To put it another way, you can have your snacks … and eat them, too.

Your Biology Loves Snacks

It's great to think that we only need 3 square meals a day. Very few of us, though, eat only 3 meals a day. Instead, many of us eat anywhere from 3 to 6 times a day.

Snacking comes naturally. Sometimes it's because our stomach growls are calling out to be heard and satisfied. Other times, it's because our stressful lives just naturally lead us into temptation whether we are hungry or not. Or our sweet tooth takes over our brains until it has been indulged. Snacks, either yucky pre-packaged versions or healthy versions, are how we satisfy these needs.

Over the past 15 years, the concept of "grazing" has become quite popular. The idea was to eat continually throughout the day, as a ruminating animal does. Grazing doesn't quite work for us humans, though. For grazing to be effective, we would need 4 stomachs, just like those cows and sheep have.

Snacking works. That's why we do it. The ideal of 3-meals-and-only-3-meals-a-day is too rigorous. The shoe, so to speak, doesn't fit. Instead, let's accept the fact that snacking is here to stay and make allowances for it.

Use snacks as a way to tide you over between meals. That way, you don't get terrifically hungry and perhaps spiral out of eating—and carbohydrate—control.

Snacking is harmful to your weight and health if you have a bad habit of snacking throughout the day without any regard to your need for food. That's simply a bad habit and one to stop. Snacking is also harmful to your weight and health if you snack just because you are bored or if you snack mindlessly, not noticing what or how a food item gets from the refrigerator into your mouth.

But mindful, conscious snacking is just fine. That way you are aware you're eating, you are enjoying the food, and you are making sure you're staying within your daily carbohydrate allotment.

The Best Low-Carb Snacks

It's easy to find snack foods—way too easy! They're everywhere, in the grocery store, the convenience store, the vending machine, and your co-worker's desk. And how easy they are to prepare! With a few deft movements of your fingers, the wrapper comes right off and, voilà, you've messed up your low-carb eating plan for the day!

The best low-carb snacks require a little forethought, planning, and preparation. They contain valuable nutrition that gives you the energy and sustenance to hold you until your next meal. They also should be eaten slowly with conscious attentiveness, so that you enjoy the total experience.

A good snack contains low-carb foods such as nuts, meat or fish, vegetables, or fruit. They are rich-tasting enough so you can eat them sparingly, and yet you get enough food value to tide you over until your next meal.

Table Talk

Many of the snack recipes in this chapter are tote-bag tested—that is, designed to take along with you. Most don't require refrigeration, although a few do. You can put them into a snack bag or small plastic container in the morning and carry them around in your briefcase or handbag. When you need a snack during the day, you can eat them at room temperature. They don't need to be warmed or cooked.

Already Ready

The time to start thinking of preparing snacks isn't when you need one. You should have them around just in case. If you have something prepared, you won't be tempted to eat a high-carb convenience food when you get hungry.

Schedule some time now to prepare Beef Jerky and Spiced Nuts and Seeds. Have the ingredients for trail mix on hand so you can put it together quickly for outings and vacations.

Rosemary Walnuts

Prep time: 5 minutes • Cook time: 15 minutes • Serves 20 • Yield: 4 cups
• Serving size: ¼ cup

Each serving has: 3 grams carbohydrate • 2 grams fiber • 1 gram nutritive carbohydrate
• 5 grams total protein • 5 grams from plant source

6 TB. butter

1 TB. dried rosemary, crumbled

1 TB. salt

½ tsp. cayenne

4 cups walnut halves

Preheat oven to 325°F.

Melt butter in a large saucepan. Remove from heat, and add rosemary, salt, and cayenne. Add walnuts and toss gently but well. Place walnuts in a shallow roasting pan in a single layer.

Bake until richly brown, about 10 to 15 minutes, shaking occasionally. These nuts are nicest served warm.

Recipe for Success

Nuts are a delicious snack containing hard-to-get healthy fat. You can eat them plain or toasted or even add just a couple spices to really jazz them up.

Pork on a Stick

Prep time: 30 minutes plus 4 hours chill time   •   Cook time: 5 to 8 minutes   •   Serves 4   •   Serving size: 3 skewers

Each serving has: 6 grams carbohydrate   •   2 grams fiber   •   4 grams nutritive carbohydrate   •   40 grams total protein   •   32 grams from animal source   •   8 grams from plant source

1 lb. lean, boneless, center-cut pork loin

½ cup red wine vinegar

2 TB. olive oil

1 clove garlic, minced

¼ tsp. fresh oregano, chopped fine, or ¼ tsp. dry, crushed

12 bamboo sticks

½ cup peanut butter

¼ tsp. crushed red pepper

Recipe for Success
This recipe is a great way to get complete protein when you're on the run. It's ideal for snacks, lunch boxes, and even for dinner. The peanut sauce simply sparkles.

Cut pork across grain into 3×1×¼-inch strips. Mix vinegar, olive oil, garlic, and oregano. Pour over pork. Refrigerate 4 hours to overnight.

Soak bamboo sticks 20 minutes in water. Drain pork and save marinade. Thread pork onto sticks. Grill 5 to 8 minutes on medium-high gas or charcoal grill, and brush with marinade.

To make sauce, warm peanut butter in a small pan with crushed red pepper. Serve hot or cold with pork on sticks.

Spiced Nuts and Seeds

Prep time: 5 minutes   •   Cook time: 5 minutes   •   Serves 14   •   Serving size: ⅛ cup

Each serving has: 7 grams carbohydrate   •   3 grams fiber   •   4 grams nutritive carbohydrates   •   8 grams total protein   •   8 grams from plant source

½ cup sunflower seeds

½ cup Spanish peanuts

½ cup toasted pumpkin seeds

1 tsp. chili powder

¼ tsp. cumin

⅛ tsp. garlic powder

⅛ tsp. cayenne

Heat sunflower seeds, peanuts, pumpkin seeds, chili powder, cumin, garlic powder, and cayenne in a skillet for about 5 minutes. Stir frequently.

Chicken Liver Pâté with Green Pickles

Prep time: 20 minutes plus chill time • Cook time: 15 minutes • Serves 8 • Serving size: 1 slice

Each serving has: 6 grams carbohydrate • 1 gram fiber • 5 grams nutritive carbohydrate • 14 grams total protein • 14 grams from animal source • less than 1 gram from plant source

½ cup (1 stick) butter	12 large fresh mushrooms
1 lb. chicken livers	¼ cup brandy
1 medium onion, chopped	½ tsp. salt
½ tsp. dried thyme	⅛ tsp. pepper
½ tsp. dried rosemary	10 sprigs fresh parsley
1 bay leaf	16 small green dill pickles (gherkins)

In a large skillet, melt butter. Add chicken livers and onion. Stir over medium heat about 10 minutes. Add thyme, rosemary, bay leaf, and mushrooms. Stir frequently while cooking for 5 minutes.

Discard bay leaf, and pour mixture into a blender. Pour in brandy, salt, and pepper. Blend 2 minutes, then pour into a 2-cup soufflé dish. Chill.

Garnish with parsley. Serve with gherkins.

Note: This dish can be covered and stored in the refrigerator for a week.

Recipe for Success

Believe it or not, a slice of this pâté is the perfect pick-me-up for late-afternoon fatigue. It resets your energy levels and seems to soothe the adrenaline surges. But it is good any time—and that also means for breakfast.

Pickled Eggs

Prep time: 15 minutes plus at least 24 hours chill time • Cook time: 10 minutes
• Serves 6 • Serving size: 1 egg

Each serving has: 4 grams nutritive carbohydrate • 6 grams total protein • 6 grams from animal source

1 cup white vinegar

½ cup water

1 TB. pickling spices

2 pieces fresh ginger root, cut into ¼-inch slices

½ tsp. salt

1 clove garlic

6 hard-boiled eggs, peeled

Boil together vinegar, water, pickling spices, ginger root, salt, and garlic for 10 minutes.

Place eggs in a jar, and cover with spiced vinegar liquid. Refrigerate at least 24 hours before eating.

Recipe for Success

Wow! You'll keep coming back for more of these. In fact, it's easy to double or even quadruple this recipe so everyone can get enough. These are terrific for late-day snacks when you need a little something to tide you over until dinner. Amazingly satisfying—the egg has complete protein and the pickling spice has great mouth appeal. You'll love these.

Beef Jerky

Prep time: 20 minutes plus overnight marinating time   •   Cook time: 7 hours   •   Serves 10
•   Yield: 10 servings of about 3 ounces each   •   Serving size: 3 ounces

Each serving has: 2 grams nutritive carbohydrate   •   16 grams total protein   •   16 grams
from animal source

2 lb. lean meat, such as brisket, flank steak, or elk steaks

½ cup red wine vinegar

1½ tsp. salt

1½ tsp. onion salt

½ tsp. freshly ground black pepper

½ tsp. minced garlic

¼ cup soy sauce

½ cup Worcestershire sauce

Slice meat as thinly as possible. Place meat in a zippered bag with vinegar, salt, onion salt, pepper, garlic, soy sauce, and Worcestershire sauce. Marinate overnight in the refrigerator. It is fine to marinate longer, as meat will get more tender.

Preheat oven to 150°F.

Drain meat. Place on oven racks in a single layer. Place foil on the bottom of the oven to catch any drippings.

Leave oven door ajar, and bake for about 7 hours until meat is chewy and/or brittle. Store in an airtight container in the refrigerator. Jerky can be safely kept for 6 months—if you can make it last that long.

Recipe for Success

Here's what to take with you when food won't be readily available. Take this on the airplane and on car trips. Take it hiking or anywhere you are going to want a high-protein snack when chances are good that the only snack you can get is filled with carbs.

Cheesy Nuts

Prep time: 10 minutes • Cook time: 5 to 10 minutes • Serves 6 • Yield: 1 cup • Serving size: ⅙ cup

Each serving has: 3 grams carbohydrate • 2 grams fiber • 1 gram nutritive carbohydrate • 5 grams total protein • 1 grams from animal source • 4 grams from plant source

1 cup walnut halves	2 TB. Parmesan cheese
2 TB. butter	½ tsp. garlic salt

Preheat oven to 350°F.

Boil nuts in water for 5 minutes. Drain on a paper towel. Spread nuts in a shallow baking dish. Dot with butter. Mix cheese and garlic salt with nuts. Roast for 5 minutes or more, stirring every 2 minutes to mix in butter.

Homemade Peanut Butter

Prep time: 10 • Cook time: 0 • Serves 6 • Serving size: 2 tablespoons

Each serving has: 7 grams carbohydrate • 2 grams fiber • 5 grams nutritive carbohydrate • 7 grams total protein • 7 grams from plant source

1 lb. roasted peanuts, unshelled, unsalted, or 2½ cups shelled

Shell peanuts, if necessary, and place nuts in a food processor. Process 3 minutes, stopping to scrape down sides as needed. Store in the refrigerator to keep oil from separating.

Recipe for Success

How more natural can you get? This is a great treat for the kids to prepare with a bit of adult supervision. There are certainly no added preservatives, sugar, or salt in this peanut butter! Use this method with any nuts to create a variety of nut butters.

Trail Mix

Prep time: 10 minutes • Cook time: 10 to 15 minutes • Serves 15 • Yield: 3¾ cups • Serving size: ¼ cup

Each serving has: 12 grams carbohydrate • 3 grams fiber • 9 grams nutritive carbohydrates • 6 grams total protein • 6 grams from plant source

4 TB. butter	½ cup flaked unsweetened coconut
½ cup sunflower seeds	1 tsp. salt
½ cup pumpkin seeds	¼ cup raisins
½ cup shelled pistachio nuts	¼ cup dates, cut into quarters
½ cup almonds	¼ cup dried apricots, cut into quarters
½ cup pecan halves	

Preheat oven to 350°F.

Melt butter in a large, shallow, glass baking dish. Place sunflower seeds, pumpkin seeds, pistachios, almonds, pecans, and coconut in the dish. Stir to coat nuts. Sprinkle with salt.

Toast in the oven for 10 to 15 minutes, stirring occasionally. Remove from the oven and let cool. Then add raisins, dates, and apricots.

Store in refrigerator.

Variation: You can make several substitutions to this recipe without changing the carb count very much. You can use pine nuts, cashews, and sesame seeds. You can use currants and dried figs in place of the raisins, dates, or apricots. But be careful. If you add chocolate morsels or wheat-, corn-, or rice-based foods, the carb count could skyrocket.

Recipe for Success

Carry trail mix with you for hiking and outdoor adventures. The salt in the nuts can help replenish body salt lost to sweating. And the trail mix itself can give you an energy boost.

Avocado-Turkey Wrap

Prep time: 10 minutes • Cook time: 0 • Serves 6 • Serving size: 2 wraps

Each serving has: 8 grams carbohydrate • 6 grams fiber • 2 grams nutritive carbohydrate • 10 grams total protein • 8 grams from animal source • 2 grams from plant source

12 thin (1-oz.) slices turkey breast	Pickle relish
1½ cups mashed avocados	Chopped jalapeños peppers
Optional seasonings:	Chopped green chilies
Capers	Nuts
Chopped olives	Spices
Pimientos	

Lay out 1 slice turkey. On 2 tablespoons avocado, sprinkle chosen seasonings and wrap securely. If needed, secure with toothpick.

Refrigerate until ready to serve.

Recipe for Success

These wraps may be made with any of your favorite thinly sliced meats and rolled around fruits as well as avocados. They make great snacks as well as accompaniments to soups and salads. Make a few extras for an easy breakfast on the run.

Spinach Wrappers

Prep time: 10 minutes • Cook time: none • Serves 6 • Serving size: 4 wrappers

Each serving has: 5 grams carbohydrate • 2 grams fiber • 3 grams nutritive carbohydrate • 16 grams total protein • 6 grams from animal source • 10 grams from plant source

2 cups spinach leaves	1 TB. minced garlic
16 oz. cream cheese, at room temperature	Black pepper to taste
2 TB. dried herbs of choice—dill, oregano, basil, etc.	½ cup pecans, finely chopped

Wash and dry spinach. Separate leaves and trim stems. Combine softened cream cheese, herbs, garlic, pepper, and pecans. Spread 1 tablespoon cream cheese mixture on 1 spinach leaf, roll, and secure with a toothpick. Stack on a platter, and refrigerate until serving time.

Eggplant Crisps for Dips

Prep time: 15 minutes   •   Cook time: 8 minutes   •   Serves 6   •   Serving size: 3 to 4 each, depending on size of eggplant

Each serving has: 3 grams carbohydrate   •   1 gram fiber   •   2 grams nutritive carbohydrate   •   less than 1 gram total protein

3 cups (3 small or 2 large eggplants) eggplant, peeled and cut into ¼-inch slices

¼ cup olive oil

2 TB. seasonings of choice—garlic powder, dill, etc.

Salt and pepper to taste

Preheat oven to 425°F.

Coat all sides of eggplant with olive oil, and sprinkle with seasonings, salt, and pepper. Lightly oil a baking sheet pan, and place eggplant slices in a single layer. Bake until browned, about 8 minutes, turning once.

Variation: If you have room in your allotted carb count for the day, you can dip vegetable slices into milk and then into breadcrumbs before baking. When highly seasoned, these make delicious appetizers all by themselves.

Recipe for Success

You can make these using zucchini slices; slice the zucchini the long way and then cut to size for larger scoopers, making them easier to dip. Make extras and keep in a closed container for munching.

Toasted Pumpkin Seeds

Prep time: 10 minutes plus ½ hour soaking time • Cook time: 10 minutes • Serves 6
• Serving size: 2 tablespoons

Each serving has: 5 grams carbohydrate • 3 grams fiber • 2 grams nutritive carbohydrates • 7 grams total protein • 7 grams from plant source

¾ cup seeds pulled from pumpkin   Salt water

Recipe for Success
This has always been one of the best things about carving the jack-o-lantern—getting to pull out the seeds and toast them for a snack after Jack was all lit up! They make great additions to salads and meat wraps as well as for eating from your hand.

Preheat oven to 350°F.

Wash seeds and remove all fibers. Prepare salt water, and soak seeds at least 30 minutes. Drain and pat seeds dry, then spread on an oiled baking sheet. Bake for 8 to 10 minutes or until golden. Watch carefully so as not to burn; they might need to be stirred so they don't stick to the pan.

Remove from pan, cool, and sprinkle with additional salt, if desired.

Stuffed Veggies

Prep time: 15 minutes   •   Cook time: 0   •   Serves 6   •   Serving size: ¼ cup

Each serving (of stuffing base) has: 2 grams nutritive carbohydrate   •   3 grams total protein   •   3 grams from animal source   •   less than 1 gram from plant source

1 (8-oz.) pkg. cream cheese, at room temperature

¼ cup sour cream

Seasonings of choice—dill, horseradish, chopped cilantro, garlic powder, red pepper, radishes, chopped olives, chopped chilies, etc.

Seafood or meat of choice—finely chopped tuna, salmon, ham, beef, turkey, etc. (optional)

Raw vegetables of choice—celery sticks, cucumber boats, zucchini boats, bell pepper strips, carrot sticks, tomato scoops, jicama sticks or rounds, turnip rounds, red leaf or green leaf lettuce leaves, etc.

Prepare stuffing by combining cream cheese and sour cream. Add 1 teaspoon each of 2 to 3 seasonings of choice and mix well. Add ¼ cup seafood or meat of choice (if using). The base is easier to stuff or spread onto vegetables if softened at room temperature.

Prepare vegetable dippers by washing and peeling vegetables of choice. Cut into dipping sticks or round circles. You can make tomato scoops by hollowing out the inside of tiny red tomatoes and filling them with cream cheese mixture. You can also use lettuce leaves to fill with cream cheese mixture and roll up as finger food.

Vegetables can be stuffed in advance and stored in covered container for quick, healthy snacks.

Table Talk

Add in carb counts for vegetables you use. The rule of thumb for quick calculations is to count an average of 5 grams carb for each 1 cup fresh vegetables. The rule of thumb for quick fiber calculations is to count an average of 2 grams fiber for each 1 cup raw fresh vegetables.

Recipe for Success

This recipe has unlimited variations! Make up small containers of the cream cheese base with various seasonings. Prepare several vegetables and refrigerate them in cold water to keep crisp. The tomato scoops can be wrapped in damp paper towels to store in the refrigerator till needed. Stuff long celery stalks with filling and stick together with fillings touching, roll tightly in wax paper; chill and cut into ½-inch pieces to serve.

Pickled Garlic

Prep time: 15 minutes • Cook time: 7 minutes plus 24 hours standing time • Serving size: 5 garlic cloves

Each serving has: 7 grams nutritive carbohydrate • less than 1 gram total protein

½ cup red wine vinegar

⅔ cup water

¾ cup sugar

¼ cup salt

8 cups peeled garlic cloves

Combine red wine vinegar, water, sugar, and salt in a large saucepan. Add garlic, making sure liquid covers garlic. If not, add more water to cover. Bring solution to a full rolling boil. Boil 3 minutes.

Cool to room temperature. Put into container, and refrigerate for at least 24 hours before serving.

Recipe for Success

These don't taste like garlic at all. They are crunchy and won't give you garlic breath. In fact, with 1 gram carbohydrate per clove, you can have several. As a special bonus, save the cooking solution—it makes an excellent salad dressing. You can often find already-peeled garlic in big jars at the food discount stores.

Garlic is so good for you. It boosts the immune system and contains antioxidants that neutralize damaging free radicals.

The Least You Need to Know

◆ Eating snacks is a natural part of today's living and eating.

◆ Keep low-carb foods on hand for when it's time for a snack.

◆ Take snacks with you for outings, vacations, work, and travel.

◆ Use snacks as a way to manage your hunger between meals.

Vegetable Side Dishes

In This Chapter

◆ The joys of vegetables in low-carb eating
◆ Delicious varieties and tastes
◆ The Big Five every day

How many times have you been told to "eat your vegetables"? About a million, right? As far back as you can remember, you have heard it from your anxious parents, your doctor, dieting authorities, and every other health practitioner you've ever met. Heck, you've even been encouraged to eat your veggies by Mr. Rogers, Big Bird, and Mickey Mouse! Most likely, you've even told your own children to eat their vegetables, too.

Well, there's good reason veggies have such a powerful fan club. Of all the foods, vegetables work the hardest per ounce to keep us healthy. They offer vitamins, minerals, antioxidants, and plenty of fiber. In this chapter, we give you another good reason to eat your vegetables: They taste great!

Not Just Broccoli

Mentioning the word *vegetable* often elicits memories of the least-appealing one a person's ever eaten. Very few people wax poetic about broccoli and certainly not about Brussels sprouts. But given a chance, even these vegetables can deliver amazing *gustatory* satisfaction.

Take a slow and observant walk down the produce aisle of your grocery store. You may be amazed. You'll likely see vegetables whose names are complete mysteries to you, and you sure don't know what to do with them! So get ready! These recipes will expand your vegetable-cooking repertoire to include a wider variety of delicious vegetables, even ones with such names as *celeriac* and *jicama*.

The Big Five

No, the "Big Five" isn't a new athletic conference; it's that magic number of fruits and vegetables we are all supposed to eat each and every day. Eating up to 10 servings is even better.

Let's face it, if you're on a low-carb eating plan for your weight, diabetes, or other aspects of your health or appearance, you care about feeling good and looking good. Eating those 5 to 10 servings accelerates your success. You'll actually feel better and likely have more energy—two things that go a long way to helping you stick with a low-carb eating plan.

Don't think of a serving of a vegetable as a giant mound of something green. Our habit of thinking of servings as some gargantuan portion is what gets a lot of us in weight trouble in the first place. A serving size of vegetables is usually about ½ cup cooked vegetables and 1 cup raw. A good-size salad is often 2 servings. It's really quite easy to eat 3 modest servings at dinner or lunch.

The list of green vegetables is long—green beans, lettuces, broccoli, spinach, kale, collard greens, celery, fennel, Brussels sprouts, cabbage, asparagus, parsley, and many others.

Think of all those vegetables in the produce section just waiting for you to take them home and try them out. Some already are your good friends, but some you have passed by week after week for years. Why not take one home and try it as a side dish? Experiment, and you may find another delicious new friend for life.

Brussels Sprouts with Pecans

Prep time: 20 minutes • Cook time: 10 minutes • Serves 6 • Serving size: ⅙ recipe

Each serving has: 10 grams carbohydrate • 6 grams fiber • 4 grams nutritive carbohydrates • 3 grams total protein • 0 grams from animal source • 3 grams from plant source

¼ tsp. salt	¼ cup chopped pecans
1 lb. Brussels sprouts, trimmed	Freshly ground black pepper
3 TB. butter	

To a large saucepan of boiling water, add salt and Brussels sprouts. Cover and cook until tender, about 10 minutes. Drain, place in a shallow serving dish, and cover to keep warm.

In a small saucepan, melt butter over medium heat. Cook until brown. Add pecans and toss until lightly browned. Pour over Brussels sprouts and sprinkle with pepper to taste.

Recipe for Success
This cruciferous vegetable takes well to just plain butter. Add in the sautéed pecans, and this is a side dish you will love.

Warm Caraway Cabbage with Carrots

Prep time: 15 minutes • Cook time: 12 minutes • Serves 8 • Serving size: ¾ cup

Each serving has: 12 grams carbohydrate • 2 grams fiber • 10 grams nutritive carbohydrates • less than 1 gram total protein

1 TB. butter	3 TB. cider vinegar
8 cups mixed green and red shredded cabbage and carrots	1 tsp. sugar
1¼ tsp. caraway seeds	¼ cup unsweetened apple juice
⅓ cup golden raisins	Salt and freshly ground black pepper

In a large, shallow skillet, heat butter over high heat. Add cabbage mixture, and stir-fry until just wilted, 2 to 3 minutes. Add caraway seeds, raisins, vinegar, and sugar. Stir-fry 1 minute. Add apple juice, and continue cooking over high heat, stirring occasionally, until most of juice is absorbed and cabbage is cooked, about 8 minutes. Season with salt and pepper to taste. Serve immediately.

Fennel and Tomatoes

Prep time: 20 minutes • Cook time: 30 minutes • Serves 8 • Serving size: ⅛ recipe

Each serving has: 9 grams carbohydrate • 3 grams fiber • 6 grams nutritive carbohydrates • less than 1 gram total protein

3 medium fennel bulbs (about 2 lb.)	¼ tsp. dried thyme
2 TB. butter	¼ cup water
1 medium onion, finely chopped	Salt and freshly ground black pepper
2 medium tomatoes, seeded and chopped	

Trim stems and bottoms from fennel bulbs. Chop fronds from stems, reserve 2 tablespoons, and discard stems. Chop bulbs and cook in boiling salted water 2 to 3 minutes. Drain and set aside.

Recipe for Success

Fennel goes well with any main dish, from beef to seafood. If you haven't yet eaten this vegetable, try it—you may just fall in love.

In a medium saucepan, melt butter over medium-low heat. Add onion and cook until just browned, 5 to 10 minutes. Add tomatoes, thyme, water, and cooked fennel. Cover and cook over low heat until tender, about 25 minutes.

Remove cover and cook until liquid evaporates, 3 to 5 minutes. Increase heat to medium, and cook 2 minutes. Season with salt and pepper to taste.

Place in a serving dish, and garnish with reserved chopped fennel fronds. Serve immediately.

Stuffed Acorn Squash

Prep time: 15 minutes   •   Cook time: 1 hour   •   Serves 4   •   Serving size: ½ squash

Each serving has: 22 grams carbohydrate   •   7 grams fiber   •   15 grams nutritive carbohydrates   •   1 gram total protein   •   1 gram from plant source

2 medium acorn squash, halved and seeded	4 tsp. packed dark brown sugar
Salt and freshly ground black pepper	Ground cinnamon
4 tsp. butter	½ cup pecans

Preheat oven to 350°F.

Season squash with salt and pepper to taste. Fill each with 1 teaspoon butter, 1 teaspoon dark brown sugar, 1 dash cinnamon, and 5 pecans. Bake 50 to 60 minutes or until tender when pierced with fork. Remove from oven.

Recipe for Success _____

Acorn squash prepared in this way is so sweet and so good. If you love wet, warm, sugary nuts, this is the side dish for you on those cold and blustery days. It's also great as a side dish for holiday feasts.

Spaghetti Squash with Italian Sauce

Prep time: 20 minutes • Cook time: 1 hour plus 5 minutes • Serves 8 • Serving size: ⅛ squash and ⅛ sauce

Each serving has: 12 grams carbohydrate • 6 grams fiber plus mushrooms and squash • 6 grams nutritive carbohydrates • 5 grams total protein • 3 grams from animal source • 2 grams from plant source

1 (3- to 4-lb.) spaghetti squash	1 tsp. minced garlic
2 TB. olive oil	1 medium red bell pepper, cored, seeded, and cut into ⅛-inch strips
1 TB. butter	
8 oz. fresh mushrooms, sliced	½ tsp. dried oregano
2 medium ripe tomatoes, chopped	¼ lb. fresh snow peas, trimmed
1 medium zucchini, cut into ¼-inch slices	Salt and pepper to taste
5 to 6 green onions, including tops, chopped	¾ cup freshly grated Parmesan cheese

Preheat oven to 350°F.

Bake whole squash 1 hour or until tender when pierced with fork. Remove from the oven and allow to cool 5 to 10 minutes. Halve lengthwise and remove seeds. With a fork, pull out spaghettilike strands, and place in a large serving bowl. Set aside.

In a large skillet, heat olive oil and butter over medium heat. Add mushrooms, tomatoes, zucchini, green onions, garlic, bell pepper, oregano, and snow peas. Cook until soft, 4 to 5 minutes. Pour mixture over squash, and toss to combine. Add salt and pepper to taste. Sprinkle with Parmesan cheese, and serve immediately.

Recipe for Success

Spaghetti squash's mild flavor blends well with the stronger tastes of Italian cuisine. Enjoy the spaghetti squash in this recipe as a hearty side dish with a meat entrée, or serve it plain with other Italian sauces, such as Alfredo or meat sauce.

Variation: Use spaghetti squash as a substitute for spaghetti or pasta in any recipe. The carbohydrate count of 1 cup cooked wheat spaghetti is about 40 grams. The same amount of cooked spaghetti squash is only 10 grams. The squash also contains more nutrients, plus each serving counts toward your 5 or more fruits and vegetables per day.

Green Peas Cooked in Lettuce

Prep time: 15 minutes • Cook time: 10 minutes • Serves 6 • Serving size: about ⅔ cup

Each serving has: 16 grams carbohydrate • 7 grams fiber • 9 grams nutritive carbohydrates
• 6 grams total protein • 0 grams from animal source • 6 grams from plant source

3½ cups frozen peas	4 Bibb lettuce leaves, cut in half
4 TB. butter	Salt and freshly ground pepper to taste
3 green onions, chopped	

Steam peas over boiling water for 5 minutes until partially cooked.

In a heavy skillet, sauté 2 tablespoons butter with green onions and lettuce. Sprinkle with salt and pepper, cover, and cook on low for 3 to 4 minutes. Add partially-cooked peas to the skillet, and cook over low heat an additional 3 minutes.

Transfer to a serving dish, and top with remaining 2 tablespoons butter.

Recipe for Success
This recipe is a simple, yet interesting side dish for meats and fish. If you've never cooked lettuce before, you will find that it softly enhances the flavor of the peas.

Variation: Substitute snow peas or sugar snap peas for the green peas in this recipe. You can also top with mint or minced fresh ginger root, or even sprinkle with toasted sesame seeds.

Colorful Broccoli

Prep time: 20 minutes • Cook time: 18 minutes • Serves 6 • Serving size: about ⅔ cup

Each serving has: 12 grams carbohydrate • 5 grams fiber • 7 grams nutritive carbohydrates • 3 grams total protein • less than 1 gram from animal source • 3 grams from plant source

1½ lb. broccoli, cut into florets	1 tsp. dried basil
2 carrots, sliced	⅛ tsp. cayenne
1 TB. butter	8 oz. *jicama*, peeled and cut into thin strips
1 small onion, thinly sliced	3 plum tomatoes, cut into wedges
½ tsp. minced garlic	2 TB. grated Parmesan cheese
½ cup water	

Steam broccoli and carrots until tender. Drain. In a heavy skillet, heat butter. Sauté onion and garlic. Add 2 tablespoons water, and cook until onion is soft, about 2 minutes. Add basil, cayenne, and remaining water and cook about 2 minutes. Add broccoli, carrots, and jicama. Heat thoroughly. Add tomatoes and mix. Remove to a serving dish. Sprinkle with Parmesan, and serve right away.

Low-Carb Vocab

Jicama is a root vegetable used in Mexican cuisine. It has a fresh and slightly sweet though bland taste. Along with the other vegetables, it adds a full rainbow of nutrients, vitamins, and antioxidants. Colorful Broccoli is an excellent accompaniment to any main course dish.

Southwestern Vegetables

Prep time: 20 minutes • Cook time: 20 minutes • Serves 12 • Serving size: 1/12 recipe

Each serving has: 18 grams carbohydrate • 4 grams fiber • 14 grams nutritive carbohydrates • 5 grams total protein • 5 grams from plant source

1 medium onion, chopped	1/4 tsp. cumin
1 clove garlic, minced	1 (16-oz.) can black beans, drained
2 TB. butter	1 tsp. salt
1 (16-oz.) can corn, drained	1/4 tsp. freshly ground black pepper
3 medium tomatoes, chopped	1/4 cup chopped fresh cilantro
3 medium zucchini, sliced 1/4-inch thick	3 TB. pine nuts
1 tsp. honey	

Sauté onion and garlic in butter over medium-high heat until tender. Add corn, tomatoes, zucchini, honey, cumin, beans, salt, and pepper; mix well. Bring to a boil and reduce heat. Simmer, covered, for 10 to 15 minutes. Remove to serving dish. Sprinkle with cilantro and pine nuts and serve warm.

Asparagus with Hollandaise Sauce

Prep time: 10 minutes • Cook time: 6 minutes • Serves 6 • Serving size: 1/6 recipe

Each serving has: 2 grams carbohydrate • 2 grams fiber • 0 grams nutritive carbohydrates • 3 grams total protein • 2 grams from animal source • 1 gram from plant source

1/2 cup (1 stick) butter	Freshly ground pepper to taste
4 egg yolks	1 lb. fresh asparagus
1 TB. lemon juice	

Heat butter in the microwave until just melted. Put egg yolks, lemon juice, and pepper into a blender. Slowly pour in melted butter, and blend for several seconds.

Steam asparagus spears over boiling water until tender. Remove to serving platter, and top with hollandaise sauce.

Ginger Carrots

Prep time: 10 minutes • Cook time: 5 minutes • Serves 6 • Serving size: ⅙ recipe

Each serving has: 5 grams carbohydrate • 1 gram fiber • 4 grams nutritive carbohydrates • less than 1 gram total protein

1 lb. baby carrots	1 tsp. honey
3 TB. butter	¼ tsp. salt
1 tsp. ground ginger	¼ tsp. coarsely ground fresh black pepper

Steam carrots over boiling water just until they are *al dente*.

In a large, heavy skillet, melt butter over medium heat. Add ginger, honey, and steamed carrots, and stir gently to coat thoroughly. Add salt and pepper.

Low-Carb Vocab

Al dente is an Italian term that indicates a stage of doneness in both pasta and vegetables. The food is cooked to the point before it becomes mushy or too soft. Al dente food has some crunch left.

Green Beans, Pecans, and Feta

Prep time: 15 minutes • Cook time: 5 minutes • Serves 6 • Serving size: ⅙ recipe

Each serving has: 13 grams carbohydrate • 5 grams fiber • 8 grams nutritive carbohydrates • 6 grams total protein • 3 grams from animal source • 3 grams from plant source

1½ lb. fresh string beans, trimmed and cut into 1-inch pieces

¾ cup olive oil

1 tsp. dried basil

⅓ cup white wine vinegar

½ tsp. minced garlic

¼ tsp. salt

¼ tsp. freshly ground pepper

1 cup coarsely chopped pecans

1 cup crumbled feta cheese

½ cup diced red bell pepper

½ cup diced red onion

Steam string beans until barely tender. In a small bowl, combine olive oil, basil, vinegar, garlic, salt, and pepper. Place beans in a shallow serving bowl. Sprinkle with pecans, feta, red bell pepper, and diced onion, and toss with olive oil dressing.

Variation: Substitute other cheeses such as Parmesan, cheddar, or Swiss for the feta in this recipe.

Recipe for Success

Even string beans become majestic when dressed up with pecans and feta cheese. Enjoy this recipe anytime you find the string beans looking terrific and fresh at the grocery store.

Baked Celery

Prep time: 20 minutes • Cook time: 30 minutes • Serves 6 • Serving size: ½ cup

Each serving has: 8 grams carbohydrate • 3 grams fiber • 5 grams nutritive carbohydrate • 7 grams total protein • 5 grams from animal source • 2 grams from plant source

4 cups sliced celery (½-inch slices)	2 TB. sherry
¼ cup butter	2 tsp. Worcestershire sauce
½ lb. sliced mushrooms	1 tsp. white pepper
2 TB. red bell pepper, chopped	¼ tsp. cayenne
1 cup Basic Cream Soup (see recipe in Chapter 14)	1 cup grated mild cheddar cheese
	¼ cup slivered almonds
¼ cup sour cream	1 tsp. paprika, for garnish

Recipe for Success
Celery is not just for dipping and seasoning—it can be a delicious hot dish all by itself. Add more Basic Cream Soup and water or broth for a soothing celery soup.

Preheat oven to 350°F.

Sauté celery in butter, remove from pan, and set aside. Sauté mushrooms and bell pepper, and add soup, sour cream, sherry, Worcestershire sauce, white pepper, cayenne, cheese, and almonds.

Mix in celery, and pour into a greased baking dish. Sprinkle with paprika, and bake 30 minutes.

Creamed Cabbage

Prep time: 5 minutes • Cook time: 20 minutes • Serves 6 • Serving size: ½ cup

Each serving has: 5 grams carbohydrate • 1 gram fiber • 4 grams nutritive carbohydrate • 2 grams total protein • less than 1 gram from animal source • 2 grams from plant source

2 TB. butter	½ cup sour cream
¾ cup chopped onion	Salt and pepper to taste
4 cups sliced cabbage	Additional seasonings as desired
½ cup water	

Melt butter in a skillet, and sauté onion until tender. Add cabbage and water and cover pan. Simmer for 5 minutes or until cabbage is tender. Remove cover and boil until water is gone.

Stir in sour cream, salt, pepper, and any additional seasonings and serve.

Recipe for Success

This is a basic recipe to allow your own natural chef ability to shine! Experiment with various herbs and vegetable combinations. Using turnips or cauliflower makes the dish a close sub for creamed whole potatoes ... without the excess carbs! Try broccoli or Brussels sprouts for your green veggie. Basil combines with most vegetables for a delightfully fragrant dish.

Eggplant-Squash Bake

Prep time: 20 minutes • Cook time: 20 minutes • Serves 6 • Serving size: ½ cup

Each serving has: 14 grams carbohydrate • 3 grams fiber • 11 grams nutritive carbohydrate • 2 grams total protein • 2 grams from plant source

3 cups peeled and chunked eggplant	½ cup water
6 small zucchini, sliced into chunks	1 tsp. basil or dill weed
3 small onions, chopped	½ lb. feta cheese
Salt and pepper to taste	5 tomatoes, chopped, or 1 (28-oz.) can diced tomatoes, drained

Preheat oven to 350°F.

Mix eggplant and zucchini chunks with chopped onions, salt, and pepper; simmer in water until tender, about 5 minutes. Remove from heat, and add basil and ½ cheese. Pour into a greased baking dish. Top with chopped tomatoes and remaining cheese. Bake until cheese bubbles, about 15 minutes.

Recipe for Success

This recipe is the perfect accompaniment to any meat dish. Leftovers are delicious as a cold lunch the next day or even for breakfast!

Tomatoes Stuffed with Blue Cheese and Mushrooms

Prep time: 20 minutes • Cook time: 25 minutes • Serves 4 • Serving size: 1 tomato plus stuffing

Each serving has: 7 grams carbohydrate • 1 gram fiber • 6 grams nutritive carbohydrates • 3 grams total protein • 2 grams from animal source • 1 gram from plant source

4 large tomatoes	½ tsp. dried parsley
2 TB. butter	1 TB. minced onion
¼ lb. mushrooms	4 TB. crumbled blue cheese

Recipe for Success

Tomatoes aren't just for salads and sauces. These baked tomatoes add lots of pizzazz to simpler meat and fish dishes.

Preheat oven to 350°F.

Cut off top of tomatoes. Take out about ½ the interior without piercing skins. Heat butter in a heavy skillet, and sauté mushrooms with parsley and onion until tender.

Divide mushroom mixture, and put into tomatoes. Top with 1 tablespoon blue cheese each. Put tomatoes into a baking dish, and bake for 25 minutes or until done.

Baked Onions

Prep time: 15 minutes • Cook time: 1 hour • Serves 6 • Serving size: 1 onion

Each serving has: 10 grams carbohydrate • 2 grams fiber • 8 grams nutritive carbohydrate • 1 gram total protein • 1 gram from plant source

6 large sweet onions, such as Vidalia	6 tsp. butter
Salt and pepper to taste	

Recipe for Success

These onions can easily take the place of a baked potato without the extra carbs. Garnish with bacon bits, green onions, and sour cream, if desired.

Preheat oven to 375°F.

Peel onions and place each on a foil square. Salt and pepper as desired. Score onion about halfway through. Place 1 teaspoon butter into each onion, and wrap onion well in the foil. Place in a baking pan, and bake 1 hour.

Broccoli-Stuffed Tomatoes

Prep time: 20 minutes • Cook time: 35 minutes • Serves 6 • Serving size: 1 tomato

Each serving has: 14 grams carbohydrate • 6 grams fiber • 8 grams nutritive carbohydrate • 4 grams total protein • 4 grams from plant source

6 large, firm tomatoes

1 TB. salt

1½ tsp. sugar

2 TB. butter

2 onions, chopped

1½ cups chopped broccoli florets or 1 (10-oz.) pkg. frozen chopped broccoli

2 TB. chopped fresh parsley

Pepper to taste

6 TB. olive oil

½ cup water

6 TB. ground pecans

Wash tomatoes and cut a thin slice from stem end. Save to use later. Scoop out pulp, drain and chop pulp, and set aside. Sprinkle inside of each tomato with ½ teaspoon salt and ¼ teaspoon sugar; invert and drain.

Recipe for Success

Tomato cups can be filled with anything. Of course they make delicious holders for fresh tuna or chicken salad. You can even bake the tomatoes with salad in them for a hot luncheon.

In a large skillet, heat butter and sauté onions and broccoli until soft. Add parsley, pepper, and ½ tomato pulp. Fill tomatoes with broccoli mixture, and set tomatoes in a baking pan. Replace tomato lids, and drizzle 1 tablespoon olive oil over each tomato. Pour water into bottom of pan, and bake 30 minutes or until hot.

Carefully remove and discard tomato lid, and sprinkle tomato with ground pecans. May serve hot or cold.

Green Bean Almandine

Prep time: 10 minutes • Cook time: 20 minutes • Serves 6 • Serving size: ½ cup

Each serving has: 8 grams carbohydrate • 2 grams fiber • 6 grams nutritive carbohydrate • 2 grams total protein • 2 grams from plant source

1½ lb. fresh green beans, trimmed (3 cups)	1 tsp. minced garlic
3 TB. butter	¼ tsp. chopped fresh rosemary or ¼ tsp. dried
½ cup slivered almonds	Salt and pepper to taste
1 small onion, finely chopped	2 TB. chopped pimiento

Bring water to boil in a large pot, and add green beans. Boil until just tender, about 6 to 8 minutes. Drain beans and run under cold water in a colander or plunge them into ice water to prevent further cooking. Pat beans dry, and refrigerate or set aside until ready to use.

Melt butter in a skillet, and sauté almonds, onion, garlic, rosemary, salt, and pepper. Add green beans and pimiento, and stir until heated through.

Recipe for Success _____

You can blanch the beans and refrigerate them the day before or earlier in the day. A few minutes before serving, sauté the seasonings and beans. If fresh beans are unavailable, you may substitute the long frozen beans and omit the first step of blanching. This is a quick and easy, yet elegant, side dish.

Hearts of Palm Spinach

Prep time: 5 minutes   •   Cook time: 45 minutes   •   Serves 6   •   Serving size: ½ cup

Each serving has: 7 grams carbohydrate   •   2 grams fiber   •   5 grams nutritive carbohydrate   •   3 grams total protein   •   1 gram from animal source   •   2 grams from plant source

2 (10-oz.) boxes frozen chopped spinach

2 TB. butter

1 TB. flour

¼ cup cream

½ cup sour cream

1 tsp. Worcestershire sauce

Salt and pepper to taste

1 (14-oz.) can hearts of palm, drained and chopped into bite-size pieces

¼ cup mayonnaise

1 TB. lemon juice

1 TB. paprika

Preheat oven to 350°F.

Cook spinach, drain and squeeze out all liquid, then set aside. In a large skillet, melt butter and stir in flour until thickened. Add cream and ¼ cup sour cream, stirring well. Add Worcestershire sauce, salt, pepper, and spinach. Stir well and simmer 10 minutes. Remove from heat, and mix in hearts of palm.

Combine mayonnaise, remaining ¼ cup sour cream, lemon juice, and paprika and set aside.

Pour vegetables into a greased baking dish, top with mayonnaise mixture, and bake for 30 minutes.

Recipe for Success

We know hearts of palm make a delicious addition to any salad, but many times we forget to cook with them. Substitute them for artichoke hearts in any dish, as they are quite versatile.

Swiss Onions

Prep time: 15 minutes • Cook time: 25 minutes • Serves 6 • Serving size: ½ cup

Each serving has: 7 grams carbohydrate • 1 gram fiber • 6 grams nutritive carbohydrate • 12 grams total protein • 11 grams from animal source • 1 gram from plant source

3 large sweet onions, such as Vidalia, quartered

2 TB. butter

2 cups (8 oz.) shredded Swiss cheese

1 cup mayonnaise

1 (8-oz.) can water chestnuts, sliced

2 TB. white wine

1 clove garlic, minced

½ tsp. cayenne

3 TB. fresh chopped parsley, for garnish

Recipe for Success

This dish is reminiscent of French onion soup. You can substitute other vegetables for the onion or cut onion amount in half and chop; add vegetables such as green beans or broccoli.

Preheat oven to 375°F.

Sauté onions in butter until tender. Combine cheese, mayonnaise, water chestnuts, wine, garlic, and cayenne. Toss with onions, and pour into a greased baking dish. Bake 25 minutes. Top with fresh parsley and serve.

Tasty Turnips

Prep time: 10 minutes • Cook time: 20 minutes • Serves 6 • Serving size: ½ cup

Each serving has: 4 grams carbohydrate • 2 grams fiber • 2 grams nutritive carbohydrate • 3 grams total protein • 2 grams from animal source • 1 gram from plant source

4 medium turnips

1 tsp. sugar

½ tsp. salt

2 cups water

2 beef bouillon cubes

1 tsp. black pepper

4 TB. butter

Peel and quarter turnips, sprinkle with sugar and salt, and set aside.

Boil 2 cups water in a saucepan, and dissolve bouillon cubes. Add turnips, pepper, and additional water to just cover turnips. Cover pot, and simmer until turnips are tender, about 15 minutes. Watch carefully, adding additional water if needed.

Drain turnips and toss with butter. Mash or leave in pieces as desired.

Recipe for Success

Turnips are a wonderful substitute for potatoes. When they are mashed with lots of butter, you can hardly tell they are not potatoes. The sugar keeps the turnips from tasting bitter. Turnips are also delicious cooked in the same pot with Southern Greens.

Vibrant Peppers and Tomatoes

Prep time: 20 minutes • Cook time: 35 minutes • Serves 12 • Serving size: ½ bell pepper

Each serving has: 6 grams carbohydrate • 1 gram fiber • 5 grams nutritive carbohydrate • less than 1 gram total protein

3 red bell peppers

3 yellow bell peppers

¼ cup olive oil

3 cloves garlic, minced

24 red cherry tomatoes

24 yellow cherry tomatoes, or if unavailable, substitute more red cherry or grape tomatoes

3 TB. drained capers

2 TB. fresh thyme leaves

Salt and pepper to taste

½ cup balsamic vinegar

Preheat oven to 425°F.

Cut red and yellow bell peppers in half lengthwise, and remove core and seeds. Keep peppers intact as they will be holders for other vegetables. Oil a large baking pan, and stand peppers up in the pan. Brush peppers with oil.

Divide garlic among peppers, sprinkling into bottom of each pepper. Place 2 red cherry tomatoes and 2 yellow cherry tomatoes into each pepper, and sprinkle with capers, thyme, salt, and pepper. Drizzle each filled pepper with olive oil.

Pour about ¼ cup water into the bottom of the pan. Bake 35 minutes, and cool to room temperature. Serve ½ pepper on each plate, drizzled lightly with balsamic vinegar.

Recipe for Success

This is the perfect dish for a BBQ or any buffet meal. Layer anchovies into the bottom of each pepper for additional flavor, or spice them up with a few slices of pickled jalapeño peppers.

Southern Greens

Prep time: 20 minutes • Cook time: 45 minutes • Serves 6 • Serving size: ½ cup

Each serving has: 4 grams carbohydrate • 2 grams fiber • 2 grams nutritive carbohydrate • 1 gram total protein • 1 gram from animal source • less than 1 gram from plant source

2 lb. mustard greens	2 TB. olive oil
2 qt. water	½ cup chopped onion
¼ cup water	½ tsp. minced garlic
1 beef bouillon cube	½ tsp. salt
2 slices raw bacon or 1 oz. ham, cut into small pieces	1 tsp. black pepper

Wash greens and tear into bite-size pieces, discarding any tough stems. In a large pot, boil 2 quarts water and add greens; boil 20 minutes until tender, then drain and set aside.

In a cast-iron Dutch oven, bring ¼ cup water to a boil, and dissolve bouillon cube. Add bacon pieces and cook. Add olive oil, onion, garlic, salt, and pepper. Stir in greens, and reduce heat to a low simmer.

Cook at least 20 minutes until greens are very tender. Stir periodically, adding water as needed to keep greens from burning.

Recipe for Success _____

Washing fresh greens to get all the sand and grit off the leaves can be a major ordeal. Now the packaged greens make it too easy not to try this simple high-vitamin dish any time of the year. Try various greens such as turnip, mustard, collard, kale, or a mixture of several. Try cooking turnips in the same pot of greens; this gives them a wonderful flavor.

Yellow Squash Casserole

Prep time: 10 minutes • Cook time: 30 minutes • Serves 6 • Serving size: ½ cup

Each serving has: 15 grams carbohydrate • 3 grams fiber • 12 grams nutritive carbohydrate
• 5 grams total protein • 2 grams from animal source • 3 grams from plant source

2 lb. fresh yellow crookneck squash	2 TB. butter or olive oil
Salted water	1 onion, chopped
1 cup Basic Cream Soup (see recipe in Chapter 14)	½ bell pepper, chopped
	2 carrots, chopped
1 egg, beaten	1 TB. chopped fresh parsley
1 (3-oz.) pkg. cream cheese, softened	1 TB. paprika
1 tsp. black pepper	2 tomatoes, chopped, for garnish

Slice squash and boil in salted water until barely tender; drain and set aside. Combine soup, egg, cream cheese, and pepper; set aside.

Recipe for Success

You just cannot beat fresh vegetables, but in a pinch frozen squash will substitute nicely in this casserole. This makes a great addition to covered dish suppers. Add cooked ground round for a meal in itself.

In a skillet, melt butter and sauté onion, bell pepper, and carrots until tender. Mix in soup mixture and heat. When all ingredients are combined, stir in squash and remove from heat.

Pour into a greased baking dish, sprinkle with parsley and paprika, and bake 20 minutes. Serve with fresh chopped tomato for garnish.

Variation: You can substitute fresh or frozen okra or even Brussels sprouts for the squash. This basic recipe is quite useful for most any vegetable.

The Least You Need to Know

- Vegetables add great variety and enjoyment to meals as side dishes.
- Eating your vegetables is certainly good for you and meets the requirements of low-carb eating.
- When purchasing vegetables, buy only the freshest and healthiest.
- Experiment with unfamiliar vegetables to increase your enjoyment of these health workhorses.

Chapter 20

Side Salads

In This Chapter

- Beyond the ho-hum salad
- Naturally low-carb salads
- Attention-getting side salads
- Dressings for all tastes

It's good for you and you order it, but you seldom get excited about it. The "it" we're talking about is the side salad that's just about always included with your entrée in sit-down restaurants. Even without asking, you know what to expect: some iceberg lettuce, maybe a few pieces of a decent leaf lettuce, a cherry tomato (if you're lucky), a couple dried croutons (if you're not), and perhaps some grated carrot or red cabbage shreds for color. Your choice of dressing usually includes ranch, blue cheese, or some kind of vinaigrette.

You can easily prepare this salad in your home—which is why you probably don't. Even though it's good for you, there's a good chance it holds little appeal after years and years of eating it.

So welcome to appetizing salads. In this chapter, we have included salads even our teen-age boys not only eat but actually request. Salads deserve their rightful place among delicious cuisine, not among the good-for-you-but-boring foods.

The Custom of Salads

Over the centuries, people have eaten salads with meals, either before, as we do in the United States, or after, as some Europeans prefer. Salads are a customary part of feasts, fancy dinners, and virtually every meal except breakfast. Of course, you certainly can eat salad for breakfast, too. A favorite restaurant of ours offers "Breakfast Salad" as an entrée.

Folk wisdom proves right again. Today, we know the reasons why salads have stood the test of time. The ingredients in salads supply important nutrients in the form of vitamins, minerals, antioxidants, and fiber. Generally speaking, the darker, more vibrant-colored lettuces have more nutrients.

Salads are excellent as side dishes for low-carb eating. You can add a salad to any main course because salads have some carbohydrates, but not many, and they add fiber to your diet. Plus, they have a refreshing quality that lightens the meal and yet satisfies.

Salad Pizzazz

A little pizzazz can turn an otherwise ho-hum salad into a delicious treat. The first time we tasted the Fiesta Confetti Salad we were in foodie heaven. Enhanced with Southwestern spices of cumin and cilantro, this salad—really a modified salsa—is sure far from boring!

The wonderful Romaine Salad with Capers and Salami also contains marinated artichoke hearts, anchovy paste, raisins, grated Parmesan cheese, and pine nuts. Remember, this is just a tossed lettuce salad but one tossed with remarkable ingredients that have our party guests practically licking the salad bowl.

The pizzazz in salads comes from adding unusual spices, vegetables, and even fruits to the standard tossed or vegetable salad. Meats, fish, and cheeses add depth and richness to a salad's taste. You'll find many good examples of salad pizzazz in these recipes.

Dressing Up Your Salads

Salad dressings are sneaky concoctions. We really only need a "splash" of salad dressing to enhance the flavor of lettuce and vegetables, but so often we tend to spoon on so much we hide the appealing tastes of the lettuces and vegetables. Too much dressing will also overload your fat intake for the day, so go easy with it.

Table Talk

Here's a basic, simple, time-tested salad dressing: Put lettuce and vegetables — the greens—into a large salad bowl. Sprinkle olive oil over the greens. Toss until each leaf is coated with a thin layer of the oil. Add more oil if needed. Then add a splash or two of your favorite vinegar and toss. Taste to make sure you have enough vinegar but not too much. Add a sprinkling of salt and some freshly ground black pepper. Then add your special pizzazz to the salad.

The dressings in these salads are low carb and contain healthy ingredients. But when purchasing salad dressing in the store, take caution to make sure you're getting the best.

♦ The best oils for salad dressings are cold expeller-pressed oils. This method of obtaining the oil doesn't use heat. Using heat to extract the oil changes the nature of the oil and creates undesirable trans-fatty acids. Some good oils to use are walnut, olive, almond, canola, hazelnut, and flaxseed. If your grocer doesn't carry cold expeller-pressed oils, find them at the health food store.

Table Talk

Store lettuce unwashed in a sealed plastic bag with a small hole or two for ventilation. Place the bag in a cold area of your refrigerator, as it lasts longest and stays crispest when stored at a temperature just above 32°F.

Table Talk

To restore partially wilted raw vegetables and lettuce, put them into a container of cold water for several minutes. This adds moisture and increases crispness.

♦ Some dressings are made with bacon fat and are quite excellent. Animal fats, including butter, can be heated without deterioration or change in quality provided you don't burn them.

♦ Avoid using low-fat salad dressings, as they are high in carbohydrates and contain both added sugars and starches.

♦ Keep freshly bottled natural lemon or lime juice in the refrigerator for salad dressings. You can also squeeze fresh lemons and limes for dressings.

♦ The tanginess of salad dressings comes from the vinegar or lemon/lime juice. If you like your dressing tangy, use more. If not, cut back on the vinegar or juice.

♦ With the exception of balsamic vinegar, vinegars contain no carbohydrates. Balsamic vinegar has 2 grams carbohydrates for 2 tablespoons.

♦ Add spices, herbs, and condiments for more flavor. Experiment with mustards, olives, hot or mild peppers, parsley, oregano, cayenne, balsam, cilantro, rosemary, and virtually anything else in your spice cabinet.

Romaine Salad with Capers and Salami

Prep time: 10 minutes • Cook time: 0 • Serves 6 • Serving size: ⅙ recipe

Each serving has: 7 grams carbohydrate • 2 grams fiber • 5 grams nutritive carbohydrate • less than 1 gram total protein

1 head romaine lettuce, washed and torn into bite-size pieces

3 TB. olive oil

3 TB. red wine vinegar

1 TB. flax seeds

2 TB. seeds or nuts—pine nuts, pumpkin seeds, sunflower seeds, pecans, slivered almonds, chopped walnuts

1 to 2 tsp. capers or to taste

2 marinated artichoke heart pieces, cut into slices

½ tsp. anchovy paste

2 TB. raisins, dried cranberries, or dried cherries

2 thin slices salami, fried

2 TB. shredded Parmesan cheese

2 TB. croutons

Recipe for Success

This is the most appealing tossed salad we know. It's even good eaten the next day. Our children who hate veggies actually want to eat this salad.

Spin lettuce until dry, put into a large salad bowl, and sprinkle with olive oil. Toss, making sure to lightly coat each leaf. Sprinkle with red wine vinegar and toss. Add flax seeds, other seeds, capers, artichoke heart pieces, anchovy paste, raisins, salami, cheese, and croutons and toss well.

Variation: To make this into a main course salad, add ½ pound roast beef, cut into strips.

Winter Salad

Prep time: 20 minutes   •   Cook time: 0   •   Serves 6   •   Serving size: ⅙ salad

Each serving has: 3 grams carbohydrate   •   less than 1 gram fiber   •   3 grams nutritive carbohydrate   •   less than 1 gram total protein

3 TB. finely chopped fresh parsley

¼ cup olive oil

¼ cup walnut oil

1 TB. white vinegar

1 TB lemon juice

1 tsp. Dijon mustard

½ tsp. salt

⅛ tsp. freshly ground pepper

½ lb. mushrooms

12 radishes

¼ jicama, peeled

4 to 6 green onions, thinly sliced by hand

1 clove garlic, minced

6 romaine lettuce leaves

Combine parsley, olive oil, walnut oil, vinegar, lemon juice, mustard, salt, and pepper in a jar and shake well.

Thinly slice mushrooms, radishes, and jicama. If not using immediately, refrigerate vegetables in separate containers covered with plastic wrap. When ready to serve, combine with green onions, garlic, and dressing, and serve in lettuce cups.

Recipe for Success

Enjoy this unusual blending of vegetables as a side dish with a heavier main course such

Spinach Salad with Hot Bacon Dressing

Prep time: 20 minutes • Cook time: 0 • Serves 12 • Serving size: 1/12 salad

Each serving has: 4 grams carbohydrate • less than 1 gram fiber • 4 grams nutritive carbohydrate • 4 grams total protein • 3 grams from animal source • 1 gram from plant source

12 slices bacon	3 tsp. flour
6 TB. bacon grease	6 TB. sour cream
9 TB. vinegar	½ tsp. salt
1 TB. water	2 TB. sugar
3 egg yolks	2 (10-oz.) pkg. fresh spinach

Recipe for Success ___
Yes, this dressing is made with bacon fat. It has no carbs, but it sure delivers a hearty taste to the spinach.

Cut bacon into ½-inch squares and cook. Drain, reserving 6 tablespoons bacon grease.

Add vinegar to bacon grease and cool. Add water to egg yolks, and blend in flour. Add this mixture to the pan, combining bacon and bacon grease with vinegar. Cook on medium heat, stirring constantly, until the mixture thickens.

Add sour cream, salt, and sugar, and bring to a boil. Pour over spinach, and serve at once.

Note: This dressing can be reheated.

Celery Root Salad

Prep time: 20 minutes • Cook time: 1 hour • Serves 6 • Serving size: 1/6 salad

Each serving has: 10 grams carbohydrate • 2 grams fiber • 8 grams nutritive carbohydrate • 2 grams total protein • less than 1 gram from animal source • 2 grams from plant source

1 celery root (also known as celeriac)	2 small bay leaves
6 small onions, peeled	4 TB. butter
6 TB. dry white wine	¼ tsp. salt
¾ cup chicken bouillon	¼ tsp. paprika
1 tsp. peppercorns	

Peel celery root, and cut into small sections like french fries. Steam for 15 minutes. Combine celery root, onions, wine, bouillon, peppercorns, bay leaves, butter, and salt in a saucepan. Simmer over low heat for 45 minutes. Remove bay leaf.

Cool in the refrigerator. Serve cold with a sprinkling of paprika.

Recipe for Success
Celery root is an excellent vegetable for salads. It has the mild taste of celery hearts, and it holds up to heat well. Unlike celery, it doesn't become really soft. You can also use celery root for crudités and even grated as a bed for meat sauces.

Fiesta Confetti Salad

Prep time: 25 minutes plus chill time • Cook time: 0 • Serves 24 • Serving size: $\frac{1}{24}$ salad

Each serving has: 7 grams carbohydrate • 1 gram fiber • 6 grams nutritive carbohydrate • 1 gram total protein • 0 grams from animal source • 1 gram from plant source

1 green bell pepper, chopped	1 (11-oz.) can corn, drained
1 red bell pepper, chopped	1 (15-oz.) can black beans, drained
2 tomatoes, chopped	1 (4-oz.) can green chilies
1 papaya or mango, peeled, seeded, and chopped	$\frac{1}{2}$ tsp. cumin
1 bunch green onions, chopped	1 tsp. salt
1 clove garlic, minced	$\frac{1}{2}$ tsp. freshly ground black pepper
$\frac{1}{2}$ cup chopped fresh cilantro	1 small jalapeño pepper, minced (optional)
	3 limes, sliced

Combine green and red bell peppers, tomatoes, papaya, green onions, garlic, cilantro, corn, beans, chilies, cumin, salt, black pepper, jalapeño (if using), and limes in a large bowl. Mix well. Chill before serving.

Recipe for Success
This recipe is a delightful surprise as a salad and also as salsa. Serve with meat, Mexican entrées, chicken, and fish. Eat for lunch and also breakfast. It's totally good for you.

Five-Day Coleslaw

Prep time: 15 minutes plus overnight chill time   •   Cook time: 5 minutes   •   Serves 6
•   Serving size: ¾ cup or ⅙ recipe

Each serving has: 9 grams carbohydrate   •   2 grams fiber   •   7 grams nutritive carbohydrate
•   1 gram total protein   •   1 gram from plant source

2 cups thinly sliced red cabbage	1 TB. white wine vinegar
2 cups thinly sliced green cabbage	1 TB. minced garlic
½ cup sliced celery	1 TB. chopped red onion
½ cup coarsely chopped bell pepper	1 TB. minced fresh ginger or 1 tsp. ground
4 green onions, sliced	1 tsp. dry mustard
2 TB. sugar	Salt and pepper to taste
2 TB. mayonnaise	

Combine red and green cabbage, celery, bell pepper, green onions, sugar, and mayonnaise. In a small saucepan, combine vinegar, garlic, red onion, ginger, mustard, salt, and pepper and bring to a boil. Pour over vegetables and mix well. Cover and refrigerate overnight before serving. This will keep well for 5 days covered in the refrigerator.

Recipe for Success

Even though the name is "Five-Day Coleslaw" we doubt you will have any left for that long. This crunchy, low-carb salad is wonderful wrapped up in meat wraps or used as a base for grilled meat salads. It is just the thing for a pick-me-up snack in the afternoon when the desire for something crunchy hits.

Asian Spinach Salad

Prep time: 10 minutes • Cook time: 0 • Serves 6 • Serving size: ⅙ recipe

Each serving has: 5 grams carbohydrate • 2 grams fiber • 3 grams nutritive carbohydrate • 5 grams total protein • 3 grams from animal source • 2 grams from plant source

½ cup soy sauce	1 (8-oz.) can water chestnuts
6 TB. olive oil	1 (8-oz.) can bean sprouts, drained
1 tsp. sesame oil (hot chili oil is best)	3 hard-boiled eggs, sliced
½ tsp. molasses	1 TB. slivered almonds, for garnish (optional)
1 (10-oz.) pkg. baby spinach leaves	1 TB. sesame seeds, for garnish (optional)

Combine soy sauce, olive oil, sesame oil, and molasses, and mix well in a blender.

Combine spinach, water chestnuts, bean sprouts, and eggs in a serving bowl; toss with dressing and serve. Garnish with slivered almonds and sesame seeds (if using).

Recipe for Success

This salad is just the treat for those who love hot-and-sour soup. The sweet and spicy flavors in the dressing make this salad irresistible; add seafood or meat for a wonderful main dish salad.

Caesar Salad

Prep time: 10 minutes • Cook time: 1 minute • Serves 6 • Serving size: 1 cup

Each serving has: 2 grams carbohydrate • 1 gram fiber • 1 gram nutritive carbohydrate • 2 grams total protein • 1 gram from animal source • 1 gram from plant source

1 egg	3 TB. olive oil
1 tsp. Dijon mustard	1 tsp. anchovy paste
2 TB. lemon juice	2 heads (6 cups) romaine lettuce, washed and torn into bite-size pieces
½ tsp. salt	2 TB. grated Parmesan cheese
1 tsp. black pepper	
1 clove garlic, minced, or 1 tsp. garlic powder	

Recipe for Success

Most Caesar salads are served garnished with high-carb croutons. For an extra crunch, try broken pieces of Parmesan crackers or sprinkle with sesame seeds or your favorite nut.

Boil egg for 1 minute, remove shell, and set aside. In a small bowl, combine mustard, lemon juice, salt, pepper, and garlic; whisk together until salt dissolves. Add olive oil, anchovy paste, and boiled egg and mix until well blended. Toss with romaine lettuce; sprinkle with Parmesan and serve.

Congealed Asparagus Salad

Prep time: 20 minutes plus overnight chill time • Cook time: 5 minutes • Serves 6
• Serving size: 1 piece

Each serving has: 18 grams carbohydrate • 3 grams fiber • 15 grams nutritive carbohydrate • 4 grams total protein • 4 grams from plant source

2 pkg. unflavored gelatin

1¾ cups water

6 TB. sugar

¼ cup white vinegar

2 (10½-oz.) cans whole asparagus spears, drained well, 1 cup juice reserved

¾ cup thinly sliced celery

2 TB. lemon juice

2 tsp. grated onion

1 (4-oz.) jar pimientos, chopped

½ cup chopped pecans or walnuts

Dissolve gelatin in ¼ cup water. Boil sugar and vinegar with 1 cup water and 1 cup asparagus juice, adding additional water if needed to make 2 cups. Cool slightly.

Line an 8-inch-square glass baking dish with drained asparagus spears. Mix gelatin mixture with celery, lemon juice, onion, pimientos, and pecans, and pour over asparagus. Chill overnight to set. Cut into 6 pieces, and serve each on lettuce leaf.

Recipe for Success

This makes a pretty salad to serve. It is so light it goes well with most meats and casseroles. You can substitute long whole green beans if desired. With the red pimientos, this salad goes well with red and green holiday decorations!

Cranberry Salad

Prep time: 10 minutes plus overnight chill time • Cook time: 0 • Serves 6
• Serving size: ⅙ recipe or ¾ cup

Each serving has: 19 grams carbohydrate • 4 grams fiber • 15 grams nutritive carbohydrate
• 1 gram total protein • less than 1 gram from animal source • 1 gram from plant
source

2 cups fresh or frozen cranberries

½ cup sugar

1 cup diced, unpeeled apples

1 cup fresh grapes, halved

1 cup fresh orange sections

½ cup pecans

¼ cup heavy cream, whipped

¼ cup mayonnaise

Recipe for Success

You can find cranberries in grocery stores in greatest abundance during the fall holiday season. Be sure to buy extra bags to freeze so you can enjoy this delicious salad all year long. Be sure to use them within a year after freezing.

Wash cranberries and chop in a food processor until coarsely chopped. In a small bowl, combine cranberries and sugar; pour into a colander, and let drain over a bowl in the refrigerator overnight.

Combine drained cranberries, apples, grapes, oranges, and pecans. Toss lightly and serve on lettuce leaf.

Blend whipped cream and mayonnaise, and serve over salad.

Guacamole

Prep time: 10 minutes plus 30 minutes chill time • Cook time: 0 • Serves 6
• Serving size: ½ cup

Each serving has: 8 grams carbohydrate • 3 grams fiber • 5 grams nutritive carbohydrate
• 1 gram total protein • 1 gram from plant source

6 avocados, peeled

⅓ cup lime juice

2 large tomatoes, chopped

4 cloves garlic, minced

1 TB. chopped fresh cilantro

Salt and pepper to taste

2 TB. chopped onion (optional)

Mash avocados, leaving a few small lumps. Stir in lime juice, tomatoes, garlic, cilantro, salt, and pepper. Mix in chopped onion (if using). Cover tightly and chill at least 30 minutes. Serve chilled over lettuce leaf or as garnish to other foods.

Recipe for Success _____

Avocados have that creamy, comfort-food texture. We assure you that the fat they contain is the good-for-you monounsaturated fat. Although this recipe makes a delicious dip for vegetables, try spreading it on your next meat wrap sandwich for a refreshing flavor. It is also great for breakfast mixed in with scrambled eggs and tomato.

Mandarin Orange Spinach

Prep time: 15 minutes • Cook time: 0 • Serves 6 • Serving size: 1½ cups

Each serving has: 18 grams carbohydrate • 2 grams fiber • 16 grams nutritive carbohydrate • 6 grams total protein • 6 grams from plant source

1 head romaine lettuce leaves	¼ cup olive oil
2 bunches spinach or other greens	2 TB. wine vinegar
1 bunch green onions	1 TB. sugar
½ bunch fresh parsley	½ tsp. salt
2 (6-oz.) cans Mandarin oranges, drained	1 tsp. Tabasco or other hot sauce
6 oz. cashews	Black pepper to taste

Mix together lettuce, spinach, green onions, parsley, oranges, and cashews in a large bowl. In a screw-top jar, mix together oil, vinegar, sugar, salt, Tabasco, and pepper and shake well. Pour over salad and serve.

Recipe for Success _____

This sweet-hot dressing is delicious served over any greens. Add chunky chicken for a wonderful main dish salad. Or add other fruits such as apples or strawberries.

Marinated Tomato Slices

Prep time: 10 minutes plus 4 hours marinating time • Cook time: 0 • Serves 6
• Serving size: ⅙ recipe or 4 slices

Each serving has: 11 grams carbohydrate • 1 gram fiber • 10 grams nutritive carbohydrate
• 1 gram total protein • 1 gram from plant source

½ cup balsamic vinegar

½ cup olive oil

¼ cup sugar

Salt and pepper to taste

2 TB. dried basil

5 to 6 firm tomatoes, each sliced into 4 to 5 slices

Mix vinegar, oil, sugar, salt, pepper, and basil until well combined. Place tomato slices in single layer, and pour marinade over all. Cover and refrigerate at least 4 hours or overnight. Serve on lettuce leaf.

Recipe for Success _____

This is a wonderful marinade to use especially for fresh tomatoes right from the garden. Add blanched carrots or cucumbers and green beans for a delightful fresh vegetable salad. Marinated tomatoes give a pungent bite to a grilled burger as well.

Marinated Vegetables

Prep time: 20 minutes plus overnight chill time • Cook time: 3 minutes • Serves 6 • Serving size: ¼ cup or ⅙ recipe

Each serving has: 6 grams carbohydrate • 2 grams fiber • 4 grams nutritive carbohydrate • 1 gram total protein • 1 gram from plant source

1 cup sliced carrot sticks	1 tsp. brown sugar
1 cup cubed yellow squash	1 tsp. spicy mustard
1 head fresh broccoli	1 tsp. Worcestershire sauce
1½ cups red wine vinegar	1 TB. dill seed
2 TB. water	½ tsp. minced garlic
½ cup olive oil	Salt and pepper to taste

Blanch carrot sticks in boiling water for 3 minutes; remove and drain. Peel off tough outer layer from squash, and cut into bite-size cubes. Cut off any tough broccoli stalks, and slice broccoli into serving-size spears. If desired, trim stalks and peel off outer tough portion; slice inner hearts into thin, bite-size pieces.

Mix together vinegar, water, oil, brown sugar, mustard, Worcestershire sauce, dill seed, garlic, salt, and pepper. Pour marinade over vegetables, cover, and chill overnight.

Variation: To make a warm marinated vegetable dish, try using halved, steamed Brussels sprouts. Heat marinade until just simmering, pour marinade over warm Brussels sprouts, add sliced green onions, mix well, and serve. If desired, refrigerate the dish overnight and serve cold.

Recipe for Success _____

You can also marinate blanched green beans or cauliflower, fresh mushrooms, jicama, and so on. It is convenient if you keep a large jar of marinade in the refrigerator; just add extra cut vegetables to the jar as you use them for other dishes. As you make another dish, you can slice an additional onion or bell pepper to add to the marinating vegetables. This vegetable mix makes tasty additions to your green salad.

Mushroom-Artichoke Salad

Prep time: 15 minutes plus overnight chill time   •   Cook time: 1 minute   •   Serves 6
•   Serving size: ⅙ recipe or ½ cup

Each serving has: 8 grams carbohydrate   •   2 grams fiber   •   6 grams nutritive carbohydrate
•   2 grams total protein   •   0 grams from animal source   •   2 grams from plant source

1 lb. sliced fresh mushrooms

1 (4-oz.) jar green pitted olives, sliced

1 (3.8-oz.) can black pitted olives, sliced

1 (10-oz.) frozen artichoke hearts, cooked as
directed, or 2 (14-oz.) cans artichoke hearts,
cut in quarters

1 TB. chopped pimiento

3 TB. chopped onion

½ cup olive oil

½ cup garlic-flavored vinegar

½ tsp. dried tarragon, oregano, or dill

Salt and pepper to taste

Sauté mushrooms 1 minute and drain. Drain green
and black olives, and mix together with artichoke
hearts and mushrooms.

Combine pimiento, onion, olive oil, vinegar, tarragon, salt, and pepper. Pour dressing over vegetables and refrigerate overnight.

Recipe for Success
This dish is delicious
served alone or added to
a green salad to give it that wilted
Italian flavor.

Buttermilk Herb Dressing

Prep time: 10 minutes   •   Cook time: 0   •   Makes: 1 cup   •   Serving size: 2 tablespoons

Each serving has: 2 grams nutritive carbohydrate   •   less than 1 gram total protein

¾ cup buttermilk

¼ cup mayonnaise

1 tsp. white pepper

2 tsp. minced fresh basil or 1 tsp. dried

2 tsp. minced fresh parsley or ½ tsp. dried

2 cloves garlic, minced

Combine buttermilk, mayonnaise, pepper, basil, parsley, and garlic until mixed well. Refrigerate.

Dijon-Lemon Vinaigrette

Prep time: 10 minutes • Cook time: 0 • Makes: ¾ cup • Serving size: 2 tablespoons

Each serving has: 2 grams nutritive carbohydrate • less than 1 gram total protein

¼ cup chicken broth or water

3 TB. lemon juice

3 TB. olive oil

3 TB. red wine vinegar

1 TB. Dijon mustard

2 cloves garlic, minced

1 TB. Worcestershire sauce

2 tsp. white pepper

Combine broth, lemon juice, olive oil, vinegar, mustard, garlic, Worcestershire sauce, and pepper until mixed well. Refrigerate.

Green Goddess Dressing

Prep time: 10 minutes • Cook time: 0 • Makes: 1 cup • Serving size: 2 tablespoons

Each serving has: 5 grams nutritive carbohydrate • less than 1 gram fiber • 3 grams total protein • 3 grams from animal source • less than 1 gram from plant source

1 cup sour cream

1 cup mayonnaise

2½ cups whipping cream

3 green onion tops, chopped

2 cloves garlic, minced

1 TB. anchovy paste

1 tsp. white pepper

2 tsp. minced fresh parsley or ½ tsp. dried

Combine sour cream, mayonnaise, whipping cream, green onions, garlic, anchovy paste, pepper, and parsley until mixed well. Refrigerate.

Recipe for Success _____

Nothing beats the taste of fresh homemade salad dressings. Perk them up with your own favorite seasonings and a variety of flavored vinegars. You know you can pronounce the name of your ingredients with no hidden harmful fats or chemicals.

Ranch Dressing

Prep time: 10 minutes • Cook time: 0 • Makes: 1½ cups • Serving size: 2 tablespoons

Each serving has: 1 gram nutritive carbohydrate • less than 1 gram total protein

1 cup mayonnaise	1 TB. minced garlic
¼ cup plain yogurt	2 TB. minced onion
¼ cup heavy cream	½ tsp. black pepper

Combine mayonnaise, yogurt, cream, garlic, onion, and pepper until mixed well. Refrigerate.

The Least You Need to Know

- Side salads make an easy, quick, and low-carb way to add texture, fiber, interest, and nutrients to a meal.
- Make dressings from cold expeller-pressed oils for taste and health.
- Add pizzazz to salads with interesting ingredients such as nuts, croutons, pieces of meat or fish, and cheese.
- Eat salads anytime—even for breakfast.

Chapter 21

Fruit Side Dishes

In This Chapter

- ◆ Adding fruit to your eating plan
- ◆ Sweetening meals with fruit
- ◆ Fitting fruit into your carb allotment
- ◆ Enjoying fruit's flavors and textures

Fruits are such an important part of a nutritionally sound eating plan that we've given them an entire chapter. Fruits are delicious, satisfying, and convenient. Many fruits, such as oranges, bananas, avocados, and apples, even come naturally packaged with a "to-go" wrapper.

Yes, fruits contain carbs, but they also contain lots of vitamins, minerals, antioxidants, and dietary fiber that are wonderful for your overall health. Perhaps you have avoided eating fruits because you thought they were too high in carbs. They're not as bad as you think. Let's do a quick calculation. One half an apple, which is considered a serving, only has 11 grams carbs and 2.5 grams dietary fiber, for a nutritive carbohydrate value of only 8.5 carbs. Obviously, your overall eating plan can easily accommodate an apple; yes, even an apple a day.

Dietitians and nutritionists recommend we eat a minimum of 5 servings of fruits and vegetables a day. They know the importance of fruits to your health and well-being. Plus, there are tastes and textures in fruits that you just can't get anywhere else. They'll add wonderful variety and interest to your meals. In other words, it's time to start enjoying fruits.

Dessert or Side Dish

Eating fruits is an excellent way to satisfy your sweet tooth. The fructose, or fruit sugar, in fruits makes them sweet. Fructose is low glycemic, meaning that it causes only a small rise in blood sugar levels, which is good. So you can eat moderate serving sizes of fruit and satisfy your sweet tooth while eating low glycemic, which is good for your heart, your weight, and your health.

Fruits are a versatile food eaten in several ways: as a snack, a side dish, or a dessert. You can serve these recipes as side dishes for breakfast, lunch, or dinner. You can also serve some as desserts or snacks. You get to choose how fruits work in your food plans.

Hot Potato
Some fruits, such as bananas, pineapple, papaya, watermelon, and apricots, are moderate glycemic. Go easier with them. Eat them in moderate amounts. You'll get the pleasure and nutrition they offer without raising your blood sugar level.

Nutritionists now recommend we "eat a rainbow." In other words, eat many colors of foods daily. Eat foods that are green, yellow, purple, red, orange, and even blue. Like vegetables, fruits have many varied colors. Both provide unique nutrients that help strengthen the immune system, protect against free radical damage, help prevent cancer, and in short, keep our bodies functioning well.

Into Your Meal

These fruit recipes have been designed to be low carb. We have taken advantage of the natural sweetness of fruit to save you carbs while letting you enjoy the benefits that cooking with fruits provides. The fruits in these recipes are mostly used raw but are sometimes cooked. Either way, they provide similar nutritional value.

If you are carefully counting carbohydrate grams, find a way to add at least 1 fruit a day. If you are more relaxed about your carb counts, then go for more.

Fresh Fruit Medley with Poppy Seed Dressing

Prep time: 25 minutes • Cook time: 0 • Serves 8 • Serving size: ⅛ recipe

Each serving has: 15 grams carbohydrate • 2 grams fiber • 13 grams nutritive carbohydrate • 1 gram total protein • 1 gram from plant source

1 orange, peeled and cut into sections	5 sprigs fresh basil, cut into 1-inch pieces
1 grapefruit, peeled and cut into bite-size sections	3 TB. fresh or bottled lemon juice
1 banana, peeled and sliced	¼ cup walnut oil, *cold expeller-pressed*
1 Red Delicious apple, cored and sliced	1½ tsp. poppy seeds
1 pint strawberries, stemmed and cut in half	1 tsp. honey
1 pear, cored and cut into 1-inch pieces	Salt and pepper to taste

Combine orange, grapefruit, banana, apple, strawberries, and pear in a large bowl with basil. Toss with 1 tablespoon lemon juice to keep fruits from discoloring.

Make dressing by combining walnut oil, remaining 2 tablespoons lemon juice, poppy seeds, honey, and salt and pepper to taste. Pour dressing over fruit mixture, and toss to coat fruits. Serve immediately.

Variation: Make this recipe with whatever fresh fruit is available locally in your grocery store. You can also add chopped or slivered nuts, such as pecans, pine nuts, walnuts, almonds, macadamias, and pistachios. Or add seeds—pumpkin, flax, sesame, or sunflower.

Table Talk

Cold expeller-pressed means the oil was pressed out of the walnuts rather than using heat. When vegetable and nut oils are heated, which is more common, they change into trans-fatty acids, which directly cause heart disease.

Apples with Raisins and Pecans

Prep time: 25 minutes   •   Cook time: 25 minutes   •   Serves 8   •   Serving size: ⅛ recipe

Each serving has: 19 grams carbohydrate   •   3 grams fiber   •   16 grams nutritive carbohydrate   •   1 gram total protein   •   1 gram from plant source

4 medium apples, cored and sliced (your favorite)	¼ cup raisins
½ tsp. cinnamon	2 TB. brown sugar
½ tsp. nutmeg	½ cup pecan halves
2 TB. fresh or bottled lemon juice	2 TB. butter

Recipe for Success

We used a favorite pie recipe and took away the crust. We think you'll love the filling as much as we do. It's a terrific combination of tastes. Use this recipe as a dessert or as a side dish with eggs for breakfast.

Preheat oven to 350°F.

Put apples, cinnamon, nutmeg, lemon juice, raisins, and brown sugar into a baking dish and mix. Spread evenly with pecans and dot with small pieces of butter. Bake, covered, for 25 minutes.

Gingered Papayas

Prep time: 10 minutes   •   Cook time: 30 minutes   •   Serves 8   •   Serving size: ⅛ recipe

Each serving has: 16 grams carbohydrate   •   2 grams fiber   •   14 grams nutritive carbohydrate   •   1 gram total protein   •   1 gram from plant source

4 firm, ripe papayas	1 tsp. ground ginger
8 TB. butter	8 thin slices lime
4 TB. fresh or bottled lime juice	Dash cayenne

Preheat oven to 350°F.

Cut papayas in half lengthwise, and scoop out seeds. Arrange in a glass baking dish with ⅛ inch warm water in the bottom. In each papaya hollow, place 1 tablespoon butter, ½ tablespoon lime juice, and ⅛ teaspoon ground ginger.

Bake for 30 minutes, basting 10 minutes before done. Place a slice of lime at the edge of each papaya half. Add a dash cayenne and serve warm.

Recipe for Success

Papayas bring the taste of the tropics into our kitchens. Baking them brings out their flavor, which also is enhanced by the butter. To ripen fruit, place in a closed container, such as a paper bag. Fruit gives off ethylene gas, which hastens the ripening process. A closed container concentrates the gas, and the fruit ripens more quickly. Serve as a dessert or side dish for brunch.

Fresh Berries with Orange Cream

Prep time: 15 minutes • Cook time: 15 minutes • Serves 4 • Serving size: ¼ recipe

Each serving has: 19 grams carbohydrate • 1 gram fiber • 18 grams nutritive carbohydrate • 1 gram total protein • 1 gram from animal source • less than 1 gram from plant source

1 pint strawberries	½ cup orange juice
3 TB. sugar	1 cup heavy cream
2 tsp. grated orange rind	

Wash and hull strawberries, cutting in half or leaving whole. Combine sugar, orange rind, and orange juice in a small saucepan. Bring to a boil, stirring only until sugar dissolves. Simmer 10 minutes without stirring. Cool completely.

Whip cream until soft peaks form. Gently fold in orange syrup. Serve over berries.

Variation: Substitute fresh blueberries or raspberries, and, instead of orange, use lemon juice and rind in the same quantities.

Recipe for Success

This recipe makes a great side dish for a meat entrée, or serve it as dessert.

Waldorf Salad

Prep time: 20 minutes • Cook time: 0 • Serves 6 • Serving size: ¾ cup

Each serving has: 11 grams carbohydrate • 3 grams fiber • 8 grams nutritive carbohydrate • 5 grams total protein • 5 grams from plant source

1 cup diced celery	½ cup walnut or pecan meats
1 cup diced apples	¾ cup mayonnaise
1 cup green grapes, halved and seeded	

Combine celery, apples, grapes, walnut meats, and mayonnaise. Mix well.

Recipe for Success _____

This crunchy, sweet, and at the same time tangy combination of ingredients goes well with virtually all main dishes. The fruits are available year-round at the grocery store, so you can serve this for Thanksgiving dinner or a summer barbecue. But remember, as this dish is mayonnaise-based, keep it refrigerated until serving and don't keep it out in the hot sun, as it will turn bad.

Avocado and Papaya Salad

Prep time: 20 minutes • Cook time: 0 • Serves 6 • Serving size: ⅙ recipe

Each serving has: 16 grams carbohydrate • 3 grams fiber • 13 grams nutritive carbohydrate • 2 grams total protein • 2 grams from plant source

1 cup avocado, cubed	1 TB. lime juice
1 papaya, peeled and sliced diagonally	¼ tsp. paprika
Bibb lettuce leaves	½ tsp. salt
½ cup salad oil	½ tsp. dry mustard
⅓ cup tarragon vinegar	1 TB. minced onion
1 TB. sugar	1½ TB. papaya seeds

Arrange avocado and papaya on a lettuce leaf.

To make dressing, place salad oil, vinegar, sugar, lime juice, paprika, salt, mustard, and onion into a blender. Cover and blend thoroughly. Add papaya seeds and blend until seeds are the size of coarsely ground pepper. Chill.

Pour dressing over fruit just before serving.

Recipe for Success

Enjoy this wonderful fruit salad with your meals. You get an extra bonus if you serve it with a hearty meat main course. The ground-up papaya seeds in the dressing plus the papaya itself offer a high amount of natural digestive enzymes.

Table Talk

Papaya seeds are edible. Most people only eat the sweet delicious flesh, but you can also eat the small, black seeds in the center of the fruit. The seeds taste like black pepper and contain papain, a digestive enzyme. The ground seeds can also be used in marinades to tenderize meat. People in some countries use papaya seeds in place of black peppercorns.

Pears with Avocado and Lime

Prep time: 20 minutes • Cook time: 0 • Serves 6 • Serving size: ⅙ recipe

Each serving has: 19 grams carbohydrate • 6 grams fiber • 13 grams nutritive carbohydrate • less than 1 gram total protein

1 TB. confectioners' sugar

2 TB. hot water

2 tsp. finely grated lime rind

¼ cup fresh lime juice

3 firm, ripe pears

1½ cups cubed avocado

1 head red leaf lettuce, leaves left whole

¼ cup chopped fresh cilantro

Recipe for Success

Enjoy avocado any way you can. It is filled with good and healthy fats and offers high nutritional value. It's great with lime, but it's fabulous with pears and lime.

Dissolve sugar in hot water. Stir in lime rind and lime juice and set aside. Peel and slice pears and avocados, brushing each slice with lime juice mixture to prevent discoloration.

Arrange lettuce leaves on individual serving plates. Alternate slices of pear and avocado over lettuce. Top with additional lime juice mixture and sprinkle with cilantro.

Fruit Salad with Passion Fruit

Prep time: 20 minutes plus chill time • Cook time: 0 • Serves 6 • Serving size: ⅙ recipe

Each serving has: 14 grams carbohydrate • 3 grams fiber • 11 grams nutritive carbohydrate • less than 1 gram total protein

3 cups strawberries, hulled and halved	3 TB. walnut oil
3 oranges, peeled and segmented	2 TB. white wine
2 passion fruit	¼ tsp. ginger

Put hulled and halved strawberries and peeled and segmented oranges into a serving bowl. Halve passion fruit and, using a teaspoon, scoop flesh into the bowl.

Mix walnut oil, white wine, and ginger in a small bowl. Pour mixture over fruit and toss gently. Cover and chill in the refrigerator until ready to serve.

Variation: You can substitute grapefruit for the oranges and raspberries for the strawberries in this recipe. Also, instead of passion fruit, you can use pomegranate seeds. For a special taste, substitute 1 teaspoon poppy seeds for the ginger.

Pear Compote

Prep time: 10 minutes • Cook time: 20 to 30 minutes • Serves 6 • Serving size: 1 pear plus ⅙ sauce

Each serving has: 16 grams carbohydrate • 6 grams fiber • 10 grams nutritive carbohydrate • less than 1 gram total protein

6 firm cooking pears	1 slice lemon
2 cups boiling water	2 TB. chopped pistachios
¼ tsp. minced fresh ginger	2 tsp. confectioners' sugar

Peel pears, cut in half, and remove cores. Drop pears into 2 cups boiling water, cover, and simmer 10 minutes. Add ginger and lemon. Cover and cook until tender, about 10 to 20 minutes. To serve, sprinkle with pistachios and confectioners' sugar.

Recipe for Success

Pears are great eaten fresh or cooked. Poached pears make a great treat, and this recipe is low carb. Serve with a slice of

Curried Fruit on Skewers

Prep time: 20 minutes plus overnight chill time • Cook time: 1 hour • Serves 8 • Serving size: ⅛ recipe (about 3 skewers)

Each serving has: 18 grams carbohydrate • 4 grams fiber • 14 grams nutritive carbohydrate • less than 1 gram total protein

1 (20-oz.) can unsweetened pineapple rings

1 (29-oz.) can unsweetened pear halves

1 (29-oz.) can unsweetened peach halves

24 green grapes

½ cup (1 stick) butter

2 TB. molasses

2 tsp. curry powder

Recipe for Success

The flavors in this recipe continue to blend for several days. You can use less curry powder if you prefer a lighter taste. Garnish with fresh basil or mint leaves.

Preheat oven to 350°F.

Drain pineapple, pears, and peaches, and pat dry with paper towels. Make fruit skewers with large toothpicks by placing 1 pineapple ring on the bottom, top with pear half, then peach half, then green grape. Secure stacks with toothpicks, and place in a shallow baking dish.

In a small saucepan, melt butter. Stir in molasses and curry powder. Spoon mixture over fruit, and bake covered for 1 hour. Refrigerate overnight before serving.

Frosty Fruit

Prep time: 15 minutes plus overnight freezing time • Cook time: 0 • Serves 6 • Serving size: ¾ cup

Each serving has: 16 grams carbohydrate • 3 grams fiber • 13 grams nutritive carbohydrate • 2 grams total protein • 2 grams from plant source

1 (8-oz.) can pineapple tidbits packed in water

½ cup walnut halves

2 TB. lime juice

¼ tsp. ground ginger

3 cups fresh or frozen strawberry halves, no added sugar

1½ cups fresh or frozen blueberries, no added sugar

¼ cup unsweetened coconut

Combine undrained pineapple tidbits, walnut halves, lime juice, and ginger. Mix well and add strawberries, blueberries, and coconut. Toss gently.

Freeze overnight. Thaw about 4 hours, and serve while frosty.

Recipe for Success

This fruit combination makes a great addition to lunchboxes. Freeze in individual containers and add to the lunchbox in the morning. By lunch time, the fruit should be partly thawed and frosty.

Microwave Cheesy Apples

Prep time: 5 minutes • Cook time: 4 minutes • Serves 1 • Serving size: 1 apple

Each serving has: 21 grams carbohydrate • 3 grams fiber • 18 grams nutritive carbohydrate • 7 grams total protein • 7 grams from animal source • less than 1 gram from plant source

1 medium cooking apple such as Gala, Macintosh, Golden Delicious, or Cortland

¼ to ½ tsp. cinnamon

¼ cup shredded cheddar cheese

Core apple and cut into quarters. Peel it, if desired. Place apple on microwave-safe plate, and sprinkle with cinnamon. Microwave on high for 3 minutes. Sprinkle with cheese, and microwave 1 minute. Let cool slightly before serving.

Recipe for Success

This recipe is a perfect snack, as it includes fiber as well as protein and no added sugar but will fill the need for healthy carbs. Try this snack with a fresh pear and Swiss cheese for a new flavor. The kids will love this quick and easy after-school snack, or serve it up for a warm breakfast to get them going—and you, too!

Minty Fruit

Prep time: 15 minutes plus chill time • Cook time: 0 • Serves 6 • Serving size: ¾ cup

Each serving has: 13 grams carbohydrate • 2 grams fiber • 11 grams nutritive carbohydrate • 1 gram total protein • less than 1 gram from animal source • 1 gram from plant source

2 TB. mayonnaise

1 tsp. sugar

1 TB. fresh or bottled lemon juice

2 TB. cream cheese, at room temperature

2 tsp. fresh mint or ½ tsp. dried

2 cups fresh strawberries, cut in half

1 cup fresh or frozen blueberries, no added sugar

1 banana, cut into chunks

1 cup cubed cantaloupe or honeydew melon or a mixture

Recipe for Success

This is a pretty dish to serve in parfait glasses with a fresh strawberry wedged on the rim of the glass. It makes a refreshing dessert or snack and is a great way to add fruit to breakfast.

In a small container, combine mayonnaise, sugar, lemon juice, cream cheese, and mint. Lightly toss together strawberries, blueberries, banana, and cantaloupe, and stir in mayonnaise dressing. Chill before serving.

The Least You Need to Know

◆ Eating fruits is a wise choice for nutritional value and mealtime variety.

◆ Most fruits are low glycemic, but some fruits fall into the moderate-glycemic range.

◆ Eat fruits any time of the day for snacks, side dishes, or desserts.

◆ Before you make fruit purchases, consider the way you are going to use the fruit.

Part 6

Extras: Treats and Starches

The "extras" are those foods you may think are forbidden in low-carb eating. They aren't forbidden here, just reformulated with low-carb ingredients that taste decadently rich!

You'll love the chocolate brownies, the peach ice cream, and the walnut torte. If bread is your passion, make up a batch of Rice Flour Rolls or Almond Crackers.

These recipes will delight you with their high-carb tastes that fit into your low-carb daily allotments.

Chapter 22

Breads and Pasta

In This Chapter

- ◆ Enjoying breads
- ◆ Low-carb bread ingredients
- ◆ Preparation hints
- ◆ Slicing it thin

Bread has been called the staff of life. Perhaps that no longer rings true for you. Your new staff of life might be a combination of vegetables, fruits, and complete protein. Does that mean that bread doesn't have a place in your life? No, of course not. But you may use a different kind of bread.

Your new bread is made with ingredients that can be filling but not high in carbohydrates. Out goes the wheat flour; in go such ingredients as nut flours, psyllium, and soy powder. You can enjoy low-carb bread in slices or rolls for such foods as hamburgers and hot dogs. You can eat low-carb crackers with cheese or nut butters. And you can make scrumptious croutons for your salads.

Eating Bread

Low-carb bread almost by definition can't contain high-carbohydrate flours. All grain-based flours such as whole wheat, white, and rye contain way too many carbohydrates for you—that is, if the breads are made the regular way. The only possible way for you to eat regular flour breads is to slice them so thin that you are actually eating only ⅓ to ½ a serving. Quite honestly, that works. Eating less of any carbohydrate-rich food reduces the amount of carbohydrates you ingest.

> **Table Talk**
>
> Some commercially available low-carb breads are made without high-carb ingredients such as wheat flour and are becoming widely available. Sample a few to see if they appeal to you. Again, the serving size is usually rather small.

Another and perhaps easier choice is to eat low-carb bread. Yes, you can purchase low-carb breads at the grocery and health food stores. Some regular wheat breads are labeled "low carb" because they deliver fewer carbohydrates per slice. This happens because the bread is sliced ⅜ inch thick rather than the usual ⅝ inch. So simply by portion control, it has fewer carbohydrates.

Components of Low-Carb Bread

In creating a low-carb version of the "staff of life," let's look at what exactly makes bread become bread. Bread dough requires the following components:

- **Leavening.** This is the ingredient that puts the air holes into the bread. For yeast breads, that ingredient is yeast; in other breads, it's baking powder or baking soda. Flat breads, such as crackers, may not use leavening. Low-carb breads use the same leavening as regular breads.

- **"Stick-together-ness."** To make bread, there has to be an ingredient that makes the ingredient mixture stick together. One of the unique qualities of wheat is that it contains gluten. When kneaded, the gluten is developed, and it causes the bread mixture to stick together. Low-carb yeast breads often forego the actual wheat but use "vital wheat gluten," available at grocery stores. For flat breads made with nut flours, the stick-together ingredient is the egg.

- **Filling.** This ingredient makes up the greatest volume of the bread. In regular bread, it is the flour; in low-carb breads, it could be a combination of bran, psyllium, soy, or whey flours. These have fewer carbs than wheat flour.

- **Sugar.** With yeast breads, some form of sugar is used for the yeast to feed upon and, thus, to grow. This can be a very small amount of sugar, honey, or molasses and is used in some of our yeast low-carb breads.

You can bake your own bread with the recipes in this chapter. We offer you yeast breads and quick breads, so you can make the kind you like the best. Plus, you can enjoy the warm satisfaction that comes from both the baking and the eating. There's nothing like fresh-out-of-the-oven bread to warm the heart and feel comforting.

Table Talk

Brushing breads with a glaze or egg wash before baking gives the final product a brown patina and crisp finish. The most basic brush is water, which gives a crust a little shine. Milk brushed on a loaf of bread gives a luster to the normally matte finish. Whole eggs beaten with a pinch of salt give an even golden finish; egg white alone gets glossy, and crusts brushed with yolks get almost burnished.

"Special" Ingredients

These recipes call for some special ingredients, which you can find at large grocery stores, health food stores, or via mail order online.

- **Vital wheat gluten.** This is the protein component of wheat that makes all the ingredients stick together. By using only the gluten from the wheat and not the wheat itself, you save many carbohydrates.

- **Psyllium husk.** Psyllium contains a water-soluble fiber that has been used for thousands of years for stomach and digestive health. It has no nutritive carbohydrates but adds plenty of good-for-you fiber to the bread.

- **Nut flours.** You can purchase these or make them yourself. To make 1 cup nut flour, process ¾ cup nuts in the food processor until they turn into a flour. Almonds, pecans, walnuts, macadamias, and hazelnuts all work well.

- **Soy powder or soy milk powder.** Soy powder or soy milk powder is made from cooked soybeans and adds a nutritional filler and wheat flour substitute for bread. Do not use soy flour, as it has a stronger taste. And don't use soy protein isolate, either; it is not the same thing. If your health food store doesn't stock soy powder, have them order it for you.

- **Whey protein powder.** Purchase this without added sugar. The plain, unsweetened version works well as an ingredient in low-carb breads, plus it adds animal protein.

- **Rice flour.** This is a great ingredient for bread. We use this in some recipes to offer you another choice if you are sensitive to wheat.

- **Oat bran.** As the outer husk of oats, the bran has lots of good-for-you water-soluble fiber.

Keep these staple ingredients in stock in your pantry just as you would wheat flour, so they'll be there when you want to make some low-carb bread.

Pastas

Some low-carb pastas are commercially available in stores. You can decide if they please your palate. Typically they are either too stiff or too pasty. But new brands are coming out continually, and hopefully, you'll find one that appeals to you.

We have found that using vegetables in place of pasta is delicious and quite satisfying. Try our zucchini pasta recipe. You can also use other vegetables in place of the zucchini. Try bamboo shoots, turnips, fennel, beets, carrots, broccoli, and cauliflower.

Vegetable pastas give you a lighter feeling after eating, and, of course, they add 1 or even 2 more vegetables to your daily fruits and vegetables target of 5 to 10 each day. To tell you the honest truth, we prefer vegetable pastas to those made with grains.

Table Talk _____
For spaghetti or fettuccine, we prefer using spaghetti squash. This recipe is Spaghetti Squash with Marinara Sauce in Chapter 19.

Rice Flour Rolls

Prep time: 10 minutes • Cook time: 20 minutes • Makes: 12 rolls • Serving size: 1 roll

Each serving has: 5 grams carbohydrate • 0 grams fiber • 5 grams nutritive carbohydrate • 10 grams total protein • 3 grams from animal source • 7 grams from plant source

3 TB. rice flour

¾ cup vital wheat gluten

¼ tsp. salt

1 cup minus 2 TB. heavy cream

6 TB. butter

2 eggs

3 egg whites

Preheat oven to 425°F.

Combine rice flour, wheat gluten, and salt and set aside. Combine cream and butter in a saucepan, and simmer until butter melts. Remove pan from heat. Add dry ingredients, and stir quickly until mixed well and dough leaves the sides of the pan.

Stir in each egg separately until well combined. Combine all egg whites together with a fork, and add to mixture, stirring well. Pour into 12 greased muffin cups, and bake 20 minutes until golden brown.

Cheese Bread

Prep time: 10 minutes • Cook time: 45 minutes • Serves 16 • Serving size: 1 slice

Each serving has: 3 grams carbohydrate • less than 1 gram fiber • 3 grams nutritive carbohydrate • 14 grams total protein • 5 grams from animal source • 9 grams from plant source

⅔ cup soy powder

⅔ cup whey protein powder

1 tsp. baking powder

4 eggs

2 TB. sour cream

2 TB. butter

½ tsp. butter flavor (optional)

1 tsp. basil or favorite herb

2 cups shredded cheddar cheese (or any type you prefer)

Preheat oven to 275°F.

Combine soy powder, whey protein powder, baking powder, eggs, sour cream, butter, butter flavor (if using), basil, and cheddar cheese, and pour into greased 4×8×4 inch loaf pan. Bake 40 minutes. Test with knife for doneness. Cover with aluminum foil if browning too rapidly.

Cool loaf completely before slicing into 16 (½-inch) pieces.

Variation: To make Asiago cheese bread, substitute shredded Asiago for the cheddar cheese. To make a sun-dried tomato bread, substitute finely chopped sun-dried tomatoes for the herbs.

Recipe for Success

The thinner the slices, the better the flavor and texture. Toasting brings out the best flavor. Instead of using herbs, you can substitute ¼ cup chopped olives, if desired. For a sweeter-tasting bread, use almond flavoring with no herbs or olives and only 1 cup of a mild-flavored cheese.

Everyday Rolls

Prep time: 10 minutes • Cook time: 12 minutes after rising • Serves 12 • Serving size: 1 roll

Each serving has: 8 grams carbohydrate • 2 grams fiber • 6 grams nutritive carbohydrates • 5 grams total protein • less than 1 gram from animal source • 5 grams from plant source

½ cup heavy cream	¼ cup rice flour
½ cup water	1 tsp. salt
2 TB. psyllium husks	1 tsp. vanilla or almond extract
¾ cup vital wheat gluten	1 TB. melted butter
⅓ cup oat bran	1 TB. sugar
½ cup whey protein powder	1 packet rapid-rise yeast

Place cream, water, psyllium husks, wheat gluten, oat bran, whey protein powder, rice flour, salt, vanilla, butter, sugar, and yeast into bread machine in that order, and set the machine for rising only. Remove dough from the pan and pull apart. Either place on a greased baking sheet and shape into rolls, or place in 12 greased muffin tins.

Directions if no bread machine: Let dough rise covered in draft-free room until doubled in size.

Preheat oven to 375°F.

Bake for 12 minutes or until set and a knife inserted into the center of a roll comes out clean.

Variations: Take the dough out of the machine after the first rising, and pat into a rectangle on a greased sheet pan. Sprinkle the dough with your favorite fillings, and roll up jellyroll style. Cover and allow this to rise, then bake in the oven until golden brown. You can do this for any of the yeast breads.

To make a cinnamon roll, lightly sprinkle the dough with cinnamon and a few nuts and raisins; if desired, mix a bit of reduced-carb jelly into the filling. Serve hot with the Pancake Syrup in Chapter 5. You can also layer cooked meats, chopped vegetables, and cheese onto the dough and bake.

Recipe for Success

Shape the rolls into hamburger or hot-dog buns if you want to serve with a summer barbecue. You can omit the vanilla or almond flavoring and use vanilla-flavored whey protein powder, if desired.

Yeast Bread with Seeds

Prep time: 10 minutes • Cook time: approximately 3 hours in bread machine • Serves 12
• Serving size: 1 slice

Each serving has: 10 grams carbohydrate • 4 grams fiber • 6 grams nutritive carbohydrates
• 10 grams total protein • 1 gram from animal source • 9 grams from plant source

1 cup heavy cream

1 TB. melted butter

1 egg, beaten

½ tsp. salt

2 TB. psyllium husks

¾ cup vital wheat gluten

½ cup oat bran

⅓ cup almond flour (¼ cup almonds, finely ground)

¼ cup sunflower seeds, coarsely chopped

3 TB. whole flax seeds

1 TB. sugar

1 tsp. molasses

1 packet rapid-rise yeast

If you're using a bread machine: Place cream, melted butter, egg, salt, psyllium husks, wheat gluten, oat bran, almond flour, sunflower seeds, flax seeds, sugar, molasses, and yeast into a bread machine in that order and bake. Remove bread from pan immediately, and allow to cool before slicing into 12 servings.

If you're using a conventional oven:

Preheat oven to 350°F.

Combine liquid ingredients. In a separate bowl, combine dry ingredients with yeast.

Make a hole in the center of the dry ingredients, and pour in liquid ingredients. Slowly stir to combine completely.

Pour into a greased 4×8×4-inch loaf pan or 2 smaller pans. Bake 25 to 30 minutes. Test with knife for doneness. Cover with aluminum foil if bread is browning too rapidly.

Variation: You can use many different kinds of seeds or nuts in this bread. Choose from pumpkin seeds, pine nuts, sesame seeds, pecans, walnuts, and even poppy seeds.

Recipe for Success
Toasting this bread makes the nutty flavor come alive. Add a slice of cheese and melt for a quick and nutritious breakfast.

Chewy Low-Carb Bread

Prep time: 10 minutes • Cook time: 3 hours • Makes: 10 slices • Serving size: 1 slice

Each serving has: 5 grams carbohydrate • less than 1 gram fiber • 5 grams nutritive carbohydrate • 14 grams total protein • less than 1 gram from animal source • 14 grams from plant source

1 TB. oil	½ cup oat flour
½ cup warm water (95 to 105°F)	½ cup plain whey protein powder
½ cup cream	1 tsp. vanilla extract
1 egg, at room temperature	¼ tsp. salt
1 cup plus 2 TB. vital wheat gluten	1 package rapid-rise yeast

If you're using a bread machine: Add oil to bottom of a bread machine pan.

Use a thermometer to determine the temperature of water; if it is too hot, it will kill yeast. Slightly warm cream, and add to water. Slightly beat egg, and add to cream mixture. Pour into bread machine pan.

In a bowl, combine gluten, oat flour, whey powder, vanilla, and salt. Mix thoroughly and gently pour onto top of cream mixture, but do not stir into cream mixture. Sprinkle yeast on top of flour mixture.

Set machine to rapid bake setting, which is usually about 2 hours with one knead cycle. Check the manufacture's directions for your machine. When bread has cooled, slice loaf into 10 slices.

If you're using a conventional oven: Preheat oven to 350°F.

Combine liquid ingredients plus vanilla. In a separate bowl, combine dry ingredients with yeast.

Make a hole in the center of the dry ingredients, and pour in liquid ingredients. Slowly stir to combine completely.

Pour into greased 4×8×4-inch loaf pan or 2 smaller pans. Bake 25 to 30 minutes. Test with knife for doneness. Cover with aluminum foil if bread is browning too rapidly.

Recipe for Success

This really is a chewy bread. Because of the texture, it is quite filling. Add your favorite nuts or cheese for variety. Slicing the loaf into thinner slices and toasting make it more flavorful.

Vegetable Pasta

Prep time: 10 minutes plus 30 minutes standing time • Cook time: 2 minutes • Serves 2
• Serving size: ½ cup

Each serving has: 4 grams carbohydrate • 2 grams fiber • 2 grams nutritive carbohydrate
• 1 gram total protein • 0 grams from animal source • 1 gram from plant source

3 (6-inch) zucchini	½ tsp. fresh or bottled lemon juice
1 tsp. salt	½ tsp. black pepper
2 tsp. olive oil	

Cut each zucchini in half crosswise and then into several lengthwise strips ½ inch thick. Cut each strip into ½-inch-thick pieces. Place in a colander, and sprinkle with salt. Let stand for 30 minutes. Rinse and pat dry.

Toss in olive oil, lemon juice, and pepper, and microwave 1 to 2 minutes until tender-crisp. Serve as is or use as "pasta" base for delicious sauces.

Variation: You can also use a vegetable peeler to make "pasta" from other vegetables such as bamboo shoots, turnip, fennel, beet, carrot, and broccoli. These vegetables will not need to be salted and set aside for ½ hour, as they do not have as high a water content as zucchini. First, peel any vegetable with a tough covering; slice thin strips and microwave about 2 minutes just until tender-crisp. Cover with your favorite sauce. Using several vegetables mixed together gives the sauce a wonderful flavor and adds multiple nutrients to your meal.

Recipe for Success

This recipe is an excellent base for serving with Italian sauces. It takes well to a sprinkling of Italian herbs when tossing. You can also use a vegetable peeler to slice zucchini into thinner strips—just peel and then rotate zucchini around as you slice off pasta strips.

Almond Crackers

Prep time: 10 minutes • Cook time: 10 minutes • Serves 6 • Serving size: ⅙ recipe

Each serving has: 9 grams carbohydrate • 6 grams fiber • 3 grams nutritive carbohydrate • 12 grams total protein • 1 gram from animal source • 11 grams from plant source

1¾ cups almond flour (1½ cups almonds, finely ground)

3 TB. vital wheat gluten

½ tsp. salt

1 egg

1 TB. olive oil

1 TB. water

Preheat oven to 350°F.

Blend together almond flour, wheat gluten, and salt and set aside. Slightly beat egg with oil and water. Make a well in the middle of flour mixture, and pour in liquid. Mix well until mixture forms a ball.

Recipe for Success

These crackers are delicious. Add spices or seasonings as desired to batter before cooking or use garlic salt. The thinner the dough is rolled out, the crisper the cracker will be. These crackers are wonderful with dips and salsa, or use them with cheese for a late-afternoon snack.

Lightly grease 2 sheets of wax paper, and place dough between sheets. Roll as thin as possible.

Cut dough into desired shapes and sizes, and place on a baking sheet. Bake for about 10 minutes or until golden brown. Watch carefully as they will burn quickly.

Cool and serve. Seal leftovers in a closed container.

Variation: Vary the taste of these crackers by substituting other nut flours. You can use pecans, walnuts, macadamias, pine nuts, and hazelnuts.

Croutons

Prep time: 10 minutes • Cook time: 15 minutes • Serves 16 • Serving size: 2 tablespoons

Each serving has: 5 grams carbohydrate • 1 gram fiber • 4 grams nutritive carbohydrate • 1 gram total protein • 0 grams from animal source • 1 gram from plant source

4 TB. butter	⅛ tsp. garlic salt
2 cups cubed day-old bread, preferably French or Asiago cheese bread, but any bread will do	⅛ tsp. dried parsley
	Salt and pepper to taste

Heat butter in a heavy skillet. Stir in bread cubes, and coat with butter on all sides. Sprinkle on garlic salt, parsley, and salt and pepper to taste. Continue to stir until bread is toasted to your preference.

Variation: Vary the seasonings in this recipe. Use crushed red peppers or hot chili powder. Or use Italian seasonings such as pesto or marinara seasonings.

Recipe for Success

Croutons are a wonderful way to get small tastes of delicious bread with very few carbohydrates. Be sure to use bread that's been sitting around for several days and is already partially dried out. Sprinkle the croutons on salads, and use the tiniest crumbs to top scrambled eggs. You can also sprinkle them over steamed vegetables.

The Least You Need to Know

◆ You can enjoy low-carb breads in many forms—sliced, as rolls, muffins, and crackers.

◆ Baking low-carb breads requires different ingredients than regular high-carb wheat-flour breads.

◆ Home-baked bread gives you the wonderful satisfaction of the baking, eating, and emotional comforts.

◆ Vegetable pastas are terrific and so far beat out commercial brands of low-carb pasta.

Chapter 23

Grains and Potatoes

In This Chapter

- ◆ Enjoying low-carb starches
- ◆ Cooking with unrefined grains
- ◆ Getting that comfort-food taste
- ◆ Sticking with serving-size suggestions

Not surprisingly, we have grown to love grains and potatoes dearly. They appeal to both "mouth and mind." In other words, they taste good and help satisfy our emotional needs as well. We often refer to such starchy foods as "comfort" foods for good reason. A big serving of them actually increases serotonin levels in the brain, which make us feel good. We get relaxed and soothed. We might even get sleepy and fall into a deep sleep faster.

Of course, all this happens subconsciously, but it helps explain our devotion to starchy foods. It's part of why many of us return, not just for second helpings of plain-old mashed potatoes but for a third mound of them, too!

When embarking on a low-carb eating regimen, the prospect of never again eating potatoes or rice isn't encouraging. Don't despair. The good news is you can have some starches, as these recipes prove. True, the carb count may be out of range if you are on a highly carb-restricted eating program, but generally speaking, you can eat them once or twice a week and perhaps more often. If you use the mock potato recipes, you can eat them even more.

Choosing Good Grains

For these recipes, we chose grains that are low glycemic and unrefined. Unrefined grains retain the outer covering of the grain and have more fiber and more B vitamins than refined grains. Our recipes call for pearl barley, quinoa, and brown basmati rice. Don't be put off by these odd names; they'll easily become family favorites.

Hot Potato

Rice and potatoes are so easy to eat and so soothing that it's not hard to overeat them. You already know this. The secret to enjoying starches and eating low carb is to eat less. Follow the serving size recommendations carefully, and you'll like the results.

But watch out. These grains still contain plenty of carbohydrates, so be sure to eat the recommended serving size to avoid a carb overload. Grains and potatoes go down easily, so don't overdo the quantity consumed. The servings in the recipes here contain around 18 to 22 carbs, so you'll need to make sure your eating plan for the day can "afford" the higher carb counts.

We think you'll like the taste of these more unusual grains and find the combination of ingredients delicious. Nuts go well with unrefined grains, as do fresh parsley, cilantro, dill, and many spices.

Sweet Potatoes Bring Smiles

With the one exception of the Jalapeño Red Potato Bowls, our potato recipes call for either yams or sweet potatoes. Both have orange-colored insides. Both are lower glycemic than white potatoes but just as delicious.

If you have any reservations about eating yams or sweet potatoes, we challenge you to bake a few, then season them with butter, salt, and pepper. Maybe even sprinkle with some cinnamon. You'll be sold on the sweet taste, the texture, and the overall satisfaction you receive. They've become such a staple at our family dinners that our children actually prefer them to white potatoes.

Table Talk

Always bake your potatoes, as opposed to boiling them, because a boiled potato has 67 percent more carbohydrates than a baked one. When boiled, more of the potato's starches and sugars become accessible to your body.

Sweet potatoes and yams have about the same carb count as white potatoes, but we recommend them because they're lower glycemic and we think they taste better. Note that the suggested serving is ½ potato.

Ingredients

Barley, quinoa, and brown basmati rice are probably not already in your pantry, as they are somewhat uncommon. Here's where to purchase these ingredients and others that we will use in this chapter:

- Brown basmati rice can sometimes be found prepackaged in the rice section, and it can often be found in bulk bins in the health food section of your grocery store. If not, try a health food store. As a last resort, search online and purchase plenty. It stores well and keeps for months in a covered container or plastic bag.

- Pearl barley is generally available at grocery stores. Be sure to purchase the long-cooking type and avoid anything that is labeled quick-cooking.

- Quinoa is available at heath food stores or online.

- Yams and sweet potatoes are available at the grocery stores. If you can't find them, ask the produce manager to get some for you.

- You already know how to find cauliflower. Right?

Basmati Rice Pilaf

Prep time: 15 minutes • Cook time: 20 minutes • Serves 8 • Serving size: ⅜ cup

Each serving has: 17 grams carbohydrate • 1 gram fiber • 16 grams nutritive carbohydrate • 2 grams total protein • 2 grams from plant source

2 cups water	1 cup brown basmati rice
1 cube chicken bouillon	2 TB. butter

Put water and bouillon cube in a microwave-safe bowl or a glass measuring cup and microwave for 4 minutes or until boiling. At the same time, sauté rice in butter in a large saucepan until hot and some kernels start to toast.

Put on a potholder mitten that protects your wrist. Turn down the heat to simmer. All at once, pour boiling water over rice and cover. Cook about 20 minutes or until fluffy.

Hot Potato

Be very careful when you pour the boiling water into the rice, and expect lots of steam and hissing. The pot might even boil over. Be sure to protect your hand. Taking this much care is worth it—the rice is the best ever.

Recipe for Success _____
Basmati rice has just as many carbs as regular rice; however, the glycemic index count is lower. So use brown basmati rice because it will keep your blood sugar levels lower than white rice. Use this rice recipe whenever you want a rice accompaniment to your meal.

Pine Nut–Barley Pilaf

Prep time: 20 minutes • Cook time: 1 hour, 10 minutes • Serves 8 • Serving size: ½ cup

Each serving has: 19 grams carbohydrate • 4 grams fiber • 15 grams nutritive carbohydrate • 5 grams total protein • 3 grams from animal source • 2 grams from plant source

1 cup pearl barley	½ cup chopped fresh parsley
⅓ cup pine nuts	¼ tsp. salt
6 TB. butter	¼ tsp. freshly ground black pepper
½ cup chopped green onions	3⅓ cup chicken broth

Preheat oven to 350°F.

Recipe for Success _____
This recipe is a nutty tasting accompaniment to main dishes. It makes a filling pilaf, so you feel satisfied with less.

Rinse barley in cold water and drain. In a heavy skillet, sauté pine nuts in butter until toasted. Remove with a slotted spoon and reserve. Sauté green onions with barley until lightly toasted. Remove from heat. Stir in nuts, parsley, salt, and pepper. Put into an ungreased 2-quart casserole.

Heat broth to boiling and pour over barley mixture, blending well. Bake, uncovered, 1 hour, 10 minutes.

Table Talk _____
Barley is one of two low-glycemic grains. The other is steel-cut oats. Even though pearl barley contains the same amount of carbs as other grains, it doesn't cause a quick rise in blood sugar as other grains do. But eat only limited amounts infrequently.

Baked Yams

Prep time: 5 minutes   •   Cook time: 1 hour   •   Serves 8   •   Serving size: ½ yam per person

Each serving has: 19 grams carbohydrate   •   3 grams fiber   •   16 grams nutritive carbohydrate   •   1 gram total protein   •   1 gram from plant source

4 small yams

Preheat oven to 375°F.

Wash yams and place directly on cooking rack in oven. Bake 1 hour or until done.

Recipe for Success _____
Serve with butter and, if you prefer, a sprinkling of cinnamon. You could find that you and your family prefer eating yams rather than white potatoes.

Stuffed Yams

Prep time: 15 minutes   •   Cook time: 1 hour plus 15 to 20 minutes   •   Serves 8   •   Serving size: ½ yam

Each serving has: 20 grams carbohydrate   •   3 grams fiber   •   17 grams nutritive carbohydrate   •   8 grams total protein   •   6 grams from animal source   •   2 grams from plant source

4 yams	½ cup sour cream
2 TB. butter	2 TB. chopped chives
Salt and pepper to taste	4 slices bacon, cooked crisp and crumbled
1 cup shredded cheddar cheese	

Preheat oven to 400°F.

Bake yams until tender, about 1 hour. Slice each yam in half, and scoop out center into a mixing bowl. Top with butter. Save yam shells. Mash yams and beat until fluffy. Fold in cheese, sour cream, chives, and bacon bits. Fill each yam shell with mixture, and bake 15 to 20 minutes.

Recipe for Success _____
Serve as a great side dish for a meat or fish main course that has almost no carbs. In that way, you can afford the 20 grams carbohydrates in these stuffed yams. Stuffed yams are perfect for holiday meals. Serve with turkey or ham or the all-around favorites, steak and roast beef.

Barley with Dill

Prep time: 15 minutes   •   Cook time: 1½ hours   •   Serves 12   •   Serving size: ⅓ cup

Each serving has: 21 grams carbohydrate   •   4 grams fiber   •   17 grams nutritive carbohydrate   •   5 grams total protein   •   3 grams from animal source   •   2 grams from plant source

1 medium onion, chopped	1 tsp. fresh dill
¼ cup butter	½ tsp. freshly ground black pepper
1¾ cup barley	4 cups chicken broth
1 tsp. salt	

Recipe for Success

Barley has lots of texture and plenty of fiber. Use it to accompany pork chops, steak, and other very low-carb main dishes.

Preheat oven to 350°F.

In a medium saucepan, sauté onion in butter until golden brown. Transfer to a baking dish with a lid. Add barley, salt, dill, pepper, and chicken broth. Mix well. Cover and bake 1½ hours.

Quinoa Pilaf with Vegetables

Prep time: 20 minutes   •   Cook time: 25 minutes   •   Serves 8   •   Serving size: ½ cup

Each serving has: 16 grams carbohydrate   •   2 grams fiber   •   14 grams nutritive carbohydrate   •   6 grams total protein   •   less than 1 gram from animal source   •   6 grams from plant source

1 cup uncooked quinoa, rinsed	2 medium carrots, diced
1¾ cup chicken broth	2 celery stalks, diced
2 TB. butter	1 tsp. minced garlic
¼ cup diced red bell pepper	1 TB. grated Parmesan cheese
¼ cup diced green bell pepper	Salt and pepper to taste
4 green onions, chopped	

In a medium saucepan, combine quinoa and chicken broth over medium heat. Bring to a boil, reduce heat, cover, and simmer until quinoa is tender and liquid is absorbed, about 15 minutes. Remove from heat.

In a heavy skillet, heat butter and add red and green peppers, onions, carrots, and celery. Cook, stirring, until just soft. Stir in garlic. Cook 1 minute longer.

Stir into quinoa. Add Parmesan cheese, salt, and pepper, and mix well. Serve hot.

Table Talk

The Incas considered quinoa (pronounced *keen-WAUGH*) the "mother grain." It has only recently been introduced into American cuisine. Find it at the health food store if it isn't available at your grocer. Quinoa is a primitive grain, so enjoy the unique taste in this pilaf. You get 1 serving of vegetables with this pilaf. Serve as a side dish with very low-carb main dishes, such as seafood, meat, or fish.

Green Brown Rice

Prep time: 20 minutes • Cook time: 40 minutes • Serves 6 • Serving size: ½ cup

Each serving has: 23 grams carbohydrate • 1 gram fiber • 22 grams nutritive carbohydrate • 8 grams total protein • 5 grams from animal source • 3 grams from plant source

2 cups cooked brown basmati rice

2 eggs

½ cup grated cheddar cheese

¾ cup chopped bell pepper

½ cup chopped fresh parsley

4 green onions, chopped

2 cups Basic Cream Soup (see recipe in Chapter 14)

1 jalapeño pepper, chopped

1 TB. red wine vinegar

1 TB. Cajun spice mix

Preheat oven to 350°F. Grease a casserole baking pan.

In a large bowl, combine rice, eggs, cheese, bell pepper, parsley, green onions, soup, jalapeño, vinegar, and Cajun spice mix, and pour into baking pan. Cover and bake 30 to 40 minutes until bubbly. Remove cover and stir well. This dish freezes well.

Recipe for Success

You can add frozen or steamed broccoli or other green veggies to this dish; add cream or water if adding vegetables. This makes a wonderful vegetable to take to a covered-dish event, as it is just as delicious at room temperature as it is piping hot.

Cajun Dirty Rice

Prep time: 30 minutes plus refrigeration time if made in advance • Cook time: 30 minutes
• Serves 6 • Serving size: ¼ cup

Each serving has: 22 grams carbohydrate • 1 gram fiber • 21 grams nutritive carbohydrate • 15 grams total protein • 13 grams from animal source • 2 grams from plant source

2 chicken livers	3 stalks celery, chopped
6 chicken gizzards	2 cloves garlic, minced
3 cups chicken broth	¼ tsp. cayenne
1 cup uncooked brown basmati rice	1 tsp. salt
½ lb. ground beef	1 bay leaf
¼ cup butter	½ tsp. thyme
1 cup chopped green onions	4 green onions, chopped
1 onion, chopped	¼ cup chopped fresh parsley
1 red bell pepper, chopped	

Boil livers and gizzards in 1 cup chicken broth, and set aside to cool. Keep broth for use later. Chop livers and gizzards very fine. It is even better to process or blend livers and gizzards so they are mashed. (They add wonderful flavor to the rice, but most folks do not enjoy actually biting into the organ meat.)

Recipe for Success

You can substitute 1 tablespoon Cajun spice mix for spices in the ingredient list. If you do not want to use livers and gizzards, substitute an additional ½ pound ground beef or sausage. Served with additional vegetables, this makes a complete meal with the protein in the rice dish.

Cook rice in remaining 2 cups broth, adding additional water if needed.

Brown meat and drain. Melt butter and sauté 1 cup green onions, onion, bell pepper, celery, and garlic until vegetables are tender. Add drained meat and mashed livers and gizzards to vegetable mixture and heat. Add cayenne, salt, bay leaf, thyme, and chicken broth left from cooking livers and gizzards. Cover and simmer 30 minutes. Remove bay leaf, and add cooked rice. Mix well and add additional 4 green onions and parsley.

This dish freezes well. It is best when it is made 24 hours in advance so the flavors can blend. Reheat when ready to serve.

Jalapeño Red Potato Bowls

Prep time: 20 minutes • Cook time: 15 minutes • Serves 6 • Serving size: 2 halves

Each serving has: 7 grams carbohydrate • Less than 1 gram fiber • 7 grams nutritive carbohydrate • 2 grams total protein • 2 grams from animal source • less than 1 gram from plant source

6 small new red potatoes	1 (3-oz.) pkg. cream cheese, at room temperature
¼ tsp. cayenne	1 jalapeño pepper, finely chopped
Salt to taste	1 TB. pimiento, chopped
1 TB. olive oil	2 slices bacon, cooked well and minced

Preheat oven to 400°F.

Cut potatoes in half, and scoop out inside, leaving a bit around edge; throw away flesh. Toss potato bowls with cayenne, salt, and oil. Place cut side down on a greased baking pan. Bake about 15 minutes until cooked through.

Meanwhile, place cream cheese, jalapeño, and pimiento into a small food processor or use an electric mixer to blend well. Fill each potato bowl with cream cheese mixture, and garnish with minced bacon.

Mock Mashed Potatoes

Prep time: 10 minutes • Cook time: 5 minutes • Serves 6 • Serving size: ½ cup

Each serving has: 3 grams carbohydrate • 1 gram fiber • 2 grams nutritive carbohydrate • 1 gram total protein • less than 1 gram from animal source • 1 gram from plant source

3 cups chopped cauliflower	¼ cup sour cream
1 TB. butter	Salt and pepper to taste

Microwave cauliflower and butter until soft enough to mash. Place cauliflower in a food processor with sour cream, and blend until texture of mashed potatoes. Stir in salt and pepper and serve.

Recipe for Success _____

A delicious lower-carb substitute for real mashed potatoes, cauliflower makes terrific mashed "potatoes." Feel free to add garlic powder and cheese to give more flavor if not serving with gravy.

Mock Potato Salad

Prep time: 15 minutes plus chill time • Cook time: 0 • Serves 6 • Serving size: ½ cup

Each serving has: 4 grams carbohydrate • 1 gram fiber • 3 grams nutritive carbohydrate • 4 grams total protein • 3 grams from animal source • 1 gram from plant source

3 cups cauliflower florets, cut into bite-size pieces	1 tsp. garlic powder
6 TB. chopped green onion	1 tsp. dill weed
1 cup chopped celery	½ tsp. dry mustard
6 TB. chopped bell pepper	¾ cup mayonnaise
3 hard-boiled eggs, chopped	2 TB. sour cream
	Paprika, for garnish

Combine cauliflower, green onion, celery, bell pepper, eggs, garlic powder, dill weed, mustard, mayonnaise, and sour cream and chill. Add a sprinkle of paprika just before serving.

Recipe for Success

No one will ever know this recipe doesn't contain potatoes! Cauliflower makes a great potato substitute. You can lightly steam the cauliflower for about 3 minutes if you prefer your salad with less crunch. For extra protein, add 8 ounces firm tofu cut into ½-inch cubes or small cubes of any favorite cheese.

Twice-Baked Potatoes

Prep time: 15 minutes • Cook time: 1 hour, 20 minutes • Serves 6 • Serving size: ½ potato

Each serving has: 20 grams carbohydrate • 4 grams fiber • 16 grams nutritive carbohydrate • 2 grams total protein • less than 1 gram from animal source • 2 grams from plant source

3 medium sweet potatoes	¼ tsp. ground cloves
¼ cup cream	2 TB. chopped pecans
¼ tsp. ground nutmeg	6 tsp. butter, sliced from stick
¼ tsp. ground cinnamon	

Preheat oven to 375°F.

Scrub potatoes and pierce skin with fork. Wrap well in foil, place on baking pan, and bake 1 hour or until done. Remove from oven and from foil. Let stand until cool enough to handle.

Slice potatoes in half, and remove flesh from skins, keeping skins intact. Place flesh into a bowl, and keep skins on the baking pan. Set aside skins until ready to fill.

Mix cream, nutmeg, cinnamon, and cloves with potato and mash well. Scoop potato mixture back into shells, and bake 20 minutes until hot.

Sprinkle with pecans, and serve with butter pat melting on top.

Variation: Freely substitute yams for sweet potatoes and vice versa. Both are lower glycemic than white potatoes and are comparable in carbohydrate counts.

Recipe for Success

This dish is a much lower-carb relative of traditional mashed potatoes. The mashed potato can also be served without re-stuffing the skins, if desired.

Sweet Potato Oven Fries

Prep time: 15 minutes • Cook time: 30 minutes • Serves 6 • Serving size: ½ potato

Each serving has: 19 grams carbohydrate • 3 grams fiber • 16 grams nutritive carbohydrate • 1 gram total protein • 1 gram from plant source

3 sweet potatoes

1 tsp. melted butter

½ tsp. salt

Additional favorite seasonings as desired

Recipe for Success

Although potatoes are a higher-carb food, the sweet potatoes cause less of a rise in blood sugar than white potatoes. These make a nice treat every once in a while, and you know they are a lot healthier than fried potatoes!

Preheat oven to 450°F.

Line a pan with foil, and coat with butter. Peel potatoes and cut into wedges. In a large bowl, toss potato wedges with melted butter, salt, and seasonings. Spread potatoes on the foil in a single layer, and bake 20 minutes. Loosen potatoes from pan, and turn to roast 10 minutes longer or until done.

The Least You Need to Know

◆ Potatoes and grains can fit into a low-carb eating plan.

◆ Sweet potatoes, yams, and even cauliflower are excellent alternatives to white potatoes—and are more delicious.

◆ Using unrefined low-glycemic grains is a healthy and delicious way to eat low carb.

◆ These foods are naturally higher in carbs, so follow serving size suggestions carefully.

Chapter 24

Desserts

In This Chapter

- ◆ That sweet end of a meal
- ◆ Sweet, yummy, *and* low carb
- ◆ Your comfort foods
- ◆ Tastes like high carb

You have taste buds that signal "sweet," which means your body seeks out sweet foods to satisfy those taste buds. It's not as accurate to say you have a sweet tooth as it is to say your sweet taste buds want satisfaction. As humans, we like to eat something sweet. In fact, your taste buds cause you to seek out all five sensations, so it's important to balance sweet with the other four—sour, salt, bitter, and protein.

We tend to eat desserts at the end of a meal, but, of course, you don't have to. You can eat dessert first. But make sure you save room for the main course. As children, we learned to save room in our stomachs for desserts. Or we had to clean our plates before our parents permitted us to eat dessert. In fact, it may not be the dessert part that is fattening, but rather the "cleaning your plate" part.

Yes, desserts can be low carb without sacrificing flavor, comfort, and satisfying ingredients. In fact, these desserts are so yummy that you can serve them with pride to your family and guests, and they won't even know they're eating low carb, which is just as it should be.

Desserts as Comfort Foods

Comfort foods, put quite simply, are any foods that make us feel good. Somehow, almost inexplicably, they elicit feelings of being loved and accepted, like a tail-wagging puppy who greets us when we get home. We turn to comfort foods when stressed, anxious, and under pressure, and they have delivered.

Desserts are among our favorite comfort foods. The good news is that you don't have to give them up, because in this chapter, you'll find cookies, puddings, mousses, cheesecake, and even ice cream!

So you can have it all—comfort foods plus healthy, low-carb eating.

Ingredients

Use high-quality ingredients for your desserts. High-quality ingredients contribute to taste and texture and to your ultimate satisfaction.

- **Nuts.** Use the freshest you can purchase. Many grocery and health food stores now offer bulk nuts, and the prices are lower than the small packages of nuts offered in the baking section.

- **Heavy cream.** If you can't find heavy cream, whipping cream will do. Other than that, there just isn't an acceptable substitute here. Don't use half-and-half, milk, or yogurt.

- **Cheese.** Use regular cheese, not low-fat cheese. Using low-fat products increases the carb count of the recipe and sacrifices quality and taste.

- **Sugar.** The recipes call for sugar. Of all the available sweeteners, it is the least controversial. Most people can easily tolerate sugar in small amounts. If you don't want to use sugar, you can substitute sucralose (brand name Splenda) in these recipes. But we don't recommend it. Sucralose has fewer carbs, but some scientific and health experts question its safety. Never substitute aspartame or stevia for sugar in these recipes. A disaster would result. Aspartame (brand name Equal) and stevia don't hold up well to heat. And they may not add enough bulk and texture to the recipe. We also find that nothing satisfies our sweet tooth like the natural real sweeteners—honey, sugar, and fruit.

♦ **Molasses.** Choose dark molasses for a stronger taste and light molasses if you prefer a softer taste. Molasses adds a brown sugar flavor to the dessert. A little molasses goes a long way, thus the recipe has fewer carbs than if it you used brown sugar.

 Hot Potato _____

If you are having intense and constant sugar cravings, chances are good that you don't need more sugar. Most likely, you need more complete protein for both breakfast and lunch. Protein keeps blood sugar levels stable throughout the day and prevents the drop in blood sugar that leads to insatiable cravings. The rule of thumb for your daily protein intake is to divide your weight in pounds by 2. So if you weigh 150 pounds, you need 75 grams of protein. It's best if you get ⅓ of that amount at each meal. For example, ⅓ of 75 is 25. So get 25 grams protein at each meal.

Low-Carbing Any Dessert Recipe

If you have a favorite dessert recipe and want to make it low carb, try some of these suggestions. Remember that the type of recipe will make a big difference in how successful you can be. In most dessert recipes, the sugar and flour contribute the most carbs.

♦ Sugar is high in carbs, with 200 in 1 cup. In most recipes, you can halve the amount of sugar and not even notice it.

♦ Flour is also high in carbs. White, all-purpose flour has 95 carbs per cup; whole wheat has 87. If you can, eliminate the flour altogether by substituting almond or pecan "flour." Flour or cornstarch is the unequalled best for thickening sauces, so don't substitute a nut flour here. But usually, if the recipe calls for 2 tablespoons flour or cornstarch, you can get by with only 1 tablespoon. Substituting nut flour for wheat flour in cakes made with baking powder may not work well, but you be the judge.

Hot Potato _____

Changing your favorite dessert recipe or comfort food into low carb requires trial and error. You may have a couple flops, but the results when you finally get it right will be, shall we say, comforting?

♦ Upgrade milk to heavy cream. One cup milk has 50 carbs; 1 cup cream has 7.

Creating a new recipe out of an old one requires working through trial and error, learning from your mistakes, and trying again until you get it right. That's why they call them "test kitchens." And sometimes even the errors taste good enough to eat.

Even Lower Carbs

Because these are dessert recipes, they have a higher carbohydrate count than other types of food, such as fruits, vegetables, and meat.

If you really want something sweet but the carb counts of the desserts would cause you to exceed your daily quota, try eating just half a serving. That way you get half the carbs and can still satisfy your sweet tooth.

Raspberry Mousse

Prep time: 30 minutes plus chill time • Cook time: 0 • Servings: 10 • Serving size: 1 custard cup

Each serving has: 10 grams carbohydrate • 1 gram fiber • 9 grams nutritive carbohydrate • 2 grams total protein • 1 gram from animal source • 1 gram from plant source

1 TB. or 1 envelope unflavored gelatin	2 egg yolks
2 TB. cold water	¼ cup sugar
¼ cup orange juice	2 cups heavy cream
2 (10-oz.) bags frozen raspberries, unsweetened	Sprigs fresh mint, or fresh fruit for garnish

Soak gelatin in cold water in a saucepan for 5 minutes. Add orange juice and raspberries, and bring just to boiling, stirring constantly. Cool to room temperature.

Beat eggs yolks and sugar in a bowl until pale yellow. Put egg yolk mixture into the top pan of a double boiler over simmering water. Stir until slightly thickened. Cool to room temperature.

Recipe for Success

This recipe has great mouth appeal. The tart taste of the berries, the rich cream, and some sugar simply feels good all over.

Add egg yolk mixture to raspberry mixture. Stir until blended. Whip heavy cream into soft peaks, and fold into egg yolk and raspberry mixture. Divide among 10 small custard-type dishes and chill.

Garnish with fresh mint sprigs or fresh fruit. Serve chilled.

Variation: You can substitute any kind of fresh or un-sweetened frozen berries—strawberries, blackberries, or blueberries. The carbohydrate count stays about the same.

Tapioca Pudding

Prep time: 5 minutes plus chill time • Cook time: 15 minutes • Serves 8 • Serving size: about ⅓ cup

Each serving has: 13 grams carbohydrate • less than 1 gram fiber • 13 grams nutritive carbohydrate • 4 grams total protein • 4 grams from animal source

3 TB. quick-cooking tapioca

½ cup sugar

¼ tsp. salt

2 eggs, beaten

2 cups milk

½ tsp. vanilla extract

Combine tapioca, sugar, salt, eggs, and milk. Without stirring, cook in the top of a double boiler over boiling water for 7 minutes. Continue to cook, stirring, for 5 more minutes. Remove from heat, stir in vanilla, and let cool. Chill.

Recipe for Success _____

Pudding is an old-fashioned comfort food and is low in carbs. You can even sprinkle toasted almonds or coconut over the pudding and still have a relatively low-carb dessert. But be careful about serving size with the dessert recipes. A second serving can overload you with too many carbs.

Crustless Cheesecake

Prep time: 15 minutes • Cook time: 50 minutes • Serves 12 • Serving size: 1 slice

Each serving has: 10 grams nutritive carbohydrate • 6 grams total protein • 6 grams from animal source

1 cup 4 percent fat cottage cheese

1 (8-oz.) pkg. regular cream cheese (not light)

1 cup sour cream

4 eggs

2 TB. lemon juice

6 TB. brown sugar

Hot Potato

Be sure to use full-fat cottage cheese, sour cream, and cream cheese. If you use low-fat products, the carb count could double and the taste won't be as delicious.

Preheat oven to 350°F.

Combine cottage cheese, cream cheese, sour cream, eggs, lemon juice, and brown sugar in a blender, and pulse until well blended. Pour into a lightly greased 8-inch springform pan, and bake for 50 minutes. Cool. Slice into 12 servings.

Variation: Because this cheesecake is plain and unadorned, you can add fruit or a favorite topping. But remember that a topping can increase the carbohydrate count.

Slow Cooker Country Apples

Prep time: 10 minutes • Cook time: 4 to 6 hours • Serves 6 • Serving size: ¾ cup

Each serving has: 24 grams carbohydrate • 2 grams fiber • 22 grams nutritive carbohydrate • 2 grams total protein • 2 grams from plant source

4 to 5 cups peeled and sliced Granny Smith or Golden Delicious apples

1 TB. flour

⅓ cup raisins

¼ tsp. cinnamon

½ cup slow-cooking oatmeal, raw

1 cup water

1 cup apple juice

3 TB. butter

1 TB. molasses

Coat apples with flour. Stir in raisins, cinnamon, and oatmeal. Pour water and apple juice into a slow cooker, and add apple mixture. Melt butter and pour over apples, then drizzle molasses over apples. Cook on low 4 to 6 hours.

Homemade Peach Ice Cream

Prep time: 10 minutes　•　Cook time: 20 minutes plus 3 hours or overnight chill time plus time for ice-cream freezer　•　Serves 20　•　Serving size: ¼ cup

Each serving has: 8 grams nutritive carbohydrate　•　3 grams protein　•　3 grams from animal source.

3 cups half-and-half

1 cup heavy cream

4 egg yolks

¾ cup sugar

1½ tsp. vanilla extract

2 cups crushed ripe peaches, fresh or unsweetened frozen

In a large, heavy saucepan, mix half-and-half and cream. Heat to boiling, and remove from heat.

In a large bowl, whisk egg yolks until foamy. Slowly beat sugar into egg yolks, beating until mixture is thick and lemon-colored. Beat cream mixture into egg mixture and add vanilla.

Pour into a saucepan, and cook over low heat, stirring constantly for 7 minutes or until thickened. Remove from heat and add peaches. Cover and chill for at least 3 hours or overnight. Stir occasionally.

Put custard into the ice-cream freezer, and freeze according to the manufacturer's instructions. Let ice cream soften slightly in refrigerator before serving.

Recipe for Success

Usually considered a summertime treat, with frozen peaches available all year long you can make this an "any time of the year" favorite. Make sure the peaches are really ripe for the best taste.

Rum-Flavored Bananas

Prep time: 10 minutes   •   Cook time: 10 minutes   •   Serves 6   •   Serving size: ½ banana

Each serving has: 13 grams carbohydrate   •   2 grams fiber   •   11 grams nutritive carbohydrate   •   less than 1 gram total protein

3 bananas	12 TB. (6 oz.) rum
2 TB. butter	Whipped cream (optional)

Peel bananas, slice lengthwise, and cut crosswise to make 4 pieces from each banana. Melt butter in a skillet, and toss bananas until warm; add rum and heat until hot. Remove from heat, and carefully light rum with a long match. Rotate pan from side to side while flaming. This allows alcohol to cook out.

Serve while hot. Add a dollop whipped cream (if using).

Hot Potato

Be cautious when flaming alcohol. Be sure the rum is hot before trying to light or it may not flame. A good safety tip would be to wear protective eye glasses or turn your head when lighting the alcohol. Definitely use a long match.

Recipe for Success

Of course this sauce is delicious over ice cream! Just remember to check the ice-cream label and count additional carbohydrates. Use other fruits instead of bananas such as peaches, cooked apples, pitted cherries, or mixed fruits. If soft fruits are too ripe, they tend to melt away during the flaming.

Strawberry Cream

Prep time: 15 minutes • Cook time: 0 • Serves 6 • Serving size: ½ cup

Each serving has: 5 grams carbohydrate • less than 1 gram fiber • 5 grams nutritive carbohydrate • less than 1 gram total protein

1½ cups heavy cream

¼ cup low-carb strawberry fruit preserves, at room temperature

½ tsp. almond or vanilla extract (optional)

Mint leaves, for garnish (optional)

Pour heavy cream into ice-cold bowl, and whip until thick and creamy. Lightly stir in preserves. If additional flavor is desired, add almond extract.

Serve in small dessert dishes topped with mint leaf (if using) or use 2 tablespoons as a luscious topping on fresh fruit or those Double Chocolate Brownies (see recipe in Chapter 25).

Recipe for Success

Substitute any flavor of fruit preserves for the strawberry. But read the label on the jar for no more than 6 grams carbohydrate per serving; avoid those made with sugar substitutes.

Hot Fruit Soufflé

Prep time: 30 minutes • Cook time: 25 minutes • Serves 6 • Serving size: ½ cup

Each serving has: 15 grams carbohydrate • 1 gram fiber • 14 grams nutritive carbohydrate • 4 grams total protein • less than 1 gram from plant source • 4 grams from animal source

2 cups fresh fruit of choice	2 TB. heavy cream
2 TB. honey	5 egg whites, at room temperature
2 egg yolks, at room temperature	Pinch salt

Preheat oven to 350°F.

In a food processor, combine fruit, honey, egg yolks, and cream. Process well.

In a separate bowl, beat egg whites with pinch of salt until very stiff peaks form. Fold in fruit mixture quickly but gently. Pour fruit mixture into a buttered 1-quart soufflé dish, and bake about 25 minutes.

Do *not* open oven door during baking or soufflé could fall. Serve immediately.

Hot Potato

This recipe can be doubled and made in a larger soufflé dish. It can be made in several smaller soufflé cups if individual servings are desired.

Recipe for Success

What a delightful ending to a meal—this light refreshing dessert is delicious following any of the heavier main courses. Fresh berries make a wonderful soufflé. If desired, use unsweetened frozen berries, but bring them to room temperature first. If frozen with sugar, you won't need the honey, but you may need to adjust the carbohydrate count. You can use dried fruit, but cook it first.

Peanut Butter Cookies

Prep time: 10 minutes • Cook time: 10 minutes • Serves 16 • Serving size: 1 cookie

Each serving has: 9 grams carbohydrate • 2 grams fiber • 7 grams nutritive carbohydrate • 3 grams total protein • less than 1 gram from animal source • 3 grams from plant source

½ cup natural peanut butter, no sugar added

½ cup sugar

1 tsp. molasses

¼ cup heavy cream

½ cup slivered almonds

½ tsp. baking powder

1½ cups almond flour (1¼ cups almonds, finely ground)

½ tsp. salt

2 tsp. vanilla extract

Preheat oven to 375°F.

Mix together peanut butter, sugar, molasses, cream, almonds, baking powder, almond flour, salt, and vanilla, and drop by teaspoonfuls onto a greased cookie sheet to make 16 cookies. If you prefer, press cookies with the tines of a fork for that peanut-butter-cookie checkerboard look. Bake about 10 to 12 minutes or until set.

Recipe for Success
We couldn't tell these were low carb. They will surely satisfy your sweet tooth. Add to sack lunches and for an after-school or after-work snack.

Table Talk
You can easily make almond flour with a food processor and almonds. Use either blanched or unblanched whole almonds. To make 1 cup almond flour, use about ¾ cup whole almonds and process until the almonds turn into a fluffy powder. Be sure to watch carefully—don't process so long that you make almond butter. You can also purchase almond flour online.

Gingersnaps

Prep time: 10 minutes • Cook time: 20 minutes • Serves 24 • Serving size: 1 cookie

Each serving has: 6 grams carbohydrate • 3 grams fiber • 3 grams nutritive carbohydrate • 2 grams total protein • 2 grams from plant source

½ cup (1 stick) butter	1 tsp. cinnamon
½ cup sugar	¼ tsp. nutmeg
1 TB. molasses	¼ tsp. cloves
1 egg	½ tsp. salt
2 tsp. freshly grated ginger or 1 tsp. ground ginger	2 cups almond flour (1½ cups almonds, finely ground)

Recipe for Success

Enjoy the aroma of fresh gingerbread when baking these cookies. And they taste just as good. Why not roll or mold dough into gingerbread men?

Preheat oven to 300°F.

Cream butter with sugar and molasses. Beat in egg. Add ginger, cinnamon, nutmeg, cloves, and salt and mix. Gradually add almond flour, and mix to a stiff dough. Form into 24 small balls, and place on a greased cookie sheet about 1 inch apart. Bake for 20 minutes.

Variation: If you like the taste of ginger without the other spices, omit the nutmeg, cinnamon, and cloves.

Baked Ricotta Cups

Prep time: 15 minutes • Cook time: 20 minutes • Serves 6 • Serving size: 1 cup

Each serving has: 33 grams carbohydrate • 2 grams fiber • 31 grams nutritive carbohydrate • 7 grams total protein • 6 grams from animal source • 1 gram from plant source

1 cup ricotta cheese	3 cups mixed fresh or frozen fruit, such as strawberries, peaches, raspberries, blackberries, or cherries
2 egg whites, beaten	
1 TB. honey	

Preheat oven to 350°F.

Place ricotta cheese into a bowl, and break it up with a wooden spoon. Add beaten egg whites and honey, and mix thoroughly until smooth and well blended.

Lightly grease 6 ramekins. Spoon ricotta mixture into the prepared ramekins, and bake for 20 minutes until ricotta cakes rise and are golden.

Meanwhile, place fruit in a pan with a little water if fruit is fresh, and heat gently until softened. Let cool slightly, and remove any pits if using cherries. Serve fruit sauce over ricotta cups.

Recipe for Success

The ricotta cups look elegant, yet are quite easy to make and are a great dessert for any time of year. Expect the berries to be slightly tart—it just adds to the intense fresh-fruit taste. Serve the fruit sauce warm or chilled.

Cherry Omelet

Prep time: 10 minutes plus 10 minutes to pit cherries • Cook time: 6 minutes • Serves 6 • Serving size: ⅙ omelet

Each serving has: 18 grams carbohydrate • 4 grams fiber • 14 grams nutritive carbohydrate • 9 grams total protein • 8 grams from animal source • 1 gram from plant source

1 pint or 2 cups fresh or frozen cherries	½ cup sugar
8 TB. butter	4 tsp. rum
8 eggs	Pinch salt

Remove stems and stones from cherries, and sauté for 5 minutes in 4 tablespoons butter. Beat eggs hard with sugar, rum, and salt. Add cherries to batter.

Heat remaining 4 tablespoons butter in a skillet or fold-over omelet pan. Tilt pan so butter coats sides of pan all the way to the top to prevent omelet from sticking. Set pan over medium-low heat. Pour batter into skillet or half batter into each side of the omelet pan. With a spatula, push egg in from the sides to allow top, uncooked egg to run over to pan. When eggs are set on bottom, fold over omelet or close fold-over pan.

Recipe for Success

The cherries in this omelet will make you forget everything you've ever heard about omelets being only for breakfast. It tastes totally indulgent.

Frozen Raspberry Soufflé

Prep time: 20 minutes plus chill time • Cook time: 1 hour • Serves 8 • Serving size: ⅓ cup

Each serving has: 30 grams carbohydrate • less than 1 gram fiber • 30 grams nutritive carbohydrate • 4 grams total protein • 4 grams from animal source

¾ cup plus 3 TB. sugar	2 cups heavy cream
¼ cup water	3 TB. sugar
8 egg yolks	1 cup fresh or unsweetened frozen raspberries

Boil ¾ cup sugar and water until it falls in a long thread from the spoon or registers 220°F on a candy thermometer, about 5 to 8 minutes.

Beat egg yolks lightly with a fork in the top of a double boiler. Slowly add hot syrup, stirring constantly with a wooden spoon. Cook in the top of a double boiler for 45 minutes, stirring frequently until sauce has consistency of thin mayonnaise.

Recipe for Success

This recipe is truly elegant for a dinner party, but you certainly can have any leftovers for lunch the next day.

Whip cream and add remaining 3 tablespoons sugar. Crush raspberries with a fork, and mix with whipped cream.

Combine mixtures and mix well. Pour into individual ramekins, or long-stemmed wine or champagne glasses. You can also pour into a bowl, and serve family-style. Chill thoroughly.

Sautéed Fruit

Prep time: 15 minutes • Cook time: 15 minutes • Serves 6 • Serving size: ¾ cup

Each serving has: 28 grams carbohydrate • 2 grams fiber • 26 grams nutritive carbohydrate • 1 gram total protein • 1 gram from plant source

2 apples, peeled, cored, and cut into thick slices (your choice)	¼ cup orange marmalade
	1 TB. Grand Marnier
1 pear, peeled, cored, and cut into thick slices	2 navel oranges, peeled and sectioned
1½ TB. fresh lemon juice	Sprigs of fresh mint (optional)
3 TB. butter	

In a small bowl, toss apple and pear slices with lemon juice. In a large skillet, melt 2 tablespoons butter, add fruit, and sauté over medium-high heat until apples are tender, stirring gently.

With a slotted spoon, transfer fruit mixture to a bowl. To the skillet, add marmalade, Grand Marnier, and remaining 1 tablespoon butter. Stir until melted. Pour sauce over fruit, add oranges and toss gently. Garnish with sprigs of mint.

> **Recipe for Success**
> This recipe is a delicious way to dress up these fruits, and they are available fresh all year long! The sauce would be dreamy served over sponge cake with or without the fruit if you have enough carbs left in your daily allotment.

Lemon Crème Custard

Prep time: 20 minutes plus 12 hours chill time   •   Cook time: 10 minutes   •   Serves 8   •   Serving size: about ⅜ cup

Each serving has: 34 grams nutritive carbohydrate   •   3 grams total protein   •   3 grams from animal source

¾ cup sugar

2 TB. cornstarch

4 TB. butter

4 tsp. freshly grated lemon rind

¼ cup fresh lemon juice

3 large egg yolks, beaten

1 cup whole milk

1 cup sour cream

In a saucepan, mix sugar, cornstarch, butter, lemon rind, lemon juice, egg yolks, and milk. Stir, cook until thick, about 5 to 10 minutes, and cool.

Fold in sour cream. Pour into a glass or ceramic serving bowl. Refrigerate at least 12 hours.

Variation: Substitute key lime juice for the fresh lemon juice in this recipe and have key lime custard.

Recipe for Success
Lemon appeals to our sense of taste for both sour and sweet—a terrific combination. If you like a lemony tart yet sweet taste, you'll love this custard dessert.

Cold Lemon and Blueberry Mousse

Prep time: 25 minutes plus chill time • Cook time: 0 • Serves 6 • Serving size: about ⅔ cup

Each serving has: 29 grams carbohydrate • 1 gram fiber • 28 grams nutritive carbohydrate • 6 grams total protein • 5 grams from animal source • 1 gram from plant source

5 egg yolks

⅔ cup sugar

⅓ cup fresh lemon juice

5 egg whites, beaten stiff

2 cups (1 pint) fresh or frozen blueberries

Recipe for Success
The blueberries add color and eye appeal and are a great way to balance the lemon flavor. Plus, all berries provide wonderful nutrition and antioxidants. Serve with mint garnish.

Beat egg yolks with sugar until light and lemon-colored. Add lemon juice and mix well. Stir over hot water in the top of a double boiler until thick. Remove from heat, and fold in egg whites. Carefully fold in blueberries. Pour into a serving dish, and chill in refrigerator.

Variation: Substitute blackberries or raspberries in this recipe, or omit the berries entirely and enjoy the singular refreshing taste of lemon.

The Least You Need to Know

♦ The sweet taste buds on your tongue like to be satisfied with desserts and sweet-tasting foods.

♦ Low-carb desserts are a tasty, sweet ending to a meal.

♦ Eat your comfort foods in comfort, knowing they are low carb.

♦ Low-carb desserts don't have to taste low carb.

♦ You can modify your favorite desserts to be low carb with some experimentation.

Chocolate

In This Chapter

- ◆ A luscious low-carb treat
- ◆ Choosing types of chocolate
- ◆ Nutritional value
- ◆ Getting picky about your chocolate

Chocolate is food fit for the gods, or so the pre-Columbian Central American natives believed. Because of its richness, exotic flavor, and intensity, chocolate was used in the ceremonies honoring the Mayan gods. It was a drink worthy of the king and nobility. They seasoned their chocolate drinks with peppers, vanilla, anise seeds, and corn. Ancient records indicate they used chocolate for religious rituals, for currency, for increasing stamina, and for daily refreshment.

Today, many of us still hold chocolate in similar high esteem. We think chocolate feeds our souls, our energy, and our hearts. It represents dreams of romance, reconciliation, and eternal love.

The reality of chocolate isn't so bad, either. It can easily fit into an overall low-carb diet. Chocolate is packed with antioxidants and other good-for-you nutrition. To honor its culinary and sensuous pleasures, chocolate has its own chapter of recipes in this book. Whether you are an avowed chocoholic, simply fond of the taste, or need a daily "fix," you can find what you are looking for—low-carb chocolate delights—right here.

Eat Your Chocolate—It's Good for You

Chocolate is actually beneficial for you. Recent studies show that its powerful antioxidants can help prevent cancer and heart disease. It even fights tooth decay! And just think, for years we thought it gave us cavities.

The cocoa bean contains antioxidants, stearic acid, magnesium, calcium, and caffeine. These plus about 300 other substances create the flavor and nutritional value of chocolate.

Chocolate contains catechins and phenols, antioxidants that are indicated in cancer and heart disease prevention. Until recently, experts thought tea had the highest concentration of these great disease fighters, but now we know dark chocolate has four times more.

The phenols in chocolate are like those in red wine. They protect against heart disease and reduce day-to-day damage to cells and DNA from free radicals. They also prevent fatlike substances in the blood stream from oxidizing and clogging the arteries. Along with all this, chocolate helps thwart mouth bacteria and stop dental decay. We must have sensed this all along as we ate our chocolate!

Table Talk

We can't imagine a worthy substitute for chocolate. In our guilt-ridden days of thinking it made us fat, we tried carob. It wasn't the same. So don't even think of using another ingredient in place of chocolate. If you did, the recipe wouldn't come close to being a food fit for the gods.

But a little goes a long way. You don't need to eat a lot of it to get the benefits. You also can get these benefits from fruits and vegetables. But it's nice to know you get value from eating chocolate. As dark chocolate is the most beneficial for your health, most recipes in this chapter call for dark or bitter chocolate.

Chocolate Choices

The varieties of chocolate are seemingly endless. You can purchase the least expensive at the store and create a wonderful dessert, or you can use the most expensive you can find, perhaps on the Internet, and enjoy extraordinary taste and aroma.

Here are some recommendations:

- **Cocoa powder (unsweetened).** For these recipes we've used both Hershey's baking cocoa in the dark brown tin and Ghiradelli cocoa powder we purchased at the health food store. And be sure that when the recipe calls for cocoa powder you do not use the sweetened kind.

- **Alkaline processed cocoa powder.** You can substitute this powder for cocoa powder in these recipes. It makes the dessert darker in color. The flavor will be less tangy or acidic, so expect a smoother, softer taste.

- **Unsweetened baking chocolate squares.** You can substitute cocoa powder for the squares by using 3 tablespoons cocoa powder plus 1 tablespoon butter for each square.

- **Chocolate morsels.** Today, you can get excellent quality chocolate in this form. We like our chocolate deep, creamy, and flavorful. Our preferences are Ghiradelli semisweet and double chocolate morsels and Guittard milk chocolate and semisweet morsels.

- **Chocolate bars.** You can substitute a good-quality chocolate bar such as Chocolove, Ghiradelli, or Guittard in many of the recipes. We have found the best quality and most variety at health food stores and at cooking supply stores. You can even purchase the best chocolate in 10-pound bars, which is quite economical. To make chocolate chunks or morsels from the bars, we suggest this: Unwrap the chocolate bar and place it in a plastic zippered bag. Take it to the front or back porch and drop it on the concrete. Or throw it on the concrete. Examine your results. Any remaining chunks that are too large you can break by hand.

Most grocery stores offer a good selection of chips and cocoa powders in the baking, spice, and flour aisle. For fancier brands of chocolate, try the larger health food grocery stores and specialty cooking stores.

 Table Talk

Chocolate can burn very easily. To melt, use one of these two methods: Cover the chocolate in a dish and use the microwave because it does not get as hot as the stove. Or if you prefer to melt on top of the stove, melt in the top of a double boiler over boiling water. Chocolate also freezes well if you have some left over. Pack it in a container or heavy freezer bag. Thaw covered in the same container so it will reabsorb the moisture given off during freezing.

The Other Ingredients

Chocolate by itself, as found in cocoa powder or bitter baking chocolate, has very few carbs. For most of us, those forms of chocolate are not palatable; in fact, they're unbearable. We need to add sugar and dairy products. But even with sugar added, chocolate's carb count is low enough to be considered low-carb when you have some—but not too much—chocolate.

We favor real full-fat dairy products in these chocolate recipes. To get the best results, use real butter, real cream, real cream cheese, and real ricotta cheese. Please don't try these with low-fat dairy products. The results will be puny compared with using the real thing. Plus, when you use low-fat dairy products, you increase the carbohydrate count of the recipe.

Absolutely do not use margarine or fake butter. You'll ruin a good recipe. These fake butters either contain trans-fatty acids or become trans-fatty acids when cooked. Beyond the taste not being as good, you are also placing your health at risk.

Chocolate Carbohydrates

The Aztecs drank hot chocolate made by mixing ground chocolate beans with hot chili peppers, water, and other spices. It was only after the Aztecs served Hernán Cortés this chocolate drink that it was brought to Europe. Later, it is thought that the Spanish first added sugar to their "hot cocoa."

If you use your chocolate as the Aztecs and Mayans did, it would contain very few carbs. Cocoa powder has very few carbs, and drinking hot chocolate without sweetener is definitely low carb.

It's the other ingredients that add carbs to chocolate desserts—most especially, the sugar and flour. We have greatly reduced and/or eliminated the flour in these recipes. We still use some sugar, but not much.

If you want to eat even fewer carbs than the recipe serving size offers, you can eat a half serving, thus halving the number of carbs you consume. Or you can purchase a dark chocolate candy bar and eat one square to get that fabulous chocolate taste with very few carbs. And the good news—a bar could last a week or more—as ¼ ounce dark chocolate has only 4 carbs.

Double Chocolate Brownies

Prep time: 10 minutes • Cook time: 20 to 25 minutes • Serves 12 • Serving size: 1 brownie

Each serving has: 13 grams carbohydrate • 2 grams fiber • 11 grams nutritive carbohydrate • 1 gram total protein • less than 1 gram from animal source • less than 1 gram from plant source

½ cup (1 stick) butter (not margarine)	¾ cup ground pecans
½ cup brown sugar	¼ tsp. salt
2 eggs	½ cup dark chocolate chips, either semisweet or double chocolate
¼ cup unsweetened cocoa powder	

Preheat oven to 350°F.

Cream butter and brown sugar in a mixing bowl. Beat eggs in well. Add cocoa powder, pecans, and salt. Stir in chocolate chips. Bake in an ungreased 9×9-inch pan for 20 to 25 minutes or until done.

Variation: Vary the recipe by adding ½ teaspoon black pepper, 1 teaspoon instant coffee, ¼ teaspoon cayenne, or ½ teaspoon vanilla extract. You can also add whole nuts or vary the type of chocolate chips by substituting milk chocolate, white chocolate, or butterscotch chips. You can even try mint chips. However, using these other kinds of chips will increase the carb count.

Table Talk

To make ground pecans, use a food processor or a blender. With a food processor, use ¾ cup pecan halves and process until you get a flour. You'll get 1 cup ground pecans. If you use a blender, do not process too long or you will end up with pecan butter. If you do get pecan butter, it is great on raw vegetables and also eaten with a spoon as a low-carb snack.

Chocolate Soufflé

Prep time: 20 minutes • Cook time: 12 to 17 minutes • Serves 6 • Serving size: ⅙ recipe

Each serving has: 10 grams carbohydrate • 2 grams fiber • 8 grams nutritive carbohydrate • 8 grams total protein • 5 grams from animal source • 3 grams from plant source

4 oz. semisweet or bittersweet chocolate	1 tsp. sugar
5 TB. butter	¼ tsp. cream of tartar
4 large eggs, separated	1 tsp. grated orange rind

Recipe for Success

Soufflés only seem hard to make until you try your first one. Even if it doesn't puff up perfectly, the results are definitely worth eating. This soufflé has a creamy center. If you want it to be less creamy, increase baking time by 4 to 5 minutes.

Preheat oven to 475°F.

Heat chocolate and butter in a saucepan over low heat until chocolate melts. Remove from heat, and stir in egg yolks. Pour into a large mixing bowl, and add grated orange peel.

Beat egg whites with 1 teaspoon sugar and cream of tartar until stiff. Fold half beaten egg whites into chocolate mixture. Add remaining whites, and fold in with a spatula. Pour into a greased soufflé dish.

Bake 5 minutes; turn temperature down to 425°F, and continue baking for 5 to 7 minutes. Serve immediately.

Chocolate Nut Pâté

Prep time: 15 minutes plus overnight freezing • Cook time: 5 minutes • Serves 18 • Serving size: 1 small slice

Each serving has: 16 grams nutritive carbohydrate • 1 gram total protein • less than 1 gram from animal source • less than 1 gram from plant source

15 oz. semisweet, bittersweet, or milk chocolate	¾ cup confectioners' sugar
1 cup heavy cream	6 TB. dark rum
4 TB. butter	½ cup cashews
4 large egg yolks	

In a heavy saucepan, slowly melt chocolate with cream and butter. Remove from heat, and beat with a wire whisk until smooth. Add egg yolks, one at a time, beating well after each. Add confectioners' sugar, stirring constantly until smooth. Mix in rum. Stir in cashews.

Pour mixture into a small 4-cup loaf pan lined with waxed paper. Freeze overnight. To remove pâté, invert pan over a serving plate, and remove waxed paper. Slice and serve.

Variation: In place of the cashews, you can use slivered almonds, pecans, walnuts, macadamias, pistachios, or pine nuts.

Recipe for Success

This highly rich dessert has the texture of fudge and can be garnished with fresh fruit, such as berries, kiwi, or peaches. You can also serve it topped with whipped cream.

Flourless Chocolate Tiramisu Cake

Prep time: 20 minutes • Cook time: 30 minutes • Serves 12 • Serving size: $\frac{1}{12}$ cake

Each serving has: 12 grams carbohydrate • 1 gram fiber • 11 grams nutritive carbohydrate • 4 grams total protein • 3 grams from animal source • 1 gram from plant source

2 tsp. butter	$\frac{1}{2}$ cup sugar
$\frac{1}{2}$ cup unsweetened cocoa powder	$\frac{1}{2}$ cup sour cream
4 eggs	1 tsp. vanilla
$\frac{1}{2}$ cup ground hazelnuts	2 tsp. instant coffee

Preheat oven to 350°F.

Prepare an 8- or 9-inch springform pan with butter and 1 tablespoon cocoa powder.

Using an electric mixer, beat eggs until fluffy and light. In another bowl, combine remaining cocoa powder, hazelnuts, sugar, sour cream, vanilla, and coffee. Care-fully fold into beaten egg mixture. Pour into prepared pan.

Bake for 30 minutes or until the cake is dry on top. Cool until warm. Loosen the edges of cake with a knife, and remove sides of pan.

Variation: For a plain chocolate cake, omit the coffee. To enhance the flavor of the chocolate, add $\frac{1}{2}$ teaspoon tarragon to the batter.

Recipe for Success

Be sure to gently and carefully fold the chocolate mixture into the eggs. The cake may sink, but this is normal. Garnish with fresh fruit or whipped cream.

Chocolate Mousse

Prep time: 20 minutes plus chill time • Cook time: 0 • Serves 6 • Serving size: ½ cup

Each serving has: 21 grams nutritive carbohydrate • 6 grams total protein • 5 grams from animal source • 1 gram from plant source

2 cups whole milk

¼ cup sugar

3 oz. semisweet chocolate morsels

4 egg yolks

½ cup whipping cream

1 tsp. vanilla extract

Recipe for Success

This recipe gives you great old-fashioned comfort and nourishment. Enhance the creamy texture and taste by garnishing with mint sprigs or berries—or simply use nothing at all.

Heat milk, sugar, and chocolate in a saucepan over low heat, stirring until chocolate is melted. Set aside and partially cool. Beat egg yolks until pale yellow. Slowly add milk mixture to egg yolks, making sure to keep stirring until blended.

Whip cream and fold into egg mixture. Add vanilla. Pour into custard cups, and chill before serving.

Chocolate Truffles

Prep time: 20 minutes plus chill time • Cook time: 10 minutes • Serves 24 • Serving size: 1 truffle

Each serving has: 5 grams nutritive carbohydrate • less than 1 gram total protein

¼ cup heavy cream

2 TB. Grand Marnier

6 oz. semisweet chocolate chips

4 TB. butter, at room temperature

Unsweetened cocoa powder

Carefully boil cream in a small pan until reduced by ⅓. Remove from heat, and stir in Grand Marnier and chocolate chips. Stir until chocolate melts.

Stir in butter, 1 tablespoon at a time until well blended. Pour into a shallow bowl, and refrigerate until firm.

Shape chocolate mixture into 24 (1-inch) balls, and roll balls in unsweetened cocoa. Store in the refrigerator. Bring to room temperature to serve.

Recipe for Success

You definitely can enjoy the wonderful luscious taste of divinely rich chocolate for only 7 grams carbohydrate. But savor it slowly; make it last. Substitute another liqueur for the Grand Marnier, or leave it out entirely and use water.

Nut Clusters

Prep time: 15 minutes plus standing time • Cook time: 0 • Serves 24 • Serving size: 1 nut cluster

Each serving has: 12 grams carbohydrate • 1 gram fiber • less than 1 gram total protein

2 cups (12 oz.) semisweet chocolate morsels	½ cup flaked or shredded coconut, unsweetened
1 cup pecans	

Melt chocolate morsels in a microwave or in the top of a double boiler over boiling water. Stir to combine. Add pecans and coconut, and stir until well blended.

Drop by teaspoonfuls onto waxed paper or aluminum foil. Cool.

Variation: Instead of pecans, substitute other nuts, such as peanuts, cashews, walnuts, pine nuts, or pistachios. You can omit the coconut, and add ½ cup more nuts.

Recipe for Success

Yes, these are actually candy. Yes, there is such a thing as low-carb candy made with real ingredients. One piece goes a long way toward satisfying your sweet tooth, or chocolate tooth, as the case may be.

Slow Cooker Chocolate-Amaretto Cheesecake

Prep time: 15 minutes plus 1 to 2 hours standing time and overnight chilling • Cook time: 2½ to 3 hours • Serves 12 • Serving size: ¹⁄₁₂ recipe

Each serving has: 20 grams nutritive carbohydrate • 5 grams total protein • 4 grams from animal source • 1 gram from plant source

1 cup ricotta cheese	¼ cup amaretto liqueur
12 oz. cream cheese	¼ cup plus 1 TB. unsweetened cocoa powder
¾ cup sugar	¼ cup flour
2 eggs	1 tsp. vanilla extract
3 TB. whipping cream	⅓ cup semisweet chocolate morsels

Recipe for Success

This cheesecake is high in complete protein and low in carbs, plus it blends two wonderful flavors into a luscious dessert. By using the slow cooker, the cheesecake comes out very moist.

Table Talk

To lower the carbohydrate count of other cheesecake recipes, eliminate the crust. Make the recipe as normal, with the same size pan and same bake time.

Because of the time involved in cooling and chilling, this dessert is best made the day before serving.

Beat ricotta cheese and cream cheese with sugar until smooth; add eggs and whipping cream, and beat with a handheld electric mixer on medium for about 3 minutes. Add amaretto, cocoa powder, flour, and vanilla; beat for about 1 more minute. Stir in chocolate chips, and pour mixture into a 7-inch springform pan.

Place cheesecake pan on a rack in a slow cooker (or use a "ring" of aluminum foil to keep it off the bottom of the cooker). Cover and cook on high for 2½ to 3 hours. Let stand in the covered cooker (after turning it off) for about 1 to 2 hours, until cool enough to handle. Cool thoroughly before removing sides of pan. Chill before serving, and store leftovers in the refrigerator.

Walnut Cake with Chocolate Cream

Prep time: 30 minutes plus chill time • Cook time: 25 to 30 minutes • Serves 12
• Serving size: ¹⁄₁₂ recipe

Each serving has: 15 grams carbohydrate • 3 grams fiber • 12 grams nutritive carbohydrate
• 7 grams total protein • 4 grams from animal source • 3 grams from plant source

10 oz. English walnuts	3 oz. unsweetened chocolate
6 eggs, separated	3 TB. sugar
¾ cup sugar	1½ cups heavy cream

Preheat oven to 350°F.

Butter and flour 2 (9-inch) cake pans. Process walnuts in a food processor or a blender until they become a fine powder.

In a large bowl, beat egg whites until stiff. In a separate bowl, beat egg yolks until pale yellow and fluffy. Gradually beat sugar into egg yolks, and fold mixture into egg whites. Fold in powdered walnuts.

Pour batter into cake pans, and bake 25 to 30 minutes or until cake is lightly browned. Remove from oven, and immediately invert the pans on racks. Cool slightly, remove cakes from pans, and cool thoroughly while preparing Chocolate Cream.

Over medium heat, melt chocolate. Stir in sugar and then cream. Stir until mixture almost boils, then remove from heat and chill.

When ready to frost cake, beat Chocolate Cream until it's the consistency of whipped cream. Spread Cream between layers, on top, and on sides of cake.

Recipe for Success

This is a fancy cake for special times and celebrations. Your guests will be amazed that this is low carb. You can substitute hazelnuts for the walnuts if you wish.

Chocolate Ganache

Prep time: 5 minutes plus chill time • Cook time: 10 minutes • Serves 48 • Serving size: 1 tablespoon

Each serving has: 4 grams nutritive carbohydrate • less than 1 gram protein

1 cup heavy cream

1 (10- to 12-oz.) pkg. semisweet chocolate morsels

1 TB. Grand Marnier

Hot Potato _____
Ganache is exceptionally rich and chocolaty, so be careful—a little goes a long way.

In a saucepan, scald cream by heating to just below boiling, when small bubbles form around the edges. Remove from heat, and gently stir in chocolate until smooth and melted. Stir in Grand Marnier. Cool and serve over ice cream, brownies, and other desserts. Yields 3 cups.

Recipe for Success _____
Use a dollop of Chocolate Ganache over brownies and cakes. Warm it up and use it as a sauce over ice cream and puddings. You can even use it as an icing for cakes. Substitute any after-dinner liqueur for the Grand Marnier. For a quick and easy treat, enjoy a single tablespoon. Keep any leftovers in a container in the refrigerator.

Rich Chocolate Brownies

Prep time: 20 minutes • Cook time: 30 to 35 minutes • Serves 16 • Serving size: 1 brownie or ¹⁄₁₆ recipe

Each serving has: 24 grams carbohydrate • 4 grams fiber • 20 grams nutritive carbohydrate • 1 gram total protein • 1 gram from animal source • less than 1 gram from plant source

12 oz. semisweet chocolate	²⁄₃ cup ground pecans
12 oz. milk chocolate	3 extra large eggs, slightly beaten
¾ cup butter	

Preheat the oven to 350°F.

Line the base and sides of an 8-inch-square cake pan with baking parchment or waxed paper.

Break semisweet chocolate and ¼ milk chocolate into pieces, and put into the top of a double boiler. Add butter. Melt over simmering water, stirring frequently. Remove from heat. Stir ground pecans and eggs into melted chocolate.

Chop remaining milk chocolate into chunky pieces. Stir ½ remaining chopped milk chocolate into the warm mixture, and pour into the prepared pan, spreading it into the corners. Milk chocolate doesn't need to melt all the way. Sprinkle with remaining chopped milk chocolate.

Bake brownies for 30 to 35 minutes, until they rise and are just firm to the touch. Let cool in the pan, then cut into 16 squares.

Recipe for Success

These are very chocolaty, very rich, and definitely satisfying. You can serve garnished with strawberries or raspberries to keep the carb count low. Or you can serve with a spoonful of ice cream, but remember to count the carbs in the ice cream as part of your daily allotment.

Chocolate Drop Cookies

Prep time: 10 minutes • Cook time: 20 minutes • Serves 24 • Serving size: 1 cookie

Each serving has: 7 grams carbohydrate • 1 gram fiber • 6 grams nutritive carbohydrate • 2 grams total protein • less than 1 gram from animal source • 2 grams from plant source

½ cup (1 stick) butter	¼ cup unsweetened cocoa powder
½ cup sugar	½ tsp. vanilla extract
1 tsp. molasses	½ tsp. salt
1 egg	1¼ cups almond flour (1½ cups almonds, finely ground)

Recipe for Success

Sometimes a chocolate cookie hits the spot. And low carbs make it better. These are richer than a normal cookie. You can frost with a teaspoon of Chocolate Ganache on top, but it will increase the carb count. Just make sure the cookies have cooled before frosting them.

Preheat oven to 300°F.

Cream butter with sugar and molasses. Beat in egg. Add cocoa powder, vanilla, and salt. Gradually add almond flour, and mix to a stiff dough. Form into 24 small balls, and place balls on a greased cookie sheet about 1 inch apart. Flatten slightly. Bake for 20 minutes.

Variation: You can add ¼ cup unsweetened coconut to the batter or even ½ cup chocolate chips. These variations will increase the carb count.

The Least You Need to Know

- Chocolate is actually good for you.
- This "food fit for the gods" can be an enjoyable part of low-carb eating.
- Use the best-quality ingredients you can find, being sure to use full-fat dairy products in these recipes.
- Enjoy eating these treats slowly and sensuously so you get the most pleasure from 1 serving.
- Eat half a serving to get fewer carbs and still enjoy the taste of chocolate.

Glossary

al dente Italian for "against the teeth," this term refers to pasta (or other ingredient such as rice) that is neither soft nor hard, but just slightly firm against the teeth. This, according to many pasta aficionados, is the perfect way to cook pasta.

all-purpose flour Flour that contains only the inner part of the wheat grain. Usable for all purposes from cakes to gravies.

allspice Named for its flavor echoes of several spices (cinnamon, cloves, nutmeg), allspice is used in many desserts and in rich marinades and stews.

almonds Mild, sweet, and crunchy nuts that combine nicely with creamy and sweet food items.

anchovies (also **sardines**) Tiny, flavorful preserved fish that typically come in cans. The strong flavor from these salted fish is a critical element in many recipes. Anchovies are a traditional garnish for Caesar salad, the dressing of which contains anchovy paste.

artichoke hearts The center part of the artichoke flower, often found canned in grocery stores and used as a stand-alone vegetable dish or as a flavorful base for appetizers or main courses.

arugula A spicy-peppery garden plant with leaves that resemble a dandelion and have a distinctive—and very sharp—flavor.

au gratin The quick broiling of a dish before serving to brown the top ingredients. The term is often used as part of a recipe name and implies cheese and a creamy sauce.

bake   To cook in a dry oven. Baking is one of the most popular methods of cooking and is used for everything from roasts, vegetables, and other main courses to desserts such as cakes and pies. Dry-heat cooking often results in a crisping of the exterior of the food being cooked. Moist-heat cooking, through methods such as steaming, poaching, etc., brings a much different, moist quality to the food.

baking pans   Pans used for baking potatoes to chicken, cookies to croutons.

balsamic vinegar   Vinegar produced primarily in Italy from a specific type of grape and aged in wood barrels. It is heavier, darker, and sweeter than most vinegars and has more carbohydrates.

bamboo shoots   Crunchy, tasty white parts of the growing bamboo plant, often purchased canned.

barbecue   This is a loaded word, with different, zealous definitions in different parts of the country. In some cases it is synonymous with grilling (quick-cooking over high heat); in others, to barbecue is to cook something long and slow in a rich liquid (barbecue sauce).

basil   A flavorful, almost sweet, resinous herb delicious with tomatoes and used in all kinds of Italian or Mediterranean-style dishes.

baste   To keep foods moist during cooking by spooning, brushing, or drizzling with a liquid.

beat   To quickly mix substances.

Belgian endive   A plant that resembles a small, elongated, tightly packed head of romaine lettuce. The thick, crunchy leaves can be broken off and used with dips and spreads.

blanch   To place a food in boiling water for about 1 minute (or less) to partially cook the exterior and then submerge in or rinse with cool water to halt the cooking. This is a common method for preparing some vegetables such as asparagus for serving and also for preparing foods for freezing.

blend   To completely mix something, usually with a blender or food processor, more slowly than beating.

boil   To heat a liquid to a point where water is forced to turn into steam, causing the liquid to bubble. To boil something is to insert it into boiling water. A rapid boil is when a lot of bubbles form on the surface of the liquid.

bouillon   Dried essence of stock from chicken, beef, vegetable, or other ingredients. This is a popular starting ingredient for soups as it adds flavor (and often a lot of salt).

braise   To cook with the introduction of some liquid, usually over an extended period of time.

bread flour   Wheat flour used for bread and other recipes.

breadcrumbs   Tiny pieces of crumbled dry bread. Breadcrumbs are an important component in many recipes and are also used as a coating, for example with breaded chicken breasts.

Brie   A creamy cow's milk cheese from France with a soft, edible rind and a mild flavor.

broil To cook in a dry oven under the overhead high-heat element.

broth *See stock.*

brown To cook in a skillet, turning, until the surface is brown in color, to lock in the juices.

brown rice Whole-grain rice with a characteristic brown color from the bran coating; more nutritious and flavorful than white rice.

Cajun cooking A style of cooking that combines French and Southern characteristics and includes many highly seasoned stews and meats.

capers Usually sold preserved in jars, capers are the flavorful buds of a Mediterranean plant. The most common size is *nonpareil* (about the size of a small pea); others are larger, including the grape-size caper berries produced in Spain.

caramelize The term's original meaning is to cook sugar over low heat until it develops a sweet caramel flavor; however, the term is increasingly gaining use to describe cooking vegetables (especially onions) or meat in butter or oil over low heat until they soften, sweeten, and develop a caramel color. Caramelized onions are a popular addition to many recipes, especially as a pizza topping.

caraway A distinctive spicy seed used for bread, pork, cheese, and cabbage dishes. It is known to reduce stomach upset, which is why it is often paired with, for example, sauerkraut.

cardamom An intense, sweet-smelling spice, common to Indian cooking, used in baking and coffee.

casserole dishes Primarily used in baking, these covered containers hold liquids and solids together and keep moisture around ingredients that might otherwise dry out.

cayenne A fiery spice made from (hot) chili peppers, especially the cayenne chili, a slender, red, and very hot pepper.

cheddar The ubiquitous hard, cow's milk cheese with a rich, buttery flavor that ranges from mellow to sharp. Originally produced in England, cheddar is now produced worldwide.

cheese boards or **cheese trays** A collection of three or four mixed-flavor cheeses arranged on a tray, platter, or even cutting board. One classic example would be at least one cheese made from cow's, sheep's, and goat's milk. Often restaurants will offer a selection of cheeses as a "cheese flight," or course.

chickpeas (also **garbanzo beans**) The base ingredient in hummus, chickpeas are high in fiber and low in fat, making this a delicious and healthful component of many appetizers and main dishes.

chili peppers (also **chile peppers**) Any one of many different "hot" peppers, ranging in intensity from the relatively mild ancho pepper to the blisteringly hot habanero.

chili powder A seasoning blend that includes chili pepper, cumin, garlic, and oregano. Proportions vary among different versions, but they all offer a warm, rich flavor.

chives A member of the onion family, chives are found at the grocery store as bunches of long leaves that resemble the green tops of onions. They provide an easy onion flavor to any dish. Chives are very easy to grow, and many people have them in their garden.

chop To cut into pieces, usually qualified by an adverb such as "*coarsely* chopped," or by a size measurement such as "chopped into ½-inch pieces." "Finely chopped" is much closer to mince.

chorizo A spiced pork sausage eaten alone and as a component in many recipes.

cider vinegar Vinegar produced from apple cider, popular in North America.

cilantro A member of the parsley family and used in Mexican cooking and some Asian dishes. Cilantro is what gives some salsas their unique flavor. Use in moderation, as the flavor can overwhelm.

cinnamon A sweet, rich, aromatic spice commonly used in baking or desserts. Cinnamon can also be used for delicious and interesting entrées.

cloves A sweet, strong, almost wintergreen-flavor spice used in baking and with meats such as ham.

coat To cover all sides of a food with a liquid, sauce, or solid.

core To remove the unappetizing middle membranes and seeds of fruit and vegetables.

coriander A rich, warm, spicy spice used in all types of recipes, from African to South American, from entrées to desserts.

count On packaging of seafood or other foods that come in small sizes, you'll often see a reference to the count, or how many of that item compose 1 pound. For example, 31 to 40 count shrimp are large appetizer shrimp often served with cocktail sauce; 51 to 60 are much smaller.

couscous Granular semolina (durum wheat) that is cooked and used in many Mediterranean and North African dishes.

cream To blend an ingredient to get a soft, creamy liquid or substance.

cremini mushrooms A relative of the white button mushroom but brown in color and with a richer flavor. *See also* portobello mushrooms.

croutons Pieces of bread, usually between ¼ and ½ inch in size, that are sometimes seasoned and baked, broiled, or fried to a crisp texture.

crudités Fresh vegetables served as an appetizer, often all together on one tray.

cumin A fiery, smoky-tasting spice popular in Middle Eastern and Indian dishes. Cumin is a seed; ground cumin seed is the most common form of the spice used in cooking.

curing A method of preserving uncooked foods, usually meats or fish, by either salting and smoking or pickling.

curry   A general term referring to rich, spicy, Indian-style sauces and the dishes prepared with them. Common ingredients include hot pepper, nutmeg, cumin, cinnamon, pepper, and turmeric.

custard   A cooked mixture of eggs and milk. Custards are a popular base for desserts.

dash   A dash refers to a few drops, usually of a liquid, that is released by a quick shake of, for example, a bottle of hot sauce.

deglaze   To scrape up the bits of meat and seasoning left in a pan or skillet after cooking. Usually this is done by adding a liquid such as wine or broth and creating a flavorful stock that can be used to create sauces.

devein   The removal of the dark vein from the back of a large shrimp with a sharp knife.

dice   To cut into small cubes about ¼-inch square.

Dijon mustard   Hearty, spicy mustard made in the style of the Dijon region of France.

dill   A slightly sour, unique herb that is perfect for eggs, cheese dishes, and, of course, vegetables (pickles!).

double boiler   A set of two pots designed to nest together, one inside the other, and provide consistent, moist heat for foods that need delicate treatment. The bottom pot holds water (not quite touching the bottom of the top pot); the top pot holds the ingredient you want to heat.

dressing   A liquid mixture usually containing oil, vinegar, and herbs used for seasoning salads and other foods. Also the solid dish commonly called "stuffing" used to stuff turkey and other foods.

drizzle   To lightly sprinkle drops of a liquid over food. Drizzling is often the finishing touch to a dish.

dry   In the context of wine, a wine that has been vinified to contain little or no residual sugar.

dust   To sprinkle a dry substance, often a seasoning, over a food or dish.

emulsion   A combination of liquid ingredients that do not normally mix well beaten together to create a thick liquid, such as a fat or oil with water. Classic examples are salad dressings and mayonnaise. Creation of an emulsion must be done carefully and rapidly to ensure that particles of one ingredient are suspended in the other.

entrée   The main dish in a meal.

étouffée   Cajun for "smothered." This savory, rich sauce (often made with crayfish) is served over rice.

extra-virgin olive oil   *See* olive oil.

falafel   Middle Eastern hand food composed of seasoned, ground chickpeas formed into balls, cooked, and often used as a filling for pita bread.

fennel   In seed form, a fragrant, licorice-tasting herb. The bulbs have a much milder flavor and a celerylike crunch and are used as a vegetable in salads or cooked recipes.

feta   This white, crumbly, salty cheese is popular in Greek cooking, on salads, and on its own. Traditional feta is usually made with sheep's milk, but feta-style cheese can be made from sheep's, cow's, or goat's milk. Its sharp flavor is especially nice with bitter, cured black olives.

fillet   A piece of meat or seafood with the bones removed.

flake   To break into thin sections, as with fish.

floret   The flower or bud end of broccoli or cauliflower.

flour   Grains ground into a meal. Wheat is perhaps the most common flour, an essential component in many breads. Flour is also made from oats, rye, buckwheat, soybeans, etc. Different types of flour serve different purposes. *See also* all-purpose flour; bread flour; whole-wheat flour.

fry   Pan-cooking over high heat with butter or oil.

garlic   A member of the onion family, a pungent and flavorful element in many savory dishes. A garlic bulb, the form in which garlic is often sold, contains multiple cloves. Each clove, when chopped, provides about 1 teaspoon garlic.

garnish   An embellishment not vital to the dish but added to enhance visual appeal.

ginger   Available in fresh root or ground form, ginger adds a pungent, sweet, and spicy quality to a dish. It is a very popular element of many Asian and Indian dishes, among others.

glycemic index   The measurement of how fast a specific carbohydrate causes a rise in a person's blood sugar level. The higher the number on the glycemic index, the faster the rise in blood sugar.

goulash   A rich, Hungarian-style meat-and-vegetable stew seasoned with paprika, among other spices.

grate   To shave into tiny pieces using a sharp rasp or grater.

grill   To cook over high heat, usually over charcoal or gas.

grind   To reduce a large, hard substance, often a seasoning such as peppercorns, to the consistency of sand.

Gruyère   A rich, sharp cow's milk cheese with a nutty flavor made in Switzerland.

gustatory   Relating to or associated with the sense of taste. Gustatory satisfaction pleases the taste buds and delights the whole sensation of taste.

handful   An unscientific measurement term that refers to the amount of an ingredient you can hold in your hand.

hazelnuts (also **filberts**)   Sweet nuts popular in desserts and, to a lesser degree, in savory dishes.

hearts of palm   Firm, elongated, off-white cylinders from the inside of a palm tree stem tip. They are delicious in many recipes.

herbs   The leaves of flavorful plants characterized by fresh, pungent aromas and flavors, such as parsley, sage, rosemary, and thyme.

herbes de Provence   A seasoning mix including basil, fennel, marjoram, rosemary, sage, and thyme.

hors d'oeuvre   French for "outside of work" (the "work" being the main meal). An hors d'oeuvre can be any dish served as a starter before the meal.

infusion   A liquid in which flavorful ingredients such herbs have been soaked or steeped to extract that flavor into the liquid.

Italian seasoning (also **spaghetti sauce seasoning**)   The ubiquitous grocery store blend, which includes basil, oregano, rosemary, and thyme, is a useful seasoning for quick flavor that evokes the "old country" in sauces, meatballs, soups, and vegetable dishes.

jicama   A juicy, crunchy, sweet, Central American vegetable that is eaten both raw and cooked. It is available in many large grocery stores as well as from specialty vendors. If you can't find jicama, try substituting sliced water chestnuts.

julienne   To slice into very thin pieces.

liver   The nutritious and flavorful organ meat from all types of fowl and animal.

low-carb spreadsheet   A chart showing the nutritional count of each recipe and used to easily plan the menu for a meal, a day, or a week and stay within a certain carbohydrate allotment.

marinate   To soak meat, seafood, or other food in a seasoned sauce, called a marinade, which is high in acid content. The acids break down the muscle of the meat, making it tender and adding flavor.

marjoram   A sweet herb, a cousin of and similar to oregano, popular in Greek, Spanish, and Italian dishes.

marmalade   A fruit-and-sugar preserve that contains whole pieces of fruit peel, to achieve simultaneous sweetness (from the sugar) and tartness (from the fruit's natural acids). The most common marmalades are made with citrus fruits such as orange and lemon.

mascarpone   A thick, creamy, spreadable cheese, traditionally from Italy, although versions using the same name are made in the United States. It is perhaps one of the most delicious and decadent dessert toppings for fruit.

medallion   A small round cut, usually of meat or vegetables such as carrots or cucumbers.

meld   A combination of *melt* and *weld*, many cooks use this term to describe how flavors blend and spread over time throughout dips and spreads. Melding is often why recipes call for overnight refrigeration and is also why some dishes taste better as leftovers.

meringue   A baked mixture of sugar and beaten egg whites, often used as a dessert topping.

mesclun   Mixed salad greens, usually containing lettuce and assorted greens such as arugula, cress, endive, and others.

mince   To cut into very small pieces smaller than diced pieces, about ⅛ inch or smaller.

mold   A decorative, shaped metal pan in which contents, such as mousse or gelatin, set up and take the shape of the pan.

mushrooms   Any one of a huge variety of *edible* fungi (note emphasis on "edible"; there are also poisonous mushrooms). *See also* cremini mushrooms; porcini mushrooms; portobello mushrooms; shiitake mushrooms; white mushrooms.

nutmeg   A sweet, fragrant, musky spice used primarily in baking.

nuts   Shell-covered seeds (or fruits) whose meat is rich in flavor and nutrition. A critical component in many dishes, many nuts are tasty on their own as well. *See also* almonds; hazelnuts; pecans; walnuts.

nutritive carbohydrate count   The actual amount of carbohydrates available in a serving. Nutritive carbohydrate count is calculated by subtracting the amount of dietary fiber in grams from the carbohydrate count of each serving.

olive oil   A fragrant liquid produced by crushing or pressing olives. Extra-virgin olive oil is the oil produced from the first pressing of a batch of olives; oil is also produced from other pressings after the first. Extra-virgin olive oil is generally considered the most flavorful and highest quality and is the type you want to use when your focus is on the oil itself. Be sure the bottle label reads "extra-virgin."

olives   The fruit of the olive tree commonly grown on all sides of the Mediterranean. There are many varieties of olives but two general types: green and black. Black olives are also called ripe olives.

oregano   A fragrant, slightly astringent herb used in Greek, Spanish, and Italian dishes.

oxidation   The browning of fruit flesh that happens over time and with exposure to air. Although it's best to prepare fresh fruit dishes just before serving, sometimes that's not possible. If you need to cut apples in advance, minimize oxidation by rubbing the cut surfaces with a lemon half.

pan-broil   Quick-cooking over high heat in a skillet with a minimum of butter or oil. (Frying, on the other hand, uses more butter or oil.)

paprika   A rich, red, warm, earthy spice that also lends a rich red color to many dishes.

parboil   To partially cook in boiling water or broth. Parboiling is similar to blanching, although blanched foods are quickly cooled with cold water.

pare   To scrape away the skin of a food, usually a vegetable, as part of preparation for serving or cooking.

Parmesan   A hard, dry, flavorful cheese primarily used grated or shredded as a seasoning for Italian-style dishes.

parsley   A fresh-tasting green leafy herb used to add color and interest to just about any savory dish. Often used as a garnish just before serving.

pâté   A savory loaf that contains meats, spices, and often a lot of fat, served cold spread or sliced on crusty bread or crackers.

peanuts The nutritious and high-fat seeds of the peanut plant that are sold shelled or unshelled and in a variety of preparations, including peanut butter and peanut oil. Some people are allergic to peanuts, so care should be taken with their inclusion in recipes.

pecans Rich, buttery nuts native to North America. Their flavor, a terrific addition to appetizers, is at least partially due to their high, unsaturated fat content.

pepper A biting and pungent seasoning, freshly ground pepper is a must for many dishes and adds an extra level of flavor and taste.

peppercorns Large, round, dried berries that are ground to produce pepper.

pesto A thick spread or sauce made with fresh basil leaves, garlic, olive oil, pine nuts, and Parmesan cheese. Other new versions are made with other herbs. Rich and flavorful, pesto can be made at home or purchased in a grocery store and used on anything from appetizers to pasta and other main dishes.

pickle A food, usually a vegetable such as a cucumber, that has been pickled in brine.

pilaf A rice dish in which the rice is browned in butter or oil, then cooked in a flavorful liquid such as a broth, often with the addition of meats or vegetables. The rice absorbs the broth, resulting in a savory dish.

pinch An unscientific measurement term that refers to the amount of an ingredient— typically a dry, granular substance such as an herb or seasoning—you can hold between your finger and thumb.

pine nuts (also **pignoli** or **piñon**) Nuts grown on pine trees, that are rich (read: high fat), flavorful, and, yes, a bit pine-y. Pine nuts are a traditional component of pesto, and they add a wonderful hearty crunch to many other recipes.

pita bread A flat, hollow wheat bread that can be used for sandwiches or sliced pizza-style. Pita bread is terrific soft with dips or baked or broiled as a vehicle for other ingredients.

poach To cook a food in simmering liquid, such as water, wine, or broth.

porcini mushrooms Rich and flavorful mushrooms used in rice and Italian-style dishes.

portobello mushrooms A mature and larger form of the smaller cremini mushroom, portobellos are brownish, chewy, and flavorful. They are trendy served as whole caps, grilled, and as thin sautéed slices. *See also* cremini mushrooms.

preheat To turn on an oven, broiler, or other cooking appliance in advance of cooking so the temperature will be at the desired level when the assembled dish is ready for cooking

presentation The appealing arrangement of a dish or food on the plate.

prosciutto Dry, salt-cured ham, rich and evocative of Italy. Prosciutto is popular in many simple dishes in which its unique flavor is allowed to shine.

purée To reduce a food to a thick, creamy texture, usually using a blender or food processor.

ragout (pronounced *rag-OO*) A thick, spicy stew.

red pepper flakes Hot yet rich, crushed red pepper, used in moderation, brings flavor and interest to many savory dishes.

reduce To heat a broth or sauce to remove some of the water content, resulting in more concentrated flavor and color.

render To cook a meat to the point where its fat melts and can be removed.

reserve To hold a specified ingredient for another use later in the recipe.

rice vinegar Vinegar produced from fermented rice or rice wine, popular in Asian-style dishes.

roast To cook something uncovered in an oven.

Roquefort A world-famous (French) creamy but sharp sheep's milk cheese containing blue lines of mold, making it a "blue cheese."

rosemary A pungent, sweet herb used with chicken, pork, fish, and especially lamb. A little of it goes a long way.

roux A mixture of butter or another fat and flour used to thicken liquids such as sauces.

saffron A famous spice made from stamens of crocus flowers. Saffron lends a dramatic yellow color and distinctive flavor to a dish. Only a tiny amount needs to be used, which is good because saffron is very expensive.

sage An herb with a fruity, lemon-rind scent and "sunny" flavor. It is a terrific addition to many dishes.

salsa A style of mixing fresh vegetables and/or fresh fruit in a coarse chop. Salsa can be spicy or not, fruit-based or not, and served as a starter on its own (with chips, for example) or as a companion to a main course.

sauté To pan-cook over lower heat than used for frying.

savory A popular herb with a fresh, woody taste.

scant A measurement modification that specifies "include no extra," as in 1 scant teaspoon.

sear To quickly brown the exterior of a food over high heat to preserve interior moisture (that's why many meat recipes involve searing).

shallot A member of the onion family that grows in a bulb somewhat like garlic and has a milder onion flavor. When a recipe calls for shallot, you use the entire bulb. (They might or might not have cloves.)

shellfish A broad range of seafood, including clams, mussels, oysters, crabs, shrimp, and lobster. Some people are allergic to shellfish, so care should be taken with its inclusion in recipes.

shiitake mushrooms Large (up to 8 inches or more), dark brown mushrooms originally from the Far East with a hearty, meaty flavor that can be grilled or used as a component in other recipes and as a flavoring source for broth.

short-grain rice   A starchy rice popular for Asian-style dishes because it readily clumps for eating with chopsticks.

shred   To cut into many long, thin slices.

simmer   To boil gently so the liquid barely bubbles.

skewers   Thin wooden or metal sticks, usually about eight inches long, that are perfect for assembling kebabs, dipping food pieces into hot sauces, or serving single-bite food items with a bit of panache.

slice   To cut into thin pieces.

slow cooker   An electric countertop device with a lidded container that maintains a low temperature and slowly cooks its contents, often over several hours or a full day.

steam   To suspend a food over boiling water and allow the heat of the steam (water vapor) to cook the food. Steaming is a very quick cooking method that preserves flavor and texture of a food.

stew   To slowly cook pieces of food submerged in a liquid. Also a dish that has been prepared by this method.

stir-fry   To cook food in a wok or skillet over high heat, moving and turning the food quickly to cook all sides.

stock   A flavorful broth made by cooking meats and/or vegetables with seasonings until the liquid absorbs these flavors. This liquid is then strained and the solids discarded. Stock can be eaten by itself or used as a base for soups, stews, sauces, risotto, or many other recipes.

Tabasco sauce   A popular brand of Louisiana hot pepper sauce used in usually small portions to season savory food. The name also refers to a type of hot pepper from Tabasco, a state in Mexico, that is used to make this sauce.

tarragon   A sour-sweet, rich-smelling herb perfect with seafood, vegetables (especially asparagus), chicken, and pork.

teriyaki   A delicious Asian-style sauce composed of soy sauce, rice wine, ginger, and sugar. It works beautifully with seafood as well as most meats.

thyme   A minty, zesty herb whose leaves are used in a wide range of recipes.

tofu   A cheeselike substance made from soybeans and soy milk. Flavorful and nutritious, tofu is an important component of foods across the globe, especially from the Far East.

tomatillo   A small, round fruit with a distinctive spicy flavor reminiscent of its cousin, the tomato. Tomatillos are a traditional component of many south-of-the-border dishes. To use, remove the papery outer skin, rinse off any sticky residue, and chop like a tomato.

turmeric   A spicy, pungent yellow root used in many dishes, especially Indian cuisine, for color and flavor. Turmeric is the source of the brilliant yellow color in many prepared mustards.

twist   A twist (as in lemon or other citrus fruit twist) is simply an attractive way to garnish an appetizer or other dish. Cut a thin, about ⅛-inch-thick cross-section slice of a lemon, for example. Then take that slice and cut from the center out to the edge of the slice on one side. Pick up the piece of lemon and pull apart the two cut ends in opposite directions.

veal   Meat from a calf, generally characterized by mild flavor and tenderness. Certain cuts of veal, such as cutlets and scaloppini, are well suited to quick-cooking.

vegetable steamer   An insert for a large saucepan. Also a special pot with tiny holes in the bottom designed to fit on another pot to hold food to be steamed above boiling water. The insert is generally less expensive and resembles a metal poppy flower that expands to touch the sides of the pot and has small legs. *See also* steam.

venison   Meat from deer or other large wild game animals.

vinegar   An acidic liquid widely used as dressing and seasoning. Many cuisines use vinegars made from different source materials. *See also* balsamic vinegar; cider vinegar; rice vinegar; white vinegar; wine vinegar.

walnuts   Grown worldwide, walnuts bring a rich, slightly woody flavor to all types of food. For the quick cook, walnuts are available chopped and ready to go at your grocery store. They are delicious toasted and make fine accompaniments to cheeses.

water chestnuts   Actually a tuber, the water chestnut is a popular element in many types of Asian-style cooking. The flesh is white, crunchy, and juicy, and the vegetable holds its texture whether cool or hot.

whisk   To rapidly mix, introducing air to the mixture.

white mushrooms   Ubiquitous button mushrooms. When fresh, they will have an earthy smell and an appealing "soft crunch." White mushrooms are delicious raw in salads, marinated, sautéed, and as component ingredients in many recipes.

white vinegar   The most common type of vinegar found on grocery store shelves. It is produced from grain.

whole-wheat flour   Wheat flour that contains the entire grain.

wild rice   Actually a grain with a rich, nutty flavor, popular as an unusual and nutritious side dish.

wine vinegar   Vinegar produced from red or white wine.

Worcestershire sauce   Originally developed in India and containing tamarind, this spicy sauce is used as a seasoning for many meats and other dishes.

yeast   Tiny fungi that, when mixed with water, sugar, flour, and heat, release carbon dioxide bubbles, which, in turn, raise bread. The yeast also provides that wonderful warm, rich smell and flavor.

Glycemic Index and Carbohydrate List

The following table lists the glycemic index ranking and the carbohydrate content of the ingredients used in the recipes in this book.

Food	Glycemic Index Value	Amount	Carbs (g)	Fiber (g)	Nutritive Carbs
Almond flour	0	1 cup	21	11	10
Almonds	0	1 cup	28	15	13
Apple	38	1 medium	22	5	17
Apple juice	40	1 cup	25	0	25
Apricots	57	3 medium	11	1	10
Apricots, dried	30	¼ cup	25	2	23
Avocado, California	0	1 medium	12	9	3
Banana	52	1 medium	29	4	25
Barley, pearl, uncooked	25	¼ cup	37	6	31
Basmati rice, uncooked	58	¼ cup	33	2	31
Beef	0	any amount	0	0	0

Food	Glycemic Index Value	Amount	Carbs (g)	Fiber (g)	Nutritive Carbs
Black beans, boiled	30	½ cup	20	8	12
Black-eyed peas, canned	42	½ cup	16	4	12
Brazil nut	0	6 large	4	2	2
Broccoli, raw, chopped	0	½ cup	2	1	1
Cabbage, raw, shredded	0	½ cup	2	1	1
Cantaloupe, cubed	65	1 cup	13	2	11
Capers	0	1 TB.	1	0	1
Carrots, raw, shredded	47	½ cup	6	2	4
Cashews	22	¼ cup	8	3	5
Cauliflower, 1-inch pieces	0	½ cup	3	2	1
Celery, diced	0	½ cup	2	1	1
Celery root, or celeriac	0	½ cup	7.2	1.4	5.8
Cheese, cheddar and Parmesan	0	1 ounce	0	0	0
Cherries, sweet with pits	22	½ cup	12	2	10
Chickpeas, canned	42	½ cup	18	7	11
Cocoa powder	55	1 TB.	3	1	2
Coconut, shredded, not packed	0	1 cup	12	7	5
Corn, sweet, boiled	60	½ cup	15	5	10
Cornmeal	68	¼ cup	25	3	22
Cornstarch	n/a	1 TB.	9	0	9
Couscous, uncooked	65	¼ cup	35	2	33
Cream, heavy	0	½ cup	3	0	3
Cucumber, sliced	0	½ cup	1.4	0.4	1

Food	Glycemic Index Value	Amount	Carbs (g)	Fiber (g)	Nutritive Carbs
Dates	50	¼ cup	32	3	29
Eggs, large	0	1 large	0.6	0	0.6
Fennel, sliced	0	1 cup	6	2	4
Figs, dried	61	¼ cup	26	5	21
Flour	70	¼ cup	22	0	22
Garlic	0	1 clove	1	0.1	0.9
Grapefruit	25	½ medium	16	6	10
Grapefruit juice	48	1 cup	23	0	23
Grapes, green	46	1½ cups	24	1	23
Green beans, cooked	0	½ cup	5	2	3
Green onions	0	¼ cup	2	1	1
Green peas, frozen	48	⅔ cup	12	4	8
Hazelnuts, diced	0	1 cup	18	7	11
Honey	55	1 TB.	17	0	17
Ice cream, high fat, vanilla	38	½ cup	16	0	16
Ice cream, low fat, vanilla	50	½ cup	18	0	18
Jicama	0	½ cup	5	3	2
Kidney beans, boiled	46	½ cup	20	7	13
Kiwi fruit	58	1 medium	11	3	8
Lamb	0	any amount	0	0	0
Leafy vegetables, raw	0	1 cup	2	1	1
Lentils, cooked	29	½ cup	20	8	12
Lima beans, frozen	32	½ cup	22	5	17

continues

continued

Food	Glycemic Index Value	Amount	Carbs (g)	Fiber (g)	Nutritive Carbs
Macadamia nuts	0	¼ cup	5	3	2
Mango, sliced	51	1 cup	28	3	25
Milk, full fat	31	1 cup	49	0	49
New potato, boiled	78	½ cup	16	2	14
Oat bran	n/a	½ cup	25	6	19
Oat flour	n/a	⅓ cup	21	3	18
Oatmeal, cooked	42	½ cup	13	2	11
Onion, chopped	0	½ cup	7	1	6
Orange, sections	42	1 cup	19	4	15
Orange juice	53	1 cup	27	0	27
Papaya, sliced	56	1 cup	14	3	11
Peach, sliced	42	1 cup	19	3	16
Peanuts, roasted	14	¼ cup	12	2	10
Pear	38	1 medium	25	4	21
Pecan flour	0	1 cup	15	15	0
Pecans, half	0	¼ cup	5	5	0
Pepper, red or green, diced	0	¾ cup	4	2	2
Pine nuts	0	¼ cup	5	2	3
Pineapple, diced	66	½ cup	10	1	9
Pinto beans, canned	45	½ cup	18	6	12
Plums, sliced	39	½ cup	11	1	10
Pork	0	any amount	0	0	0
Potato, white, baked	85	in skin, 4¾ by 2½ inches	51	5	46
Psyllium husks	0	3 TB.	8	8	0
Raisins	64	¼ cup	31	2	29
Rice, brown, uncooked	50	¼ cup	37	3	34
Rice flour	n/a	¼ cup	31	1	30

Food	Glycemic Index Value	Amount	Carbs (g)	Fiber (g)	Nutuve Carbs
Salami	0	1 ounce	0	0	0
Shellfish, seafood	0	any amount	0	0	0
Soy flour	n/a	½ cup	16	8	8
Split peas, uncooked	32	¼ cup	27	11	16
Squash, cooked, cubed	0	1 cup	15	2	13
Sucrose, table sugar	68	½ cup	100	0	100
Sweet potato, mashed	44	½ cup	24	3	21
Tomato, chopped	0	1 cup	8	2	6
Tuna and fish	0	any amount	0	0	0
Veal	0	any amount	0	0	0
Vital wheat gluten	n/a	1 TB.	3	0	3
Walnuts	0	¼ cup	3	3	0
Wild rice, uncooked	57	¼ cup	34	3	31
Whey powder	n/a	⅓ cup	2	0	2
Wheat germ	n/a	2 TB.	7	4	3
Whole-wheat flour	71	¼ cup	21	3	18
Yams, cooked, cubed	37	½ cup	19	3	16

Each ingredient has a glycemic index ranking (GI). This tells how much your blood sugar level increases when you eat this food. The ranking is based on 100—that the blood sugar rises from eating glucose. The lower the number, the less likely the food will trigger a quick rise in blood sugar.

A quick rise in blood sugar stimulates the pancreas to secrete the hormone insulin. Insulin lowers the blood sugar level to a safe range. When the body has a high increase in blood sugar as when eating a high-glycemic food, the pancreas, in a sense, produces more insulin than needed. Excess insulin results in …

◆ A person getting hungry again soon after eating.

◆ Increased body-fat storage.

Because you don't want those two things to happen in your body, it's best to eat low- to moderate-GI foods.

High	> 70
Medium	56 to 69
Low	< 55

The only ingredients we use in this cookbook that are high GI are white potatoes and wheat flour. However, we have used them in such small quantities that their overall effect is minimal.

Listed with the GI of each ingredient is the carbohydrate count based on the amount of food. Use this information to figure the carbohydrate count of other recipes and foods you might eat.

Menu Planning Spreadsheet

No matter how large or small your daily carbohydrate allotment, this chart helps you plan your meals for the day. Save yourself the hassle of last-minute scrambling and counting and make each meal more relaxing and enjoyable by using this step-by-step approach.

1. Using the Menu Planning Spreadsheet

The Menu Planning Spreadsheet that follows gives you the following information for each recipe:

◆ **Nutritive Carbohydrate Count per serving.** This is the difference between the total number of carbohydrates in grams less the fiber in grams. Use this number to make your calculations to figure your daily carbohydrate allotment.

◆ **Total Grams of Animal Protein per serving.** As a rule of thumb, you need about half a gram of complete protein per pound of body weight per day. If you weigh 150 pounds you need 75 grams complete protein every day. The complete protein on this chart is listed as animal protein. Plant proteins are deemed incomplete as they don't contain all nine essential amino acids, so they don't count as complete protein.

Recipe	Type of Dish	Chapter	Nutritive Carbs	Carbs	Fiber	Protein	Animal	Plant
Almond Crackers	Starch	22	6	9	3	12	1	11
Apples with Raisins and Pecans	Side	21	16	19	3	1	0	1
Artichoke Chicken with Mushrooms	Main	10	7	9	2	33	31	2
Artichokes Stuffed with Shrimp	Main	16	5	8	3	6	5	1
Asian Smoked Turkey	Main	16	15	18	3	3	0	0
Asian Spinach Salad	Side	20	3	5	2	5	3	2
Asparagus Cheese Pie	Main	15	6	6	<1	20	19	1
Asparagus Tart	Breakfast	5	3	3	<1	11	10	1
Asparagus with Hollandaise Sauce	Side	19	0	2	2	3	2	1
Avocado and Papaya Salad	Side	21	13	16	3	2	0	2
Avocado Margarita	Side	17	2	4	2	<1	0	0
Avocado-Turkey Wrap	Side	18	2	8	6	10	8	2
Baked Avocado	Side	17	8	12	4	8	3	5
Baked Celery	Side	19	5	8	3	7	5	2
Baked Onions	Side	19	8	10	2	1	0	1
Baked Ricotta Cups	Dessert	24	31	33	2	7	6	1
Baked Salmon with Spinach Sauce	Main	12	1	1	0	29	28	1
Baked Swiss Onion Dip	Side	17	6	6	<1	4	4	<1
Baked Yams	Starch	23	16	19	3	1	0	1
Barley with Dill	Starch	23	17	21	4	5	3	2
Basic Cajun Flour Roux	Main	14	5	5	<1	1	0	1
Basic Cream Soup	Main	14	7	7	<1	2	1	1
Basic Gumbo and Variations	Main	14	13	14	1	32	30	2
Basil Pot Roast	Main	13	12	15	3	31	29	2
Basil Stuffed Chicken	Main	10	3	3	0	34	34	0
Basil Turkey with Peppers	Main	16	9	12	3	27	22	5

Recipe	Type of Dish	Chapter	Nutritive Carbs	Carbs	Fiber	Protein	Animal	Plant
Basmati Rice Pilaf	Starch	23	16	17	1	2	0	2
BBQ Shrimp	Main	11	2	2	<1	26	26	0
Beef and Pork Skewers	Lunch	6	<1	<1	0	16	16	0
Beef Fajitas	Main	7	2	3	1	32	32	0
Beef Jerky	Side	18	2	2	0	16	16	0
Beef Jicama Chalupas	Main	7	5	14	9	19	16	3
Beef Ratatouille	Main	13	13	15	2	24	21	3
Beef Salad with Capers	Main	16	4	6	2	30	28	2
Beef Soup with Vegetables	Main	14	4	6	2	30	29	1
Beef Steak Over Greens	Main	7	7	9	2	35	33	2
Beef Stroganoff	Main	7	2	2	<1	32	32	0
Beef Tandoor	Main	7	5	5	0	32	32	0
Beef with Vinaigrette	Main	7	1	1	0	32	32	0
Beef-Vegetable Burgundy Stew	Main	14	5	9	4	29	29	>1
Beer Bottom Smoked Chicken	Main	10	2	2	0	30	30	0
Blackened Fish	Main	12	1	1	0	30	30	0
Bleu Cheese Rib Eyes	Main	7	<1	<1	0	43	42	1
Boiled Eggs	Breakfast	4	<1	<1	0	6	6	0
Braised Beef with Italian Herbs	Main	13	6	6	<1	43	43	0
Brie Stuffed with Sun-Dried Tomatoes and Basil	Side	17	4	5	1	9	8	1
Broccoli Stuffed Tomatoes	Side	19	8	14	6	4	0	4
Broccoli-Seafood Dip	Side	17	3	3	<1	10	10	<1
Brunch Egg Casserole	Breakfast	5	12	12	<1	30	27	3
Brussels Sprouts with Pecans	Side	19	4	10	6	3	0	3

continues

continued

Recipe	Type of Dish	Chapter	Nutritive Carbs	Carbs	Fiber	Protein	Animal	Plant
Buttermilk Herb Dressing	Side	20	2	2	0	<1	0	0
Cabbage Rolls	Main	8	8	10	2	10	8	2
Caesar Salad	Side	20	1	2	1	2	1	1
Cajun Black Bean Soup	Main	14	11	19	8	7	2	5
Cajun Dirty Rice	Starch	23	21	22	1	15	13	2
Catfish Stew	Main	14	10	12	2	35	33	2
Celery Root Salad	Side	20	8	10	2	2	0	2
Cheese Apple Bake	Main	15	16	16	0	2	2	>1
Cheese Bread	Starch	22	3	3	<1	14	5	9
Cheesy Baked Eggs	Main	15	3	3	0	11	11	0
Cheesy Nuts	Side	18	1	3	2	5	1	4
Cherry Omelet	Dessert	24	14	18	4	9	8	1
Chewy Low Carb Bread—bread machine version	Starch	22	5	5	<1	14	<1	14
Chicken and Fresh Fruit Salad	Main	16	19	20	1	33	32	1
Chicken Breasts Stuffed with Mushrooms and Spinach	Main	10	6	6	<1	38	35	3
Chicken Cole Slaw	Main	16	8	9	1	15	13	2
Chicken Couscous	Lunch	6	7	9	2	17	15	2
Chicken Liver Pâté with Pickles	Side	18	5	6	1	14	14	<1
Chicken Macadamia	Main	10	16	18	2	35	33	2
Chicken Picatta	Main	10	4	4	<1	31	30	1
Chicken Quesadillas	Side	17	3	6	3	27	22	5
Chicken Soup with Paprika	Main	14	2	2	<1	32	32	>1
Chicken Stir-Fry with Fruit	Main	10	8	9	1	33	30	3
Chicken with Olives and Capers	Main	10	5	5	<1	45	45	0
Chile Relleno and Crab Casserole	Main	15	8	8	0	38	37	1
Chili Meatloaf	Main	8	7	9	2	33	31	2
Chinese Chicken	Main	10	9	10	1	32	30	2

Recipe	Type of Dish	Chapter	Nutritive Carbs	Carbs	Fiber	Protein	Animal	Plant
Chinese Meatballs	Main	8	20	26	6	29	28	1
Chocolate Chip Cheese Ball	Side	17	3	4	1	1	1	0
Chocolate Drop Cookies	Dessert	25	6	7	1	2	<1	2
Chocolate Ganauche	Dessert	25	4	4	0	<1	0	0
Chocolate Mousse	Dessert	25	21	21	0	6	5	1
Chocolate Nut Pâté	Dessert	25	16	16	0	1	<1	<1
Chocolate Soufflé	Dessert	25	8	10	2	8	5	3
Chocolate Truffles	Dessert	25	5	5	0	<1	0	0
Chocolate-Amaretto Cheesecake	Dessert	25	20	20	0	5	4	1
Chorizo Omelet	Main	15	5	6	1	18	18	0
Clam Chowder with Mushrooms	Main	14	8	8	<1	5	5	0
Cold Cut Rollups	Lunch	6	1	1	0	14	14	0
Cold Egg Cream Salad	Main	15	5	5	0	8	8	0
Cold Lemon and Blueberry Mousse	Dessert	24	28	29	1	6	5	1
Colorful Broccoli	Side	19	7	12	5	3	<1	3
Company Chicken Spaghetti	Main	10	5	6	1	38	36	2
Congealed Asparagus Salad	Side	20	15	18	3	4	0	4
Country Pâté	Main	9	1	1	<1	13	12	1
Crab Cakes with Creole Sauce	Main	11	8	8	0	21	20	1
Crab Stuffed Eggplant	Main	11	4	8	4	17	17	0
Crabmeat au Gratin	Main	11	7	7	0	30	30	0
Crabmeat Florentine	Main	11	4	6	2	13	10	3
Cranberry Eggs	Breakfast	5	19	25	6	5	2	3
Crawfish Creole	Main	11	8	9	1	28	26	2
Crawfish Étouffée	Main	11	9	10	1	37	34	3
Creamed Cabbage	Side	19	4	5	1	2	<1	2

continues

continued

Recipe	Type of Dish	Chapter	Nutritive Carbs	Carbs	Fiber	Protein	Animal	Plant
Creamed Cajun Seafood	Main	11	6	7	1	26	25	1
Crispy Black Pepper Salmon	Main	12	6	6	<1	37	35	2
Croutons	Starch	22	4	5	1	1	0	1
Crustless Cheesecake	Dessert	24	10	10	0	6	6	0
Crustless Quiche	Breakfast	5	4	4	0	23	23	0
Curried Chicken	Main	10	8	9	1	7	6	1
Curried Fruit on Skewers	Side	21	14	18	4	<1	0	0
Curried Pork Chops with Apricots	Main	9	9	9	<1	43	42	1
Deviled Eggs	Side	17	1	1	0	13	13	0
Dijon-Lemon Vinaigrette	Side	20	2	2	0	<1	0	0
Double Chocolate Brownies	Dessert	25	11	13	2	1	<1	<1
Easy Cheese Breakfast Soufflé	Breakfast	5	5	5	0	17	17	0
Egg Pancake	Breakfast	4	1	1	0	13	13	0
Egg Roll	Breakfast	4	11	13	2	15	13	0
Egg Salad and Variations	Lunch	6	2	2	0	13	13	0
Eggplant and Meat Casserole	Main	13	14	14	<1	29	21	8
Eggplant Crisps for Dips	Side	18	2	3	1	<1	0	0
Eggplant Spread	Side	17	5	5	<1	<1	0	0
Eggplant with Ground Beef	Main	8	7	9	2	20	18	2
Eggplant-Squash Bake	Side	19	11	14	3	2	0	2
Eggs Benedict	Breakfast	5	5	5	<1	27	26	1
Eggs with Spinach	Breakfast	5	8	8	<1	14	13	1
Eggs with Spinach	Main	15	13	13	<1	19	18	1
Everyday Rolls	Starch	22	6	8	2	5	<1	5
Fennel and Tomatoes	Side	19	6	9	3	<1	0	0

Recipe	Type of Dish	Chapter	Nutritive Carbs	Carbs	Fiber	Protein	Animal	Plant
Fiesta Confetti Salad	Side	20	6	7	1	1	0	1
Five-Day Coleslaw	Side	20	7	9	2	1	0	1
Five-Pepper Tuna	Main	12	7	7	0	69	69	0
Flourless Chocolate Tiramisu Cake	Dessert	25	11	12	1	4	3	1
Fresh Berries with Orange Cream	Side	21	18	19	1	1	1	4
Fresh Cranberry Salad	Side	20	15	19	4	1	<1	1
Fresh Fruit Medley with Poppy Seed Dressing	Side	21	13	15	2	1	0	1
Frosty Fruit	Side	21	13	16	3	2	0	2
Frozen Raspberry Soufflé	Dessert	24	30	30	<1	4	4	0
Fruit Salad with Passion Fruit	Side	21	11	14	3	<1	0	0
Fruit Stuffed Meatloaf	Main	8	14	16	2	32	30	2
Garlic Roast	Main	7	6	6	0	32	32	0
German Pancakes	Breakfast	5	9	9	0	10	10	0
Ginger Snaps	Dessert	24	3	6	3	2	0	2
Gingered Carrots	Side	19	4	5	1	<1	0	0
Gingered Papayas	Side	21	14	16	2	1	0	1
Granola	Breakfast	4	16	20	4	10	0	10
Green Beans Almandine	Side	19	6	8	2	2	0	2
Green Beans, Pecans, and Feta	Side	19	8	13	5	6	3	3
Green Brown Rice	Starch	23	22	23	1	8	5	3
Green Goddess Dressing	Side	20	5	5	<1	3	<1	3
Green Peas Cooked in Lettuce	Side	19	9	16	7	6	0	6
Green Tomatoes and Ham	Main	9	11	13	2	30	26	4
Grilled Catfish with Mustard	Main	12	4	4	0	32	32	0
Grilled Fish Salad	Main	16	12	13	1	32	29	3

continues

continued

Recipe	Type of Dish	Chapter	Nutritive Carbs	Carbs	Fiber	Protein	Animal	Plant
Guacamole	Side	20	5	8	3	1	0	1
Halibut Salad with Carrots and Fennel	Main	16	9	11	2	23	23	0
Ham Flan	Breakfast	5	2	2	<1	10	10	0
Ham Rollups	Breakfast	4	3	4	1	28	28	0
Hamburger with Mushrooms and Cream	Main	8	3	4	1	9	9	0
Hearts of Palm Spinach	Side	19	5	7	2	3	1	2
Herbed Pork Chops	Main	9	3	3	<1	42	42	0
Home Made Peach Ice Cream	Dessert	24	8	8	0	3	3	0
Home Made Peanut Butter	Side	18	5	7	2	7	0	7
Hot Chicken Salad	Main	16	6	8	2	20	17	3
Hot Crab Dip	Side	17	2	2	<1	10	10	0
Hot Fruit Soufflé	Dessert	24	14	15	1	4	4	0
Italian Baked Chicken	Main	10	<1	<1	0	28	28	0
Italian Meatballs	Main	8	1	7	6	35	34	1
Jalapeño Red Potato Bowls	Starch	23	7	7	<1	2	2	<1
Jambalaya	Main	13	27	30	3	34	30	4
Lasagna	Main	8	6	6	<1	17	16	1
Layered Roast Salad	Main	16	16	20	4	25	22	3
Layered Salad	Lunch	6	7	10	3	30	26	4
Lemon Cheese Pie	Main	15	18	18	0	3	3	>1
Lemon Cream Custard	Dessert	24	34	34	0	3	3	0
Lentil Soup	Main	14	13	23	10	4	0	4
Lobster Pâté	Side	17	2	2	0	17	17	0
Lobster with Mango	Side	17	13	14	1	27	27	<1
Luncheon Egg Ring	Main	15	10	10	0	35	34	1
Make Ahead Italian Bake	Breakfast	4	9	11	2	9	7	2
Mandarin Orange Spinach Salad	Side	20	16	18	2	6	0	6

Recipe	Type of Dish	Chapter	Nutritive Carbs	Carbs	Fiber	Protein	Animal	Plant
Marinated London Broil	Main	7	2	2	<1	33	32	1
Marinated Beef Kabobs	Main	7	6	8	2	33	32	1
Marinated Crab Fingers	Side	17	4	4	<1	5	5	0
Marinated Pork Tenderloin	Main	9	1	1	<1	30	30	0
Marinated Tomato Slices	Side	20	10	11	1	1	0	1
Marinated Vegetables	Side	20	4	6	2	1	0	1
Meat and Cheese Loaf	Main	13	6	7	1	29	29	<1
Mediterranean Halibut	Main	12	5	6	1	42	41	<1
Mexican Chicken Avocado Soup	Main	14	7	9	2	15	13	2
Mexican Layers with Veggies	Lunch	6	10	15	5	15	2	13
Mexican Meat Soup	Main	14	4	4	<1	31	30	1
Mexican Omelet	Breakfast	5	15	18	3	7	5	2
Microwave Bacon	Breakfast	4	0	0	0	5	5	0
Microwave Cheesy Apples	Side	21	18	21	3	7	7	0
Microwave Scrambled Eggs	Breakfast	4	1	1	0	10	10	0
Minty Fruit	Side	21	11	13	2	1	<1	1
Mock Mashed Potatoes	Starch	23	2	3	1	1	<1	1
Mock Potato Salad	Starch	23	3	4	1	4	3	1
Mushroom "Caviar"	Side	17	2	2	<1	<1	0	0
Mushroom-Artichoke Salad	Side	20	6	8	2	2	0	2
Mushroom-Gingered Baked Ham	Main	9	12	12	<1	29	28	1
Mustard Brisket	Main	7	2	2	0	32	32	0
Nut Butter Spreads	Lunch	6	0	0	0	4	0	4
Nut Clusters	Dessert	25	11	12	1	<1	1	<1

continues

continued

Recipe	Type of Dish	Chapter	Nutritive Carbs	Carbs	Fiber	Protein	Animal	Plant
	Side	17	3	3	<1	1	0	1
Open-Faced Canadian Bacon	Breakfast	4	1	1	0	14	12	2
Oriental Spinach Salad	Main	16	7	8	1	10	9	1
Oven BBQ Ribs	Main	9	18	18	0	44	42	2
Pacific Seafood Salad	Main	16	14	18	4	24	22	2
Pancake Syrup	Breakfast	5	12	12	0	0	0	0
Paprika Chicken	Main	10	5	6	1	33	32	1
Parmesan Snacks	Side	17	1	1	0	8	8	0
Party Cheese Log	Side	17	3	4	1	14	13	1
Peanut Butter Cookies	Dessert	24	7	9	2	3	<1	3
Pear Compote	Side	21	10	16	6	<1	0	0
Pears with Avocado and Lime	Side	21	13	19	6	<1	0	0
Peasant Beef Casserole	Main	13	10	13	3	31	28	3
Pecan Trout	Main	12	2	8	6	37	33	4
Peppered Tenderloin Casserole	Main	13	10	11	1	29	28	1
Picadille Dip	Main	8	8	11	3	32	28	4
Pickled Eggs	Side	18	4	4	0	6	6	0
Pickled Garlic	Side	18	7	7	0	<1	0	0
Pine Nut Barley Pilaf	Starch	23	15	19	4	5	3	2
Pine Nut Chicken	Main	10	6	7	1	38	32	6
Pork Chops and Cabbage	Main	9	7	9	2	32	31	1
Pork Chops with Apples	Main	9	16	21	5	42	42	<1
Pork Chops with Raisins and Walnuts	Main	9	11	12	1	47	42	5
Pork Chops with Sauerkraut	Main	9	5	9	4	43	42	1
Pork Chops with Spaghetti	Main	9	11	14	3	46	44	2

Recipe	Type of Dish	Chapter	Nutritive Carbs	Carbs	Fiber	Protein	Animal	Plant
Pork on a Stick	Side	18	4	6	2	40	32	8
Portobello Pizza	Main	8	7	9	2	17	11	6
Pot Roast with Caraway	Main	7	4	5	1	32	32	0
Quinoa Pilaf with Vegetables	Starch	23	14	16	2	6	<1	6
Ranch Dressing	Side	20	1	1	0	<1	0	0
Raspberry Mousse	Dessert	24	9	10	1	2	1	1
Red Bean and Ham Soup	Main	14	16	23	7	19	12	7
Red Snapper with Mango Salsa	Main	12	17	18	1	30	29	1
Rice Flour Rolls	Starch	22	5	5	0	10	3	7
Rich Cheesy Soup	Main	14	11	12	1	11	10	1
Rich Chocolate Brownies	Dessert	25	20	24	4	1	1	<1
Roast Beef Scoop	Main	16	7	8	1	18	16	2
Roasted Turkey Breast	Main	10	1	1	0	25	25	0
Roasted Vegetable-Fruit-Beef Salad	Main	16	18	19	1	35	32	3
Romaine Salad with Capers and Salami	Side	20	5	7	2	<1	0	0
Rosemary Roasted Chicken	Main	10	8	8	0	30	30	0
Rosemary Walnuts	Side	18	1	3	2	5	0	5
Rubbed Beef Steak	Main	7	4	4	0	32	32	0
Rum Flavored Bananas	Dessert	24	11	13	2	<1	0	0
Salad to Go	Lunch	6	25	30	5	24	18	6
Salmon in Dill Sauce	Main	12	4	4	0	35	35	0
Salmon Salad with Pickles and Raisins	Main	16	7	8	1	14	13	1
Salmon Soufflé	Breakfast	5	4	4	0	19	19	0
Salmon with Macadamia Lime Butter	Main	12	3	3	<1	31	30	1
Salmon with Olives and Lemon	Main	12	<1	<1	0	35	35	0

continues

continued

Recipe	Type of Dish	Chapter	Nutritive Carbs	Carbs	Fiber	Protein	Animal	Plant
Sausage Muffins	Main	15	3	3	0	22	22	0
Sautéed Fruit	Dessert	24	26	28	2	1	0	1
Sautéed Shrimp in Artichoke Sauce	Main	11	12	15	3	23	20	3
Sautéed Steak with Green Peppercorns	Main	7	<1	<1	0	42	42	0
Scallop Salad	Main	16	6	8	2	6	4	2
Scotch Eggs	Lunch	6	3	4	1	24	23	1
Scrambled Eggs with Tomatoes and Basil	Breakfast	5	3	3	<1	13	13	0
Seafood Mold	Side	17	10	10	<1	10	8	2
Seafood with Curried Chutney Dressing	Main	16	14	17	3	29	25	4
Shrimp Dinner Boil	Main	14	12	15	3	18	17	1
Shrimp Scampi	Main	11	3	3	0	26	26	0
Shrimp with Fennel and Green Beans	Main	11	4	5	1	20	19	1
Shrimp with Sun-Dried Tomatoes and Pineapple	Main	11	7	9	2	14	13	1
Shrimp, Crab, and Artichokes au Gratin	Main	11	8	10	2	32	30	2
Sirloin with Lemon Sauce	Main	7	2	2	<1	33	32	1
Slow Cooker Country Apples	Dessert	24	22	24	2	2	0	2
Slow Cooker Italian Brisket	Main	13	5	5	0	30	30	<1
Slow Cooker Pot Roast	Main	7	0	0	0	32	32	0
Smoked Salmon Cheesecake	Main	15	5	5	0	14	14	>1
Smoked Salmon Spread	Side	17	<1	<1	0	4	4	0
Smothered Pork Chops	Main	9	8	8	<1	44	42	2
Southern Chili	Main	14	18	23	5	31	27	4
Southern Greens	Side	19	2	4	2	1	1	<1

Recipe	Type of Dish	Chapter	Nutritive Carbs	Carbs	Fiber	Protein	Animal	Plant
Southwestern Vegetables	Side	19	14	18	4	5	0	5
Spaghetti Sauce	Main	8	7	9	2	14	7	7
Spaghetti Squash with Italian Sauce	Side	19	6	12	6	5	3	2
Spiced Nuts and Seeds	Side	18	4	7	3	8	0	8
Spicy Seafood Stew	Main	14	10	11	1	21	19	2
Spinach and Ricotta Pie	Main	15	8	8	<1	19	18	1
Spinach Cheese Squares	Side	17	4	4	0	8	7	1
Spinach Salad with Hot Bacon Dressing	Side	20	4	4	<1	4	3	1
Spinach Wrappers	Side	18	3	5	2	16	6	10
Spinach-Artichoke Dip	Side	17	3	5	2	9	8	1
Steak Salad	Main	16	4	6	2	23	22	1
Stewed Chicken	Main	13	3	4	1	28	28	0
Strawberry Cream	Dessert	24	5	5	<1	<1	0	0
Stuffed Acorn Squash	Side	19	15	22	7	1	0	1
Stuffed Green Peppers	Main	8	7	10	3	34	30	4
Stuffed Steak	Main	7	0	0	0	42	42	0
Stuffed Veggies	Side	18	2	2	0	3	3	<1
Stuffed Yams	Starch	23	17	20	3	8	6	2
Summer Quick Shrimp	Main	11	4	4	0	18	18	<1
Sweet and Sour Stew	Main	14	14	16	2	37	35	2
Sweet Potato Oven Fries	Starch	23	16	19	3	1	0	1
Sweet Red Pepper and Crab Bisque	Main	14	7	8	1	16	13	3
Swiss Onions	Side	19	6	7	1	12	11	1
Tamale Pie	Main	8	19	23	4	11	7	4
Tapioca Pudding	Dessert	24	13	13	<1	4	4	0
Tasty Turnips	Side	19	2	4	2	3	2	1

continues

continued

Recipe	Type of Dish	Chapter	Nutritive Carbs	Carbs	Fiber	Protein	Animal	Plant
Toasted Pumpkin Seeds	Side	18	2	5	3	7	0	7
Tomatoes Stuffed with Blue Cheese and Mushrooms	Side	19	6	7	1	3	2	1
Trail Mix	Side	18	9	12	3	6	0	6
Trout Dinner in a Bag	Main	12	11	15	4	32	29	3
Tuna Fish Cakes	Main	12	1	1	0	13	13	0
Turkey-Apple Salad	Main	16	17	19	2	35	32	3
Twice-Baked Potatoes	Starch	23	16	20	4	2	<1	2
Veal Chops with Tarragon	Main	9	2	2	0	30	30	0
Veal Italian Style	Main	13	3	3	0	28	28	<1
Veal Marsala	Main	9	13	13	<1	39	35	4
Veal Parmigiana	Main	9	18	20	2	42	38	4
Vegetable Pasta	Starch	22	2	4	2	1	0	1
Vibrant Peppers and Tomatoes	Side	19	5	6	1	<1	0	0
Waldorf Salad	Side	21	8	11	3	5	0	5
Walnut Cake with Chocolate Cream	Dessert	25	12	15	3	7	4	3
Warm Caraway Cabbage	Side	19	10	12	2	<1	0	0
White Chili	Main	14	17	22	5	32	28	4
Wild Rice and Beef	Main	8	10	10	<1	30	26	4
Winter Salad	Side	20	3	3	<1	<1	0	0
Yeast Bread with Seeds	Starch	22	6	10	4	10	1	9
Yellow Squash Casserole	Side	19	12	15	3	5	2	3
Your Choice Stir-Fry	Main	13	0	7	7	25	21	4

2. Using the Daily Planning Worksheet

On the Daily Planning Worksheet, keep track of the following information:

◆ Write down what you'll eat for breakfast and calculate the amount of carbs and protein for that meal.

◆ Write down all snacks, lunch, and dinner foods, and calculate the amount of carbs and protein.

◆ Add up your daily totals for both carbohydrates and proteins. If they match your allotment, you are done with your carb and protein planning for the day.

◆ If your totals are higher in your allotment of carbs, or lower than your requirement of complete protein, readjust your menu and recipes until you reach your goals.

3. Getting Balanced Meals

Review your Daily Planning Worksheet to assure that:

◆ You are eating at least 5 servings of vegetables and fruits. Do this by having 2 servings per meal. You can also eat servings of vegetables and fruits for snacks.

◆ Your carbohydrates allotment is spread throughout the day and not all spent on one or two meals.

◆ Your protein intake is balanced at breakfast, lunch, and dinner. Plan to eat about one-third of your protein requirement at each meal.

◆ You are eating foods that appeal to you and to all of your senses. Include different textures and aromas. Also, have some hot foods and some cold ones.

◆ You are eating a rainbow throughout the day. Eat vegetables and fruits with many colors of the rainbow.

You can copy the following Daily Planning Worksheet and plan a day ahead or a week ahead, based on your needs.

Daily Planning Worksheet

Meal or Snack	Recipe Choice	Page #	Nutritive Carbohydrate	Complete Protein
Breakfast				
Snack				
Lunch				
Snack				
Dinner				
Snack				
Total for the day:				

Index

Y–Z